Sir John Hawkins

Sir John Hawkins

QUEEN ELIZABETH'S SLAVE TRADER

Harry Kelsey

YALE UNIVERSITY PRESS   NEW HAVEN AND LONDON

For Parry and Jane

Title page image: English school (sixteenth century), *Sir John Hawkins, 1532–1595*.
Copyright © National Maritime Picture Library.

Published with assistance from the foundation established in memory of
Oliver Baty Cunningham of the Class of 1917, Yale College.

Designed by Sonia L. Shannon.
Set in Bulmer type by Temple Graphics.
Printed in the United States of America by R. R. Donnelley & Sons Company.

Library of Congress Cataloging-in-Publication Data

Kelsey, Harry, 1929–
Sir John Hawkins : Queen Elizabeth's slave trader / Harry Kelsey.
p.   cm.
Includes bibliographical references and index.
ISBN 0-300-09663-1 (cloth : alk. paper)
1. Hawkins, John, Sir, 1532–1595. 2. Great Britain—History,
Naval—Tudors, 1485–1603—Biography. 3. Great Britain—History—Elizabeth,
1558–1603—Biography. 4. Slave trade—History—16th century.
5. Slave traders—England—Biography. I. Title.
DA86.22.H3K45   2002
942.05'5'092—dc21
[B]
2002010995

A catalogue record for this book is available from the British Library.

The paper in this book meets the guidelines for permanence and durability
of the Committee on Production Guidelines for Book Longevity of
the Council on Library Resources.

10 9 8 7 6 5 4 3 2 1

Contents

List of Illustrations vii
Acknowledgments ix
Introduction xiii

ONE
The Uses of Duplicity 1

TWO
Robbing Portugal and Selling to Spain 34

THREE
Slave Trading 52

FOUR
San Juan de Ulúa 70

FIVE
Counting the Cost 94

SIX
Turning Defeat into Victory 116

SEVEN
Changing Course 142

EIGHT
War with Spain 183

NINE
There Is No Other Hell 227

TEN
Weighing Hawkins 266

Appendixes

ONE

Latin Text of Hawkins's Claim for Losses
at San Juan de Ulúa 283

TWO

Account of the Battle at San Juan de Ulúa
Alvaro de Flores 286

THREE

Inscription on the Memorial to Hawkins
at St. Dunstan in the East 299

FOUR

Portraits of Hawkins 304

Notes 307
Bibliography 371
Index 389

Contents
{vi}

Illustrations

Figures

1. View of Plymouth in the sixteenth century   3

2. The Hawkins coat of arms   32

3. View of Myncing Lane, London   40

4. The *Jesus of Lubeck*   48

5. The *Minion*   55

6. Alvaro Flores title page   85

7. List of English prisoners in Mexico   92

8. Hawkins testimony, 1569   105

9. *Troublesome Voyadge,* title page   109

10. William Cecil, Lord Burghley   121

11. File on Robert Barrett, "Lutheran heretic"   134

12. *Rare Travailes of Job Hortop*   135

13. Letter to Lord Burghley, 1576   140

14. Letter offering ships to serve the queen, 1577   152

15. Royal shipwright Matthew Baker   158

16. Dom Antonio   162

17. John Hawkins and Richard Hawkins   192

18. The *Elizabeth Bonaventure*   203

19. Charles Howard, lord high admiral   215

20. John Hawkins (Holland's *Herωologia Anglica*)   224

21. Will of John Hawkins   257

22. Principal castle at Gran Canaria   259

23. John Hawkins (Boissard)   305

Maps

1. Voyage of William Hawkins to "Brazil"   5
2. The Hawkins voyages to the Canary Islands   11
3. The route to Africa   14
4. Slave raids on the Guinea Coast, 1564   22
5. Voyage to the Caribbean   25
6. Voyage of Lovell and Drake   43
7. The slave raids of 1568   65
8. Voyage to the Caribbean, 1568   72
9. The Medway anchorage   175
10. The Hawkins raid of 1586   180
11. The Armada battles   211
12. The Hawkins voyage of 1590   238

Acknowledgments

By ancient tradition an author must reveal his final feelings about the book at the very beginning, where everyone can see them. There is a good reason for this, because the final feelings usually involve gratitude to the people who helped put the work together. Heading the list of those who helped me is Giles Mead, followed immediately by Martin Ridge and Roy Ritchie. These three have made it possible for me to have a working place at the Huntington Library in San Marino, California, where much of the research and most of the writing was done. Other staff members have also given advice and assistance, including Christopher Adde, Romaine Ahlstrom, Alan Jutzi, Susi Krasnoo, Anne Mar, Mona Noureldin, Barbara Quinn, Bert Rinderle, and Mary Robertson.

In addition, staff members from other archives and libraries have gone far beyond the demands of duty. They include, in England, the very efficient but ever-changing staff in the Manuscript Department of the British Library, the equally competent professional staff at the Public Record Office, and the helpful librarians at the National Maritime Museum. In Spain the archivists at the Archivo General de Indias gave their usual cordial welcome, as did those at the Archivo Historico Nacional and the Archivo General de Simancas, where Isabel Aguirre presides over the best archival research room in Europe. In Dublin the staff at the National Library introduced me to collections of manuscript and printed sources that were both unknown to me and not easily available in other research collections. Officials of Duke Humphrey's Library in the Bodleian Library at Oxford allowed me to consult their marvelous collection, as did the officials of the Pepys Library, Magdalene College, Cambridge. The librarians at the Guildhall Library, London, permitted me to use original manuscript and printed materials in that fine collection. The archivists at the Devon Record Office in both Plymouth and Exeter helped me once more to find my way around their catalogues. The librarians at the West Country Studies Library in Exeter and the Plymouth Public Library again gave me free use of their extensive collections of local history materials. The staff of the Bayerische Staatsbibliothek in Munich helped me during a personal visit and later by mail when it turned out I had neglected some important items. The Biblioteca Apostolica Vaticana again allowed me to consult manuscript materials, as did the Pius XII Library at St. Louis University, which has a valuable microfilm collection of many Vatican Library materials. The librarians at the Folger Library in Washington allowed me to use their important materials. All of this research was made possible by a grant from the Giles W. and Elise G. Mead Foundation.

In Málaga, Spain, Maria Soledad Santos Arrebola helped me untangle the wording of a poorly printed copy of the Alvaro Flores poem and kept me from making several silly mistakes in translation. Robert Bromber reviewed the sections concerned with the English prisoners in Mexico and then made suggestions based on his own research in this area. Geoffrey Parker read the entire manuscript and made many helpful comments. In addition, he very kindly sent me prints of documents I had missed at Simancas (AGS Estado 153) and gave me copies of his notes on the financial reports submitted by Hawkins as treasurer of the navy (PRO E 351 and AO 1). I had avoided consulting these latter documents on purpose, because they are both voluminous and difficult to decipher. He convinced me that this was a mistake.

My son Joseph helped me solve nagging computer problems, and my son Matt advised me on the preparation of computer-generated illustrations and maps (the latter of which were prepared with Cartesia software and Corel Draw). My daughter Sarah Forrest kept me supplied with a steady stream of photocopied materials from libraries at the several universities where she studied and worked. My wife, Mary Ann, helped with research at the Public Record Office, the British Library, and the Archivo General de la Nación. Sadly, Barney found the duties involved in the preparation of this volume to be more onerous than a dog should bear. I trust he is now reading the results in another, better place.

While involved in the research I made every effort to record proper names just as they were in the original documents. Men of the Elizabethan age spelled their names in diverse ways at various times, sometimes differently in the same document. This was not the case for John Hawkins and his brother, though. They consistently spelled their name Hawkyns, and their clerks did the same. Even so, most of their contemporaries wrote it as Hawkins, and the practice has continued to this day. Someone ought to have the courage to change it back to Hawkyns, but that someone is not me. However, I have kept the original spelling of this and other terms in quotations from original documents and have preserved all original spellings, accents, and abbreviations to the extent that such things are reasonably possible.

There is a similar problem with English names in foreign documents. Spanish writers tended to refer to Hawkins as Aquins or a similar variant, while his friend Fitzwilliams was regularly called Fizulians. The meaning in both cases is clear, but other men are not so easy to identify. Guillermo Verde could be William Green or Bird or Baird. Some Englishmen captured by Spain gave fictitious names; other men apparently had both an English and a Spanish name. In several cases two men had the same or very similar names, and at least one man used two different English names. Spanish officials often did not know what the real names might be, and this confusion is manifest in the official sources. To minimize the problem for readers who want to consult the original manuscripts I have tried to match the footnote references with the names used in the documents.

Printed collections of English documents commonly modernize grammar and spelling, sometimes changing word order or adding words that appear to have been omitted in the original. Although this approach makes the text easier to read, it also alters the meaning. Beyond that it makes men of little learning appear to be more literate than they really were. I have tried to avoid the problem by consulting the original documents in every case of importance and by taking all quotations from the original texts.

A final problem has to do with dates. In England the new year began on 25 March, but Spain and other countries started the new year on 1 January. When it seems likely that this difference might confuse the reader who wants to consult the original source, the new style is noted in parentheses following the date that appears on the document. A similar matter involves dates after 15 October 1582, when Spain and other Catholic countries began to follow the Gregorian calendar. This change produced a ten-day difference with England and other countries that continued to use the Julian calendar. These conflicts are also noted in parentheses.

Even so, there is no such thing as a perfect book, as Donald Cutter has observed. I ask the reader in advance to forgive any errors in copying or clumsiness in style.

Introduction

This is a nation of overwhelming audacity, courageous, impetuous,
unmerciful in war, warm on first acquaintance, sneering at death, but
boastful about it, cunning, and completely given to dissimulation,
whether in word or deed; above all they possess prudence,
along with great eloquence and hospitality.
Emanuel van Meteren

Ask a man from Devon to name the greatest mariner of the
Elizabethan age, and he is likely to say Sir Francis Drake.
But Drake's cousin and mentor, Sir John Hawkins, argu-
ably knew more about seamanship and did more for his
country than Drake. During several voyages in the
1560s Hawkins demonstrated to his countrymen that good profits
could be made trading in the Spanish ports of the West Indies. He also
introduced his queen and his fellow merchants to the loathsome business of slave trading, where even greater profits could be made by men
whose consciences were not of exceeding tenderness.

His interest in the West Indies was sharply diminished at the end
of that decade, when his ships were set upon by a Spanish fleet under
orders from a new Spanish viceroy. In the end each side saw the conflict
differently. Hawkins called the attack a piece of treachery. The viceroy
said Hawkins was a pirate who deserved what he got. With much of

his fleet lost and a great number of his men in Spanish custody, Hawkins spent the next few years trying to secure freedom for his men and reimbursement for his losses. In the process he concluded agreements with the Spanish crown that looked very much like treason to authorities in England. Even so, he was a man of such ability that he could not be ignored. Because of this he was appointed to oversee the reorganization of the naval service, turning it into a fleet capable of challenging Spain, the greatest empire of the day.

His loyalty was tested later, during the Armada battles. Hawkins proved to be a patriot, and the fleet he built defeated the enemy. Despite this success, Hawkins was never fully trusted again. He was nonetheless kept in service for the rest of his life, largely because the queen could think of no one to replace him. It was too long. Hawkins outlasted his usefulness and ended his life at sea as joint commander of an expedition he did not want to lead.

Hawkins was excoriated by later generations for his involvement in piracy and slave trading. He lived in an age of religious and political change, when prudent men kept their options open. Even so, his apparent willingness to shift loyalties marked his reputation with an indelible hint of treason and a suspicion of religious indifference. By the time he died, Hawkins was a thoroughgoing Protestant, loyal to queen and country. In his earlier days, this may not have been true, as we shall see.

1

The Uses of Duplicity

To harpe no longer upon this string, & to speake a word of
that iust commendation which our nation doe indeed deserue: it can not
be denied, but as in all former ages, they have bene men full of actiuity,
stirrers abroad, and searchers of the remote parts of the world, so in
this most famous and peerlesse gouernement of her most excellent
Maiesty, her subiects through the speciall assistance, and blessing
of God, in searching the most opposite corners and quarters
of the world, and to speake plainly, in compassing the vaste
globe of the earth more than once, haue excelled
all the nations and peoples of the earth.
Richard Hakluyt

Plymouth sits on the edge of England. In Elizabethan times the outer bay was wide open to every gale sweeping across the Atlantic. But wooden ships blown into the bay found a town nestled in the lee of a hill called the Plymouth Hoe. Off to one side the weary mariners could see a snug harbor whose narrow entrance would keep out the worst of the wind and the waves. Stout timber wharves lined the shore, along a strand where storerooms, forges, brew houses, and shops faced the water. Narrow streets ran down the back of the hill, lined with the houses of leading merchants. The buildings faced inward toward courtyards where servants and family members went about their business, cleaning stables, tending gardens, handling goods brought in by the ships. Frequent driving rains sluiced down the streets, pouring all their effluvia into the harbor. Warmed later by the sun, this floating mass raised a stink that made the name Catwater seem like an apt description.

1

Sixteenth-century view of Plymouth. Adapted from British Library Cotton Augustus I.1.38.

In the sixteenth century Plymouth was home to a rough breed of Englishmen who were sometimes merchants, sometimes pirates, and often both at the same time. Located alongside one of the major trade routes of Europe, the town attracted goods and traders from all the known world. Almonds, raisins, wine, and fine cloth came from lands bordering the Mediterranean. Timber, iron, and cordage came from Holland, the Dansk ports, and Muscovy. Ships from the East Indies brought spices, silks and damask, fine porcelain, and jewels. Others coming from the west brought hides and great stores of precious metal. Shipmasters who had friends in Plymouth were usually welcome, and their cargoes were safe. Others took their chances, coming into range of the cannons on the Hoe with their own guns loaded and men ready to serve them.

John Hawkins was born here in the early years of the sixteenth century. His grandfather, for whom he was named, came from Tavistock, an abbey town a few miles inland from Plymouth on the southeast coast of England. The older John Hawkins went to sea as a youth, then came home to marry Joan Amydas, who bore him two sons, Henry and William. Both boys became merchants and seamen. William was a rowdy lad and seemed to like a good brawl. In the spring of 1528 he and several others beat a neighbor, John Jurdon, so badly that he nearly died.[1]

Not much is clear about this fracas, but another is better known, largely because the Hawkins boys enjoyed battling in court as much as fighting in the street. A running feud with Peter Grisling was partly religious, partly political, and very personal. There were threats and arrests and appeals to the crown before the parties finally gave up the argument. In most of their scuffles drink was a major factor, but money was always at the root of things.[2] When there was a fight in Plymouth harbor between French and Spanish ships, William Hawkins helped to man the bulwarks. But he was still a merchant. Before he reported to the fortress, William sold the town 196 pounds of powder for its guns, then sold the town a few more guns as well.[3]

An ambitious and adventurous man, William Hawkins sailed with his own 250-ton ship, the *Pole of Plymouth,* to the Guinea coast of Africa. There he met Portuguese traders loading slaves for transport to "Brazil," a term then used to describe the islands and mainland in the

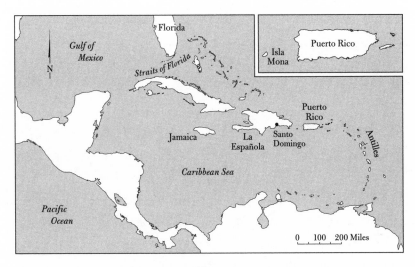

Map 1
Area visited by William Hawkins during his 1527 voyage to "Brazil."

northeastern part of South America. English records are silent about the date of his voyage, but it can be extracted from contemporary accounts. Richard Hakluyt, the great chronicler of early English exploration, mentioned the trip in different ways. Hakluyt first said that William Hawkins made "a voyage to Brasill . . . in the yeere 1530." He then went on to describe "three long and famous voyages unto the coast of Brasill" made by William Hawkins.[4] With the discrepancy called to his attention, Hakluyt clarified matters in a later edition of his work, saying there were two voyages to Brazil, in 1530 and 1532, as well as an earlier voyage of unspecified date.[5]

This earlier trip was almost certainly the one reported by Spanish witnesses in 1527. In one of the reports the captain of a Spanish caravel saw a 250-ton English ship arrive at the island of Mona on 19 November 1527. The Englishman commanding this vessel told the local people various stories about his journey. To one man he said he had been on a voyage to Newfoundland but had lost his pilot and become confused, and needed provisions. To another he said he was on a voyage to Brazil and had gone off course. No one knew which story to believe. The captain said that he wanted only to trade, but his vessel bristled with heavy guns, and his crewmen were armed with crossbows, lombards, pikes, and targets. He needed supplies and a pilot, said the English captain, but those who went aboard his ship saw that it was well manned by experienced seamen and good pilots, and well supplied with food and trade goods. The ship belonged to the king of England, he said. If the Spanish captain could read Latin, the English captain would be glad to show him the orders from his king. Alas, said the Spanish captain, "Because I could not read, I did not see it."[6]

While the authorities in Santo Domingo mulled the English captain's request to trade, the commander of the local citadel got nervous and fired his cannon at the English ship. The unnamed English captain promptly sailed away, with an oath and a threat to return and level the place. As it turned out, he did not go very far, just to Puerto Rico. There he conducted a more successful trade, and as the Spanish authorities later surmised, he scouted the ports and defenses of the area. The authorities also learned that during the entire visit, which lasted for some weeks, no one seems to have had the good sense to record the name of the English captain or the name of his ship. Even so, the records now gathered in Seville make it almost certain that the captain was William Hawkins and the ship was the *Pole of Plymouth,* the first foreign vessel ever allowed to stop in the West Indies ports.[7]

With his early trips to America and his other trading ventures, William Hawkins made a great deal of money. By 1532 he was rich enough and influential enough to begin a year of service as mayor of Plymouth. In 1540 he was listed as one of "the xiii persones that always be of the privy Councell and Chyffe men of the burgh and Towne of Plymouthe."[8] This was an impressive achievement for a man who was probably still in his thirties.

Some years earlier William Hawkins had married Joan Trelawny, who eventually gave him two children, named William and John. Marriage and birth records are nearly nonexistent for this period, but William is usually said to have been born about 1520. For John Hawkins the records are also silent, as was John himself. Always reticent, he said little more about his origins than that he was born in Plymouth.[9] Even so, inscriptions on his portrait and on his monument in Chatham church make it possible to arrive at a more exact birth date, with a slim degree of precision. The monumental inscription said he was sixty-three years old at his death in November 1595. The inscription on the portrait gives his age as fifty-eight in 1591. In those days the calendar year began on 25 March. Assuming that both statements are correct, it can be supposed that John Hawkins was born between November 1532 and 25 March 1533.[10]

Although details about his birth and childhood are skimpy, details about the town are more plentiful. In 1538, when William Hawkins was mayor for the second time, he purchased a tenement and garden on Woolster Street, near the quay where the family trading business was located.[11] Old John Hawkins lived several streets away, between St. Katherine's Lane and Finewell Street, though he also owned a house and garden in the same block as William.[12]

To judge from the few architectural fragments that remain today, this was a neighborhood of imposing houses, with sufficient room for a large family. The main hall probably had an adjoining parlor, and there were additional sleeping rooms upstairs. Interior walls and ceilings may have had plaster ornamentation. The attached gardens were intended as much for enjoyment as for the production of fruits and vegetables. Outbuildings provided room for servants and storage.[13]

But Plymouth was not an urban paradise. The town authorities struggled to provide fresh water, and sanitation was always a problem. The fresh smell of the sea and the stunning harbor views of modern Plymouth do not necessarily reflect the Plymouth of the sixteenth century. In those days Plymouth authorities had to warn ship captains not to discharge bilge into the harbor, and citizens were admonished not to throw dead animals or "any kynd of stingkyng thyng" into the water.[14]

The house of William Hawkins was a busy place, with merchants, foreign visitors, and government officials coming and going every day. There was talk of foreign lands, goods to be bought and sold, money to be made, political and religious matters to discuss. Other young relatives joined the household to profit from meeting important people and to be trained as merchants and seamen. One such lad was young Francis Drake, a cousin from Tavistock, who later recalled that there were a dozen such fellows in the Hawkins establishment when he lived there in the 1550s.[15] While the children in the Hawkins household learned to read and write, they learned more from watching their elders. They saw that money could be made in trade, that goods on the sea belonged to the man who was strong enough to take charge of them, and that reluctant customers could be coerced into buying. They learned to ignore the voice of authority when it came from a distance, and they found that a decision made in a burst of anger might very well have to be changed after sober reflection. Moreover, they found religious belief changing with changing circumstances.

During a period of twenty years the Hawkins family seems to

have moved easily from Catholic to Protestant and back again, following royal whims. Thus in 1538, after the crown confiscated ecclesiastical property, William Hawkins took charge of the ecclesiastical plate from the Grey Friars church, including several chalices, silver cruets, a silver pyx, silver candlesticks, the rood shoes and crown for the image of Our Lady, and a cross from the image of Saint Savior.[16] These he sold from time to time, buying armaments and other materials for the town defenses, but not making a final accounting to the town for at least another seven or eight years. When he served in Parliament under Henry VIII, he no doubt took the oath of supremacy.[17] Still, he seemed to think it wise to avoid being a leader of either religious faction. During the Prayer Book Rebellion of 1549, when rebels in Devon demanded a restoration of traditional religious practices, William Hawkins apparently did not join them, and royal officials in London thought he might really be loyal to the crown.[18] Even so, he managed to serve again in Parliament when Mary became queen and restored the old religion.

This sort of moral flexibility may have been what Raynold Wendon had in mind when he called William Hawkins "a traytor a thyff & a very vyllayne."[19] If so, William Hawkins had the best of this dispute, for the borough court found damages in his favor in the amount of two thousand marks.[20] In other disputes he was not so fortunate.

Piracy had been a popular calling in Plymouth for as long as any seaman could remember. If a plundered shipowner complained to the authorities, the Plymouth pirates usually said that the ships and goods were prizes that had been taken from the king's enemies. In May 1545 William Hawkins and his partner the mayor of Plymouth were called before the Privy Council to answer a charge of piracy. They declined to appear but sent word to London that there was nothing to worry about, because the goods belonged to Frenchmen, with whom England was then at war. Ordered to return the property forthwith, Hawkins and his partner sold them instead. Ultimately, the two were summoned to appear before the Admiralty Court, where William Hawkins was found to be in contempt and sent to prison "there to remaine untill he shoulde fulfill all and singulier the premisses, or otherwise agre with the saide marchaunt."[21]

In the rough and ready society of Plymouth seamen it was probably inevitable that young John Hawkins would acquire some of the same rowdy tendencies his father showed. Drunken fights were common, and William Hawkins was probably not greatly surprised to find his son John involved in these, just as old William himself had been. Still, the father could not have been pleased when he heard that one brawl in the summer of 1553 had gotten badly out of hand, and John Hawkins had killed his opponent. Details are sketchy, but Nicholas Slannyng, the Plymouth coroner, finally decided that John had acted in self defense "and not feloniously or with malice aforethought." Thereupon, money was paid, and a royal pardon was issued.[22]

By the time old William Hawkins died in 1554, both of his sons were established as merchants in Plymouth. William was older than John by a dozen years, married, and apparently living on Kinterbury Street in Plymouth in a house purchased a decade earlier. A few other English merchants were then establishing permanent bases in the islands of Gran Canaria and Tenerife, where sugar and fine Canary wine could be had in exchange for English goods. The Hawkins brothers chose a somewhat different course. Rather than stationing a factor in the Canaries, they forged a close alliance with the Ponce and Soler families, prominent Canarian merchants. Young Hawkins probably cemented these ties during several trips made to the Canaries in the 1550s.[23]

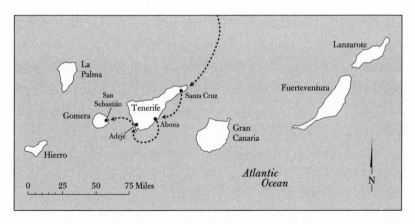

Map 2
Route taken by John Hawkins during his voyages to the Canary Islands.

John Hawkins went to other ports as well, trading, and representing family interests in foreign countries. In December 1556, when he
was only twenty-four years old, Hawkins went to Brest on a mission to
reclaim family property. During the recent war with France the
Hawkins brothers had seized the ship *Peter* from its French owners,
who promptly took it back when the ship ventured into a French
port.[24] The outcome of his mission is not entirely clear, though one
Canary Island historian thinks John Hawkins used the *Peter* for a trip
to the Canaries in 1560.[25]

On this journey Hawkins traded English textiles to the Soler family for a shipload of Canary island sugar. But he also engaged in a
shady affair, helping some English sailors hire a small vessel, ostensibly
for a trip to Granada. Instead, they glided quietly into the harbor at
Santa Cruz one dark night, then stole aboard a Spanish merchant vessel
heading for the Indies and sailed it home to Plymouth. There was
strong evidence that the pirates came from the Hawkins ship. Perhaps

the Soler and Ponce families were involved as well. They certainly remained his firm friends, and not just friends, but coreligionists. A priest from the family, Padre Pedro Soler, was convinced that Hawkins was not only an honest man, but a faithful Catholic, for he saw him go to church, hear Mass, and conduct himself in such a way that everyone assumed he was Catholic.[26]

Back home in Plymouth there was a surprise waiting for young John Hawkins, a baby boy named Richard. Nothing much is known of the child's mother. Richard later said through a Spanish interpreter that her name was Catalin Aquinza, very likely Catherine Hawkins.[27] Some writers have supposed the name to be a hispanicization of Katherine Gonson, who married John Hawkins five years later, in 1565. This is possible, though Richard himself called Katherine his mother in law, a term often used in those days to mean stepmother. Clearer evidence that Katherine Gonson was not Richard's natural mother comes from a contemporary who referred to Richard Hawkins as the "base sonne" of John Hawkins—or, in less polite terms, a bastard.[28]

Despite the circumstances, John Hawkins took his new responsibilities seriously. When Plymouth municipal officials established a grammar school in 1561, the young man contributed eight shillings toward the annual salary of the new schoolmaster, a contribution that put him in the top 20 percent of the donors, and may have indicated a new interest in caring for children.[29]

During the last trip to the Canaries young John Hawkins concluded an arrangement with the Ponce family, making them his partners in a new enterprise, the slave trade. According to the Spanish ambassador who saw the letters, the Ponces agreed to provide food, water, warehouse space, and vital information about the trade. They would even arrange for other Spanish merchants to accompany his ships. Most important, they would find an experienced pilot, who could guide Hawkins to the slave coasts of Africa and then to the ports of the Indies.[30]

With the agreements in hand, Hawkins was able to gain the support of Benjamin Gonson, the treasurer of the navy for Queen Elizabeth. Gonson proceeded to organize a syndicate of London merchants and investors to equip ships for the slaving voyage. These financiers included William Winter, who was then surveyor of the navy and master of ordnance, Sir Lionel Ducket, Sir Thomas Lodge, and others.[31] If any of them had qualms about involving themselves in the slave trade, no such record has survived. The same might be said about their attitude toward Spanish law. Under Spanish statutes no unregistered goods or slaves could be taken to the Indies, nor could anyone go to the Indies without the king's license.[32] Although no Englishman had tested Spanish resolve in these points, Hawkins and his backers probably thought that the goodwill of influential citizens in the Canaries and the Indies would help to ease any official sanctions that might later be imposed.[33]

With these hazards in mind, the partners equipped three or four ships for the journey. Even the largest was small, the 140-ton *Salomon*. The *Jonas* was a 40-ton vessel, and the *Swallow* a 30-ton ship. The first two belonged to the Hawkins brothers, and perhaps the third did as well. John Hawkins was captain of the largest ship; Thomas Hampton, another Plymouth merchant, commanded the *Swallow*. Aware of the heavy losses from sickness on overcrowded slave ships, Hawkins kept his crew to a bare minimum, one hundred men or fewer.[34] Young Francis Drake, on his first trip to the Canary Islands, was probably one of that number.[35]

Sailing from Plymouth in October 1562, Hawkins reached Tenerife, where he stopped to visit with his partners, the Ponte family, who

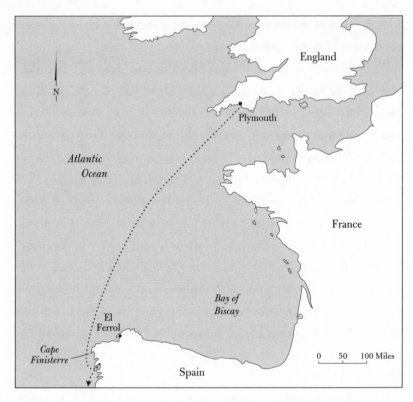

Map 3
The usual route to Africa and the West Indies went along the coast of Spain.

doubtless gave him the most recent news about Portuguese ships on the slave coasts. Pedro de Ponte had secured the services of an experienced pilot. Juan Martínez knew the routes to the Guinea coast and to the Indies, and because he was from Cádiz, where many foreign merchants lived, he could speak English. Martínez joined the fleet in Tenerife, where water and supplies were taken on board. No doubt the ships also carried the usual woolens and other trade goods from Devon, plus a supply of beans that would be cooked to feed the slaves.[36] Continuing to Sierra Leone, Hawkins captured several Portuguese vessels and a huge number of slaves. It was a brutal affair, one that Hawkins did not talk much about. To Richard Hakluyt he said only that he had "stayed some good time, and got into his possession, partly by the sword and partly by other meanes, to the number of 300. negroes at the least, besides other marchandises, which that country yeeldeth."[37] Spanish and Portuguese records tell a fuller story. According to those accounts Hawkins took half a dozen Portuguese ships on the way to Sierra Leone, plus cargoes of cloves, wax, ivory, and nearly four hundred black slaves.[38] When all this was finished, Hawkins sent one of his ships home, loaded with goods from Africa and the Canaries. Francis Drake returned home with that vessel.[39]

Guided by Juan Martínez, Hawkins had his augmented fleet in the Indies in early April 1563. Crammed into the holds of the ships and given a meager diet of beans and water, the slaves suffered horrible torments on the crossing. Nearly half seem to have perished on the way, if the totals listed in Spanish accounts are credible. The good planters on the island of Española were accustomed to seeing slaves who looked miserable, so they snapped up the wares Hawkins offered. He had acquired his goods and his slaves for next to nothing, and he could sell at bargain prices.[40]

While trade continued at Puerto de Plata, Monte Christi, and Isabela, authorities in Santo Domingo became aware of what Hawkins was doing. For a while nothing happened. Then, after most of the merchandise was sold, the Spanish officials in Santo Domingo decided that it was time for action. They dispatched Lorenzo Bernáldez with orders to arrest the Englishmen and seize their ships and goods. Crossing the island on horseback, Bernáldez arrived at Isabela in mid-April. There he managed to take two English sentries into custody. Of course, his horsemen could not capture the English ships, and perhaps they were not supposed to. By the time they arrived, Hawkins had only 140 slaves left, no doubt those who were too old or too young or too sick to be sold. There was a brief skirmish, then Bernáldez and Hawkins conferred. The Spanish officer insisted that license fees and duties be paid on all the slaves sold during the voyage. In response Hawkins offered to give three fourths of his remaining slaves to the crown, mostly those who attracted no buyers. In return Hawkins wanted the release of the captive Englishmen and a license to sell the other thirty-five slaves. The Spanish officer said no. Then Hawkins added the captured caravel to his offer, and Bernáldez accepted the terms.[41]

The license is a curious document, issued by a young officer who probably thought he could get no better terms but still suspected that the authorities at home might not approve of what he had done. The license would be valid, he said to Hawkins, "in so far as I can and by right ought to give it, and no more."[42] Of course he had no authority to give any trading license at all. It was cleverly done, said Bernáldez. "I agreed to mislead them, granting them the license they asked for, but doing it in such a way that it would have no value at all." Hawkins nonetheless proceeded to sell his remaining slaves, even while Bernáldez advised the colonists that the license was "worth nothing."[43]

Despite the loss of slaves to sickness and ransom, the Hawkins profits were huge. After loading his own three ships with gold, silver, pearls, ginger, sugar, hides, and other goods he had collected in trade with the colonists of Española, Hawkins found that he had more than he could conveniently carry home. Because of this he consigned the rest of his goods to two Spanish hulks that were in port at Isabela. To the captains he gave instructions to deliver the goods to Hugh Tipton in Seville, with Cristóbal de Santiesteban acting as intermediary. The ships belonged to the Martínez family, merchants in Seville, and the arrangements for their use were probably made by Pedro de Ponte before the journey started. One carried 1,300 hides, the other 476 hides and two chests of sugar.[44] There has been some speculation as to why Hawkins would send these shipments to Spain, where the goods were immediately confiscated.[45] The answer is twofold. First, the Martínez ships were the ones that were available. Second, Hawkins hoped that Spanish authorities would think the goods were legitimate Spanish trade items coming from the Indies in Spanish vessels. The plan might have succeeded, but colonial jealousies, plus a generous measure of bigotry, intervened. A local official, a licenciado named Echegoyan, wrote several letters of complaint, calling the trade with Hawkins a "scandalous affair." In his reports to Seville, Echegoyan give copious details about the visit of the Englishman. He called Bernáldez a recently converted Jew who was not to be trusted. Moreover, he said that all the local people called the trading license "a great joke." More than this, Echegoyan thought that something sinister might be afoot. "Tomorrow all this land could become part of England," he said, "if steps are not taken."[46]

Armed with Echegoyan's information, royal officials in Seville seized one of the ships as contraband as soon as it arrived. Officials in Lisbon seized the other ship when it landed there. Thomas Hampton, sent by Hawkins in command of the first vessel, just managed to escape imprisonment in Spain, but others were less fortunate and landed in prison. Hawkins and his London partners tried for several years to secure reimbursement for the lost goods, but nothing came of their efforts.[47] Instead, this first Hawkins voyage, with all the chicanery and secret negotiations, contributed substantially to the deterioration of relations between Spain and England.

What about the losses? Even if the goods Hawkins sent to Spain were worth the thousand pounds or so he later claimed, they were really excess profits from a voyage that had already made a great deal of money. When Hawkins arrived in Plymouth in late summer 1563, his ships were loaded with Spanish coins, jewels, and trade goods. These brought a handsome return to the London investors, so much so that plans were soon afoot for further trips to the Indies.[48]

Some three or four months elapsed between the time Hawkins left Española and the time he arrived in Plymouth. To account for this, the Spanish historian Rumeu de Armas has suggested that Hawkins stopped in the Canaries and arranged with the Ponte family for a new voyage.[49] The evidence is circumstantial but convincing. Two unidentified English ships stopped in Santa Cruz, Tenerife, in June 1563, and the captain met with local civic and religious officials.[50] At about the same time, royal officials in the Canaries confiscated slaves, church vestments, and other items of cargo that belonged to Hawkins, placing them in bond with Pedro de Ponte. Ponte later wrote to tell Hawkins that he could have everything back, as Ponte had convinced the officials that the goods belonged to somebody else.[51]

No doubt Ponte family members were partners of some sort in the slave trader's newest plans. Queen Elizabeth also took a share, unconcerned that it involved buying and selling human beings. As her contribution to the new venture, Elizabeth gave Hawkins the use of the *Jesus of Lubeck,* a vessel of 700 tons. Originally bought secondhand for the navy of Henry VIII, the *Jesus* was in poor condition, but Hawkins could see distinct advantages in adding it to his fleet.[52] First, there was plenty of room for a huge cargo of goods and slaves going to the Indies and room as well for all his profits going home. He would not have to pretend that the cargoes he sent home belonged to Spanish merchants in Spanish ships going to Spanish ports. Best of all, the royal standard flew from its mast. As on the first voyage, Hawkins also took the 140-ton *Salomon* and the 30-ton *Swallow,* as well as a 50-ton ship named the

Tiger. Following what seemed to be a proven standard, he took fewer than 150 men in his greatly expanded fleet.[53] A smaller crew meant fewer losses to sickness and battle, and lower expenses as well.

Almost as soon as the plans began to be discussed, the Spanish ambassador, Guzmán de Silva, heard that Hawkins intended to go once more to the Indies. English pirates were haunting the Channel, looking for merchant vessels sailing between Spain and the Netherlands. Guzmán de Silva seemed to think that Hawkins intended to join the raiders. When the ambassador complained to the queen's officials, he was told that Hawkins had royal permission to make the trip. Guzmán de Silva thereupon wrote directly to the queen, asking her to stop Hawkins, lest some harm be done to Spanish subjects. She replied that Hawkins was no pirate, but a good man and rich besides. He simply wanted to trade. If this was so, asked the ambassador, why did he go in such heavily armed ships, with a full complement of soldiers, artillery, and munitions? Responding for the queen, William Cecil, her chief minister, repeated her previous assurances. Unable to do more, Guzmán de Silva reported all of this to the Spanish king. Philip, for his part, decided that nothing else should be done for the moment.[54]

By 18 October 1564 Hawkins was ready to leave Plymouth. This second slaving voyage for John Hawkins was probably the first West Indies trip for his twenty-two-year-old kinsman Francis Drake, who sailed again as an ordinary seaman.[55] A few miles from port the fleet met with two royal ships, the *Minion* and the *John Baptist,* both bound for the Guinea Coast. The first ship soon sailed off, but the *John Baptist* stayed with Hawkins until a storm three days later drove this ship away as well, along with his own tiny *Swallow.* Gathering his fleet again off Cape Finisterre, Hawkins put in at El Ferrol on the coast of Galicia.

Here the ships remained for several days, during which time Hawkins drew up a set of instructions for his fleet. Hawkins ordered "the small shippes to be alwayes a head and a weather of the Jesus, and to speake twise a day with the Jesus at least." As a signal he said, "If in the day the Ensigne bee ouer the poope of the Jesus, or in the night two lightes, then shall all the shippes speake with her. If there be three lights aboord the Jesus, then doeth she cast about." There were also provisions for other emergencies. "If the weather be extreme, that the small shippes cannot keep companie with the Jesus, then all to keep companie with the Salomon, and foorthwith to repaire to the Island of Teneriffe, to the Northward of the road of Sirroes." The other ships were to have their own signals: "If any happen to any misfortune, then to shewe two lights, and to shoote off a piece of Ordinance. If any loose companie, and come in sight againe, to make three yawes, and strike the Myson [mizzen] three times." The final order bade them "Serue God dayly, loue one another, preserve your victuals, beware of fire, and keepe good companie."[56]

The day after the fleet arrived at El Ferrol, the *Minion* came into port with a tragic tale. A nearby ship, the *Merlin,* had suffered an explosion in its powder magazine, then caught fire and promptly sank. A few badly scorched survivors made their escape in a small boat that happened to be towed at the stern. With this sobering news Hawkins ordered his own vessels to put their brigantines astern. He then gave some signal guns to the *Minion* and with his augmented fleet left once more on 30 October.[57]

Reaching the island of Madeira on 4 November 1564, Hawkins at first thought he was in the Canaries. Quickly grasping his error, he sailed on. After some additional confusion on the coast of Las Palmas and Gomera, Hawkins reached the port of Adeje in Tenerife on 8

November. The *Swallow,* separated from the fleet two days earlier, awaited him there, just as his sailing orders had directed.

Expecting the usual cordial reception from the Ponte family, Hawkins immediately rowed for shore in his pinnace. Much to his surprise, the local militia, armed to the teeth, suddenly appeared at the shoreline. Taking the Hawkins ships for a pirate fleet, the Canarians were prepared for battle. Hawkins quickly called to them, saying that he was a good friend of Pedro de Ponte's. As it happened, Pedro's son Nicolaso was in the militia group. When Hawkins saw Nicolaso, he jumped out of the boat and waded onto the beach for the usual festive welcome.[58] The confiscated slaves and vestments were returned to him shortly thereafter. Hawkins promptly sold the vestments to Pedro de Ponte, who passed them on to a local curate. There was a scandal about this later, when it became apparent that the vestments had been taken from a church in England. When that was revealed, some of the local people suddenly recalled that they had thought all along that Hawkins and his men were *luteranos*—the term applied in Spain to all Protestants.[59]

Taking advantage of the opportunity to resupply his vessels, Hawkins purchased firewood, fresh water, and provisions from the local merchants. He also made necessary repairs to the ships in his fleet. His flagship, the *Jesus,* for example, had sprung its mainmast in a recent storm, and the mast had to be reset. A week later, on 15 November 1564, Hawkins and his fleet put to sea once more.[60]

Heading for Cabo Blanco, Hawkins and his ships passed ten or so Portuguese fishing boats, which fled at the first sight of the suspected English pirates. Then one of his little pinnaces capsized in a squall, and before anyone on the *Jesus* had noticed, the overturned boat was a mile or two behind, with survivors perched gloomily on the keel. Hampered by wind and current, his ships could not easily turn about or sail

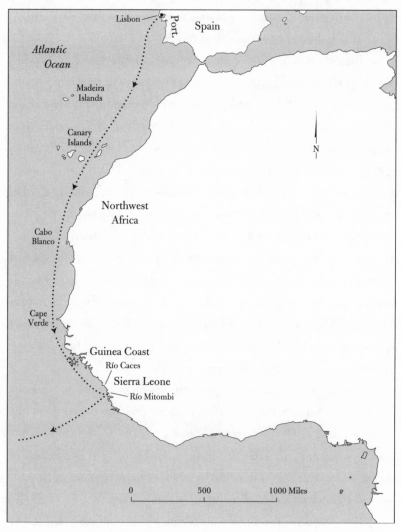

Map 4
The slave raids on the Guinea Coast in 1564.

into the wind. But Hawkins had the presence of mind to order a great boat put into the water with two dozen men at the oars. Rowing hard against the current, the oarsmen eventually reached the stricken vessel and brought both men and pinnace back to the *Jesus*.[61]

The next port of call was Angla de Santa Ana, somewhat south of Cabo Blanco, on 25 November. Previously mistaken for a pirate, Hawkins now decided to be one. The Portuguese fishermen who worked from this harbor made regular tribute payments to the local king, who was supposed to protect them from intruders. But the fishermen and their Moorish protectors were armed only with bows and arrows and not prepared for an artillery bombardment. After Hawkins fired a few well-aimed cannon balls, he was able to take all the provisions that he wanted without any argument.[62]

At Cape Verde, reached on 29 November, Hawkins rescued a French seaman, Martin Atinas, who had been shipwrecked a few weeks earlier. From this point he began to form his men into raiding parties, sending them ashore to hunt for slaves. The best pickings were in an island called Sambula, where they went ashore every day, shooting, burning, and looting. The slaves they captured at Sambula had already been enslaved by the ruling Samboses, who had conquered the place some three years earlier.

Late in December 1564 Hawkins took his fleet to the Río Callousa, where Portuguese traders sold him two caravel loads of slaves on Christmas Day. At their advice he sailed on to a town called Bymba, where the Portuguese said he could probably take another hundred slaves and gold as well from the peaceful inhabitants. Relying on this information, Hawkins took forty armed men ashore and soon found himself under fierce attack. Barely escaping to the boats, Hawkins found that he had gained ten new slaves but had suffered nearly thirty wounded and seven killed, including the captain of the *Solomon*. The same day some of the sailors bathing near the ships were attacked by sharks. Losses in the sea amounted to five killed and one grievously injured.[63]

Several years later the Portuguese merchants submitted their claims in London. They said that Hawkins and his men took gold, ivory, wax, and at least sixty slaves from them in the rivers Mitombi and Caces in Sierra Leone. He also seized some of their ships and left the mariners on the beach. One merchant, Francisco dal Varenga, claimed that Hawkins "confiscated and extorted a ship named the *Cola,* loaded with merchandise to the value of 4,000 ducats, in the river called Caces."[64] Others made similar claims. No doubt they exaggerated, but the basic facts are probably true, for Hawkins always considered Portuguese ships and cargoes fair game. After a further month on the coast at Tagarín, Hawkins departed for the West Indies on 29 January.

The crossing was miserable for slaves and seamen alike. For three weeks the fleet was becalmed and nearly ran out of water. Then the winds came up, a series of storms that threatened to send every vessel to the bottom. At last the weather changed, as the chronicler of the voyage said, because "Almightie God . . . never suffereth his elect to perish." The slaves were not numbered among the elect. Of four hundred or so who started the voyage, only 370 seem to have reached the Indies.[65]

Finally, on 9 March the fleet arrived at La Dominica, reputed to be the "Island of Cannybals." Fortunately for Hawkins the landfall was entirely deserted, and his men were able to fill their water casks without molestation. A few days later they came to the island of Margarita, where the citizens and officials sold them both beef and mutton but would not trade for merchandise or slaves. When they learned that Hawkins had a local man as pilot for the voyage through the Indies, the officials tried to keep the man ashore. Then they sent word to the viceroy in Santo Domingo, and a message was forwarded to the other ports, forbidding the inhabitants to trade with Hawkins. A few days later Hawkins stopped his ships at a place called Santa Fe, where the

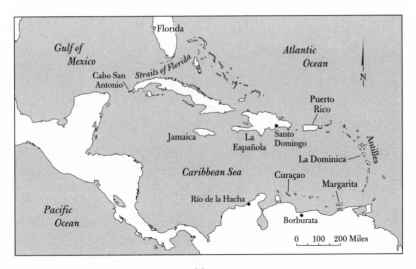

Map 5
The Hawkins voyage to the Caribbean in 1565.

Indians traded maize cakes, chickens, potatoes, and a variety of pineap-
ple for the "beades, pewter whistles, glasses, kniues, and other trifles"
carried in the ships.[66]

On 3 April 1565 Hawkins brought his fleet into harbor at Borburata and began to negotiate with the local officials. Told at first that he
could not trade without a license from the governor, Hawkins said he
was willing to wait for such a license to arrive. In the meantime he
wanted to sell some of the "lean and sicke Negroes." This, he said,
would give him enough money for supplies and would give the sick
slaves a chance to recover. After several days of discussion, the locals
agreed to let him sell thirty slaves, but there was further bickering over
price. At one point the locals told him that permission had been granted not for poor negroes, but for poor purchasers, for they had little
money. Finally on 14 April the governor arrived. Getting down to busi-

ness, Hawkins gave the governor his well-rehearsed story that he was the *capitán general* of Queen Elizabeth, whose ensign graced his flagship. He had been to Guinea on a mission for the queen but had been driven off course by contrary wind and sea. Now he needed to sell his slaves just to pay for supplies and repairs on his ships.[67]

Hawkins made it sound so reasonable. After all, the countries were at peace and traded freely with each other. Surely in this emergency situation the royal officials of Spain could stretch the law somewhat to help a royal official of their friends the English, especially when everyone would benefit. Spanish colonists would be able to buy slaves and goods at prices considerably lower than Spanish merchants could offer, and naturally there would be gifts for everyone. Governor Alonso Bernáldez wanted to allow the trade, but he also wanted to spread the responsibility. First he took testimony from several witnesses, including one who claimed to have heard Hawkins say he would devastate the entire coast if he were denied a license. After this, the governor agreed to grant the license, but the two men disagreed about the terms. Hawkins refused to pay the royal treasury a license fee of thirty ducats per slave. The governor dropped this provision but inserted a clause saying that the license was effective only insofar as he had authority to grant it. Disgusted with the whole proceeding, Hawkins ripped the license to shreds. He then put a hundred armed men ashore and threatened to march on the town. In the end the governor agreed to all his demands. Hawkins then insisted upon receiving the hostages before he would land his slaves and merchandise.[68] There was no more difficulty. The governor became one of his best customers, buying so much that Hawkins had to take his promissory note for a six hundred–peso balance, payable later in Río de la Hacha.[69]

After all the negotiations, the citizens at Borburata proved to be reluctant buyers, so much so that at one point Hawkins took his fleet out of the harbor, pretending to leave in disgust. No sooner had he done so than the French pirate and slave trader Jean Bontemps approached the town with his own ships full of slaves and trade goods. Stopping the French vessel, Hawkins met briefly with Bontemps, then returned to Borburata and finished his sales with no further interruption. But the obviously friendly association between Hawkins and the French pirate left some local people convinced that Hawkins was a close ally of Bontemps's, and was probably a pirate himself.[70]

Others had different opinions. In the course of his many conversations with Spanish officials Hawkins boasted that he was "a very fine gentleman and servant of his majesty [King Philip] whose vassal he had been when he was king of England."[71] This transparent exaggeration was rooted in Philip's tenure as king of England during his marriage to Mary Tudor. But Hawkins repeated the story many times, telling Governor Bernáldez, "I am a great servant of the majesty of King Philip, whom I served when he was king of England."[72] The story lost nothing in the retelling, and those who heard it added embellishments of their own. A few years later one of the local men, Juanes de Urquiza, stated that he knew for a fact that Hawkins was the first man knighted by Philip when he came to England.[73]

Once matters were settled at Borburata and the slaves were sold for what Hawkins considered to be a fair price, he demanded a testimonial letter from the officials and sailed for Río de la Hacha. His reception there followed the same scheme: the royal officials refused at first to trade, Hawkins threatened, the officials relented, and the planters said his prices were too high. Early in the morning of 21 May 1565, Hawkins fired a cannon to alert the townspeople, then put a hundred armed men ashore. The citizens armed themselves and marched out to meet him, drums rolling, a flag bearer in the lead, and horsemen prancing to one side. A few more cannon balls were fired from the ships, and the citizens decided that they had shown all the resistance advisable. In fact, the entire affair was a charade, or so the investigating officials in Spain concluded later. They found that the spectacle was arranged in advance between the citizens of Río de la Hacha and Hawkins. In any case, the local people proved to be eager customers, granting hostages, purchasing all the rest of the slaves, perhaps as many as three hundred, and taking most of the other goods as well. They even gave Hawkins special orders for merchandise to be brought on the next voyage and provided him with a written testimonial of his good conduct and fair dealing.[74]

With his entire cargo disposed of for a good price, Hawkins sailed to Curaçao, where he purchased 1,500 hides from the cattle drovers who lived there. The animals had been introduced a quarter of a century earlier and had flourished beyond anyone's dreams. The few inhabitants of the island existed on a marvelous diet of beef, vegetables, and fruit, slaughtering additional cattle simply to harvest the hides and tongues. John Sparke, a prominent merchant and later mayor of Plymouth, was also the chronicler of this expedition. He asserted that he saw a field strewn with a hundred rotting beef carcasses from which only the hides and tongues had been removed.[75] A receipt for one of the transactions shows how trade was accomplished before the day of bank transfers:

> I received from Señor Lázaro de Peserano of the Island of Curasau 978 hides, each hide valued at 10 reales of silver, for which I paid to Artur Noios six slaves, two men, two women, and two children, and 344 varas of Ruan [a measure of cloth]; and since it is true that the said Artur received payment, he verified it by signing his name. 13 May 1565,

Artur Mue   Laçaro Peseraro

More: I received my payment of 707 hides, four slaves, 214 varas of Ruan, and 30 varas of telillas. 15 May 1565 años. artur mue.[76]

Obviously, Lázaro Peserano was delighted to have a customer for his hides. Hawkins had wanted a thousand hides, and Peserano apologized for being short by twenty-two. He also asked Hawkins to take delivery on shore, as he was reluctant to bring the hides out in his canoes.[77]

After this stop Hawkins took his fleet to Jamaica, where he had promised to take Llerena, a Jamaican captive he had freed in Guinea. As it turned out, Llerena could not recognize the coastline, so the fleet sailed past the island without stopping. Hawkins stopped once more for water at the Isla de Pinos, then proceeded to Cabo San Antonio on the western tip of Cuba, where Llerena again failed to recognize landmarks. Hawkins thus missed an opportunity to purchase an additional cargo of hides and to replenish his supply of food, while the poor Jamaican merchant ended up going back to England with the rest of the crew.[78]

From this point the details of the journey are less clear. An informant in England later told the Spanish ambassador that for the next two weeks Hawkins kept his fleet in the Florida channel, hoping to pick off a straggling Spanish ship. John Sparke, on the other hand, said that they were simply looking for a good place to fill the water casks and trying to find the French settlement recently established by René Laudonnière. Whatever the reason, after fifteen days, Hawkins and his ships reached the Río de Mayo on the Florida coast, where the French colony was located.[79]

On this leg of the voyage the French pilot rescued in Guinea proved his worth. Martin Atinas of Dieppe had previously come to Florida with the expedition of Jean Ribault in 1562. Having secured his services as pilot, Hawkins was repaid when the man led him as ordered to the French settlement at Fort Caroline on the Río de Mayo. There Hawkins was received cordially by the Huguenots, and he responded in kind. Seeing that Laudonnière needed a ship, Hawkins sold him the smallest one in his fleet. In exchange, Laudonnière gave Hawkins four cannons and a supply of powder and shot, plus a promissory note for the remainder of the purchase price.[80]

The trip home was long but not terribly difficult. Leaving on 28 July, Hawkins sailed north to catch the winds and currents. As supplies ran low, he stopped off the Newfoundland banks to fish for cod. On St. Bartholomew's Eve, 23 August, he managed to purchase a good supply of fish from two French vessels, whose captains were no doubt astonished at his willingness to pay for something he could easily have taken by force. Finally, on 20 September 1565 Hawkins brought his ships into port at Padstow in Cornwall. From there he sent a note to the queen, advising her of his arrival, and giving a few details of the voyage. There was just the slightest exaggeration in his description of events involving citizens of Spain and Portugal: "I have always been a help to all Spaniards and Portugals that have come in my way without any harm or prejudice by me offered to any of them."[81] Not true, perhaps, but Hawkins had letters of good conduct from officials in Borburata and Río de la Hacha, and he was quick to show these to anyone who asked.[82]

Of the 170 men who began the journey, all but twenty returned, a remarkable record for those days. The twenty deaths came in the usual ways for sailors. The first day out an unnamed officer was struck in the head and killed by a pulley swinging from a sheet. In Guinea a carpenter went ashore to harvest wood, was ambushed, and had his throat cut. Seven men were killed in battle, and four were eaten by sharks. At least twenty-eight others were injured, and there were unnumbered losses from disease in Sierra Leone. But it was a good record for a slaving voyage, on which the slave deaths were not even counted.[83]

Sparke's record of the journey is laced with many tales about the natives and their customs, some of which may be true. Among his stories is a description of potatoes, which he called "the most delicate rootes that may be eaten." He also includes a famous account of natives in Florida smoking tobacco. "The Floridians when they trauel haue a kinde of herbe dryed, which with a cane, and an earthen cup in the end, with fire, and the dried herbs put together do sucke thoro the cane the smoke thereof, which smoke satisfieth their hunger, and they liue foure or five days without meat or drinke." Relying no doubt on this information, early English chroniclers credited Hawkins with introducing both the potato and tobacco to Europe or at least to England, and the story is still repeated. But Sparke also noted that "all the Frenchmen" were already using tobacco, which considerably undercuts any presumption that might be made in favor of Hawkins.[84]

Profits from the second Hawkins voyage were marvelous, though no one would say just how much they were. Guzmán de Silva heard from his informants that Hawkins "brought back more than 50,000 ducados in gold, plus some pearls, hides, and sugar in payment for his slaves." Later, when he had more complete information, including some from Hawkins himself, the Spanish ambassador said that the business was so profitable Hawkins could afford to pay the governor of Río de la Hacha 1,600 pesos for the license to trade there and to take a promissory note from the governor of Borburata for another 600 pesos' worth of merchandise. Total profits, he said, were a whopping 60 percent.

2

The new Hawkins coat of arms featured a slave bound with a rope. Ellis, "Life of Sir John Hawkins," 206.

"They tell me that the profits have boosted the spirits of some merchants for another expedition," Guzmán de Silva wrote to the king. "They even say that the same Hawkins will go again in May, a matter of importance that needs some resolution."[85]

With such marvelous profits from slavery, the investors seemed to lose all sense of shame. William Garvey, Clarenceux king of arms, agreed. His grant of arms noted that Hawkins was "lineally descended from his ancestors a gentilman" of "couragious worthe and famious enterprises." The arms feature a black slave bound with a rope.[86]

Meeting the newly minted gentleman in the royal palace by chance on 20 October, Guzmán de Silva spoke to him at some length about the voyage. The two hit it off immediately and began to visit regularly thereafter. Guzmán de Silva enjoyed entertaining the young slave trader in his London home. This was a man who was easy to like. Just as had happened with officials in the Canary Islands, in Borburata and in Río de la Hacha, Guzmán de Silva found many redeeming qualities in the young English slave trader. He was clever and dynamic. Not overly concerned with truth or morality, he was nevertheless a fine seaman and certainly a persistent trader. Guzmán de Silva thought Hawkins ought to be watched, but he also thought the man lacked a firm commitment to Queen Elizabeth. Perhaps he could be brought into the service of the king of Spain. Was Hawkins interested? Well, he said, he might be.[87]

2

Robbing Portugal and Selling to Spain

Dame Katharine,
His first religious wife,
Saw yeeres thrice tenne
And two of mortall life,
Leaving the world the sixth,
The seventh ascending.
Margaret Hawkins

When Ambassador Guzmán de Silva invited John Hawkins to dinner, he had more in mind than pleasant conversation, though there was plenty of that. Voluble as ever, Hawkins told the ambassador that his voyage to the Spanish ports in the Indies was approved in advance by the queen, whose instructions he had followed strictly in all his dealings. For proof he offered to let Guzmán de Silva see the licenses granted by the local governors, though truthfully he had only one, having destroyed the other in a fit of anger. If Guzmán de Silva noticed the omission, he did not say so in his report to King Philip, largely because Hawkins also claimed to have testimonial letters from these same officials. But Guzmán de Silva was no fool. He knew that Hawkins glossed over certain details, especially his method for dealing with local people: initial threats, often bogus, followed by a negotiated agreement to trade. In a coded section of his report Guzmán de Silva said that he was certain the governor of Borburata had made a secret agreement with Hawkins. "He had a private discussion with the governor," said Guzmán de Silva, "and they agreed between them that the next day he would put men ashore, and they would make a show of entering the place and causing damage. Then the governor would march out, and so that Hawkins would not damage the place, he would be allowed to carry on his business. And so it was done."[1]

By the time they met again the following February, Guzmán de Silva had become a great admirer of Hawkins. "He is rated as a good pilot," said Guzmán de Silva, "and he appears to be a clever man." Then in cipher Guzmán de Silva added that Hawkins had said that he was unhappy in England: "He is not content with things as they are here." This was just the opening Guzmán de Silva wanted, for he had an idea of recruiting the English seaman for service in the Spanish navy. "I told him that he does not belong in this country, but would be better off in the service of your majesty, who would be able to employ him as he has other Englishmen."[2] To this proposal Hawkins replied that he could scarcely serve in Spain, for he had gone to the Indies without the permission of King Philip. And anyway, he was more interested in getting back the goods that had been confiscated in 1563.

A few days later the two met again. This time Hawkins brought the documents he had received from the governors in the Indies and allowed Guzmán de Silva to make copies, which may still be seen in the Spanish archives.[3] Guzmán de Silva again suggested that Hawkins ought to be in the service of the Spanish king, with her majesty's permission, of course.

Hawkins replied that the suggestion appealed to him, especially because the Turkish fleet was threatening to raid the Mediterranean ports once more. "He would serve at his own cost," Guzmán de Silva reported, "with three ships each of two hundred tons or more, with one of three hundred tons, all of them very good, and manned by five hundred very able men." Only two problems remained to be solved. First,

Hawkins wanted assurance that the king of Spain had forgiven his prior infractions of Spanish law; and second, he would need some token payment. "As a reward for his service, he would be content with the hundred slaves, or the value thereof, that he left with your majesty's ministers in Santo Domingo, for which a certain sum of money was paid, and he used this to buy some hides that he sent in a ship to Seville." Eager for a response from Madrid, Hawkins told Guzmán de Silva a few days later that he still wanted to go and might even be able to get another ship, this one belonging to the queen, who would surely give it to him. Guzmán de Silva must move quickly, said Hawkins, because many of his best men knew the way to the Indies and might decide to go there with other merchants if he did not sign them for the king's service very soon. At the end of March, Hawkins again went to see Guzmán de Silva, telling the ambassador that certain merchants were preparing in secret to send two ships to the Indies. He promised to keep Guzmán de Silva informed of developments, but said he really needed to know what the king would do.[4]

All these negotiations were supposedly secret, and it seems clear that Hawkins used them to mask his preparations for another trip to the Indies. In May, with no approval yet from the Spanish king, Hawkins told Guzmán de Silva that he was getting his ships ready for the sea, just in case Philip should approve his plan to sail against the Turks. Guzmán de Silva wanted to believe Hawkins, though he realized that all the activity might simply be another bit of dissembling. In fact Spanish agents at Plymouth were reporting that Hawkins intended to go to the Indies once more. Hearing this, Guzmán de Silva began to worry. If the stories were proven true, he would break his promise of secrecy and immediately ask the queen to ban another such voyage. As the summer progressed, Guzmán de Silva's suspicions grew, but

Hawkins managed to keep the ambassador guessing. It was not as easy to fool King Philip, who told Guzmán de Silva, "Keep an eye on what he is doing, and determine what intentions he might have for the ships he has fitted out."[5]

By October the truth was apparent. Hawkins was indeed ready to go to the Indies. When Guzmán de Silva complained to Queen Elizabeth, she simply told him that she did not know much about the matter. She thought some members of her council had invested in a previous trip, but Hawkins had not intended on that occasion to go to the Indies. He had simply been forced there by bad weather. And he traded only after the local governors had given him a license. In the end Guzmán de Silva showed the queen that he knew exactly what was going on. George Fenner had three ships at Portsmouth, with 150 men and artillery pieces from the queen's own arsenal. John Chichester had another ship ready at Bristol, and the well-known pirate William Cook was going with him. John Hawkins had three ships ready at Plymouth. Hearing this from Guzmán de Silva, Elizabeth summoned her chief minister, William Cecil, and in Guzmán de Silva's presence ordered him to find out where Hawkins and the others intended to go and to take whatever steps might be necessary.[6]

So orders were given, but no one took them very seriously. Dr. David Lewes of the Admiralty Court said that he could do little; John Chichester at Bristol and Hawkins at Plymouth were both outside his jurisdiction. George Fenner had already been forbidden to go, and Lewes did not even know William Cook. Hawkins was finally summoned to appear in London, but only, Guzmán de Silva believed, after a delay designed to allow Hawkins to send his fleet to sea. "It's the sort of thing they do here," said Guzmán de Silva. At the end of the month Dr. Lewes wrote to say that he was still uncertain whether they wanted him to deal with Hawkins. "If the power be referryd to me," he said, "I shall accordingly se it accomplished."[7]

A few days later Lewes wrote that he had taken a bond from Hawkins in the matter. The "bond" is an interesting document, unsigned, and incomplete:

> quingentas libras bone et Legalis monete Anglie
> The condicion of this recognizance is suche, that where the abovebounden John Hawkens hathe preparid a shipp of his callid the Swallowe of Plimouthe foresaid to be sent unto the parttes of Guinea for merchandizes, If the said John Hawkens do forbere to send the same shipp or any other shipp or shipps at this tyme into any place or places of the Indias, whiche are privilegid by the Kinge of Spayne to any person, or persons there to traficque, And also if the master, and company of the said shipp, and the master, and company of any other shipp, or shipps, to be sett further in this voyadge by the said John Hawkens do not robbe, spoyle, or evill handle ennye of the Quenes maiesties subiects Alies, confederates, or ffrends. That then go or ells go [document ends abruptly here][8]

Hawkins, of course, had no intention of going himself. Rather, he planned to marry and move to London, where he was in the process of establishing his home and his business. The bride was Katherine Gonson, the eighteen-year-old daughter of Benjamin Gonson, who was treasurer of the navy board.[9] If the Hawkins and Gonson families were not already well acquainted, Hawkins probably became familiar with them in 1564, when he arranged to take the queen's ship *Jesus of Lubeck* to sea. The Gonsons were an important family of merchants and seafar-

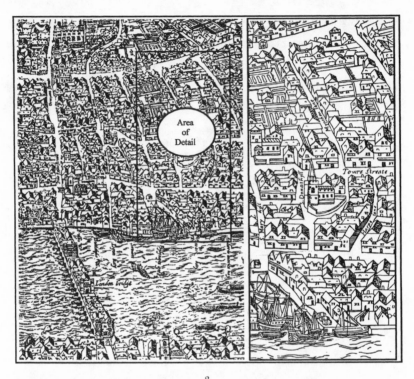

3

John Hawkins and his new bride lived on Myncing Lane, shown in the upper center of
the inset. Detail from Agas, *Civitas Londinum*.

ers whose connections with the admiralty dated from the time of Henry
VIII. The family lived on Myncing Lane in the London parish of St.
Dunstan in the East, and the wedding took place in the parish church
on 20 January 1566. The newlyweds seem to have remained in the
parish, perhaps in the Gonson home at first, though Hawkins soon purchased his own home on Myncing Lane.[10]

　　To command his new expedition to the West Indies, John
Hawkins chose a relative named John Lovell. In the first years of their
business arrangements in the Canaries the Hawkins brothers had often

sent Lovell as their representative, and he is probably one of those Hawkins had in mind when he told Ambassador Guzmán de Silva that "ten or twelve of his men knew the way" to the Indies as well as he did.[11]

The fleet consisted of four ships, including the *Salomon,* commanded by James Raunce; the *Paul,* commanded by James Hampton; the *Pascoe,* commanded by Robert Bolton; and the *Swallow*. The *Paul* and the *Salomon* were about the same size, 140 tons or so, depending on the method of measurement.[12] The *Pascoe* was a 40-ton vessel and the *Swallow* 80 tons.[13] Another Hawkins relative, Francis Drake, went on the voyage as well, but as an ordinary seaman, not a commander. The fleet left Plymouth on 9 November 1566.[14]

Lovell was a convinced adherent of the new religious rites in England, and he tried to see that the rest of the men followed his example. Seaman Miguel Morgan later declared, "They recited psalms in every ship, along with the other things that are specified in . . . the books the Protestants use in England."[15] On Lovell's ship the prayers were read by one of the merchants, probably Thomas Hampton, the brother of James Hampton, commander of the *Paul*. Firmly convinced of his own righteousness, Lovell refused to allow opposing religious views. While John Hawkins had always been careful to conform to the religious practices of the Canary Islands, Lovell refused to do so. In fact, he seems to have gone out of his way to scandalize and offend the local people. When Lovell stopped in Tenerife for supplies, he told a local official that "he had made a vow to God that he would come to these islands, burn the image of Our Lady in Candelaria, and roast a young goat in the coals."[16]

Some members of his crew still practiced the old Catholic religion. Miguel Morgan was one, but he later said that he converted to

Protestant doctrines on the Lovell voyage. A Spanish notary recorded his testimony this way: "Francis Drake, a firm English protestant, came in the ship and converted him to his law." According to Morgan, Drake said that "God would receive the good work that he might perform in either law, that of Rome or that of England, but the true law and the best one was that of England." These ideas were "taught and discussed every day" on the flagship.[17] Morgan's experience seems to reflect the ideas of many ordinary people in sixteenth-century England, that God could see good in either religious viewpoint, but He probably preferred one over the other.

Leaving the Canaries, Lovell sailed on to Guinea, where he spent two or three months, following the example of John Hawkins, gathering a cargo of slaves and merchandise worth perhaps thirty thousand ducats. In documents presented later in London, Portuguese merchants claimed that Lovell gathered his cargo and slaves in the same way that Hawkins had, by purchase, intimidation, and outright theft. Operating "under the pretext of war," Lovell attacked "the great ship *Sacharo,* loaded with slaves, within sight of the island of Saint James." In the process the captain and crew were "gravely injured and forced ashore, except for several Portuguese cruelly slain by the English." Among the other ships attacked was the *Sale,* taken near the island of Maio and then sunk. Another was seized as it sailed from the island of Fogo. Even allowing for the exaggeration normally found in such claims, it is clear that Lovell used Portuguese merchant ships as a supply depot where no payment was required.[18]

Details about the voyage through the West Indies are sparse. Stopping probably at the island of Margarita, Lovell took on wood, water, and food, but he was not allowed to trade. At his next stop, Borburata on the coast of Venezuela, he established the trading methods he

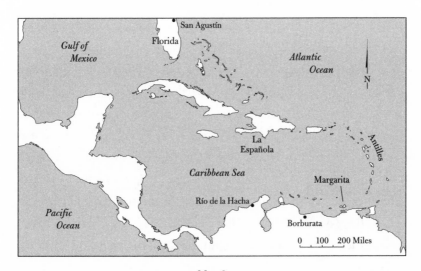

Map 6

Hawkins sent Lovell and Drake to the Indies in 1567, and they created problems there for
Hawkins to solve the following year.

used for the rest of the voyage. Two French pirate fleets had been on
the coast ahead of him, and the fleet of Jean Bontemps was in the harbor when he arrived. Knowing the man well from previous experience
on the Hawkins voyages, Lovell quickly determined to join Bontemps
in demanding permission to sell his slaves and merchandise.[19]

Anchoring their ships in the harbor at Borburata, Lovell and Bontemps sent representatives to Governor Pedro Ponce de León in the
nearby port of Coro. Because the governor had given a license to
Hawkins the previous year, Lovell half-expected to receive one as well.
However, the governor had very strict instructions from Spain, forbidding trade with foreigners, and he refused to grant the license. Meanwhile, the two traders told the local officials in Borburata that they were
peaceful merchants who planned to donate a hundred slaves to the

royal treasury and then to sell another two hundred to the local citizens. They also seem to have arranged a standby plan.[20]

When the request for a license was refused, Lovell and Bontemps took an armed party ashore. They seized two government officials and several other citizens of Borburata, whom they carried off to their ships. Two of the hostages, merchants from Nuevo Reyno de Granada, just happened to be carrying 1,500 pesos in their purses. Lovell and Bontemps took the money, gave the men twenty-six slaves in exchange, and set everyone free. The local officials thereupon "confiscated" the slaves and required the merchants to pay a fine to the crown before the slaves were returned, thus settling the matter of royal tax collection.[21]

It was the old pattern established by John Hawkins: English offers to trade met by Spanish refusal, then secret negotiations that satisfied both the traders and the colonists, and even some of the officials. Much of the trading was done by night, when the officials were absent. If questioned later, the colonists "covered for one another." The officials for their part seemed reluctant to interfere. They hated to force the colonists to testify under oath about their trading activities. As one of them reported, "We think they only perjure themselves."[22]

On 18 May 1567 Lovell and his ships arrived in Río de la Hacha, where he again sent an agent ashore, requesting a license to trade. The local commander, Miguel de Castellanos, had negotiated openly with John Hawkins during the previous visit. This time he said that trade was forbidden by the crown.[23] Even so, arrangements were made.

Baltasar de Castellanos, brother of the commander, wrote a letter signed by several other citizens and describing what had happened. These good people affirmed that the Englishman spent nearly a week in port, trying to get the citizens to trade. Faced with their refusal, Lovell simply unloaded "ninety or ninety-two slaves" on the far side of the river, then sailed away in the middle of the night. As the citizens explained it at first, these slaves were old, sick, and half-starved. In any case they were unloaded where no one could put a stop to it.[24]

A few months later, when doubts began to surface about the strict truthfulness of this account, Miguel de Castellanos and other citizens wrote another report, describing events somewhat differently. According to this new story, Bontemps arrived first with his fleet, was met on the beach by armed citizens, and was driven back to his ships. A few days later Lovell arrived and said he wanted to trade. When this was not permitted, Lovell sent a message threatening to land his forces and lay waste the town with all its inhabitants. "Come ashore," Castellanos replied, "I would like to see you try."[25] When Lovell tried to land his men, the local people, only sixty-three able bodied men in all, met him at the water's edge and forced him back to his ships. The gallant Spanish defenders even managed to kill or wound a considerable number of Lovell's people, or so they said. A few days later, Lovell landed "ninety-six slaves that were old and weak and on the point of dying" and sailed away. Surely, said the colonists, they had worked so hard and so bravely to defend the port that the king would want them to keep the slaves as part payment for all their trouble and expense.[26]

All this looked suspiciously like the sort of arrangement that had been made in Borburata. Official resistance, followed by several days—and nights—of unofficial business dealing. As far as the colonists were concerned, merchandise was no problem, for it could be hidden away, then brought out as needed for use. Slaves, however, could be seen by royal officials, and they had to be accounted for in some way. Very likely the transactions involved secret payments, followed by the midnight delivery of the slaves at a place agreed upon across the river. The colonists could then pick them up, claiming that the slaves had been abandoned by Lovell.[27]

With his business concluded at Río de la Hacha, Lovell took his fleet to Española to sell the remainder of his cargo. Spanish records give only the briefest mention of Lovell's dealings there. Writing to the king a few months later, several citizens at Río de la Hacha said, "He then departed and sailed on to the island of Española, where they say he wrought great evil and destruction."[28] Perhaps so, perhaps not. He may have managed to take on a load of hides, as Hawkins had tried to do a year earlier. Whatever he accomplished at Española, Lovell's voyage was not a great success. Hawkins later blamed this on "the simpleness of my [deputies], who knew not how to handle these matters."[29] In other words, Lovell lacked the tact and diplomacy of Hawkins. His arrogance with the Spanish authorities almost certainly cost a few English lives, just as the later Spanish reports say. This conclusion seems to be confirmed in a passage published by Philip Nichols in 1626, mentioning Francis Drake's "wrongs received at Río de Hacha with Captaine John Lovell . . . not onely in the losse of his goods of some value, but also of his kinsmen & friends."[30]

By the time Lovell brought the Hawkins fleet back to Plymouth in September 1567, other plans were afoot. Queen Elizabeth was so pleased with the success of previous slaving ventures that she determined to back Hawkins in his efforts to continue trading with the Spanish Indies. As a mark of her favor, the queen recently had granted Hawkins the reversion of the office of clerk of the ships, to be effective whenever it might be vacated by the present incumbent, George Winter. In fact, Winter continued to hold the office for another dozen years or so, but the appointment is evidence that Hawkins was beginning to wield some influence in London naval circles.[31]

However, commerce was his main interest, and the slave trade was a proven moneymaker. The arrival of several Portuguese adventurers soon presented Hawkins with a convenient way to continue selling slaves, while hiding his plans from the inquiring eyes of the Spanish ambassador. These rogues had spread stories around London that they knew the location of a great gold mine near the coast of Portuguese Africa, but in an area not claimed by any Christian prince. Some parts of their stories seemed doubtful, but the queen and her advisers appeared to believe them and instructed Hawkins to cooperate. For his part, Hawkins saw the gold-mine story as a way to disguise his real plans. Perhaps as part of the deception, when Hawkins requisitioned guns, powder, shot, bows and arrows, and pikes, he wrote that they were to be used in "the fort at Genoia [Guinea], if there shalbe nede of fortyficacion."[32]

However, these weapons were just what Hawkins was accustomed to use on his ships. Guzmán de Silva heard of the requisition and immediately complained to Queen Elizabeth and to Secretary Cecil, who told him that the ships were simply going to the African mines. Guzmán de Silva remained dubious, but Cecil swore "a great oath." In any case, before the summer was over, Hawkins had his ships in the harbor at Plymouth, ready either to sail for the Portuguese mines and fill his ships with gold or, as seemed more likely, to purchase, capture, or steal several shiploads of slaves for sale in the Indies.[33]

In the midst of these preparations, on 30 August 1567, a Spanish fleet under the Flemish admiral Adolf de Bourgoigne, Baron DeWachen, arrived at the port of Plymouth heading for Spain but driven off course by bad weather. At Dover a few days earlier the Flemish admiral had been treated like a visiting dignitary. The mayor told him that the queen knew he was coming and had notified all ports in the

4

Queen Elizabeth invested in the 1567 voyage, allowing Hawkins to use the royal ship *Jesus of Lubeck*. Sketch adapted from a drawing in PL2991, Pepys Library, Magdalene College, Cambridge.

kingdom to welcome his ships. The reception at Plymouth was different. Hawkins, awaiting the queen's authorization to begin his voyage, saw the Spanish banner on DeWachen's flagship and immediately concluded the fleet had come to attack his own ships. As DeWachen took his to the anchorage in the Cattwater, the inner harbor, Hawkins ordered his own guns and those in the nearby fortress to open fire. DeWachen immediately lay to, sending a messenger to the mayor to determine why the ships and the fort had fired on him. The messenger was told that the ships in question belonged to the queen and were commanded by John Hawkins; he would have to ask Hawkins why the guns had fired. Going then to the *Jesus of Lubeck*, the messenger found Hawkins surrounded by armed men. With the proper courtesies, he repeated his question, and Hawkins replied that he had not been apprised of DeWachen's coming, "my mystres not gevging" advance notice. Beyond this, he did not want the other ships so close to his own. DeWachen's Spanish fleet thereupon anchored outside the Cattwater, but the hostilities were not over. A day or so later some sailors boarded a Spanish ship in the harbor and freed a group of Flemish prisoners being sent to Spain to serve in the galleys.[34]

Complaints were lodged immediately with the queen and Cecil, though Hawkins himself kept a strange silence about the matter. Toward the middle of September, Cecil wrote, via George Fitzwilliams, an aide to Hawkins, to say how unhappy the queen was with Hawkins's behavior. Hawkins replied that his guns had fired on DeWachen only because he thought the Spanish fleet had been sent by King Philip to destroy his ships and thus keep him from going to the Indies again. In any case, the queen's own ships were the ones most at risk, and he had simply been trying to defend them. "I had rather her hyghnes found fault wth me for kepynge her shippes and people, to her honour," he wrote, "then to lose them to the glory of others." He went on to explain that if DeWachen had been allowed to enter the Cattwater, where the queen's ships were anchored, he could have sunk them at will. "I greatly fearyd ther warlyke workynge," said Hawkins. As for the Flemish prisoners, Hawkins claimed to be innocent of any wrongdoing, suggesting that perhaps they had been freed by countrymen from the Spanish fleet. Warned that the Spanish and Flemish sailors were out for revenge, Hawkins replied, "I know they hate me and yet without cause for they are the better of me by great sommes, and I the worse by 40000 dockaetts." Then, for the first time informing Cecil that he had been negotiating privately with the Spanish ambassador, Hawkins added that the debt "ys not unknowen to thembasador of Spayne. I hope one day they wyll make me recompense of their owne cortesy."[35]

Years later, when Richard Hawkins wrote his memoirs, he asserted that his father fired on the ships because of their failure to salute the royal ensign.[36] This can hardly be the case, or John Hawkins would surely have mentioned that fact in his report to Cecil, rather than the weaker argument that he thought the ships might be hostile. In any case, Hawkins sent gifts to DeWachen and on several occasions invited him to a feast aboard his own vessel, just as a mark "of cortesye for the quenes ma^ties honoure, wch I had so great a regard unto."[37]

Before anything was settled about the fracas in Plymouth harbor, the three Portuguese gold miners fled, claiming Hawkins had mistreated them. It did not matter to Hawkins, who did not believe their story anyway, but Cecil and the Queen were embarrassed, or so they said. Hawkins wrote to reassure them. "This enterpryse cannot take effecte," he said, "which I thinke god hathe provided for the beste." Still, his ships were ready for a trip to Guinea, where he could find a cargo of slaves and trade them in the West Indies for "golde pearles and essmeraldes wherof I doute not but to bring home great abundance."[38] Suspecting something like this, DeWachen asked Hawkins just where he intended to go. His reply was typical Hawkins casuistry. As the admiral reported to King Philip, Hawkins "does not know where he is going, or so he says, because the queen has not told him." As it turned out, the queen agreed to the new Hawkins proposal—so quickly, in fact, that it seems very likely that this had been her plan all along.[39]

Over half a dozen years Hawkins had learned to deal with government officials and ambassadors, sometimes carrying out independent negotiations without the knowledge of the queen or her ministers. He was a shrewd negotiator, careless with the facts, and he knew how to use force to conclude a business deal. If circumstances seemed to require the use of arms, he preferred to shoot first and think about an excuse later. In his personal life Hawkins had established his home and a branch of the family business in London, where he married the daughter of a leading naval figure. Even so, he kept his base in Plymouth. His son was born there and seemingly continued to live there with the family of William Hawkins after John Hawkins moved to London.[40]

3

Slave Trading

Master Iohn Haukins . . . being amongst other particulers assured, that
Negroes were very good marchandise in Hispaniola, and that store of
Negroes might easily be had upon the coast of Guinea, resolved
with himselfe to make trial thereof, and communicated
that deuise to his worshipfull friends of London.
Richard Hakluyt

On the new trip to the West Indies, Hawkins intended
to lead the fleet himself, with the queen furnishing
two ships, and the usual array of London investors
backing the venture. In fact, thirty or more merchants invested in the voyage, and some of them sent
their own representatives along.[1] The most important investor was the
queen, whose ships were the largest in the fleet. More important, her
participation gave Hawkins an excuse to style himself a naval commander. At the very least, this was an exaggeration, for his commission
came from the merchant syndicate, not from the queen.[2] The leaders of
the merchant syndicate were Sir William Garrard of London and
Alderman Rowland Heyward.[3] Other investors included William
Hawkins, William Winter, and a dozen or so gentlemen who went on
the voyage and whose identities are known largely from their later testimony before Spanish tribunals.

The undisputed head of this group was Anthony Godard, a citizen of Plymouth, where he later served as treasurer. Because Godard
was fluent in French and Spanish, Hawkins put him on the flagship to
serve as official interpreter on the expedition. In Spanish records
Godard often appears as Antonio Tejeda, perhaps because he was a

dealer in woolen cloth *(tejido)*.[4] The three Portuguese adventurers later claimed that they deserted the expedition because Godard seized some of their goods and would not return them.[5]

Some of the Englishmen named in the Spanish records are difficult to identify. The merchant called Valentín Verde in Spanish may have been named Green or Bird, for example. We know Thomas Fuller's and Christopher Bingham's names from their signatures, though the Spanish notary wrote the names phonetically. George Fitzwilliams is well known from English records, which make it possible to identify him as the man called Jorge Fizullens by Spanish notaries. The man known as Ricardo Tempul is pretty clearly Temple, an assumption that is affirmed by the notice of his death in a Spanish prison. The facts are not so clear for Enrique Quince, whose name is given as Quin in the death record.[6] But Tomás Benito is probably Bennet, though another man's name was also written as Tomás Benito.[7] Juan Brun is no doubt Brown, and there seems to be little reason to confuse the name of Gregorio Simon. Spanish investigators were anxious to know just how John Hawkins was able to come and go as he pleased in the Indies. Their careful questioning of these men elicited hundreds of pages of information about the voyage, documenting it more completely than any other English voyage of the day.

Shortly after John Hawkins returned home, an account of the voyage appeared under his name. Whether he wrote it himself is doubtful, though much of it seems to be based on his recollection of events. Some of the narrative has been copied from other records, the chief of which is a journal that seems to be the work of an unnamed gentleman on the flagship who acted as secretary for Hawkins. The extant copy of that manuscript is a rough draft that has been badly damaged by fire. Several of the earlier pages are entirely gone. But much of the missing

5

The royal ship *Minion*. Sketch adapted from a watercolor in PL2991, Pepys Library, Magdalene College, Cambridge.

material can be found in other English sources or the more plentiful Spanish and Portuguese manuscripts.[8] Together, these give a fairly complete and nearly unique picture of a voyage in the sixteenth-century English slave trade.

For his flagship, Hawkins took the queen's 700-ton *Jesus of Lubeck,* with Robert Barrett as master and William Saunders as mate. The other royal vessel was the 300-ton *Minion,* which Hawkins had seen on his earlier trips. John Hampton was captain and master, and John Garrett was mate. Taking these two vessels to Plymouth, Hawkins joined them with four others belonging to him and his brother William. The *William and John,* 150 tons, had Thomas Bolton as captain and master, with James Raunce as mate. A ship from Lovell's fleet, the 80-ton *Swallow,* was nearly new and still in good condition.[9] Quickly refitted, it became part of the new Hawkins slaving fleet, along with fifty or so slaves brought back in its hold. Two other ships, the 50-ton *Judith* and the 33-ton *Angel,* completed the fleet, along with a tiny pinnace of 7 tons that was towed by the *Swallow.* The *Judith* may have been commanded by Francis Drake, though this is not certain.[10]

The flagship carried 166 people, including soldiers, sailors, and merchants. There were 99 more on the *Minion.* In all, some 400 men went on the ships, as officers, sailors, merchants, and servants, along with several dozen slaves left over from Lovell's trip. By the first of October 1567 the fleet was ready to sail.[11]

English testimony recorded in Spanish documents gives a clear picture of the way sailors and gentlemen were recruited and how they expected to be paid. While some went voluntarily, a great many others were pressed into service.[12] One seaman said that he "was taken by force by command of the queen." The practice applied even to gentlemen, for several later told their Spanish captors that they went only because they feared the queen's wrath.[13] The queen and the merchant investors had contractual arrangements for sharing the profits. None of the seamen and soldiers had written contracts, but some expected to share in a third of whatever might be gained on the journey. The gentlemen apparently had nothing more than an understanding that John Hawkins would give them a just recompense when they returned. One "gentleman-soldier," though forced to go, said that "upon returning to England, John Hawkins would reward him as befit the quality of his person."[14]

The fleet departed from Plymouth on 2 October 1567.[15] On the third day at sea, following his usual practice, Hawkins assembled his ships and issued sailing orders. Although these are not recorded in detail, they were probably similar to those issued in 1564. If the ships were separated, the fleet should reassemble at Tenerife, where supplies and water could be obtained. Not everyone understood the orders, perhaps because Hawkins did not write them out but relied on the captains to recall his usual practice for sailing to the Canaries. In fact, Hawkins kept most of his plans secret, and neither the gentlemen nor the sailors knew what their exact destination might be.[16]

Four days out of Plymouth, the fleet was battered by a great storm, and for several days the *Judith* was separated from the rest of the fleet. The *Angel* managed to rejoin the *Jesus of Lubeck* near Cape Finisterre, but the other ships seemed to be lost. Almost overwhelmed by the extensive damage to his vessels, Hawkins thought about returning to Plymouth. A day later, the storm ceased altogether, and things looked much better. Hawkins thereupon gave orders to resume the voyage. The *Minion,* the *William and John,* and the *Swallow* sailed on to Gomera, while the *Jesus* and the *Angel* sailed to Tenerife. When the storm began, the *Swallow* had the pinnace in tow, but the line parted in the heavy seas, and the pinnace was lost, with its two-man crew. Very nearly the same thing happened to the the longboats of the *Minion* and the *Jesus,* though Hawkins was able to bring his two drowning sailors back aboard the *Jesus.* Unable to locate the other ships, the *Judith* kept sailing alone but still headed for the Canaries. On 11 November, when the *Jesus* and the *Angel* were within sight of Gomera, the *Judith* came sailing up, firing a salute to the flagship.[17]

From Gomera, Hawkins took his ships to Santa Cruz on Tenerife, where he intended to reassemble his fleet, purchase supplies as usual from his friend Pedro de Ponte, and take on a fresh supply of water. This time he found conditions drastically changed. In a number of pointed letters the authorities in Spain had directed local officials to treat Hawkins with circumspection. As soon as his ships came into view, local militia units were mobilized. When the *Jesus of Lubeck* entered the harbor, the officials saw that it was too heavily armed for any direct attack. Instead, they kept the militia drawn up in battle order, just outside the town. Hawkins, for his part, kept a guard on the alert throughout his stay in Santa Cruz, and only good friends like Pedro de Soler and a few others came out to visit with him. Among those others was Gregory Stevens, a native of Plymouth who had been in Tenerife for the past year, working as agent for an English merchant whose name appears in the Spanish records as Enrique Nuñez. When Hawkins arrived, Nuñez came with him. Once Stevens had loaded the wine and provisions, he joined the fleet, his work in Tenerife ended.[18]

With no further advantage to be gained by pretending to be Catholic, Hawkins abandoned his former attempts to conform to local religious practices. Rather, he invited his friends to a feast of Canary Island partridge, scandalizing everyone by serving meat on Friday and joking that he had a special papal dispensation for everyone aboard his ships.[19] But the crews were confined to their vessels, and a quarter-mile away the local militia remained armed and ready. In this state of tension discipline suffered on the *Jesus of Lubeck,* and fights broke out among the men. Two of them, Edward Dudley and George Fitzwilliams, argued so bitterly that they agreed to go ashore for a duel. Hearing of this in the nick of time, Hawkins ordered Fitzwilliams to remain on board and sent word to Dudley that he should return immediately. When Dudley came aboard, Hawkins gave him a stern lecture. Dudley answered with a rude remark, and Hawkins struck the man with his fist. Dudley drew his knife, and Hawkins did the same. Before they could be separated, both men were cut and bleeding. Dudley was immediately placed in irons and after a time was brought before Hawkins for punishment. The insult to himself could be forgiven, said Hawkins, but not the insult to the queen, whose ship they were on. Having said this, Hawkins took a loaded harquebus, pointed it at Dudley, and told the man to say his prayers and prepare to die. Dudley begged for mercy, and many of the bystanders urged Hawkins to forgive him. Among those asking clemency for Dudley was the Canarian priest Pedro de Soler, who later said that it was entirely through his own efforts that Hawkins decided to pardon Dudley.[20] This was typical Hawkins behavior, though, blazing anger followed by remorse and a willingness to forgive and forget.

Other members of the crew took the Hawkins jokes about religion as a signal that they could do likewise. During a brief trip ashore William Benit, the baker from the *Jesus,* entered a chapel at Santa Cruz, took a crucifix from the wall, and threw it on the floor. The vicar was a friend of Hawkins's, so he wrote to report the matter, and Hawkins called Benit to task. First rebuking him in front of everyone, Hawkins then had the man tied to the mast and suspended there for two hours as an example to the others.[21]

For the next few days Hawkins kept his seamen busy repairing and resupplying the ships, although his main concern was to find the three missing vessels. After a time he learned they were waiting for him at Gomera.[22] With the entire fleet located once more, Hawkins sailed out of the harbor at Santa Cruz, and his ships traded cannon salutes with the local fortress. Perhaps by accident, one of the guns on the *Jesus of Lubeck* fired a shot into the town, and the house of Juan de Valverde was partly destroyed. Local people insisted that the only accident was that Hawkins had missed the church and hit Valverde's house instead.[23]

Once arrived at Gomera, Hawkins had his fleet back together for the first time in weeks. Away from the officials on Tenerife, members of the crew were greeted as old friends by the merchants on shore, who traded freely with them and allowed them to refill the water casks on all the ships. One of the young gentlemen who traveled aboard the *Minion* stayed as a guest for a week or so in the house of the governor of Gomera while he waited for Hawkins to arrive with the rest of the fleet. During this time he heard local merchants talking about the French pirates who seemed to prey without fear on their ports and ships. When Hawkins arrived, they asked him to keep a lookout for these rascals and to punish them if possible.[24]

The ordinary seamen seem to have enjoyed themselves at Gomera in the ways sailors usually do, though a man from Tenerife later said he had heard that they burned images of saints looted from the local church. Confronted with this charge, the English sailors denied having done anything of the sort, and perhaps they did not. Several men, including the same George Fitzwilliams who was involved in the argument with Dudley, secretly attended Mass in the local church. At least one of the men went to confession—perhaps Fitzwilliams himself sought forgiveness for the near-duel. Most of the officers did not attend Mass, and most of them were considered by the locals to be *luteranos*.[25]

On 4 November all was finished, so the reunited fleet departed for the coast of Africa. Two weeks of monotonous sailing brought the ships to Cabo Blanco. Here Hawkins took on supplies of fish, bread, and wine, perhaps from stores that had been assembled and shipped there earlier by Stevens.[26] In the harbor at Cabo Blanco, Hawkins found four Portuguese vessels abandoned by their crews, who had been attacked by French raiders and forced to take refuge in the nearby fort. Three of the ships were bare hulls, stripped of sails, masts, and rigging and slowly filling with water. The other ship had been set afire, and nothing was left but a burned-out hulk. Hawkins immediately confiscated the best caravel, pumped out the hull, refitted it, and added it to his fleet. When the Portuguese owner, a captain named Maya, came down from the fort to ask what was happening to his ships, Hawkins said, "They are all mine under the laws of the sea." Hawkins then told Maya he would have to buy his other two vessels back, but it quickly became clear that everything the man owned had been taken by the French. Not one to lose a sale, Hawkins had Maya sign a contract to pay forty ducados, due in England in two years, and Hawkins threw in sufficient equipment to put the two ships back into service.[27]

Coasting south along the African mainland, the Hawkins fleet met six French merchant ships trading in the local settlements. With a brief exchange of gunfire Hawkins subdued the French merchantmen and boarded their ships. Five of the Frenchmen convinced him of their good intentions, but he decided that the sixth was one of the pirates involved in the raids on the Canary Island merchants and the Portuguese vessels at Cabo Blanco. Hawkins added the ship to his fleet. Antonio Godard said later that "five of the Frenchmen, who were captains and masters, had licenses from the admiral of France to go where they would," but the other did not.[28] One gentlemen traveling with Hawkins recalled hearing about French pirates during the stay in Gomera, and he said that Hawkins felt he was doing his Canarian friends a favor by taking the unlicensed ship. Another equally close to Hawkins and equally well informed said that Hawkins had the ship searched for contraband, found a shipment of almonds stolen from the Portuguese, and thus knew it was a pirate ship.[29] Perhaps all three were correct.

The next day one of the French merchantmen volunteered to accompany Hawkins to the Indies. Not trusting the pirate crew of the seized ship to man the French vessels, Hawkins removed them to his flagship and replaced them with good English sailors.[30] The ship that volunteered, the *Don de Dieu,* was commanded by Paul Blondel, known in the English accounts as Captain Bland and in the Spanish documents as Planos or Plones. Blondel served valiantly with Hawkins in this voyage and was associated with Drake in a later journey.[31]

While anchored at Cape Verde, about 18 November 1567, Hawkins assembled his first shore party to hunt for slaves. Marching inland a few miles with 150 men, he attacked a large village and took some captives. In the process Hawkins and about twenty-five of his seamen were wounded with poisoned arrows. At first everyone seemed to recover, but a few days later they began to sicken, and seven or eight died in great agony, jaws clamped tight from pain and paralysis. "I myselfe had one of the greatest woundes," said Hawkins, "yet, thanks be to god escaped." The secret remedy was a clove of garlic, which a slave advised him to apply to the wound and thus draw out the venom.[32]

From Cabo Verde, Hawkins headed southeast to the Guinea Coast and Sierra Leone, dealing with French captains and Portuguese merchants in the neighborhoods of Cabo Rojo and the Río Grande. In his own account of the journey Hawkins neglected to describe his business here, and the other English witnesses stayed remarkably silent. One of the sailors recalled the visit with a brief observation: "The Portuguese didn't want to do business."[33] The Portuguese themselves had a much more vivid recollection of events. According to their ambassador in London, Hawkins captured or looted seven Portuguese ships, along with their cargoes of ivory, wax, and slaves. Then Hawkins forced the captains under threat of death to sign documents saying that they had willingly sold him the goods he seized. Beyond this they said that Hawkins and his men burned a town and in the process killed a number of the Portuguese inhabitants. Total damages amounted to more than 70,000 ducados.[34] The official list of damage claims tells the story.

> The list of those whose goods Joannes de Canes [John Hawkins] has stolen and their true value amounts to the following sum.
>
> From the vessel whose captain was Emanuel da Veiga he stole six thousand ducados   6000
>
> From the vessel called Our Lady of the Conception the sum of four thousand ducados   4000
>
> From another vessel the sum altogether amounted to ten thousand ducados   10000
>
> From another vessel of Anthony Cadoso, Portuguese, he seized ten thousand ducados   10000
>
> From another such [vessel] of Ferdinand Gundalsavo he took the sum of two thousand gold [ducados]   2000
>
> In the river of Saint Dominic he boarded another ship belonging to Alvaro Gundisalvo whom he spoiled of two thousand gold   2000
>
> In the same river John Hawkins with the rest of his army landed and burned the town called Chacheum, in which he killed many Portuguese and caused damage and destruction in excess of thirty thousand gold   30000
>
> Then leaving this river he journeyed to the river of Sierra Leone, where he spoiled the vessel belonging to Antonio de Olivera, from which he took the sum of five thousand ducados.   5000
>
> In the same Sierra he spoiled a vessel belonging to Luis Faire, which amounts to the sum of five thousand gold
>
> 5000

In the same place he seized a vessel belonging to Francisco
de Alvarenga, amounting to four thousand ducados

4000

Seventy thousand ducados . . .[35]

These Portuguese claims, paired with the anonymous journal,
give a graphic picture of the Hawkins approach to slave trading and
incidentally help to explain why the journal remained unpublished. At
Cabo Rojo, Hawkins tried to entrap local people "with margaritas
[cheap trinkets] and other wares which the negros esteme," but the people had evidently seen this trick before and fled when his men
approached. Sailing on to the Río Santo Domingo, Hawkins sent
Robert Barrett, the master of his flagship, upriver with some of the
smaller boats. Exactly who started the fighting is unclear. One of the
men with Hawkins said the plan all along had been to "make war on
whatever Portuguese they might encounter."[36] According to the anonymous journal, Barrett tried to trade peacefully, but the Portuguese captain refused to do so and fired on Barrett's boats. Barrett thereupon
boarded the Portuguese ship and forced the commander to trade. The
vessel was apparently the one belonging to Alvaro Gundisalvo, who
claimed damages of 2,000 ducados.[37]

Once this matter was settled, Hawkins determined to try to capture a town a mile or so away, Cacheo apparently, where about 6,000
blacks were said to live. Barrett and Dudley with 250 well-armed men
marched boldly on the town and set it afire. Only then did they notice
that an army of blacks and about 100 Portuguese were standing in the
road, blocking their way back to the ships. "The fight was cruell," said
the anonymous chronicler, "and 4 of oure menne were slaine by and by
and many of oure menne hurt." The river at this place was so shallow
that Hawkins could not bring in his larger vessels to offer assistance, so

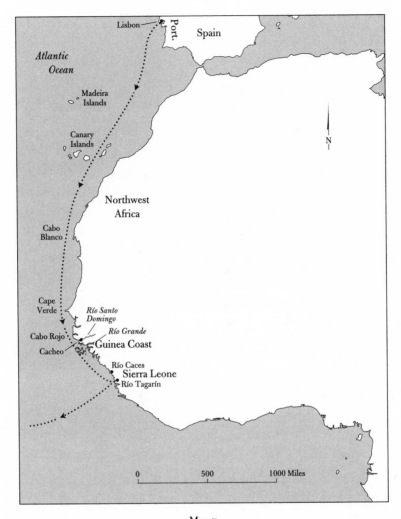

Map 7

Hawkins captured slaves at many of the same places he had visited earlier, some called by
different names. The Río Santo Domingo was called the Cacheo in the lower reaches.
Río Mitombi was also called the Tagarín.

Barrett and Dudley had to fight their own way out. In retaliation for the
defeat Hawkins seized a few more Portuguese caravels and went elsewhere for the special human cargo he sought.[38]

The fleet sailed to the Río Tagarín in Sierra Leone, where Hawkins hoped that slave hunting might prove to be a less difficult occupation. Arriving there just before Christmas 1567, he dispatched some of his smaller vessels to the nearby rivers of Calowsa and Casteos, but results were still discouraging. Not only were slaves unavailable in the nearby villages, the country was inhospitable as well. Disease decimated the crews, and one caravel was attacked by hippopotamuses, which supposedly stove in the planks, sank the vessel, and devoured two of the men before help could arrive.[39]

After several discouraging days at Río Tagarín conditions changed. Hawkins was approached by an emissary for two local kings, Sheri and Yhoma, who asked for aid against their enemies, the kings Sacina and Setecama. Describing a weak and populous foe, the two rulers promised to give the Englishmen an equal share of any prisoners they might take. With this agreement, on 15 January the kings began an overland march on the enemy village, while the Englishmen rowed upriver in the smaller vessels of the fleet, including one commanded by Francis Drake. Attacking from both land and water, the Englishmen and the blacks burned the town and took several hundred prisoners, though the kings kept the larger share of slaves and dared Hawkins to do anything about it.[40]

For several days, while Hawkins continued to negotiate for more slaves, the Englishmen watched in fascination as their allies feasted on the bodies of their enemies. The anonymous chronicler thought that this was done partly to torture the poor wretch whose flesh was peeled away and roasted before his eyes. But it was also done for "sustenaunce having as in d[eed they] have no manne[r] of cattayle." By this account, fear of torture was a major factor in native relationships. A black prince who had committed adultery with one of the wives of his king willingly surrendered himself to Hawkins as a slave rather than face the miserable death his lord would surely inflict as punishment. The Englishmen also recorded remarkable deeds of bravery by their native foes, including the story of a warrior who ran through a hail of bullets to seize an oar from one of Barrett's rowers. Once he had the oar, the unarmed man then ran forty yards, holding the oar above his head, before collapsing and dying from his wounds.[41]

In addition to the fifty slaves left over from Lovell's voyage, Hawkins had managed to round up about four hundred or five hundred miserable souls for transport to America.[42] In the various battles he probably lost about sixty men killed and many more wounded. Edward Dudley, who fought with Fitzwilliams and Hawkins at Santa Cruz, was wounded at Cabo Verde. He recovered sufficiently to lead a slaving party at Tagarín, but he later sickened and died on the way to the Indies.[43]

The journey across the Atlantic lasted from early February to the end of March, seven or eight weeks of unbroken ocean travel.[44] There are no contemporary accounts of the accommodations provided for slaves on the Hawkins ships, but conditions can scarcely have differed much from those on later voyages. The fleet was well supplied, so there was no shortage of provisions. Food for the slaves was simple but had to be provided by the crew, who probably tried to keep the slaves fed so they would remain healthy and command a good price. Still, discipline was strict, and for the security of the crew the slaves were usually packed tightly in the hold. Because it was not always possible to bring them on deck for necessary bodily functions, the foul stench from perspiration, vomit, and feces soon made the air below decks nearly unbreathable.[45]

The seamen fared better, managing to entertain themselves in various ways. Hawkins insisted on setting a good table, with fine linen and silver, and dishes cooked to his liking. A group of five or six musicians on board the *Jesus of Lubeck* played fiddle music for the enjoyment of the captain and the crew. The leader of the group was a tiny youth named William Low, twenty years old, though he looked like a freckle-faced boy.[46]

In addition to all this, every morning between seven and eight and again when the watch changed at nightfall, the mate William Saunders gathered all the men before the mainmast and had them kneel to recite psalms, the Lord's Prayer, and the Creed. On Sunday morning at eight they said the same prayers, and a literate crew member read the epistle and the gospel appointed for that day. Saunders, or sometimes Barrett or Hawkins, then gave a homily, reading from the *Paraphrases* of Erasmus, then expanding upon the theme in his own words. The whole observance took forty-five minutes or an hour. A similar ritual was observed on each of the other ships in the fleet, and when time allowed, the Sunday observances were also read during the week.[47]

Attendance was compulsory. When some of the men on the flagship refused to attend services, Thomas Williams, the second mate, was sent with a whip to force them to come on deck and participate in the prayers. Even the slightest hint of "papistry" was forbidden. A man on the *Minion* who blessed himself before taking the helm was roundly excoriated before all the crew. "There are on this voyage such evil papist Christians," said Saunders, "that we cannot avoid having a pestilence visited on this armada."[48]

Certainly, pestilence was a problem, and medical care was important, if rudimentary. Without being aware of germs and viruses, people of the day still understood that disease could be transmitted by personal contact. As a result, any crew member who became ill on the flagship was immediately transferred to the *Minion* until he was fully recovered. The reasoning was that the flagship was a floating fortress, and the crew had to be in perfect health, ready for action at any time.[49]

The slaves caught the same diseases as the crew, but probably in more virulent form because of the crowded conditions below decks. Loss of life among the slaves from illness or even suicide might have been very high, though there is no way to be certain of this. The various accounts of the voyage suggest that Hawkins probably sold about 325 slaves during the journey. Taking Lovell's experience as a guide, and tempering this with information from English and Spanish witnesses, it seems likely that Hawkins ended his voyage with fifty or so slaves still unsold. If he "obtayned betwene 4 & 500" in Africa, then Hawkins lost more than a hundred slaves on the journey.[50]

On the journey Hawkins followed his usual plan, with a generous allotment of food and supplies but a modest complement of men. The queen contributed two ships, armaments, and perhaps even funds for the journey, and Hawkins was not allowed to leave port without her express approval. Thus, by exaggerating just a little, he could claim a royal appointment as fleet commander, even though his commission was from the merchant syndicate. During the voyage Hawkins treated Spanish subjects with some circumspection, but he looked upon Portuguese citizens and possessions as fair game, taking ships, supplies, and slaves at will, sometimes paying and sometimes not. When these efforts failed to produced the desired numbers for a human cargo, Hawkins allied himself with two native rulers who promised to fill the holds of his slave ships in return for his help against their enemies. Neither Hawkins nor the queen nor any of the merchant investors expressed reservations then or later about involving themselves in such a loathsome business.

4

San Juan de Ulúa

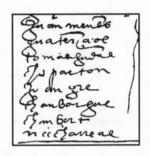

If all the miseries and troublesome affayres of this sorowefull
voyadge shoulde be perfectlye and
throughlye written, there shoulde
nede a paynfull man with his penne, and as greate a tyme as he
had that wrote the liues
and deathes of the
martyrs.
Finis.
John Haukins

W hen Hawkins left the coast of Africa, his fleet
consisted of ten ships. The six original ships
were the *Jesus of Lubeck,* the *Minion,* the *William
and John,* the *Swallow,* the *Judith,* and the *Angel.*
Along the way he had acquired a caravel at Cabo
Blanco, two French ships added near Cape Verde, and another Portuguese caravel taken at the Río Santo Domingo.[1] Apparently he abandoned or burned another ship or two seized at Río Santo Domingo.

With years of experience at sea and particularly on the West
Indies voyage, Hawkins was able to act as his own pilot, a skill not then
common among sea captains. He had his own ballestilla, astrolabe,
compass, and other instruments, and best of all, he had good charts of
the region.[2] The first landfall after two months at sea was the island of
Dominica, where Spanish charts marked a safe passage through the
Antilles. Here the fleet took on fresh water but nothing else, for the

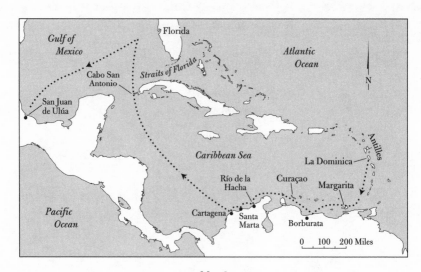

Map 8
Hawkins traded at seven ports in the Spanish Indies before a storm forced him to stop at San Juan de Ulúa.

local Indians had nothing to trade. Turning south, they landed at the Caribbean island of Margarita, just off the coast of Venezuela. Hawkins immediately sent a messenger ashore to tell the local governor that he wished to trade peaceably, restock his ships with food and water, and rest his crew. This letter and the other correspondence that Hawkins had with local officials during his journey survive only in the anonymous narrative. The narrative copies are clumsily worded, apparently translated from Spanish originals, with corrections made during the translation process. The most obvious candidate as author of the letters and the narrative is Anthony Godard, the official interpreter of the fleet. Hawkins assured the governor of Margarita:

> worshipfull I have touched in your Ilond only to thentente
> to refresh my menne w^{t}h fresh victualles w^{c}h for my mony
> or wares you shall sell me meanyng to staye only but 5 or 6

dayes here at the furthest In the wch tyme you maye asure youre selfe and so all others that by me or any of myne there shall no domadge be done to any manne the wch alsoe the quenes ma^tie of Inglond my mystres at my departure out of Inglond comaunded me to have great care of and ~~also~~ to serve wth my navye the kinges ma^tie of Spaine my olde m^r if in places where I came any of his stoode in neade/³

The response came in unexpectedly cordial terms, so Hawkins kept the fleet at Margarita for more than a week. This is how the interpreter recorded the governor's greeting:

Right worshipfull [your] [presence] [with] your navye [i]s as joyfull vnto vs as ~~if~~ of any other capt[ain] [you havin]g ~~for your excellent dedes~~ deserved by youre excele[nt dedes, the st]atly beautye the majesty of the quene youre [mistress possesses] ~~and youre the fame of~~ youre great worthines is [so well known in t]hese partes that not only all menne wolde gladlye [serve you but] alsoe I am sure ~~that no~~ any navye of the kinge [would yiel]de you mejority and bycawse you shall ~~se the~~ perceave the [willingness I have] ~~you~~ to serve you I will ~~come~~ be at ~~the~~ the towne at 9 of the clocke before none to receave you thowghe [I am so si]~~ck~~ wolde not that I showlde rase oute of my bedde [what things] that are in this Ilond and may pleasure you shalbe [at your c]omaundement wth desire that you showlde tarye here longer [unless your v]ioadge requyreth you showlde depart/⁴

As good as his promise, the governor came to greet Hawkins, along with a number of leading citizens. When the English ships departed on 9 April 1568, Hawkins took with him a certificate of good conduct signed by the governor. He left behind a town full of happy colonists, who had traded island oxen, sheep, and produce for good Devon and Rouen cloth at attractive prices. In fact, the islanders could scarcely have refused to trade, for they numbered no more than fifty souls, and their town had been very nearly destroyed by French pirates a few months earlier.[5]

Souvenirs of the French visit were evident everywhere. Godard noticed their work when he toured the settlement. "Walking through the town of Margarita with some of the citizens I discovered a phrase," he said, "written with charcoal on the wall of a house in French, which I understand very well: Vengeance for Florida."[6] In getting even for the 1565 Spanish destruction of Port Royal, the French pirates also created some of the earliest graffiti reported in the New World.

The first mainland destination was Borburata, the Spanish pearl fishery where Hawkins had traded profitably on earlier voyages. Arriving on Holy Saturday, 17 April 1568, Hawkins again wrote to ask for permission to trade. Lying a little, stretching the facts a little more, Hawkins suggested a way the local authorities could circumvent the royal prohibition on trade. Repeating a story he had used successfully on earlier voyages, Hawkins said that he had not really intended to come to the Indies, but as long as he was there, he needed to sell a few slaves and a small amount of goods to make expenses. Surely the Spanish king would have no objection to that:

> worshipfull this vioadge on the wch I am [come was
> ordered] [by] the quenes matie of Inglond my mystres
> another [way and not to] [th]ese partes and the charges
> being made In In[glond before] [I] sette sayle the pretence
> was forcablye overtorned [therefore I am] comaunded by

the quenes matie my mystres to seeke [some other] trafique
wth the wares wch I all readye had and negros [wch I made
to] procure in guynea to lighten the great chardges he[re-
tofore made] in the setting out of this navye/ I knowe the
[king of] spaine your mr unto whome alsoe I have bene a
servaun[t and am] comaunded by the quene my mystres to
serve wth my navye [as need] requyreth hathe forbidden
that you shall geve ~~any~~ licen[ce to any] straunger to trafique
I will not therefore requeste any su[che] thinge at your hand
but that you will license me to se[ll 60] negros onlye and a
parcell of my wares wch in all is but littell [for] the payment
of the soldiers wch I have in my ships/ In this you you shall
~~pleasure me and~~ not break the comaundement of youre
prince ~~againe you shall showe doe your mr~~ but doe him
good servyce ~~and cause not~~ and advoyd divers inconven-
iences ~~for some thinkinge~~ wch happen often tymes thor-
oughe ~~ii observe~~ beyng to precise in observing precepts wth
out consideracion I ~~wolde you wolde take the paynes and~~ If
you may I most instantlye desire y[ou] that you will take the
paynes to come hether that I might conferre wth you my
self[e] trewly it wolde be lever to me then 10000 doccatts
~~and alsoe I~~ if you come you shoulde not fynde me Ingrate-
full nor counte youre travayle lo[st][7]

The exaggerated claim that "I knowe the [king of] spaine your m[r]
unto whome alsoe I have bene a servaun[t]" is probably something
Hawkins repeated later to Spanish officials, based no doubt on the fact
that Philip was king of England for four years during his marriage to
Mary Tudor. In fact, Hawkins may have expanded on this claim in his
conversations with local officials, who were always thrilled by intima-

tions of royal favor. This sort of story loses nothing in repetition. Within a short time, people were saying confidently that Hawkins was a Spanish cavalier. Juanes de Urquiça later declared that he had "heard it said many times . . . that [Hawkins] was the first cavalier that the king Don Phelipe his lord knighted in England."[8] It is probably worth noting that Philip had a totally different opinion of John Hawkins. In instructions to his new ambassador Guerau de Spes, Philip warned about the depredations of "the English pirate named John Hawkins, who has gone through the Indies committing great robberies and destruction." He recommended that the ambassador press the queen and her council to punish "this pirate . . . in a manner befitting his escapades."[9]

After several days, with no response from the governor, Hawkins addressed a similar letter to the bishop of Valencia, a town nearby. He began his letter with the traditional English salutation for a prelate:

> right reverend father in God I arived [here] in this port of
> borboroata 4 dayes agone where I have [und]erstood of
> youre good fame the wch had stirred me [to] write unto
> you and to desire you that I may have [b]roughte hether to
> the porte /100/ oxen to serve my torne while I am in this
> porte and I will pay for them and for the bringing of them
> hether as you shall appoincte I have to sell /60/ negros and
> a percell of my wares to helpe to lighten the chardges of
> this vioadge whereon I nowe am and was not thought to
> have bene made to any of these partes but that thinges have
> happened contrarye I ~~truste~~ beseche you ~~wilbe~~ to be a
> meane to the governor all that you maye that my request to
> him may take effecte and any thing that I may pleasure you
> in you shall comaund it the wch you shall have the better

proofe of if you wolde doe me so muche honer as to visite me in this port.[10]

Hawkins had not intended to come to the Indies, he said, but "thinges have happened contrarye." The bishop, for his part, encouraged Hawkins to stay and see what could be worked out. "I will doe wth the gover[nor all that I m]ay," he wrote, but he declined the invitation to visit the ship, so "that I maye not be suspected."[11]

Thus encouraged by the bishop of Valencia, Hawkins kept his fleet in the harbor for several weeks, trying to extract a trading license from the authorities. After a time the governor of Venezuela wrote to say that he absolutely could not allow Hawkins to trade. "I sawe the governor my predecesser caryed awaye prisoner into spaine," the anonymous English witness quoted him, "for ~~trafiquyng~~ geving license to the countrye to trafique wth you at your laste being here." When the local merchants learned of the governor's refusal, they quietly arranged for Hawkins to land a few armed men and take them captive. They could then claim that they had traded with Hawkins only because they were forced to do so. Accordingly, Hawkins sent Barrett ashore with sixty men to seize the waiting merchants. Before Barrett reached Valencia, however, local officials got wind of the plot, took the merchants into custody, and marched everyone out of town.[12]

While waiting in vain at Borburata, Hawkins took the time to recaulk some of his ships. Other vessels were dispatched on trading missions to Coro and Curaçao, but with little success.[13] Finally, in late May, Hawkins sent Francis Drake with two of the smaller ships, the *Judith* and the *Angel*, to inspect the port at Río de la Hacha. This is the port where Lovell had caused such a problem the previous year, trying to force the local people to buy his slaves. Warned in advance by advisories from Borburata, the local commander, Miguel de Castellanos, had new defenses ready near the town, with a hundred harquebusiers mobilized to defend the approaches. As Drake's small ships came into the harbor, the Spanish batteries opened fire, and the two English vessels withdrew.[14] For the next few days the *Judith* and the *Angel* rode just out of cannon range, blockading the port and waiting for Hawkins to arrive with the rest of the fleet.

Entering the harbor on 10 June, Hawkins followed his usual practice of sending a messenger to the local commander to ask formal approval for a bit of trading. In this case, the commander was an old friend and trading partner. But things had changed, and the commander was unwilling to break the clear royal prohibition of trade with the English pirates.[15]

Again, attempting to provide a rationale for trade, Hawkins reminded Castellanos that the slaves Lovell had delivered to Río de la Hacha in 1567 were the ones Castellanos had asked for earlier. Still, all that was in the past, and Hawkins would not ask for payment, for the slaves had been confiscated by royal officials. "This I desire," he wrote, "that you will geve me license to sell /60/ negros onlye towards the payment of my soldiers ~~that I have~~ to help to lighten the chardges of this vioadg wch was appoincted to be made otherwayes ~~by~~ and to none of these partes." He apologized for the rash behavior of Lovell, but warned that he intended to put his men ashore, subtly reminding him that he could avoid a conflict by meeting Hawkins's terms. "If you se in the morninge armed men[ne] alond lett it nothing troubell you for as you shall comaund they shall retorne abourde againe."[16]

Castellanos, unpersuaded by the argument and the veiled threat, replied that Hawkins and his men had better be prepared for a fight. Going ashore the next morning with two hundred armed men and some artillery, Hawkins was met by Castellanos leading about sixty

men, some of them on horseback.[17] Trading shots and killing one Englishman, the overwhelmed Castellanos soon abandoned the town.[18]
What happened then is a matter of dispute between two accounts. The
anonymous narrative says that Hawkins occupied the place and sent a
message to Castellanos under a flag of truce, asking once more for the
trading license. When Castellanos still refused, Hawkins threatened to
burn the town. Castellanos told him to proceed, saying that "thoughe
he sawe all the India afyre he wold geve no license."[19]

The alternate version says that some of the sailors searching
through the town found a few chickens and a barrel of wine and decided to celebrate. Helping themselves to the wine while the chickens
cooked, they managed to set a grass house on fire. Before Hawkins
could have the blaze extinguished, the wind rose, and the fire spread,
and several dwellings burned to the ground.[20]

In the meantime a few sailors went into the church, where they
stole the brocaded vestments from the sacristy and hid them on board
the ship. Others took the wooden statues out of the church and burned
them. Once he had the situation in hand, Hawkins sent a messenger to
Castellanos, noting the damage and demanding a ransom for the rest of
the town. Two slaves approached while Hawkins waited for a reply.
They knew where a valuable store of merchandise had been hidden
and would lead Hawkins to the place in return for a guarantee of freedom. Hawkins agreed and was led to the place, where he found cases
of soap, clothing, and other things, all of which he took, along with a
few hostages.[21]

This was enough to bring Castellanos to the bargaining table.
Riding into town alone on his horse, he went into a building with
Hawkins, and the two had a long conversation. No one knows exactly
what was said by either man. As Hawkins reported the discussion, his

firmness had the desired effect on Castellanos, who agreed to let the people trade. The local planters bought about 200 of his slaves, and as usual, Hawkins distributed gifts to Castellanos and other officials. He then sent for the sailors who had stolen the vestments, demanded their return, and delivered the goods to Castellanos. Declaring that he himself was a "Catholic Christian" and did not approve of what his men had done to the church, Hawkins made other gifts of merchandise to Castellanos, saying that he hoped it was sufficient for the replacement of the statuary.[22]

Castellanos gave a very different account of events in his report to the king. He claimed that Hawkins required him to pay a ransom of four thousand pesos for the release of the hostages, then left about seventy-five sick and dying slaves on shore to repay the damage done to the dwellings. These were mostly children and old people, said Castellanos, and they were distributed among local planters who had agreed to provide food and shelter. They were being sold off gradually, he wrote, though the value did not approach the cost of repairing the damaged dwellings. In any case, he thought the ransom well spent. He was able to execute the two slave deserters, one by hanging, the other by quartering. If this is really what happened to the blacks, it was a great act of betrayal on the part of Hawkins, who had promised them their freedom for the information they had provided.[23]

It is difficult to know exactly what took place at Río de la Hacha. Perhaps the truth lies somewhere between the various accounts. The Spanish colonists no doubt bought a large number of slaves while government officials looked the other way. Hawkins left a smaller number of slaves in the hands of the local treasurer, who might have been expected to keep sales records on these unfortunates in order to confuse the government inspectors who would inevitably be sent later. The

Hawkins trade pattern had become a familiar one: his formal request for a license to trade; a formal refusal by the local officials; a brief battle, with perhaps a few men killed and injured on each side; and finally two or three weeks of profitable trade in slaves and merchandise, carried out under the guise of ransom payments on one side and reimbursement for damages on the other. In his printed version of events Hawkins claimed to have concluded "a secrete trade" with his friend Castellanos, but the friendship could not have been very close, for Hawkins captured and kept the ensign carried by the Spanish officer. Secret or not, the trade was profitable. Thomas Fuller said that Hawkins sold 120 slaves for a total of twelve or thirteen thousand ducados in pearls, gold, and silver, or about £18 each.[24]

When he finished at Río de la Hacha, Hawkins sailed with his fleet to Santa Marta, reaching there about the end of June. Following his standard pattern of request, refusal, scuffle, and trade, Hawkins addressed his usual letter to the governor:

> worshipfull
>
> I ~~have~~ browght oute of guynea certaine negros the w^{c}h I had there by trafique to helpe to lighten the chardges of this vioadge wch was determyned to ~~be made~~ wth ~~the w^{c}h~~ I have in a manner solde them all saving a fewe I beseche you being as ~~it is~~ they are a small ~~matter~~ nomber that ~~he have~~ are lefte yo[u] will license me to sell ~~them for~~ or ~~to~~ trucke them here for suche necessaryes that you maye helpe me to w^{c}h I lacke/[25]

With the message delivered, Hawkins landed for a private talk with the governor, where he arranged the usual show of force. Returning to the ships, Hawkins had a few shots fired over the town, then landed once more. This time he had 150 men, led by himself in battle armor. Marching into the town square, Hawkins and his troops found the governor and the leading citizens under a flag of truce, waiting to deliver the license. The captain and officers then began to enjoy the usual round of feasts ashore, followed by entertainment for the locals aboard the flagship. The men ate fresh meat and vegetables, and some went ashore in work parties. In two weeks of trading Hawkins sold 114 slaves, collecting another twelve or thirteen thousand ducados for them.[26]

Leaving Santa Marta on 13 July, Hawkins took his fleet farther along the coast to Cartagena, arriving three days later. Once more the usual battle ensued, but this time the Spanish colonists put up a stiff defense, and the English managed only to secure a supply of oil and wine. The Spanish commander at Cartagena refused to enter into any negotiations with the pirates, telling the messenger, Anthony Godard, that if he were not a messenger he would be punished severely. In fact, the governor had two citizens who had brought Godard into his presence thrown into the stocks. He ordered his guns to fire on the ships, ten or twelve shots in all, hitting nothing. Still, the message was clear. With a good fortress to defend his town, the governor had no need to worry about Hawkins and his fleet.[27]

By this time the fleet needed water, wood, and fresh provisions. Luckily a boy Hawkins had taken at Borburata knew of a nearby island with a pleasure garden and a spring that local citizens often used. There Hawkins found not only a good supply of water but also about a hundred jars of oil and others of wine, which he paid for by leaving some trade goods behind.[28] After spending another week at the island near Cartagena, Hawkins decided further delay was pointless. He left on 29 July, taking the fifty or so slaves and the small quantity of trade goods that remained in his ships. "Our trade was so neare finished," said Hawkins, "we thought not good eyther to adventure any landinge, or to detract further tyme."[29]

Shortly after leaving the harbor at Cartagena, the fleet was becalmed for a day or two. With the hurricane season well advanced and his supplies running low, Hawkins decided to abandon one of the vessels seized on the African coast and sail home with a smaller fleet. The English sailors who had been sent to man the French pirate ship came back to the *Jesus of Lubeck.* The original French crew returned to their own vessel with supplies sufficient for a quick trip home. Leaving them and sinking the Portuguese vessel taken on the coast of Guinea, Hawkins then sailed north with his remaining eight ships.[30]

Heading for the Yucatán Channel and the Straits of Florida, the fleet had scarcely rounded Cabo San Antonio when a terrible storm bore down on the ships. The *Jesus,* old and rickety, sprung its planks and began to take on water by the bow and stern, where the seams opened so wide that fish swam into the bilge and fouled the pumps. The *William and John* simply disappeared in the storm and made a separate voyage home. Four days later, when the storm blew itself out, the fleet lay hundreds of miles north off the coast of Florida. For two weeks Hawkins searched for a port in which to repair his battered vessels. Finally, he decided to sail south for New Spain, where he expected to find a haven. Along the coast of Campeche, Hawkins captured two Spanish ships belonging to Francisco Maldonado and Agustín de Villanueva. A brief conversation with their pilot was enough to show that the ships were going to San Juan de Ulúa, the port town for Vera Cruz.[31]

The pilot, Bartolomé González, told Hawkins that the harbor at Vera Cruz was broad and open, but slightly sheltered from the weather by the low-lying island of San Juan de Ulúa.[32] When González said that there was no better port nearby, Hawkins decided it was a good enough spot to refit and reprovision his fleet. He thereupon added the two Spanish ships to his fleet, took the commanders and their Portuguese pilot on board, and headed for San Juan de Ulúa. A few days later, he captured a third Spanish ship and added it to his fleet as well.[33]

On 16 September, with badly faded banners flying from its masts, the *Jesus* led Hawkins's ten ships into port to the thundering welcome of a five-gun salute by local officials who expected a Spanish merchant fleet and mistook the faded banners for the Spanish ensign.[34] Taking advantage of the confusion, Hawkins returned the courtesy with a salute of his own. When the local delegation came on board, Hawkins greeted them in Spanish, "Enter, Señores, the lord general wishes to speak to you." After a brief discussion, he took one of the officials, Martín de Marçana, as a hostage. The other, Francisco de Bustamante, he released to carry the bad news back to shore. Warned by the pilot González to guard his mooring lines, Hawkins sent a party ashore, seized the island, and established his headquarters "in a large building called the House of Lies."[35] Most of the troops manning the Spanish guns appear to have been blacks who made up the labor force on the island. They either fled to the mainland or were sent there by Hawkins, who feared that they might cut the cables and loot his ships.[36]

For a while the Englishmen went about freely on shore, trading with local merchants and generally enjoying themselves. One sailor recalled that "he had gone ashore once or twice to drink." According to the account published later by Hawkins, there were a dozen ships in the harbor, which may be true. However, the story that the great hulk of Diego Felipe was loaded with 200,000 pounds sterling in gold and silver, awaiting shipment to Spain, must be taken as a seaman's tale.[37]

¶ Obra nueuaméte compuesta so-
bre vna admirable victoria que bouo Don Francisco Lu-
çan contra Don Juã D Acle lutberano capitan de la
Reyna de Jnglaterre. Compuesto por Aluaro
de Flores natural de Malaga y vezino de
Seuilla. E ftay examinada por el do
cto: millan, r con licécia impresta
en Burgos por Pedro de
Sátillana impresto:.
Año. M.D.XII.

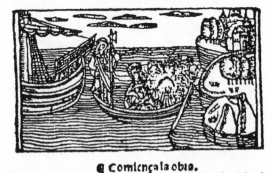

¶ Comiença la obra.

Emperadora del cielo
Rosa fresco linda auroxa
pues que soys nuestro côsuelo
alcançame en este suelo
de la gracia que en vos mora,
Sagrada virgen Maria
madre de mi redemptor
dame gracia en este dia
porque no la historia mia
diga con vuestro fenor.

¶ Porq todos los christianos
que en el mundo son nascidos
dexen los vicios mundanos
que los ciegos lutberanos
vean como descreydos,
Porque tengan en memoria
lo que ahora acontescio
contar e en aquesta historia
la gran batalla y victoria
que ahora en Jndias subcedio,

6

An account by the soldier-poet Alvaro Flores, with an illustration presumably showing
the arrival of the Hawkins fleet at San Juan de Ulúa.

The following morning, 17 September 1568, lookouts from the English fleet were startled to hear a signal gun. Looking out to sea, they saw the sails of the real Spanish fleet on the horizon. Hawkins reacted just as he had when the fleet of DeWachen arrived off Plymouth, though he clearly should have expected trouble. Some of his men said later that everyone thought that it might be the fleet of Pedro Menéndez, who had destroyed the French settlement at Port Royal. Hawkins immediately sent fifty men ashore to man the fortifications, reinforcing the shore batteries with guns from his own ships. Within a short time the shore party was well dug in, and Hawkins was determined to defend this strong position.[38]

While all this was going on, Antonio Delgadillo, who had been in charge of the defenses at San Juan de Ulúa, sent a messenger to inform the Spanish fleet commander that Hawkins had occupied the port with seven armed vessels. Shortly thereafter Delgadillo himself arrived at the flagship with a message from Hawkins proposing a truce.[39]

No doubt Hawkins addressed his message to the commander of the fleet, Francisco de Luxan, whose name he did not know. With his usual mixture of truth and fiction Hawkins told the Spanish commander that bad weather and severe damage to his ships had forced him to take refuge in San Juan de Ulúa, where he needed to make repairs and purchase additional supplies. Similar circumstances had brought him to the Indies in the first place, forcing him to trade his shiploads of slaves for sufficient supplies to victual his men and return home with a small profit. Hawkins assured the commander that his visit had been entirely peaceful, with no damage to Spanish citizens or possessions. Hawkins concluded with an offer to sign a truce "with his owne hand" and a threat of a fight if Luxan would not agree to the terms.[40]

The most important passenger in the Spanish fleet was Martín

Enríquez, the freshly appointed viceroy of New Spain. Lacking military experience but outranking Luxan, Enríquez was determined to participate in all decisions. These two had a difficult choice to make. If they attacked Hawkins, they risked losing their fleet along with the other ships in the harbor. Yet the weather was threatening, and it was necessary to bring the fleet into port after the long and difficult voyage. Calling his officers into conference, Enríquez finally agreed to let Hawkins remain in port for a brief time, repairing his ships and buying necessary supplies. Hawkins and Enríquez then exchanged hostages as a guarantee of good faith. Hawkins also released Delgadillo and Marçana, the latter of whom he had kept with him on the island.[41]

Bad weather continued for three more days, during which time the Spanish fleet delayed entry into the harbor. Meanwhile, both veiled threats and friendly overtures passed back and forth between the two commanders. Hawkins took advantage of the delay to improve his fortifications on the island, apparently keeping the Spanish fleet commander ignorant of what he was doing. In his letter of acceptance Enríquez had said that he expected to put his own men on the island, where they would mingle freely with the Englishmen.[42] But when Luxan arrived at the mooring on 21 September, the defenses were occupied by English gunners ready to fire. Although Hawkins told him he was "as safe as if he were in his own house," both Luxan and the viceroy felt that Hawkins had deceived them. Within a few days plans were complete to eject the Englishman from his fortified position.[43]

The ships were docked on alternate sides of the harbor, the Spanish fleet on the west and the English next to the island. Keeping up a pretense of friendship, the Spanish commander promised to send carpenters and caulkers to help Hawkins recondition his fleet. Hawkins, for his part, dispatched his four musicians to the viceroy's ship to give the Spanish officers a taste of English culture. Not giving up all precautions, but relaxing somewhat, Hawkins began to put his men to work on the ships. The *Jesus of Lubeck,* in the worst condition, was the first to receive attention. The seamen hauled down all the canvas in preparation for careening.[44]

Plans for the Spanish attack were made quickly and not too carefully. On the night of 22 September, with the fleet in harbor for only a day, a hundred and fifty soldiers, armed with harquebuses and targets, crept silently aboard the empty hulk belonging to Diego Felipe. Sailors on the ship then attached a mooring line to the same bollard that held the lines from the *Jesus* and began towing the vessel into position alongside the English flagship.[45]

Early in the morning, while the men were still at breakfast, Hawkins saw a ship nearby with Spanish soldiers on board. Immediately suspecting some sort of treachery, he sent Robert Barrett to ask Viceroy Enríquez what the Spanish were doing. It was just practice, he was told. But the practice continued, so Hawkins sent Barrett once more. This time Barrett met General Luxan, who ordered him taken into custody, chained hand and foot, and confined below deck.[46]

While this was going on Hawkins was at table in his own cabin with the Spanish hostages. One of them, Agustín de Villanueva, picked up a knife, and the guard thought he intended to stab the English commander. Immediately disarmed, the man was taken below and put in irons. Hawkins then went on deck to see why Barrett was delayed. There he saw Admiral Juan de Ubilla aboard the approaching hulk and called to him that he was a trickster and no gentleman. Other words were exchanged, as some witnesses have recorded, no doubt improving upon them as time passed.[47] Suddenly, an arrow from the *Jesus* landed near Ubilla, while a man at his side fell from a harquebus shot. Seeing that the plot was discovered, Ubilla gave the attack signal to the Spanish flagship, which was some distance away. It was only 10 A.M., an hour before the time agreed upon, and the attacking forces were not in position. Even so, the viceroy ordered a trumpet sounded. This done, the commander of the Spanish flagship, Don Luís Zegri, gave the traditional battle cry, "Santiago!" On his own disabled flagship Hawkins responded with the English battle cry, "God and St. George, upon these false traitors, for my trust is only in God that the daie shall be ours."[48]

Antonio Delgadillo, Pedro de Yerba, and Francisco de Bustamante with reinforcements from Vera Cruz were waiting in boats drawn up alongside the hulk. As soon as they heard the trumpet, they rowed to shore and easily occupied the three fortifications Hawkins had established at the House of Lies, La Ventanilla, and the smithy. The startled Englishmen were put to the sword, no quarter given and none asked, for it all happened too quickly. A few managed to escape aboard the *Jesus,* and a few more badly wounded men were captured, but most died at their guns. The attackers then turned the still-loaded guns on the English ships and began firing.[49]

As soon as they heard the first shot, cannoneers on the *Minion* ran to their guns and lit their matches, but it was difficult for the officers to believe that the Spanish would attack. Thomas Anthony told the gunners to hold their fire, the Spanish were simply practicing. Then a shot from the Spanish guns shattered the foremast yard on the *Jesus of Lubeck,* and everyone could see that it was not practice. Crying, "Treachery! Treachery!" the English gunners began to fire, and the soldiers who were not already under arms ran to their battle stations.[50]

Although the Spanish troops quickly slaughtered the men guarding the moorings, Hawkins was able to cut the cables of the *Jesus* and drift away from the anchorage. With a little distance between the vessels, Hawkins trained his guns on the decks and rigging of the Spanish ships, battering them badly and setting fire to the Spanish flagship. As a result the Spanish commander prepared a fire ship to drive Hawkins away. The first such ship failed to ignite, and Hawkins gained valuable time while his attackers prepared another. With a second fire ship bearing down on the *Jesus,* Hawkins called the ten Spanish hostages on deck, where they underwent a few moments of uncertainty. Hawkins soon calmed their fears, saying he had "given his word to leave them in peace in their own land." Thus he abandoned them, along with many of his own luckless men, mostly wounded, who remained on the flagship. After drifting away to the Isla de Sacrificios, Hawkins began to transfer his valuables to the *Minion.* Taking a little too much time, he and a few others barely managed to escape, leaping aboard the *Minion* at the very last moment.[51]

Drake, who was nearby in the *Judith,* was ordered to come alongside the *Minion* to take on some of the extra men and equipment saved from the *Jesus of Lubeck.* "He did," said Job Hortop thirty years later, though Hawkins himself told a different story, reflecting less credit on Drake. While the *Minion* lay in the lee of the island outside the range of the Spanish guns and loaded with more English survivors than it could carry, Drake sailed off in the darkness, heading for home. "The Judith," said Hawkins, "forsoke us in oure greate miserie."[52]

Five ships from the Hawkins fleet were abandoned in the port, four captured and one destroyed by the Spanish militia.[53] In fact, these sea-worn prizes made it possible for Hawkins and the others to escape. As soon as the *Minion* and the *Judith* were out of the harbor, the undisciplined Spanish militiamen ended their pursuit and spent the rest of the day looting the English ships and fortifications.[54]

An honored tradition in most maritime communities, this practice of looting abandoned stores was something of an art at San Juan de Ulúa. When Hawkins first arrived with his fleet, all the wealthy merchants fled with whatever they could carry. Those who stayed behind then helped themselves to what was left. As one man described the scene, "Those who had little wanted to help those who had something save what they had, so it seems they put it away for themselves."[55]

Exactly what and how much Hawkins left behind is a matter of dispute. One of the prisoners told his Spanish captors that "all the gold and silver and pearls that John Hawkins possessed on the day of the battle was taken by the Spaniards."[56] Another said that when Hawkins fled from San Juan de Ulúa, "he abandoned in the ships he left behind much gold and silver and slaves and merchandise."[57] Viceroy Enríquez, on the other hand, reported to his government that Hawkins had escaped with "the greater part of his possessions and loot."[58] Among the items left behind were the guns Hawkins had moved to the island and those on the ships abandoned in the harbor. To his men the flagship had seemed like a floating arsenal, with thirty or forty guns, twenty-two of bronze and the others iron. The Spanish officials later made an inventory of the guns and other loot, arriving at a total in more or less agreement with this. There were four or five vessels carrying nearly sixty guns of various types. In addition, the vessels still carried a supply of trade goods, along with about fifty slaves and perhaps some gold and silver coin. All of these fell into Spanish hands, either to the looters or to the royal officials. Hawkins and his investors later claimed their losses were great, while the Spanish officials reported much lower totals.[59]

While Drake and his men in the *Judith* saved themselves, Hawkins remained on the coast of Mexico with an overloaded ship and

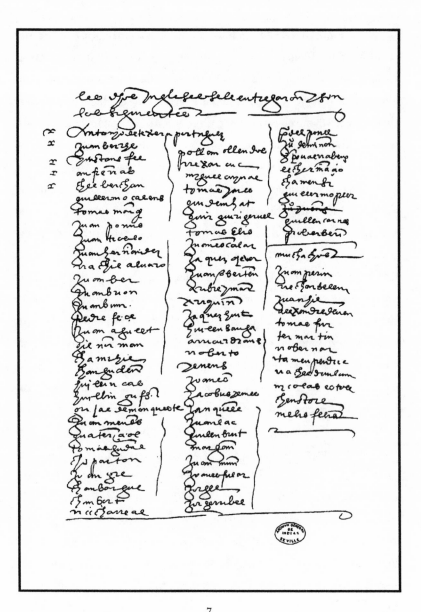

7

The Spanish list of prisoners taken after the battle at San Juan de Ulúa begins with
Antonio de Texera Portuges, the Spanish name of Anthony Goddard. España,
Ministerio de Educación, Cultura, y Deporte, Archivo General de Indias,
Patronato 265, ramo 12, fol. 9.

San Juan de Ulúa

insufficient food. As their suffering increased, nearly a hundred men asked to be put ashore, reasoning that it was better to surrender to the Spanish officials than to face death by starvation on the voyage home. Realizing that he could not take them all home, Hawkins set them ashore in Campeche, near the town of Tampico, giving those who asked for it a bit of money and a supply of cloth for trading.[60] Hawkins promised to do what he could for the abandoned men but most of them never saw England again. The scandal of desertion haunted Drake for the rest of his life, though Hawkins himself refused to dwell on the incident, perhaps because he was also being criticized.[61] Instead Hawkins and Drake both nursed their feelings of bitter betrayal, claiming that the Spanish viceroy had broken a clear and solemn promise to let them refit and leave peacefully. The Viceroy for his part felt Hawkins had tricked him into the agreement, not only lying to conceal his attacks on Spanish ports and citizens, but also in his armed occupation of the island at San Juan de Ulúa.

5

Counting the Cost

¶ A true
declaration of the
troublesome voy-
adge of M. John Hau-
kins to the parties of
Guynea and the west
Indies, in the yea-
res of our Lord
1 5 6 7. and
1 5 6 8.

I also saw another Englishman, a well-dressed young man, with
slippers of crimson velvet, fine stockings, and a scarlet leather jacket
with silver fringe. He was of medium height, with a sunburned face,
and they said he was Captain John Hawkins.

Gregorio Sarmiento de Valladares

O n 16 October 1568, when John Hawkins left the coast
of Mexico, his slaving fleet was reduced to one small
ship and fewer than a hundred hungry men. Another month of miserable sailing brought him through
the Bahama Channel. No doubt he stopped along the
way for wood and water, perhaps at Cabo de San Antonio on the eastern tip of Cuba, where Drake watered his own beleaguered fleet some
years later. Sailing north to catch the wind that would take him home,
Hawkins watched helplessly as the weather turned colder and his men
sickened and died. Supplies were so short that nearly every mouse, rat,
dog, cat, parrot, or monkey that could be found in the ship was cooked
and eaten, and when everything else ran out, the men began eating the
leather fittings and drinking salt water.[1] Finally, convinced that the
ship could not reach England, Hawkins headed for Galicia on the
northwest coast of Spain, where he had friends among the Spanish and
English merchants. Just off the coast of Spain, according to the story
told a few weeks later by a slave from the *Minion,* Hawkins met three
Portuguese vessels. In a swift battle he captured the ships, cut off the
legs of the surviving seamen, and threw the men into the water, still
alive. Then he helped himself to the supplies and sent the ships to the
bottom.[2] Whether or not this really happened, there is no doubt that

Hawkins was very desperate by the time he neared the Ría Pontevedra in Galicia.

On the first day of January 1569 a fisherman named Gregorio de Sias noticed the *Minion* at anchor in the mouth of the estuary near Porto Nuevo. Seeing a signal flag, Sias approached the ship and was invited to come aboard. There he saw some fifty people, black and white, sick and well. The captain asked Sias to guide the ship to Pontevedra, or a closer port if possible, for the sailors were dying of hunger. The fisherman thereupon led the *Minion* to the port of Marín, a few miles downstream from the town of Pontevedra. Anchoring there, the *Minion* fired signal guns to attract attention, and several boatloads of local men came out to give assistance. Only a magistrate and two or three local merchants were allowed to come aboard. Once on deck they found Hawkins standing on the gratings dressed in his finest clothes. A Portuguese merchant, Juan de la Torre, described him: "He was dressed in a coat trimmed with marten skins, with cuffs of black silk. He had a scarlet cloak, edged in silver and a doublet of the same material. His cape was silk, and he wore a great gold chain around his neck."[3]

All the healthy crewmen were standing at their arms, and the guns were rolled out as though the ship were ready for war. As soon as the visitors came aboard, Hawkins demanded that the local merchants be allowed to sell him supplies, saying that if they could not do so, he would simply take what he needed from the ships in the harbor and leave without paying. Somewhat intimidated, the officials quickly agreed. Then, using his considerable charm, Hawkins entertained the officials on deck. By the time they went ashore he had convinced them to tell everyone that there was a pestilence on the ship, a tale that he hoped might keep potential marauders away.[4]

A sort of pestilence actually did come aboard the *Minion* along with the new supplies of meat, bread, and wine. The famished seamen, unable to control their hunger, gorged themselves, and as a result many died.[5] Hoping to keep his losses secret, Hawkins had the bodies put into the sea at night with stones tied to their feet. In spite of these precautions, some of the stones came loose, and a few bodies washed ashore, where the locals could guess what had happened. Officers were luckier than ordinary seamen. Some of them spent a few days recuperating in the local inn, among them James Raunce, the old captain, who told people he was suffering from gout. Hawkins himself did not go ashore, saying that he had sworn not to leave the ship until he reached England. But faced with the loss of so many crewmen, Hawkins might have ended his journey at Marín, had not an English trader named Duarte Boronel brought ten or twelve seamen from some English ships in the nearby port of Vigo to fill the vacancies. When these new crewmen arrived, Hawkins ordered those who had gone ashore to return, and the *Minion* departed for England.[6]

Even then the "troublesome voyadge" was not over. Sailing out of the Ría de Pontevedra, the *Minion* ran directly into the teeth of a storm. Once more, Hawkins brought his ship back to land, sheltering at the Islas Cies in the mouth of the Ría de Vigo. During the few days he stayed in the islands, Hawkins sent men ashore at Vigo, where they met Tomás Olanda and other English traders. With new supplies Hawkins again went to sea, and again a storm forced him to return. Anchoring this time in the harbor of Teys, a mile or so from Vigo, Hawkins sent another supply party ashore, where the men stayed for a few days as the fortunate guests of Olanda and other English merchants.[7]

Well aware that he would be subjected to great criticism for losing so many ships and men, John Hawkins deliberately avoided sending any written report home. Even so, news about the voyage arrived in Ply-

mouth before he did. Late in December, William Hawkins had a gar-
bled account of the battle at San Juan de Ulúa, and shortly thereafter he
knew that his brother was in the harbor near Vigo.[8] When William
Hawkins wrote to Secretary Cecil to report the arrival of Francis Drake
in late January, he declared that John Hawkins also seemed to be safe.
"God hathe p[re]servyd" him and will "sende [him] well home in
salfeyte." Even so, his arrival was still "very daungerouse and doutfull."
With this in mind William sent a bark loaded with spare anchors,
cables, and thirty-four mariners to help sail the *Minion* the rest of the
way to Plymouth.[9]

Thus when John Hawkins returned to the harbor at Vigo, he
found two ships from England loaded with food, anchors, and cables.[10]
A few of the ill and badly wounded seamen from the *Minion* were
moved to these vessels. In spite of the precarious condition of his ship
and crew, Hawkins remained a canny trader. He kept his treasure under
guard and paid his bills with the slaves and bolts of cloth that remained
in the hold, and even one parrot that had somehow escaped the clutch-
es of the hungry crewmen.[11]

During this stay among friends at Vigo, Hawkins felt more
secure, so he allowed a number of people to come aboard the *Minion*.
One of the visitors left this description of the old ship captain and of
John Hawkins as well: "On that ship I saw that there was an old man
dressed in sheepskin, and he said he was the captain of the ship *Minion*. I also saw another Englishman, a well-dressed young man, with
slippers of crimson velvet, fine stockings, and a scarlet leather jacket
with silver fringe. He was of medium height, with a sunburned face,
and they said he was Captain John Hawkins."[12]

Resupplied once more, the *Minion* sailed out of the harbor at
Vigo on 20 January 1569, accompanied by a smaller English vessel,

apparently the one sent by William Hawkins to see his brother home safely. Still unchastened, John Hawkins stopped a ship outside the harbor and helped himself to an extra supply of wine. Four days later he landed at Mounts Bay in Cornwall, whence a messenger came quickly to his brother in Plymouth, saying that John Hawkins had returned with the *Minion*.[13]

Hawkins himself arrived on the other vessel, as he noted in a letter sent the next day to London. "The 24th day of Januarii thanks be to god we aryved in a place in cornewall called mounts bay and by us the mynion w[ch] ys last us of all our fleet." Only a few survivors were in the *Minion*, no more than fifteen mariners, according to the Spanish ambassador. In the first detailed account he received of the voyage William Hawkins learned that forty-five men had died of hunger and were buried at sea.[14] Some of the casualties probably were the tragic deaths from overeating at Marín.

In his first report to Cecil, John Hawkins sent a lengthy account of the voyage, "not all our mestryes that hathe past yet the greatest matters worthe of notynge." Using a metaphor he seemed to like, Hawkins said, "yf I shold wryt of all our calamytes I ame sure a volome as great as the byble wyll scarcly suffyce." Once the people at Plymouth recovered from their joy at seeing the survivors, the recriminations began. Some wondered how it was possible for Hawkins to have brought home unsold slaves but not possible to have brought home all his seamen. By March, John Hawkins was in London, defending his own conduct of the expedition. "Ther are some w[ch] cane be contentyd to spek the warst in eny thynge & to fynd many faults wher yf they had bynbe present pardventure wold have done worse."[15]

Relations between England and Spain were very different in the early months of 1569 than they had been when John Hawkins had departed on his ill-fated voyage to the Indies. While Hawkins and his fleet headed for the coast of Africa, the duke of Alba began marching through the Netherlands with a huge Spanish army in an attempt to restore Philip's authority and suppress Protestant disturbances there. Protestant leaders in France, Germany, and England saw these Spanish troops as a distinct threat to their own security. William of Orange took direct action to assist the Dutch rebels, but Queen Elizabeth contented herself with providing other forms of aid to the enemies of Philip II, who was still a nominal friend and trading partner. Late in 1568 French Huguenot raiders based in La Rochelle intercepted a fleet of small ships sent by Genoese bankers with a loan to pay the Spanish troops in the Netherlands. Escaping from the raiders, the ships took refuge in Plymouth and Southampton. Seeing the largely unprotected treasure, English port officials, William Hawkins among them, argued that it was still vulnerable to pirate raids, took it off the ships, and ultimately sent it to the queen in London.[16] Whether Elizabeth intended to keep the funds or simply send them on to the Netherlands is not clear, but Alba thought that she had taken his money and in retaliation ordered the immediate confiscation of English ships and goods in the Netherlands. At this point William Hawkins heard of his brother's losses in the battle of San Juan de Ulúa, and he asked Secretary Cecil to reimburse those losses from what he supposed was a hoard of Spanish money.[17]

Authorities in Spain were also taking action. In February 1569 a formal inquiry was made in Vigo and Ponte Vedra to determine why John Hawkins had been so well received there after his belligerent excursion through the Spanish ports in the West Indies. At the same time, restrictions were imposed on English merchants and goods in Seville and elsewhere.[18]

Perhaps because so many of his men were still in Spanish hands,

John Hawkins seems to have taken a more moderate position than his brother on the matter of reimbursement. With so many lives and so much money at stake he preferred to settle matters by negotiation rather than confrontation. In March 1569 he journeyed to London, where he joined with other survivors of the expedition in a declaration before the High Court of Admiralty, outlining the events at San Juan de Ulúa and establishing a claim against the government of Philip II. The list of damages covered twenty-seven items ranging from fully equipped ships to cargoes of slaves and even a bale of taffeta. Realizing that such claims were automatically negotiated downward, Hawkins and his associates set their valuations at the highest possible levels, with numerous separate listings of items clearly included in other broad categories. The claim was summarized as follows:

1   First the specified ship called The Jesus of
    Lubecke with its equipment and accouterments
    as sent out from England   5000^{li} ster.

2   Item instruments of war, or guns of bronze and iron,
    which were part of the accouterments, equipment,
    and muniments installed in the same ship called the
    Jesus and sent out from England   2000^{li}

3   Item gun powder, iron balls, arms and other
    instruments or guns installed in the same ship and
    dispatched from England   2000^{li}

4   Item two anchors and three anchor lines, called
    cables, from the equipment of the ship called The
    Mynion, which were lost when the said ship escaped
    from forcible seizure by Spaniards   200^{li}

5   Item the specified ship called The Swallowe with

its equipment, accouterments, and muniments
sent out from England, and the victuals and
seamen's goods carried in it   850^{li}

6 Item the specified ship called The Angell, with
its equipment, accouterments, and muniments
sent out from England, as well as the victuals
and seamen's goods carried in it   180^{li}

7 Item the specified ship called The Grace of
God, with its equipment, apparatus, and
muniments, as well as the victuals and seamen's
goods placed in it   400^{li}

8 Item in the specified ship called The Jesus, and
the three other ships, or some of them, 57 black
Ethiopians, commonly called negros, of the best
sort and stature, each of whom is worth 400 gold
pesos in the region of the West Indies   9120^{li}

9 Item in the said ship called The Jesus and the
other three ships, or some of them, 30 bales of
linen cloth, each worth 3000 rials   2250^{li}

10 Item in the said four ships, or some of them,
1000 pieces of dyed cloth, each of which is
worth 15^s ster   750^{li}

11 Item in the said four ships, or some of them,
400 pounds of that kind of merchandise
commonly called margaritas, each pound of
which is worth v^s ster   100^{li}

12 Item, in the said four ships, or some of them,
300^{li} of pewter, each pound of which is
worth ii^s ster   30^{li}

13 Item a bale of cambric commonly called

taffata, containing 40 *varas* 40^{li}

14 Item four bales of woolen cloth called
hampshires and northerns, each of which is
worth viii^{li} ster 340^{li}

15 Item six bales of cottons 90^{li}

16 Item a chest containing 30 swords decorated
in gold 120^{li}

17 Item 12 quintals of wax

120^{li}

18 Item seven tuns of manillios, commonly vii
tonnes of arm and wrist bands, each of which
is worth 50^{li} 350^{li}

19 Item in the said ship called The Jesus a little
sack of gold and silver containing 600 pesos
of gold and silver 2400^{li}

20 Item in the said ship a chest containing various
pieces of silver work, commonly called silver
plate 200^{li}

21 Item in the said ship silver called currency

500^{li}

22 Item in the said four ships, or some of them,
twenty jars of Cretan and Spanish wine,
commonly xx butts of malmeseys & secks 300^{li}

23 Item, in the said four ships or some of them
36 containers of flour, commonly xxxvi barrells
meale, each of which is worth 4^{li} 144^{li}

24 Item in the said four ships or some of them,
other victuals and necessaries to the value of

150^{li}

25 Item in the said ship called The Jesus clothing
   belonging to the said John Hawkins and other
   things brought for his personal use   300^{li}

26 Item in the said ship called The Jesus chests
   and trunks of seamen's belongings   900^{li}

27 Item, in the said ship called The Jesus a bale
   of 20 mantles, commonly called a packe of
   xx clokes, each of which is worth 4^{li} 80^{li} [19]

The five men who testified with Hawkins were an ill-assorted lot. They included Thomas Hampton, the forty-four-year-old captain of the *Minion,* the "old man" described by the witnesses at Vigo; William Clarke, age twenty-eight, one of the four merchants in the fleet, who sailed home in the *William and John* and thus avoided the battle at San Juan de Ulúa; John Tommes, age twenty-seven, the personal servant of John Hawkins; Jean Tureen, age thirty, trumpeter on the *Jesus;* and Humphrey Fones, age twenty-five, steward on the *Angel.*[20] Perhaps these men were chosen because they were the only survivors available. Still, the captain could testify about the ships and their value, while the merchant could be presumed to know costs and selling prices. The servant, the trumpeter, and the steward would probably know what Hawkins himself might have lost. Interestingly enough, Francis Drake was not among those who testified. Gossips in Spain said he was in prison because he refused to give an accounting of the goods and treasure brought home on the *Judith,* but no English source confirms this. A better guess might be that Drake was in the Indies once more, trying to recover some of the profit that had been lost at San Juan de Ulúa.[21]

When first reporting possible losses in the voyage, William Hawkins thought the totals for the two brothers might amount to £2,000, but two months later John Hawkins swore the total was close to

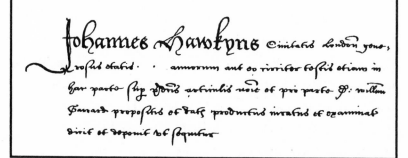

8

In his testimony of March 1569 John Hawkins missed a perfect opportunity to leave a record of his age. Alderman William Garrard neglected to ask him, so the notary left a blank space where the age should be. Public Record Office, SP 12/53, fol. 33v.

£30,000. That included a generous £5,000 for the old and leaky royal vessel, *Jesus of Lubeck* (valued at £2,000 in 1563), and £850 for the *Swallow*. There was even a claim of £180 for the *Angel*, though that vessel was smaller than the *Judith*.[22] A few weeks earlier William had valued the *Judith* at £100 because "she is a very good sayler." There was a claim of £9,120 for the slaves Hawkins could not sell, and £900 for the baggage belonging to the sailors.[23] There was even a claim of £400 for the *Don de Dieu* or *Grace of God*, the French ship that had joined Hawkins's fleet voluntarily. If the valuations given by Hawkins were reduced by 80 percent, the total might be nearly correct.

While the material losses on the voyage were great, the human losses were enormous. Hawkins left 130 dead at San Juan de Ulúa, plus 52 taken prisoner. In the crippled vessels he took from the battle there were fewer than 200 men, perhaps substantially fewer. An unknown number went home with Francis Drake, while a few others came home in the *William and John*. Hawkins abandoned about 90 on the beach near Tampico and lost another 45 to disease and starvation on the way home, arriving in Cornwall with 15 survivors. Staggering as they are, the figures seem correct, adding up to about 370, the number said to have been in the fleet at Borburata.

By the time Hawkins entered his claim, the king of Spain had his own reports on the Hawkins matter, which was just a small part of the problems arising between England and Spain. The new year brought a complete embargo on trade between the two countries. English ships and merchants were under guard in Spanish ports, while Spanish vessels and subjects suffered equally in English ports. The Spanish ambassador Guerau de Spes was under guard in his own house. His correspondence with the king and the duke of Alba still continued, some reports intercepted, but others apparently not. Several messages sealed in a tin can inside a flask of beer, for example, appear to have come through unchecked.[24]

Philip wanted de Spes to know the Spanish version of the battle at San Juan de Ulúa. "We doubt not that they will interpret very much in their own way what happened in New Spain and the punishment that my viceroy Don Martín Enríquez gave to Captain John Hawkins, the pirate, native of that kingdom, who went there with seven ships of war." Because of this the king sent a copy of the Spanish account of the battle to the duke of Alba, who would forward a copy to de Spes. "In this way," he said, "you can supply the truth wherever and whenever it may be lacking."[25]

The Spanish report did not reach England because the duke of Alba decided not to send it on, given the precarious conditions in which the ambassador was held.[26] Even so, de Spes was determined to complain about the Hawkins depredations in the Indies. Through the good offices of his guard, George Speake, de Spes sent a note in Latin to the Privy Council, which summarized his views as follows:

Considering the harm inflicted upon the friendship of the Catholic king by John Hawkins, who they say took the royal fleet with the support and encouragement of the other councillors, now for the fourth time, and undertook an expedition to the western [area] (namely the Indies[)], contrary to treaties and royal laws, taking ships by surprise, plundering and burning towns, capturing people, natives as well as Spanish, among whom is Don Juan Mendoza, now captive in Ireland; Hawkins ought to be punished for all of this, and all the gold and silver and captives ought to be restored; in addition the other depredations made by English and French pirates sailing out of English ports ought to be entirely satisfied and the sea made free once more.[27]

A marginal note on the document shows the skepticism of the Privy Council. "There is more cause to complaine of iniuries done to Jhon Hawkins, wher of when time serveth, there shal be declaration." The "declaration" was not long in coming. By the middle of May printed copies of the report Hawkins had given to Cecil were available on the streets of London.[28] The new publication was called *A true declaration of the troublesome voyadge of M. John Haukins to the parties of Guynea and the west Indies, in the yeares of our Lord 1567. and 1568.* Whether Hawkins wrote it all himself is not clear. At the very least he had an editor who managed to correct some of his more enthusiastic variations in spelling and syntax. Still, his authorship seems to be verified by a new version of a favorite metaphor inserted on the final page. "If all the miseries and troublesome affayres of this sorowefull voyadge shoulde be perfectlye and thoroughlye written," he declared, "there shoulde nede a paynfull man with his penne, and as greate a tyme as he had that wrote the lives and deathes of the martyrs." This latter remark was a reference to the work of John Foxe, whose compendious tale of Protestant heroes had appeared in English a few years earlier and was about to be issued in a substantially revised and enlarged edition.[29]

Hawkins's own small booklet of fifteen unnumbered folios seems not to have had a wide distribution, perhaps because Hawkins had been a little too frank in describing his trading methods. Forwarding a copy of the booklet to the duke of Alba, the Spanish ambassador remarked, "After having published the book, they are going around gathering up whatever copies they can find, revealing their embarrassment at having made it." Surviving examples of the booklet are now so rare that most historians use the text reprinted by Richard Hakluyt twenty years later. Even so, a copy did find its way to the court of Philip II, where a translation was ordered for the king's perusal.[30]

The Hawkins claim for damages had to be submitted through diplomatic circles as part of a total settlement of the dispute between Spain and England. The High Court of Admiralty finished taking testimony on the claim in July 1569.[31] There was no immediate attempt to submit the specific list of damages, but news leaked out that the claims would be large. In September the Spanish ambassador wrote to his king that John Hawkins planned to claim a "ridiculous" 500,000 ducats.[32] Still, no one knew how Hawkins would proceed. The French ambassador heard that Hawkins was planning to go to sea once more, to take revenge for the defeat at San Juan de Ulúa.[33] In December 1569 gossips in Seville were saying that Hawkins had a fleet of twenty-two ships off the northwest coast of Spain, but de Spes soon put that rumor to rest.[34] Others said that Hawkins was in the Canary Islands robbing Portuguese merchants.[35] Early in 1570 Juan de Mendoza, still a prisoner in Dublin, reported that John Hawkins was headed back to the Indies to rescue the men he had left there a few months

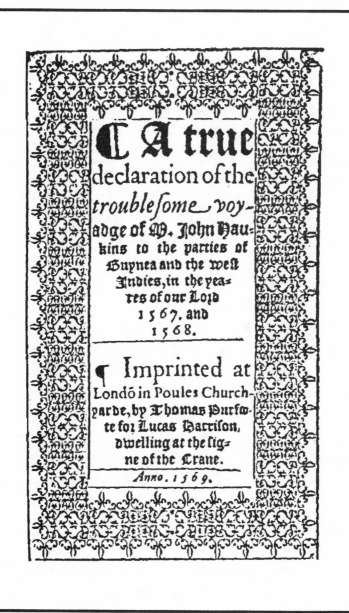

¶ A true declaration of the troublesome voy-adge of M. John Haukins to the parties of Guynea and the west Indies, in the yeares of our Lord 1567. and 1568.

¶ Imprinted at Londõ in Poules Church-parde, by Thomas Purfote for Lucas Harrison, dwelling at the sig-ne of the Crane.

Anno. 1569.

9

A report of "all the miseries and troublesome affayres" of the 1568 voyage, written by John Hawkins a few months after his return.

Counting the Cost

earlier, and other reports seemed to confirm the rumor.[36] Even so, it was not true.

Uncertain where his men were being held and convinced that he could use his proven technique of negotiation and threat, friendship and hostility, Hawkins went to London in February 1570 to talk about the prisoners with the Spanish ambassador. Guerau de Spes reported the Hawkins approach to his king, as Hawkins no doubt knew he would.[37] At about the same time an English adventurer and former Hawkins sea captian named Thomas Stucley began talking to Hawkins about a possible deal with Spain.[38] Others also became involved, and the pattern of plot and counterplot became so convoluted that it is no longer possible to determine the motives or objectives of all the participants. Hawkins was clearly interested in freeing his men from prison, but at times he played the role of a traitor to queen and country.

This was a familiar role for Stucley, who had been jailed for a time in Dublin and there met Juan de Mendoza. The Spanish prisoner was the son of an important family, or claimed to be, and a prisoner of John Hawkins as well. It happened this way. After the Hawkins ship *William and John* had been separated from the *Jesus of Lubeck* in the storm of August 1568, it stopped at a nearby port for supplies. There they met the survivors of a Spanish merchant ship captained by Mendoza. This vessel had been robbed "on the island of Ucatan" by French pirates, perhaps the same Frenchmen who had been released by Hawkins near the Yucatan Channel in August 1568. Through a ruse the Englishmen captured Mendoza and took him to Ireland, where he stayed, unable to go home. Mendoza found a kindred soul in Stucley, a man of great experience and cunning, with connections in Spain as well as England. Together they concocted a scheme to convince Philip II that Stucley could use English ships and men to take control of Ireland.[39]

At this point the plot did not involve Hawkins or the prisoners. Then, in March 1570, a letter arrived in London from Seville, reporting that some thirty of the Hawkins sailors were in prison there, barely clinging to life. This was the first direct news anyone in England had from the men. The Englishmen were not alone in their suffering. Prisoners were not treated well in either country. Early in his captivity Mendoza had written to the Spanish ambassador in London, saying he was sure that John Hawkins would release him soon, though de Spes was not so certain. "They guard prisoners very strictly here," he reported. "They treat the Spanish very badly, and many of them are kept in chains."[40] No doubt this was true, but the Spanish could have given English jailers lessons in cruelty. As Hawkins became more fully aware of the plight of his men, he determined to do whatever was necessary to release them.

Of the 400 men who had started the voyage with Hawkins, scarcely a dozen were with him when the *Minion* arrived in England in January 1569. Another dozen may have come home with the newly minted Captain Francis Drake in the *Judith,* and Captain Thomas Bolton may have had 15 or 20 in the *William and John.* All the others were either dead or in prison. If Hawkins lost 45 men to starvation and disease on the voyage home, as his brother claimed, then he must have had about 60 on board when he left Tampico.[41] After the battle at San Juan de Ulúa Spanish officials counted 130 English dead and took another 52 English prisoners.[42] In addition there may have been as many as 50 slaves on the English vessels left in the harbor, numbered in the records only because these poor souls were considered as commodities, as were the slaves in the three vessels that escaped to England.[43]

Of the hundred or so men put ashore at Tampico, two drowned and eight were killed in a battle with local Indians. The rest escaped

with their lives and little more. About half of the English fugitives headed north along the coast. Three of them, including David Ingram, were
eventually rescued by one of the many French ships raiding Spanish
settlements in the area, and they reached home before the end of 1569.[44]
Some two dozen returned to the main group, while another twenty or so
disappeared without a trace. Led by Anthony Godard, the seventy-
seven surviving Englishmen made their way to Tampico and surrendered.[45] Spanish officials then chained them and packed them into a
tiny jail. After several days of heavy-handed interrogation, the local
magistrate confiscated all their money, then sent them on to Mexico City,
using their own funds to pay the travel expenses. Several more died on
their way and fifteen or sixteen perished after reaching the capital.[46]

At first the ten English hostages apparently received more lenient
treatment, possibly because Hawkins had released the ten Spanish
hostages before leaving San Juan de Ulúa. With only a brief delay they
were taken to Mexico, where they lodged in the house of the viceroy.
The rest of the men captured at San Juan de Ulúa were kept for a time
on the island in the harbor.[47] After a week the able-bodied prisoners
were transferred to Vera Cruz for interrogation then sent on to Mexico
City.[48] The wounded men were interrogated at San Juan de Ulúa.[49] By
the time most of them had recovered sufficiently, the fleet was ready to
leave for Spain. The hostages, plus a few of those who surrendered at
Tampico, joined a number of the prisoners taken at San Juan de Ulúa.
Numbering forty in all, they were loaded onto a ship and sent to Spain.
When they arrived in Seville late in 1569, they were jailed at the Casa de
Contratación. Six died there from their wounds, from starvation, and
from general ill treatment.[50]

All of them might have died had their luck not changed. The
English merchant Hugh Tipton, jailed for debt, met them in prison and

apparently notified his friends about their condition. Beyond this, one of the prisoners, George Fitzwilliams, was a relative of Jane Dormer, the duquesa de Feria, who made it her business to care for Englishmen stranded in Spain. When the duchess learned of the plight of these poor prisoners, she immediately arranged a cash allowance so each man could purchase his own food.[51] She also began to work for their release, making it possible for Fitzwilliams to send that letter to Cecil, the first direct news received from the prisoners.

The plaintive plea of the surviving prisoners seems to have goaded Hawkins into greater activity. Perhaps to remind the Spanish government what a serious annoyance he could be, Hawkins began in June 1570 to prepare a new fleet at Plymouth. At one point he said he planned to attack and capture Spanish vessels in the Channel. At another he let the Plymouth agent of the Spanish ambassador believe that he either intended to go once more to the Indies and establish a base or that he might waylay the Spanish fleet returning from there. To cap it all, Hawkins told a Spanish agent that he was "determined to avenge the damage the Spaniards had done him."[52]

These were empty threats. There was really no possibility that Elizabeth would allow John Hawkins to leave England on any such venture. Instead, he and other ship captains were kept close to home to defend against a possible Spanish attack. It seems that a great Spanish fleet had suddenly appeared in the Netherlands. By all reports, the fleet was supposed to escort Philip's new bride, Anna of Austria, back to Spain, but the English feared a more sinister purpose.[53] Even after the fleet did just that in September 1570, the English ships were still kept close to home.

During this period of enforced idleness Hawkins continued his meetings with Guerau de Spes, pointing out that he could be either an enemy or a friend. On 19 August, Hawkins admitted he had been ordered by the Privy Council to abandon his plans for a voyage to the Indies. As he told the ambassador, he would comply with the order, but with great reluctance, because he remained angry about the losses he had suffered at San Juan de Ulúa and concerned about the prisoners. At the end of the meeting de Spes concluded that Hawkins would be happy to forget the loss of his ships and merchandise. "It would be sufficient to free his men," he reported.[54]

On various occasions in the past Hawkins had told the Spanish ambassador that he was unhappy with the religious and political conditions in England. He would like nothing better, he had claimed, than to serve the Spanish king. He must have said the same things to Stucley and Mendoza, for they looked upon him as one sympathetic to their cause. In March 1570 Mendoza reported that Stucley was about to join John Hawkins in an effort to bring about the release of the prisoners. At the same time Stucley began talking about a plan to bring his "very good friend" into the king's service.[55]

The effort by Hawkins to secure the release of the prisoners quickly became entwined in another plot. Roberto Ridolfi, a Florentine banker resident in London, had managed to get papal backing for his own plot to depose Elizabeth and put Mary Queen of Scots on the English throne. As it turned out, Ridolfi was or soon became a double agent, reporting to Cecil on every change of plan.[56] While both these schemes were afoot, in April 1570 Stucley was allowed to leave Dublin, ostensibly to go to London and establish his innocence. Instead, he sailed directly to Spain and renewed his offer to serve King Philip. It would be possible, he said, to bring some of the major English pirates into Spanish service and use them against the English government. "I mean Hawkins," he wrote later, recalling for Philip the role he had played in organizing the plot. "As your majesty knows, he is my very great friend, and I was primarily responsible for bringing him into your service with his ships."[57] Shortly after Stucley's arrival in Spain, Fitzwilliams was released from prison. The royal cedula ordering his release is dated 27 July 1570, and he seems to have left the prison a few days later. A month after that he was back in England, speaking with Hawkins and with the Spanish ambassador.[58]

This was the end of Hawkins's slaving career but the beginning of new things for him. After the disastrous loss at San Juan de Ulúa he had made his way home with only a few survivors. Two other vessels from his fleet had made it home as well. Thomas Bolton brought the *William and John* back to Ireland, with a Spanish prisoner, Juan de Mendoza. And Francis Drake had sailed back with the *Judith,* arriving in Plymouth just a day before his commander. Dejected at first and feeling betrayed, Hawkins shook off his depression and renewed his contacts with the Spanish ambassador. One way or another, he would recover the men abandoned in Mexico and the ships and goods he had lost there. At first he threatened to free the men by force. Later, in conversations with Thomas Stucley and with the Spanish ambassador, Hawkins began to devise a plan for bringing his own ships and a good part of the queen's fleet into Spanish service.

6

Turning Defeat into Victory

John Hawkins and his brother . . . are Catholics, and they regard the
Queen of Scotland as their true queen. With Elizabeth they are
oppressed and treated badly.

George Fitzwilliams

George Fitzwilliams, one of the last survivors of the
ten hostages, was the first to return home. Seven others had lived to reach Spain with him, but by summer 1570 only three were still alive. Fitzwilliams was
one. The two others were Juan Berin and Thomas
Fuller.[1] The detailed background for his release is lacking, but it clearly
involved the plans of Stucley and Mendoza. There was also an agreement that Fitzwilliams would tell Hawkins that the rest of the prisoners
could be freed if Hawkins would perform some service in return. Once
back in London in early September 1570, Fitzwilliams visited the
ambassador, apparently carrying information about the Spanish proposal. He probably had reported to Hawkins first, for Hawkins
approached de Spes at almost the same time with a sweeping conces-
sion. He would disarm and give up all idea of trading in Spanish territory, expecting in return the release of his prisoners and the repayment
of his losses. In this he misjudged the credulity of the Spanish ambassador, who reported the offer to his government but said, "I just don't
believe him."[2]

His skepticism was well placed. At the very time Hawkins began
his new conversations with de Spes, he was working closely with
French pirates who raided Spanish shipping, and he had retained the
services of a Portuguese pilot who was an expert in sailing through the

Spanish Indies. Even when the Privy Council ordered him to cancel his planned trip to the Indies, Hawkins simply dispatched the ships elsewhere, loaded with materials for construction of a French pirate base. And his offer of peace was not made until news reached England that the French had ended their civil war and thus removed some of the Hawkins allies from the sea.[3]

Negotiations about the English prisoners cooled for a time, while Elizabeth and Philip began to negotiate their larger disputes. The French legate, Cardinal Châtillon, had been in London recruiting English shipowners to serve the cause of the Huguenots in France. With that conflict settled, he was ready to return home. In October 1570 the Hawkins brothers were ordered to transport the cardinal and his party to Rochelle or whatever other French port they might want to reach.[4]

Meanwhile, the condition of the prisoners in Seville remained grim. They had been questioned under oath, along with other witnesses, and the royal officials were about to enter judgment in their cases. Faced with the threat of serious punishment, the prisoners asked several English and Spanish merchants living in Seville to testify that to their knowledge the prisoners had never committed crimes against the Spanish crown.[5] Several did so, saying that in San Juan de Ulúa they were simply defending themselves against a treacherous attack by the Spanish fleet.[6] Unmoved by such pleas, the Spanish officials levied a fine on each of the twenty-three surviving English prisoners: 100,000 maravedis or a hundred lashes apiece in the public streets of Seville. In addition, they were forbidden to go again to the Indies without a special license from the king. The penalty for violating the last provision of the sentence was to be two hundred lashes and a life sentence on the rowing benches of the royal galleys. Moved, it seems, by illness and hunger, the prisoners accepted the sentence, then immediately entered a plea for nullification on the ground that they were too poor to pay the fine and too miserable to do otherwise.[7]

When information about these new developments reached Hawkins, he got in touch once more with the Spanish ambassador, promising that he would agree to everything if the prisoners were released. Following this, in early March 1571 he dispatched George Fitzwilliams to Spain to see what could be arranged. At this point in the negotiations it seems pretty clear that Hawkins was acting without the approval of the queen, who was about to send her own emissary to Madrid, telling the king that she wished to reopen her embassy there.[8]

At the same time, Ridolfi left for the Continent, armed with a special passport from Queen Elizabeth but carrying as well secret messages and documents from supporters of Queen Mary. These men begged the king of Spain to help place Mary on the English throne. These secret pleas coincided exactly with Spanish plans. For some time Irish chiefs and bishops had kept an ambassador in Madrid, urging Philip to occupy Ireland and to send Don Juan of Austria or some other Catholic to rule there. When Stucley arrived in the Spanish capital he managed to convince Philip that he was just the man to bring this about. In the plan he described, Stucley would ally himself with John Hawkins, seize the port of Plymouth, and then take an army to invade Ireland. Fascinated by this convincing rogue, Philip rewarded Stucley in January 1571 with a new title, Duke of Leinster. Stucley, though, preferred to call himself "duke of Ireland."[9]

Just as news of this appointment arrived in London, Elizabeth announced that Stucley's close friend William Cecil would henceforth be Lord Burghley. A former supporter of Stucley, the new English lord certainly knew the general outline of Spanish intentions. His agent in Spain, Robert Hugins or Hogan, sent regular reports through the English ambassador in Paris.[10] Beyond this, Spanish Ambassador de Spes, in his frequent chatty and ill-protected messages home, gave broad hints of what was being done. One of his letters, for example, referred to the role of George Fitzwilliams in bringing messages from Spain. "A relative of the duchess of Feria," he wrote to Philip, "brought me letters from the duke." De Spes also reported that Elizabeth and Cecil were extremely annoyed by the reception Stucley had received in Spain, so much so that Juan de Mendoza was confined in Dublin Castle for plotting with him.[11]

Arriving in Madrid in early April 1571, Fitzwilliams went to see the duke of Feria, who had been assigned to deal with him. In order to keep matters secret, Fitzwilliams had memorized a list of ideas that Hawkins had authorized him to put into writing following his arrival in Spain. In the written submission he reported first that "Captain John Hawkins, seeing the great ruin of his native land increase each day, due to the heresies that are tyrannically sown there, wishes for the exaltation of the glory of God to serve the Catholic King in behalf of Queen Mary of Scotland, helping her to the just possession and dignity of the kingdom of England, whereby God may be served and glorified in that land, as He ought." In order to accomplish this, Hawkins wanted to join with his friend Thomas Stucley "in this most fitting enterprise, for the great love that has always existed between the two" of them. He promised to bring with him "an armada of at least twenty-five very good ships, supplied with everything necessary, except the salary of the men and the costs from now until the enterprise is concluded, which with the help of God will not amount to much." In return all he asked was "an honorable pension sufficient for the year while the enterprise lasts; or, if he should not prevail (which God forbid) and he believes to be impossible, that then he should be entitled to such a grant during his lifetime. If he should die in the undertaking, then his brother William

William Cecil, Lord Burghley. From Granger, *Biographical History of England*, vol. 3, part 1, no. 44. This item is reproduced by permission of the Huntington Library, San Marino, California.

Hawkins, who will also accompany him in the voyage, should succeed to the said pension." Thinking it unlikely that he would get a written reply from the king, he asked instead that "the Duke and Duchess of

Feria should be obligated by their words and signatures," so that if "anything untoward might be befall him" or his people, "a liberal and generous treatment might be accorded them, as befits a most powerful king."[12]

Fitzwilliams also brought a letter from Hawkins to the duchess of Feria, thanking her for her role in freeing the three surviving hostages and asking her to do whatever she could to arrange the release of the other eighteen or twenty men still in jail in Seville. Fitzwilliams brought at least two other letters, one from Margaret Douglas, the mother of Lord Darnley, Mary's late husband. Thomas Fuller, one of the released hostages, had been a Darnley servant, and the good lady thanked the duchess for working in his behalf. During his stay in Madrid, Fitzwilliams made the usual rounds, including, no doubt, visits with Stucley, who had made himself a close friend of the Feria family.[13]

After waiting nearly a week with no word from anyone, Fitzwilliams again called on the duchess of Feria. This time he said very plainly that Hawkins was most anxious to see the prisoners released, or, barring that, at least to see them kept in more comfortable circumstances. He also asked her "very particularly about the manner in which Thomas Stucley had been received and what arrangements had been made with him," implying that Hawkins expected to be rewarded in the same way. Beyond this, Fitzwilliams asked about the king's attitude toward the queen of Scotland and the condition of Catholics in England. "John Hawkins and his brother . . . are Catholics," he said, "and they regard the Queen of Scotland as their true queen. With Elizabeth they are oppressed and treated badly."[14]

There was a reason for the delay in negotiations. Feria could not be rushed, probably because he was ill.[15] Finally, he recovered sufficiently to talk with Fitzwilliams and to outline his principal concerns.

He wanted to know just how close Hawkins was to Queen Mary and exactly what military force he could command. Fitzwilliams told the duke that his information about the queen came mainly from the former prisoner Thomas Fuller, who was "very close" to the Scottish queen. He then described the fleet in general terms, saying the Hawkins brothers owned "seven or eight ships of 25 to 28 toneladas, others of 150 to 130, others of no more than 30." The whole town of Plymouth would follow the Hawkins brothers, he said, for they owned much property there and in London and were well liked in both places. They also had some of the queen's artillery and could get more, and once the fighting started many people would join them.[16] Feria was not satisfied with the vagueness of the replies, and in the end he put his concerns into a list of questions that Fitzwilliams should take to Hawkins.

> The things about which George Fitzwilliams needs to bring clarity.
>
> Since the principal goal intended in this business is the service of God and the restoration of the Roman Catholic religion in the Kingdom of England, delivering it to Queen Mary of Scotland to whom it rightly belongs, John Hawkins must see just how he can and should proceed to this goal.[17]
>
> What persons of the kingdom will assist and help him, and what quality are they, and what are their names and where do they reside?
>
> Whether he has any intelligence with the principal Catholics who have fled to Flanders and whether he is joined with them.
>
> Whether he has any intelligence from the Queen of Scotland, and by what means, and whether he has communicated this concept with her, and how the queen responded to it.

What number of ships he has for this purpose and what size they are, all together, and each one by itself, and whether they are his, and whether there are more than the 25 George Fitzwilliams has spoken of, [and whether] any other Catholics are joining him and in what number and what persons.

What pieces of artillery are placed in his ships and of what quality.

How many men of war he would be able to embark and carry in the said ships that can go with the convenience necessary.

Should the enterprise not succeed, what pension would satisfy him and his brothers, if they also come as has been said.

What salary is needed for this armada and for how long a time?

He must bring clarity and resolution about these particulars, along with a letter of authorization from the said John Hawkins, to negotiate and resolve and agree in this matter, in the fullest and most final manner that might be required.[18]

Fearful of discovery, Fitzwilliams was reluctant to take such a document back to England. When he told Feria this, the document was recopied for him in invisible ink, which, as Hawkins explained, "was not to be redde Before it came to the fyre."[19] This meager attempt at concealment was not much help, for Burghley had captured a messenger from Ridolphi and knew about the plans in considerable detail.

When Fitzwilliams returned to England in late April, he tried without success to arrange a clandestine visit with the queen of Scotland, who was being kept under close guard at Sheffield. First he reported to the Spanish ambassador. This diplomat immediately got in touch with the bishop of Ross, Mary's ambassador in London. He told the bishop that Fitzwilliams had brought messages from Spain for the queen. If the bishop could simply arrange for Fitzwilliams to see the queen, Fitzwilliams would obtain permission for the visit. He had a sister or a cousin who was in the service of Lady Shrewsbury at Sheffield, and he could travel to Sheffield on the pretense of a visit to this relative. From the Spanish ambassador the bishop learned that Hawkins and Fitzwilliams were deeply involved in a plot to free Mary and spirit her out of England. According to Guerau de Spes, the duke of Feria was trying to arrange for Hawkins to take Queen Mary to Spain in one of his ships. Though suspicious, as he confessed a few months later, the bishop finally wrote to tell the queen about the plan, but it is not certain that she received the letter.[20]

Annoyed by the delay, Fitzwilliams decided to ask Hawkins for help. Perhaps Queen Elizabeth would allow him to see Mary, for a letter from her might persuade Philip to release the prisoners. Writing to Lord Burghley on 13 May 1571, Hawkins asked for this approval. The tone of his letter seems to imply that Hawkins had talked to Burghley some time earlier, giving him full details about the conspiracy, and shifting all the blame to Fitzwilliams. "He hath devised with me that I should make some means to obtain him license to have access to her," said Hawkins, "which device I promised him that I would follow." Burghley understood the treasonous implications of this and might not have asked the queen's approval had not Hawkins reminded him that something else was at stake. It was not just a matter of releasing a few prisoners. Money was involved, too. "Unless she be first spoken with," said Hawkins, "and an answer from her sent to Spain, the credit for the treasure cannot be obtained." Burghley thereupon asked Queen Elizabeth about the matter, and she approved a meeting between Fitzwilliams and Mary.[21]

At last, permission in hand, Fitzwilliams visited Sheffield in the first days of June 1571. There he delivered a few small gifts from the duchess of Feria and Thomas Stucley and secured in return the letters that he needed, plus a present that Mary asked him to deliver at the Spanish court.[22] Fitzwilliams then went back to London and reported to Hawkins. The letters from Queen Mary were innocuous, so Hawkins suggested that Fitzwilliams show them to Burghley. The gift was less innocent. It was a missal, written in gold, intended as a present for the duchess of Feria, and inscribed by the queen in Latin: "Absit nobis gloriari, nisi in cruce Domini nostri Jesu Christi. Marie R."[23]

On 7 June 1571 Hawkins wrote once more to Burghley, telling him that Fitzwilliams would be arriving, and asking for a belated royal approval of "the course which I have begun." This time he did not even bother to mention the prisoners. Instead, he listed three principal results that might be expected: "(1) The practices of the enemies will be daily more and more discovered. (2) There will be credit gotten for a good sum of money. (3) The money shall be employed to their own detriment." Fitzwilliams was unaware that he had been betrayed, and Hawkins was careful to remind Burghley of this fact: "I pray you to carry this matter so that Fytzwylliams may not have me in suspicion." And so it was done. The queen gave her consent once more.[24]

Fitzwilliams returned to Madrid some time in July 1571, but he was dogged by reports from London advising caution, for both Fitzwilliams and Hawkins had been seen consulting with Lord Burghley.[25] At the same time King Philip began to entertain serious doubts about Hawkins. In the middle of July he wrote to de Spes saying,

"What is Hawkins doing? Where is he? How many ships does he have and of what type and size, and has he opened up to you in such a way that we can be sure that, once rewarded, he would serve me loyally?"[26] Philip already knew about the pressure put on Elizabeth by Count Ludovic, brother of William of Orange, asking that Hawkins be sent with his ships to help resist the Spanish in Flanders. Members of the royal council shared Philip's doubts about Hawkins, but Fitzwilliams was able to reassure them. According to a letter from Feria, "His majesty is so ardent about the English negotiations that I am made to seem uninterested in them."[27] From this point negotiations for the release of the prisoners went forward rapidly.

No doubt the duke and duchess of Feria and Thomas Stucley helped Fitzwilliams in this regard. A report from Burghley's spy in Madrid noted a frequent visitor at Stucley's house, a mysterious Englishman, who accompanied Stucley to secret meetings with the king and Cardinal Siguenza but kept away from other Englishmen.[28] The results of the meetings were reported in council and a resolution taken either to remove Elizabeth or to see her dead. It seems unlikely that either Fitzwilliams or Hawkins contributed directly to this decision. On the other hand, communications from Guerau de Spes probably had something to do with the council's idea to use Hawkins and his ships "to safeguard the armada of the Indies." Were they laughing when they dreamed up this role for the man they had been calling a pirate?[29]

Early in August 1571 the king wrote to Guerau de Spes, saying, "Fitzwilliams has arrived here with a reply to the articles he carried to John Hawkins. Negotiations with him are going forward in order to see clearly whether he brings anything of substance. If he does, and Hawkins comes on an honest footing, there is no doubt that he will be of service. But if we are to grant him credence, many guarantees are necessary."[30] At this point Roberto Ridolfi was asked for his opinion of Hawkins. His reply suggests that Ridolfi had no more than a vague awareness of the Hawkins involvement. Guerau de Spes himself said that the Hawkins-Fitzwilliams plot was separate from the work of Ridolfi, though he thought it might be a good idea to consolidate the two schemes.[31]

On this second trip from London to Madrid, Fitzwilliams brought only a few documents. One was a letter to the duke of Feria, signed by John Hawkins on 14 June 1571. Hawkins thanked the duke for his past efforts on behalf of the prisoners and asked him for one further favor: their release from prison. "For this not only will they be indebted to your excellency," said Hawkins, "but I will stand ready for service to your excellency all the days of my life." This was not Hawkins writing, but Fitzwilliams writing for him. "For the rest of our negotiations," he continued, "I commend you to the bearer, whom you should credit as though I were present myself."[32] When he met with the duke on 28 July 1571, Fitzwilliams presented this letter, then proceeded to discuss the replies to the specific questions he had been given in April. For this purpose Hawkins had supplied him with rough outlines of both the questions and the answers, written in a peculiarly fractured Spanish. Hawkins could not give more ample replies, he said, because of the danger of discovery. However, once he was in Spain with his fleet, they could all get together to decide what might be accomplished. Support for the plan was not nearly as clear as Fitzwilliams had previously said. Hawkins had not discussed the matter with anyone in England, not even his brother William, "lest he be discovered." For the same reason he could not name a port that could be used or a friend who would dare to help him. He did think that the queen of Scotland had sufficient popular support that if a fleet of six warships were to sail into the Humber near York, the entire north country would rally to her banner. On the other hand, the only connection he had ever had with Mary was when George Fitzwilliams went to ask for a letter from her on behalf of the prisoners.[33]

The other information that Fitzwilliams brought was a list of the ships, men, and supplies Hawkins could furnish, along with an estimate of costs. Sixteen ships were named in the list, the fourteen contained in the estimate given by Fitzwilliams in April, plus the 500-ton *Savior* and the 100-ton *Antelope*. Three of the listed vessels were said to be bound for Terra Nova (Newfoundland). The tonnages attributed to each ship are the same as or slightly higher than those given in April. Hawkins gave no estimate of the number of sailors he would need to man his ships, simply saying that the ships would be manned. Soldiers were estimated at one man for every two tons, roughly 1,500 men. Armament was estimated on a sliding scale. The 500-ton *Christóval* and *Salvador* were said to carry fifty guns each. The 40-ton *Clara* had ten. In all Hawkins claimed to have 406 pieces of artillery, 300 of them cast iron. Salary and victuals would cost £2 per man per month, and an additional £1,500 would be required for the ships. Hawkins would need £9,340 to begin fitting out the ships, plus an additional £3,000 for one month's salary for the soldiers.[34]

Hawkins sent a ring to the duke of Feria "as a countersign." For any other information he referred the duke to George Fitzwilliams, assuring him that he would fulfill "whatever promise might be made by Fitzwilliams in his name, insofar as possible, and advising him that he would not write nor send any further word except through George Fitzwilliams or Ambassador don Guerau."[35] Regarding the prisoners, Fitzwilliams reported that Hawkins considered them to be of no value to his enterprise. "It seems better to set them free, so each one can go where he will," he said. "They are not worth the expense he has with them. Only charity has moved him to be concerned with them, and the same applies to those who are still in the Indies."[36]

Obviously, some of the questions raised in April had not been answered satisfactorily. There were not twenty-five ships but sixteen, and some of these were not immediately available. It seemed impossible that 1,500 soldiers could do the work required. Moreover, Hawkins had no direct contact with Queen Mary or other Catholic leaders. And he appeared to have no friends who would help, not even his brother. Finally, the proposed budget was too high. These points were covered in the ensuing discussions and a satisfactory agreement reached. Hawkins proposed to come to Spain first, then to see whether it would be necessary to have more than 1,500 soldiers. "If more should be necessary," Feria wrote in his notes, "they can be placed in other ships, up to ten of which he can get from his friends and acquaintances." This could be done without raising any suspicion in England, by simply saying that he intended to join Count Ludovic, for which purpose Queen Elizabeth had just given him a license. Ridolfi suggested that it might be possible to send the Hawkins fleet to Rochester to burn the queen's galleons moored there practically unguarded. "This will be a good beginning for his service," said Ridolfi, "and for him it will be easy." The council agreed. Having settled the question of the number of ships and possible help from friends, Feria turned to the budget. The cost estimates were reduced by about a third. The matter of an advance for preparing the fleet was omitted from the budget, though it was tacitly agreed that nothing would be done until the money was forthcoming.[37]

On one point Hawkins made a suggestion that probably coincided with royal intentions. Negotiations would be much easier, he said, if the duke of Feria were made governor of Flanders. While not putting these exact words into the final contract, Feria and Fitzwilliams did agree that any further action to free Queen Mary and put her on the English throne could come either from the king or from "whoever his lieutenant in the states of Flanders might be at that time." In some ways the most important part of the agreement had to do with the losses Hawkins claimed to have suffered in the battle at San Juan de Ulúa. Article twelve of the fifteen articles covered this point. "Since John Hawkins and George Fitzwilliams claim they have suffered loss and damage in the event in the port of San Juan de Ulúa in New Spain in the year 1568, his majesty will order that they be heard in court, and that they should be repaid if they have [suffered any loss]."[38]

The final agreement was signed by the duke of Feria and George Fitzwilliams on 10 August 1571. For some reason Fitzwilliams did not take a copy of this signed agreement to England for Hawkins. According to one of the draft copies, the original was to be kept by the duke of Feria, while Fitzwilliams "would take a copy." This was written both at the beginning and the end of the draft. Then, apparently, there were second thoughts, because the words were crossed out in both places, and Hawkins did not receive a copy.[39] An annex to the agreement listed the sixteen ships, the 406 guns, the 1,585 soldiers, and the budget of 16,981 ducados. The annex was signed by Fitzwilliams alone, for there was still some doubt about the totals, which Hawkins was to certify within thirty days after Fitzwilliams returned home.[40]

On the same day that Fitzwilliams and Feria signed their names to the agreement, King Philip signed a document approving the arrangement. At the same time he signed a pardon for Hawkins, Fitzwilliams, and the Englishmen who accompanied Hawkins to the Indies. The king and the royal council still did not trust Hawkins, so certification from him was demanded before any money was paid or other action taken. As one of the council members wrote, "If he is deceiving us, he will not spill much of our blood."[41]

The prisoner release did not mention the negotiations with Fitzwilliams and Hawkins. Moreover, the correspondence of one of the council members shows that the prisoners were freed largely to please Queen Mary, and also because the duchess of Feria had urged Philip to free the men. The royal cedula of 21 August 1571 gave the official reason for freeing the prisoners: "Her most serene majesty the Queen of Scotland our very dear and very beloved sister has written to ask for the release of the twenty Englishmen" taken prisoner in New Spain. The order reached Seville at the end of the month, and on 3 September eighteen men were set free. A few days later the beds and other things they had been given earlier were sold, and the proceeds were distributed among them.[42]

Not all the prisoners were so fortunate. Heretofore the negotiations had concerned only the forty prisoners who had come to Spain in the fall of 1569 in the fleet of Francisco de Luxan. For some reason not clear now the other prisoners were considered as a separate group. Juan Bono of Saltash and Tomás Ellines of London arrived in Seville a year after the first group but were kept in prison and interrogated as though they belonged with the earlier arrivals. Even so, they were not included in the pardon. Later it was claimed that they were kept in jail because they were French. The king and council thought the French prisoners ought to be the subject of separate negotiations with their own monarch. Still, two men who were clearly identified as "franceses" were released with the eighteen Englishmen who went home in September 1571. The two other Englishmen were still in jail the following summer and still petitioning for release.[43]

Those prisoners who remained in Mexico were treated at first with surprising leniency. After a time spent in religious houses or private homes, they were allowed to take up trades, and some even married local women. Everything changed after 1571, when the Inquisition was brought to Mexico. All the English seamen were rounded up and put into prison. About a dozen of them were still boys, and they were jailed for a brief time, then released. Those who were older were treated as lapsed Catholics. Many were tortured repeatedly to force them to confess their failings or to incriminate others. They were then sentenced, usually to two hundred lashes and several years of service in the galleys.[44] Others faced a grimmer fate.

Robert Barrett and a dozen of his companions, implicated in various acts considered at the time to be blasphemous, were sent to Spain for trial. After a year in jail at the Casa de Contratación in Seville, all managed to escape. Six were recaptured almost immediately: Robert Barret, Job Hortop, John Emery, Thomas Marks, Humfrey Roberts, and John Gylbart. Barrett and Gylbart were subsequently burned at the stake. Job Hortop and a man named John Boone were condemned to the galleys for ten years. The others received lesser terms, according to their ranks as officers. Hortop escaped some years later and returned to England to write about his adventures. Miles Phillips, who remained in Mexico, avoided torture because of his youth. He escaped as well, and he also wrote an account of his years in captivity.[45]

The prisoners released from jail in Seville were effectively excluded from the future plans, particularly after Hawkins said that they would be of no use in his conspiracy. In fact, it is difficult to know exactly who was party to each of the several plots. Hawkins pretty clearly was not directly involved in schemes with Ridolfi, nor were Fitzwilliams or Stucley. Stucley has sometimes been thought of as a

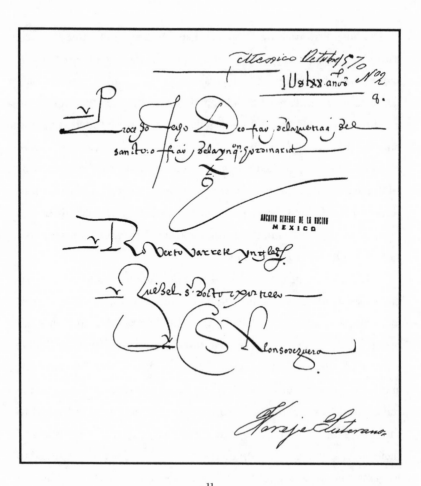

11

Robert Barrett was one of two English prisoners tried, condemned, and executed for heresy. The notation on his file in the Mexican archives calls him a "Lutheran heretic." Archivo General de la Nación Inquisición 49, exp. 2, fol. 8.

sort of double agent in the negotiations, though this is probably not so. The best that can be said of the prisoner Juan de Mendoza is that he was not who he seemed to be. After his release from England, Mendoza revealed that his real name was Juan de Salvatierra. As he explained it, early in his captivity an English officer remarked that he had once

THE RARE

Trauailes of *Iob Hortop*, an Englifhman,
who was not heard of in three and
twentie yeeres fpace

Wherin is declared the dangers he efca-
ped in his voiage to Gynnie, where after hee was
fet on fhoare in a wildernes neere to Panico,
hee endured much flauerie and
*bondage in the Spanifh
Galley.*

*Wherein alfo he difcouereth many ftrange and wonder-
full things feene in the time of his trauaile, as well concerning wilde and fauage people, as alfo of fundrie
monftrous beafts, fifhes and foules, and*
alfo Trees of wonderfull forme
and qualitie.

LONDON
Printed for William Wright.   **1591.**

Condemned to serve in the galleys, Job Hortop later escaped, returned to England, and
wrote about his experiences.

known a Juan de Mendoça, a good friend of King Henry VIII. Thus prompted, the prisoner said, "That was my father." He continued to use the new name until he was returned to Spanish territory. Then he found that the Spanish officials refused to believe that he was Juan de Salvatierra. The use of a pseudonym seems to have been common for English prisoners as well. The sailors taken captive at San Juan de Ulúa used such a variety of names that it is still not possible to identify all of them or to say exactly how many were present at any given time. Given such circumstances, it must have been difficult for prison officials in either country to know exactly who was in jail or for the conspirators to know who was spying and who was not.[46]

Fitzwilliams reached Plymouth by 4 September, bringing Hawkins a copy of the royal cedula confirming the agreement he had made with the duke of Feria. He carried as well an answer from the duke of Feria to the Hawkins letter of 14 June. In this brief message Feria said that Fitzwilliams had accomplished everything he had been sent to do, adding that the man himself would explain all the details. He also described himself as "a true friend," adding in English that his wife wished "w^t all her hart" to be remembered to him. His son added another line in English, "I pray you to know mi for your good frind as mi father is."[47]

Fitzwilliams apparently failed to tell Hawkins about the need to send a written guarantee about his fleet, or about the ordnance, the men, and the names of the ports where the ships were located. Perhaps he had forgotten the details. He also neglected to mention that when he left Spain, the prisoners had not been released. No doubt this explains why Hawkins wrote to Burghley on 4 September, saying that the prisoners were out of jail and that a great sum of money was even then on its way to his coffers. Perhaps thinking of the royal reception given to

Thomas Stucley, Hawkins reported he would also be receiving a few honorary titles from King Philip.[48]

Once Fitzwilliams arrived in London, he gave the Spanish ambassador the same account he had given Hawkins, asking whether the money had arrived yet. De Spes thereupon wrote to the king, asking about the money and other details of the agreement. Neither the money nor a copy of the agreement ever arrived. On 6 September 1571 the duke of Feria suddenly died, and their agreement, which depended on Feria's supervision, was in a shambles. At first Philip wrote to de Spes, saying that he should reassure Hawkins that the agreement would continue in force and referring him to the duke of Alba for further instructions. But at the end of October Philip advised his ambassador that the whole business was at an end. "There is nothing more to say about the John Hawkins matter, for it was dependent on the principal business. You should proceed with him in the manner and form that the duke advises and orders."[49]

With no direct word from Spain, Hawkins and Fitzwilliams began to have their own doubts about the matter. They told de Spes that they were being used by the privy council in an attempt to trap Queen Mary in some act of betrayal. Fitzwilliams thought of returning to Spain, if only to find out exactly where matters stood. Hawkins kept in touch with de Spes as well, but he reported all their conversations to Burghley.[50] It is impossible to say just what his intentions were at this point, because he also told de Spes everything he learned from Burghley and the council. Probably Hawkins was like other double agents, faithful to one side, but keeping his options open.

While this was going on, conditions in England changed dramatically. Many but not all of the Englishmen involved in the Ridolfi plot were imprisoned, and Mary herself was placed in much closer confinement. After the discovery of his Spanish negotiations in April 1571, Hawkins had kept Burghley fully informed, so he and Fitzwilliams were among those initially left undisturbed. For several more months they kept in touch with de Spes, and Hawkins kept his fleet in the harbor at Plymouth, ready to go to sea. This gave rise to a vague suspicion in court circles that he was not a faithful subject of the queen.[51] In December the discredited Spanish ambassador was expelled, largely because of his involvement with Ridolfi. With a fine sense of irony Burghley ordered Hawkins to take one of the queen's ships and transport de Spes and his party to Calais. When Hawkins, Fitzwilliams, and de Spes met for the last time, they devised a cipher for sending coded messages, determining that if a message could not be sent safely, then George Fitzwilliams would be sent to Spain once more to deliver the message in person. Burghley knew that Hawkins and de Spes were "well enough agreed," but somehow Hawkins managed to stay in Burghley's good graces, as did a few other conspirators. Fitzwilliams was not among this group, for once de Spes was out of the country, Fitzwilliams was sent to the Tower, or so the ambassador said.[52]

There is no evidence that Hawkins ever made an effort to free Fitzwilliams from that English prison or his other men from their Spanish prisons. Apparently happy to have kept himself out of jail, Hawkins simply worked to recast the record of his own part in the affair. Writing to Burghley in early September 1571, he remarked that he expected soon to have word of "great tytells and honours and tytells from the kinge from wch god delyver me." Perhaps feeling that this was not a clear enough declaration of loyalty, he added, "Ther practyses be very myscheyvous and they be never idell, but god I hope will confound them & torne ther devyses upon their owne necks."[53]

Hawkins must have been convincing, for he soon received an augmentation to his arms. This came not for his defeat at San Juan de Ulúa but for his victory a few weeks earlier at Rio de la Hacha, where he forced a reluctant royal official to trade for his slaves and merchandise. Hawkins wanted only to "furnyshe himselfe of suche necessaryes as he wanted, viz. water and fuell," wrote Robert Cooke, Clarenceaux. "He was by Michell de Castillanos, a Spanyard, in warlyke wise resisted wth 1000 harkabushers," said Cooke, with considerably more enthusiasm than accuracy. "Nevertheles the sayd John Hawkins, wth 200 men und^r his conducton and valiantnes, entred the sayd towne, and not only put the sayd Captayne and his men to flight, but also toke and brought his enseigne away."[54]

A few years later, in response to continuing rumors about his negotiations with Spain, Hawkins composed an even more innocent interpretation of his role as a secret agent. In this document he described the agreement with Feria as something concocted by the duke and Fitzwilliams without his knowledge or consent, omitting any reference to his own earlier overtures to Guerau de Spes. "When George fytzwylls was sent by me into Spayne to obtayne lybertye for ~~for~~ soche men as I had in captyvytye," he wrote, "the duck of feria and secretary sayas pracctysed wth him, that I myght be woon to joyne w^t the rebles of the northe." Having thus established his innocence, Hawkins claimed that Queen Elizabeth had authorized him to continue the negotiations, implying that her approval came before he started negotiating with Spain. He also said that de Spes gave him a code for communication, exactly the opposite of what the ambassador wrote in his own recollection of the matter. A year later, in a final effort to clear his record, Hawkins submitted a claim for reimbursement for his expenses in sending Fitzwilliams to Spain. "I was at the sole charge of sendynge fytzwylls into spayne twyse for intellygence w^t her ma^{ties} consent w^{ch}

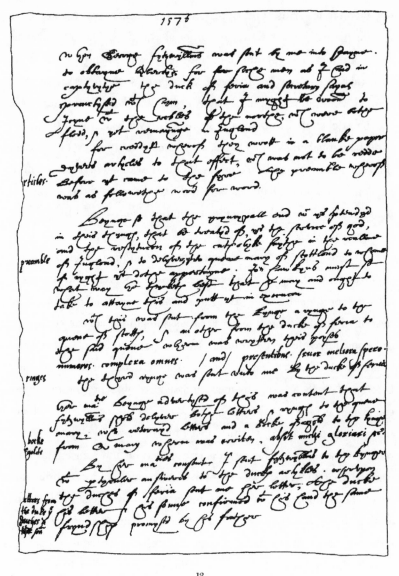

In 1576 Hawkins wrote to Burghley, suggesting that his recent negotiations with
Spain were really the work of George Fitzwilliams and the Duke of Feria.
British Library Cotton Galba C.V.263.

cost me 500 d°s." Again, without directly saying so, Hawkins implied that the whole thing was done with the prior approval of the queen, rather than her later acquiescence in the matter.[55]

None of this was unusual in sixteenth-century Elizabethan society. Loyalties, whether national or personal, could change rapidly and then change back again. John Hawkins found it easy to pose as a convinced Catholic and a faithful servant of the Spanish king, when doing so made it possible to earn a profit. Equally, he found it convenient to work for the release of a few of his men who were languishing in a Spanish jail, when this was part of a larger scheme to get money from the Spanish king. But Hawkins was always careful not to put himself in jeopardy in the process. When Burghley discovered the real nature of his private negotiations with Spain, Hawkins let his friend George Fitzwilliams continue to believe the matter still a secret. If he had any qualms about deserting his friend, no record of that has survived. Perhaps this is why Hawkins managed to understand and then forgive Francis Drake for abandoning him and his men in the harbor at San Juan de Ulúa. He could understand betrayal.

7

Changing Course

Amonge a nomber of tryfflinge crossings and slaunders, the verye
wauls of the Realme have byne brought in questyon; and their slaunder
hathe gone veryee farr and generall, to thincoraidgement of the
Enemyes of god and o^r countrye. onlye to be avenged of me
and this servis, wch dothe discover th^e coruptyon &
ignoraunce of the tyme past.
John Hawkins

The death of the duke of Feria and the departure of Spanish ambassador Guerau de Spes left Hawkins without the means to communicate with Spain. Then in the summer of 1572 Sir Humphrey Gilbert went to the Low Countries, and Hawkins managed to contact de Spes through him. Following this de Spes suggested that Juan de Salvatierra (alias Mendoza) might be used as a go-between. Salvatierra had left England with the queen's blessing, and he was either a friend or a relative of Gilbert's. As it turned out, the duke of Alba disapproved, and he had the final word. Alba thought that Feria had been too generous in his contract with Hawkins, and he felt that any operation involving the Hawkins ships would have little chance of success.[1] The agreement was not canceled, but it was allowed to lapse, while both Hawkins and de Spes worked to bring it back to life.

Meanwhile, both Hawkins and Gilbert went to Parliament in April 1571 as representatives from Plymouth. A year earlier Pope Pius V had issued a bull of excommunication against Queen Elizabeth, raising the hackles of Protestant Englishmen. As a result, both houses gave speedy approval to several bills on religion, including one to prohibit the publication of papal bulls. None of this involved John Hawkins, who completed his first session in Parliament without attracting much attention. According to the minutes, his only official work was done on Monday, 21 May, when he sat on a conference committee to reconcile differences with the House of Lords regarding a "Bill for the Increase of Tillage, and Maintenance of the Navy." When Parliament met again the following year, Hawkins went once more, with about the same result. His name appeared in the official record only when he asked to be absent, and the request was granted.[2]

During the next few years Hawkins stayed close to home, or rather to both homes, the one in London and the other in Plymouth. This was not entirely voluntary. Authorities in London did not quite trust him. Together with his brother William, Hawkins began to concentrate on the Low Countries and France, where good profits could be made in piracy and in trade with both Protestants and Catholics. When he took the Spanish ambassador to the coast of France in January 1572, John Hawkins improved the occasion by attacking and looting a ship that belonged to Bartel Entens, who sailed for the prince of Orange. A year later, the Hawkins brothers had ships on station near the Isle of Wight, capturing French merchant vessels and running supplies to the Huguenots at La Rochelle. From time to time one Hawkins or another was rumored to be at sea or to be preparing a new expedition for the Caribbean. In September 1572 Hawkins gathered most of the men he had rescued from jail in Seville and sent them on a voyage to the Spanish Indies, but Hawkins himself did not go. A Spanish agent reported that Hawkins was fitting out three ships to sail for Guinea, where they would load slaves for the Indies. Again Hawkins did not go himself. Another report said he was in Flushing with Gilbert's troops, but this was idle gossip. In early 1573 Spanish, French, and Portuguese agents in London reported that the Hawkins brothers were contributing nearly a dozen ships to a fleet intended to relieve the siege of La Rochelle. But in the accounts of this expedition the name of John Hawkins is notable only by its absence.[3] Not Europe but Ireland was the focus of his attention.

The Irish had been up in arms since 1494, when Henry VII tried to subordinate the local parliament. Irish resistance rose to a fury after 1541, when Henry VIII assumed the title of king of Ireland and attempted to enforce his ecclesiastical changes there. For the next thirty years the English government squandered huge sums of money and great masses of men in a furious effort to subdue Ireland, but with little success, except in the Pale around Dublin. The campaign languished for a time during the reigns of Edward and Mary but was renewed with vigor by Elizabeth, whose major objective was to extend English control in Ireland beyond the Pale.[4]

In assorted attempts local English officials embarked on a program to eliminate the Irish nobility and to reduce the "Irish churl" to servitude. One of the more colorful men to try his hand at suppressing the recalcitrant Irish was the Hawkins friend Thomas Stucley, whose name kept appearing in reports for years afterward. Chief among the problems of the would-be conquerors were bickering and jealousy, but poor planning was involved as well. In 1573 Walter Devereaux, earl of Essex, conceived a scheme to subjugate Ulster. Mortgaging his English lands to the queen for £10,000, Essex agreed to use the money to pay four hundred foot soldiers and two hundred horsemen to serve in Ireland. In return the queen agreed to contribute the same numbers of men and to grant Essex a large estate in County Antrim, along with sweeping governmental powers. Private individuals were encouraged to invest in the project with the promise of smaller grants for their trouble.[5] Much like the slave trade, it was a nasty business.

When the local chief, Sir Brian MacPhelim O'Neill, heard the details of the scheme, he organized a protest, though he remained loyal to the queen and for a time worked with Essex. For his part Essex saw that he would need to eliminate O'Neill if his Irish expedition was to be a success. Thereupon, Essex lured the man's followers into a grand feast. Once he had them trapped, Essex slaughtered them all, men, women, and children. Afterward, he sent Sir Brian himself to Dublin, where he was hanged and quartered, along with his wife and brother. There was great indignation in Antrim, but Essex was proud of the clever way he had eliminated his enemy. And there was no public reproach from the queen. The role of John Hawkins in all this is unclear. When it was all over and the earl was dead, Hawkins said very little about the Essex enterprise. His whole investment was £950, "the wch her ma^{tie} toke [in] her hand wthout any recompence," or so he claimed. To do her justice, Queen Elizabeth may have had good reason for keeping the money. In the Irish expedition the men from Devon were noted mainly for their lack of enthusiasm—understandable perhaps, because many of them were conscripts. Hawkins summarized his own role in a single sentence: "I adventured w^t therle of essex by see and by land." He may have been in Ireland, or he may have done no more than gather conscripts in Devon and send them to Ireland.[6]

Back in London once more, in mid-October 1573 John Hawkins and William Winter walked out one morning for a bit of air. Passing up Middle Temple Lane toward Fleet Street, they entered the Strand, where they stopped in a crowd of perhaps twenty other people. Here a man named Peter Birchet caught up with them, muttering to himself as he did, "Shall I do it? What, shall I do it? Why then I will do it." At that he lifted a dagger and stabbed Hawkins several times. In the confusion Birchet managed to escape, but he was captured almost immediately and taken to the Tower. There his interrogators heard a strange if rambling tale. He had mistaken Hawkins for Christopher Hatton, the captain of the queen's guard and a man rumored to be a secret Catholic. With no one else taking steps to eliminate this papist, Birchet decided that God wanted him to remove the offender. Asked if he was sorry, Birchet said he was sorry he had got the wrong man. Then he picked up a cudgel and struck his jailer on the head, killing the poor fellow. This was enough. Crazy or not, Birchet was summarily beheaded.[7]

When Queen Elizabeth heard about the attack, she immediately assumed that it was another plot to remove her from the throne. A special commission investigated the matter, but the results were not published, and rumors continued to spread. Some involved members of "the new sect, those who call themselves puritans or unblemished," who wanted to promote dissension in the country. Another rumor was that Hatton had given the queen a little book from the Netherlands that named Lord Burghley and other principal advisers as part of the new plot. Of course the queen defended her ministers and said no one should pay attention to such "seditious slanders."[8]

Aside from Birchet himself and his hapless guard, the only man actually injured in the affair was John Hawkins, who lay at death's door for several days. If suspicion of Hawkins lingered after the Ridolfi plot, the attack by Birchet ended it, so far as the queen was concerned. "Hir ma^{te} taketh hevily the hurting of hawkyns," wrote one observer. "Neither hir ma^{te}, nor allmost eny one here can thynk otherwyse, but that ther is a big conspiracie." The victim Hawkins could hardly have been a party to the conspiracy. The queen sent her own surgeons to care for Hawkins, and she watched anxiously for reports of his improving health. With his reputation on the mend, Hawkins regained his health as well. Antonio Guaras, the Spanish representative in London, reported on 15 November 1573 that the man was "out of danger."[9]

His recovery was probably a long and slow process. If local records can be taken as a guide, he went to Plymouth for part of that time. He was there in January 1574, sending a few ships to join the other pirates based on La Rochelle. The French ambassador complained about this to Elizabeth, but she continued to allow the Hawkins brothers to work with the pirates and with the Comte de Montgomery, who was trying to relieve the besieged Huguenots. There is some indication that William Hawkins may have commanded one or another of the ships the brothers had at sea, but apparently John Hawkins did not.[10]

For a time John Hawkins used Plymouth as both home and headquarters. In partnership with his brother he took charge of the town mills at Plymouth, improving the operation. He had a weighing house at Popes Head and kept a man with a horse on duty there, to fetch the grain from the houses of the inhabitants. He owned a house, garden, stables, wharf, and forge at Plymouth, later granting a half-interest to his son when he was old enough to have his own household there. But John Hawkins's main business was piracy, and Plymouth was one of the favorite haunts of English pirates. During the next few years there were complaints of piracy by Hawkins ships as well as inquiries in Madrid about one of the Hawkins men still kept in prison. But there is no indication that John Hawkins actually sailed aboard any of his ships, nor any way to be certain why he did not.[11] Still, it is possible to make a guess.

John Hawkins was a man of forty-one when Peter Birchet stabbed him. He had been a pirate and a slave trader, wounded several times in brawls and battles. At his advanced age a slow recovery could be expected. In addition, he had been involved in shady dealings in

Madrid and London that raised serious doubts in both places about his integrity. For some months after Fitzwilliams visited Madrid, Hawkins hesitated to take any action that might alienate the Spanish king. Then attitudes in both capitals began to change. The queen started showing a new affection for Hawkins, while Philip failed to send the expected funds.[12]

From late November 1569 to early August 1573 Francis Drake made several increasingly bold raids on the West Indies. After a time the Spanish began to suspect that John Hawkins had something to do with this.[13] Well they might. Hawkins and Drake were known to be partners in trade with the Ionian island of Zante, and Hawkins ships were openly attacking Spanish vessels. Early in 1575 Hawkins sent a small squadron to hunt down stragglers from the Indies fleet, but without success. In the summer he tried again, but again without notable success. Even so, his renewed activity was enough to earn John Hawkins a place in the Spanish list of English pirates. At the end of 1575 Philip sent Elizabeth a pirate roster that included the Hawkins brothers and Francis Drake and his brothers, plus Sir William Winter, Lewis Lader, and others.[14]

Things were not going well for King Philip. He was bankrupt at home and frustrated abroad. Revolt still smoldered in the Netherlands, where rebellious Protestants and Catholics demanded a change in Spanish rule. The Ottoman fleet, seemingly crushed at Lepanto in 1571, had reappeared to threaten Philip and his allies in the Mediterranean. Faced with these problems, the king determined to settle some of his differences with Elizabeth, even ordering the expulsion of the English Catholics who had taken refuge in the Netherlands.[15] Elizabeth, for her part, sent two of her ships to suppress the pirates operating in the channel and issued a new order forbidding English enlistment in armies or fleets in the Low Countries. Perhaps even more astonishing, when vessels from a Spanish Netherlands fleet were blown off course and took refuge at Plymouth and elsewhere, Elizabeth ordered the ships to be reprovisioned and then sent them on their way.[16]

Hawkins and the other merchant-pirates were not at all happy with this development, which drastically reduced their opportunities for profit without at the same time opening the Spanish Indies to English ships. Putting the worst possible interpretation on events, Hawkins wrote to Burghley and urged a complete change in policy. Citing his own recent negotiations with the Spanish king, Hawkins said, "The p[re]mysses consyderyd me thinks yt dothe suffycyently prove that the Kynge wysheth as myche hurt as he can to her ma[tie], if he know whiche way to put her dystruccion in practice." Rather than waiting for this to happen, Hawkins suggested that he be allowed to make a preemptive attack on the Spanish fleet as it sailed home from the Indies. He could handle this with three royal ships, the *Dreadnaught,* the *Foresight,* and the *Bull,* plus five smaller merchant vessels "of 120 ton or ther abouts," which he and his brother happened to have available. The profit would be enormous, £2 million. The cost would be minimal, no more than £3,750, including £100 apiece to the owners of the merchant ships.[17]

His advice was not taken. Hawkins was not allowed to go to sea or do anything else that might constitute official recognition. For years his father-in-law, Benjamin Gonson, had been treasurer of the navy, serving as part of a board that included the Winter brothers and William Holstocke. In February 1577, with an eye on Gonson's post, Hawkins wrote once more to Burghley, listing seven specific instances of his recent service to the crown. His journey returning Cardinal Châtillon to France had taken eleven weeks and cost him £238 (even though he sailed in the *New Bark,* which belonged to the queen). He had been promised £100 "to clere the co[a]st of piratts," he said, but the money was never paid. Sending a rescue ship to Rochelle added another £50 to his list of expenses, and caring for Guerau de Spes at Canterbury for five weeks had cost him £50 as well. As we have seen, Hawkins claimed a loss of £950 for his part in the Irish expedition of the earl of Essex. Putting a bold face on a doubtful undertaking, Hawkins even listed his expense in negotiating with the king of Spain for the release of his men. First, he said it had cost £150 to send Fitzwilliams to Spain in 1571. And the fleet that Hawkins had gathered at Plymouth and offered to King Philip he now said was really being kept in reserve for the queen. "I kept in order 10 shipps by the space of tow yere, & was allwayes in good hope at her ma^ties hand that a pese of service shold have byne done to recompence yt wch I wyll not valew." Despite the disclaimer, Hawkins expected something in return. "I doubt not but her highnes wyll accept the rather my resonable sewts."[18]

These "resonable sewts" were probably drawn up in consultation with Burghley. After first gathering information from Gonson's accounts, Hawkins met with the two master shipwrights Peter Pett and Matthew Baker. He then laid out a series of charges against members of the Navy Board and particularly the Winter brothers. Saying that the Winters were making unjustified profits, Hawkins claimed that he could provide a better navy for less money. Where the "ordinarye" charge per year for keeping the royal fleet in harbor was about £6,000, Hawkins said that he could do it for £4,000 "and farre better." The "extraordinarie" charge for rebuilding seven ships during the past year was nearly £5,000, which should have been more than enough. Even so, the work was not finished, and Hawkins thought the final cost in 1578 might very well be double that amount. New ships, which were

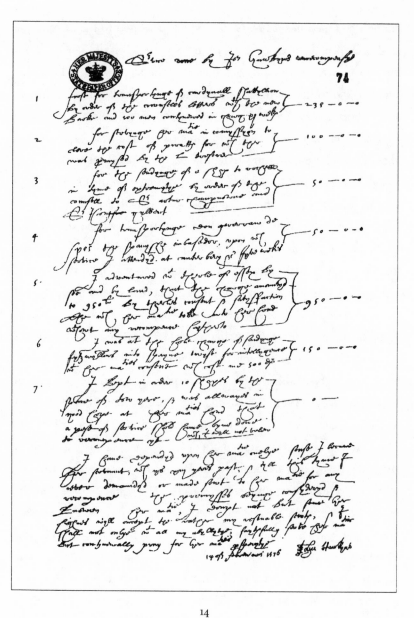

14

In 1577 Hawkins claimed that he kept ten ships ready to serve Her Majesty, no doubt the same ships he had offered to King Philip. Public Record Office, SP 12/111/33, fol. 74.

costing £3,000, could have been done better for £2,200. Lumber that cost £900 per load could have been provided at £500. Probably the biggest discrepancy Hawkins found in the books was in the amounts charged for timber and planks. Of £9,000 spent since 1570, less than half had gone into the royal ships. The rest was used to build ships and pinnaces for William Winter, Drake, and Frobisher. Other timber had gone into wharves at Woolwich and Wapping. Masts from the royal supply were sold and the money pocketed, and at least once the queen was charged for timber that came from her own stock.[19]

Hawkins submitted his report in high hope, but for a time nothing happened. At the request of the earl of Lincoln, lord high admiral of the navy, Hawkins joined with the Winter brothers in mediating a dispute between two other navy men.[20] He invested £500 in Drake's proposal to sail to the Indies. At one point he seems to have written a fictitious letter to help Drake conceal his real destination, but he had no major role in preparing the expedition. Instead, Hawkins waited confidently for some recognition from the queen. His reward came on 18 November 1577, when Elizabeth gave him the right to succeed his father-in-law as "treasurer of the marine causes." It was an important post, but the problems were enormous. Gonson warned him, "I shall plucke a thorne owt of my fotte & put yt into yours." Shortly thereafter the old man died, and Hawkins assumed the office at the beginning of the following year.[21]

Although the charges Hawkins made were probably true, they were not very serious. Royal office holders expected to earn a profit in the course of their work. The crown expected only that the work would be done efficiently and with reasonable economy. Members of the Navy Board usually had to furnish materials for the crown and look for reimbursement later, either in cash or in kind. The Hawkins report did not imply that Winter should have worked for nothing. Rather, Hawkins said that if he were given the job, he could do it for less and still make a profit. Because Hawkins had established such a close relationship with Burghley in the latter part of the Ridolfi negotiations, it seems likely that his report was the result of conversations he had with Burghley. All the other members of the board kept their positions, but the close association between Hawkins and Burghley meant that Hawkins would be the lord treasurer's representative in the group. Within a short time Hawkins was effectively in charge of the board.

During 1578, his first year as treasurer of the navy, Hawkins received a special warrant for £150 to construct a set of floodgates at Deptford Strand. Considered to be among the earliest drydocks with movable gates, the design was almost certainly the work of the shipwrights. Still, Hawkins was probably involved in the request for funds, and he certainly had to approve the work. The new drydock was an important innovation in shipyard operation. Before that time it was common to construct a semipermanent earthen dike at the entrance to a dock. Once construction was finished, the dike had to be dug away. Thus the drydock could be out of service for long periods of time. With the movable gates, the pool at Deptford Strand could be filled and drained almost at will.[22]

As treasurer of the navy Hawkins received from the queen £5,714 each year "for the kepinge and repayringe of our said shipps in harborowe."[23] This was the "ordinary" budget, covering items of general maintenance. There was also an "extraordinary" budget for new construction and major rebuilding, and this amount varied from year to year. Total receipts and expenditures for 1578 amounted to £14,000, the difference being the special warrants for major expenditures.[24] One of these was a warrant of £3,000 for the "repair ordinarie of her mat[ies] shippes in decay and for the new making of boots and cockes to the same." In spite of the word "ordinarie," this warrant was intended for completion of the repair work on the *Triumphe*, the *Victory*, the *White Bear*, the *Hope*, the *Philip and Mary*, and the *Antelope*, six of the seven ships Hawkins had previously noted as still needing repairs.[25] This work was finished in 1578, and Hawkins then submitted a proposal to perform much of the maintenance work on the fleet for a fixed annual sum. Money left unexpended at the end of the year would be profit for the contractor. Something similar had been done before when Edward Baeshe began to supply rations and "purser's necessaries" for the navy at a fixed price. Aimed at stabilizing costs of fleet construction and maintenance, the contract seems to have been the result of conversations between Hawkins and Burghley, who quickly approved the arrangement. Under the new terms Hawkins agreed to keep the twenty-four ships and other vessels of the queen's navy safely moored in harbor, providing cables and other equipment at his own expense. The new contract described Hawkins as "tresorer of her highnes navye" and listed the ships by name, the earliest such listing during his administration:

The names of the Queenes Ma[ties] ships and vessells w[ch] the said John Hawkins undertakith to keepe in manner following:

The triumph	The Antelop
The Elizabeth Jonas	the Swallow
The white Beare	the Ayde
The Victory	The Bull
The Mary Rose	The Tigre
The hope	The Skoute
The Phillip and Mary	The Achates

The Elizab. Bonaventure	The handmayde
The Lyon	The new small bark
The Revenge	The galley Elenor
The Dreadnaught	The George Hoye
The Swiftsure	The great Lighter

Signed on 10 October 1579, the new agreement was actually effective from 29 September, the Feast of Saint Michael. In return for the mooring services, Hawkins received £100 per month "for his own use without any accounting." In addition, he was given all the old cables from the ships, "the old invocing & Jonks of this yeere 1579 . . . for the making of taklings platte sinett & rope yarn." The ink was scarcely dry on the contract before Sir John Perrott, captain of the *Revenge,* complained that Hawkins had furnished him with ropes made from old cables. This Hawkins vehemently denied: "No man hathe taken that care I have done to fine that corroption banyshed."[26]

In a second agreement the master shipwrights, Pett and Baker, agreed to perform many of the "ordinary" repairs for a payment of £1,000 per year. Under this contract the shipwrights would ground the five largest royal vessels every three years, the second five every two years, and the others every year. They would replace a certain number of strakes, ransack and caulk the hulls, and keep the small boats in repair. Certain supplies could be taken from the queen's stores; others were the responsibility of the shipwrights, who also had to provide necessary workmen. The shipwrights were not left entirely to their own devices. Hawkins was required to check and approve their work. In turn, his own accounts were to be countersigned by the other members of the Navy Board. The "ordinary" maintenance budget would stay at £5,714, but Hawkins promised Burghley that he would make every effort to reduce expenditures to £4,000. The other £1,714 would then be available for use in replenishing warehouse stocks, which were dangerously low.[27]

By this time rumors were rife in England that Drake was on his way home with a ship stuffed full of Spanish treasure. The delighted investors named representatives in all the major English ports to assist Drake whenever and wherever he might arrive. At the same time Spanish and English diplomats met in Bristol to negotiate an end to piracy. The meeting had scarcely opened when it became obvious that English merchants would not be required to return their stolen Spanish goods. Foreseeing a likely reversion to old practices, John Hawkins once more proposed to mount a raid on the Spanish fleet sailing home from the Indies. Under his new plan five merchant ships and eleven pinnaces would join four of the lightest royal vessels, the *Lyon* and *Philip and Mary* of 200 tons, and the *Swallow* and *Aide* of 130 and 100. In addition to the usual supplies and a cash advance to each captain, all the ships would be sheathed at a cost to the royal treasury of £1,000, and the queen would furnish artillery and other weapons from the Tower. In return she could expect treasure that would make Drake's rumored 600,000 ducats seem like a small sum. "The bo[o]tty that is of ordynary to be stryken upon the yndyes flete ys 2000000[li] w[ch] ys *two myllyons of pounds*," Hawkins wrote, with considerably more enthusiasm than usual. Every port in the Indies could be destroyed, with little or no risk to the English fleet. "Ther ys to be stryken w[th] this company all the townes upon the cost of the yndies, & ther nede not to be sufferyd one shipe barke, frygatt, or gallye, to stayne untaken." As with the other Hawkins suggestions for ships to raid the Spanish fleet, nothing came of this. A month later, though, four royal warships were dispatched to Bristol, perhaps in part to encourage the negotiators to complete their work, but also to patrol the coast of Ireland. These were the *Dreadnought*, the *Revenge*, the *Swiftsure*, and the *Foresight*.[28]

15

The royal shipwright Matthew Baker seems to have left a self-portrait in his manuscript
on Elizabethan ship construction. Adapted from the drawing in PL 2820,
Pepys Library, Magdalene College, Cambridge

All part of the new Elizabethan navy, none of these ships was
built by Hawkins. Although he is commonly credited with the development of a lower, faster English galley, there is no indication that he was
really responsible for the new design. Rather, the "race built" ship
seems to have been the work of royal shipwrights Peter Pett and
Matthew Baker, whose drawings and notes can be found in a manuscript now called "Fragments of Ancient Shipwrightry."[29] On the
other hand, Hawkins and the rest of the board certainly made it possible for work on the new designs to proceed under their supervision.

Shipbuilding in Elizabethan England was partly a science, but
mostly an art. Shipwrights relied on intuition and experience, selecting
from available material and developing the design as they went along.
The complaint of a mariner in Spain probably typified conditions in
England as well. "Some ships start in the yards as small ones and end as

large ones, while others start out large and end up small." One of Baker's major contributions was the preparation of a plan, using mathematics to calculate the dimensions of various parts of a ship. His manuscript includes an illustration of a master shipwright, presumably himself, at work on the drawing of a ship. No doubt it is an idealized depiction of the way ships were designed and built in those days, but there is no question that Baker was widely regarded as an accomplished shipwright who could and often did use mathematical principles in the construction of his ships.[30]

Where older ships like the *Jesus of Lubeck* had high castles for guns at the bow and stern, race-built vessels were much lower, with long, low gun decks, and a good deal of "tumble home" from the main deck to the top of the stern castle. Not everyone liked the design. Richard Hawkins, John's son, later criticized the "Race-ships of Warre." He thought them "tender sided, and unable to carry sayle in any fresh gaile of wind." Beyond that, there was little protection for the men at the guns and in fact little "place for accommodating their people to fight, labor, or rest."[31]

The first vessel in the new design was the *Foresight,* launched in 1570. This was followed by the 700-ton *Dreadnought,* the 550-ton *Swiftsure,* and the smaller *Achates* and *Handmaid,* all launched in 1573. The *Revenge* and the *Scout* were laid down in 1575 and launched in 1577.[32] A major program for rebuilding began that year, but of seven ships started only the *Elizabeth Jonas* was finished. As Hawkins pointed out, the expense of reconstructing these ships greatly exceeded the original authorization. Work on the other six, the *Triumphe,* the *Victory,* the *White Bear,* the *Hope,* the *Philip and Mary,* and the *Antelope,* was finished in 1578. Although some of these were among the first constructed, or rather reconstructed, under the supervision of John

Hawkins, not all of them were changed to the new design, which in any case evolved during the next decade or so. Richard Hawkins said that at the time of the battles with the Spanish Armada in 1588, the *Elizabeth Jonas,* the *Triumph,* and the *Bear* still retained the old configuration.[33]

No doubt other improvements in nautical design can be traced to the administration of John Hawkins. The best known is his method for sheathing ships with a thick coating of tar and horsehair smeared between the planks and the sheathing. "Some hold the opinion that the tarre killeth the worme," said his son Richard. "Others [say] that the worme, passing the sheathing, and seeking a way through, the hayre and the tarre so involue him, that he is choked therewith; which me thinkes is most probable." John Hawkins is also credited with the introduction of the chain pump, which Richard says was used on the *Jesus of Lubeck* in 1568. In addition to these novelties, Sir Walter Ralegh, in a long list of new developments that came into widespread use during his lifetime, described a capstan for raising the anchor. He did not specifically credit any of the innovations to John Hawkins, but they could scarcely have been used on royal vessels without the approval of the treasurer of the navy.[34]

Whatever Hawkins was doing must have pleased Burghley, for the treasurer was trusted with doling out large sums of money and supervising an ever-growing list of marine projects. Incomplete figures for 1578 show a startling variety of activities in the four royal shipyards. Some hundred and fifty officers, mariners, shipwrights, clerks, bricklayers, and others were at work building and repairing nearly two dozen royal ships stationed at Gillingham at various times during the year. A new mast pond was dug at Chatham, where lodgings were available for the lord admiral, for the members of the Navy Board, and for workmen as well. Hawkins by this time had bought a house and other buildings there. The *Philip and Mary,* the *Hope,* and the *Antelope* were moved to Deptford, once the repair work at Chatham was complete. The old-style drydock at Woolwich handled the repairs on the *Elizabeth Jonas.* When this work was finished, laborers spent two weeks digging out the dockhead so that the ship could float free.[35]

Even though the master shipwrights had separate contracts with the crown, Hawkins supervised them, releasing the money only when he was satisfied with their work. This led to charges that he retained some of the money for himself, and no doubt he did. A persistent problem for contractors was the long delay in getting funds from the royal treasury. Faced with continual demands for payment, Hawkins often found himself paying the contractors and then waiting for reimbursement. In the end he adopted a system of offering quarterly payments to contractors in return for a fee of three pence per pound. Hawkins thought the charge justified, telling one man that "by reason of such disbursement he was sometimes £3,000 or £4,000 out of purse." Reasonable as this may seem, critics managed to interpret the fee as dishonesty on the part of the treasurer of the navy.[36]

Other members of the Privy Council showed a liking for Hawkins, and he worked closely with them on projects that seemed to be only peripherally related to his work with the navy. In 1580, for instance, he supervised the repair and cleaning of the armor and personal weapons stored in the Tower. In 1582 he joined a commission that included Burghley, the earl of Warwick, Christopher Hatton, Walter Mildmay, and others to conduct a "survey of all ordnance, shot, munition, powder, saltpetre, artillery, etc. now in charge of the officers of the ordnance."[37] Francis Walsingham often chose to work directly with Hawkins, reporting the matter to Burghley later, if at all.[38]

During this time the Hawkins brothers continued their usual

ANTHONIUS de ± Coninck van Portugael
en Algarben.

16

In the 1580s Hawkins and Drake negotiated with Dom Antonio, pretender to the throne
of Portugal. Prince, *Damoni Orientales Illustres,* vol. 1, opp. page 273 (rare book no.
313163, extra-illustrated). This item is reproduced by permission of the
Huntington Library, San Marino, California.

trading activities. When Horatio Pallavicino chartered four ships and kept them for an extended time beyond the terms of the contract, the brothers sued, claiming damages of £1,550. Seemingly their loss was not nearly so large. After presenting evidence to support their claim, the brothers settled in April 1581 for a fraction of that amount.[39]

In the same period Dom Antonio, pretender to the throne of Portugal, was in England seeking assistance in his dispute with Philip II of Spain. The Hawkins brothers joined with Burghley, Walsingham, and Leicester, as well as the merchant-mariners Drake, Frobisher, Winter, and others in a plan to send ships to establish Dom Antonio in Terceira in the Azores. Once there, Antonio would be safely out of England, but in a position to provide English ships with a base for raids on the Spanish treasure fleet and the ports in the West Indies. Claiming poverty at first, Dom Antonio asked Elizabeth to fund the project. For a time she toyed with the idea, encouraging the English partners to meet with the pretender at his lodgings in Greenwich. Soon there was a plan. Drake would command a fleet of eight ships, Dom Antonio paying a fourth of the cost and the investors paying the rest. The fleet gathered at Plymouth, but for no very clear reason Elizabeth lost interest. Antonio then produced bundles of jewels, including a diamond of eighty carats. These he offered as pledges to cover the expenses of the fleet. Even so, the project soon collapsed. The crews were discharged, the supplies were sold, and all the proceeds went to pay off the investors. A second plan quickly evolved, calling for the establishment of an English presence in Calicut on the Malabar coast. Dom Antonio promptly gave his blessing to the new plan, which involved an area that was nominally Portuguese. Most of the previous investors joined once again, though John Hawkins stayed out this time, rightly concluding that the project was risky and unlikely to succeed.[40]

Instead, John seems to have backed his brother William in a separate voyage to the coast of Brazil. This was also Portuguese territory, and this scheme was also approved by Dom Antonio. William's own son John had joined the earlier expedition of Captain Edward Fenton, and the family connections were preserved when Richard Hawkins decided to accompany his uncle William on the voyage to Brazil. The seven-ship fleet included the 300-ton *Primrose* and two smaller vessels furnished by Sir Francis Drake. Loading the ships with trade goods at Plymouth in November 1582, William headed for the West Indies, presumably stopping on the coast of Africa for a cargo of slaves. On 3 June 1583 he was at Margarita dredging for pearls. Six weeks later he was at San Germán in the island of Puerto Rico. Using his family's proven approach to West Indian officials, William told the local officials that "they were English driven up from Brazil." All they wanted was "a river mouth with water sufficient to allow them to overhaul their vessels." He seems also to have tried to sell slaves, for some of the ships were said to have "many women aboard" who were offered to the islanders in trade.[41] In November 1583 reports from Plymouth said that William arrived home with a huge profit, at least part of which was rumored to be from the treasure fleet.[42]

At last, life for John Hawkins looked wonderful. Business was good. An important government job brought him £220 per year in salary and allowances and kept him in close contact with the most important men in the country. Still, he was not entirely happy. In a letter written by one of his new clerks, Hawkins confessed to Burghley that he felt like "a sheepe among wolves." The report he had written to secure his appointment to the Navy Board had turned Winter and others into enemies. As treasurer of the navy, Hawkins endured constant criticism from these adversaries, making his work "doblyd in tedyousnes & verye combersom." While the letter explaining all this to

Burghley was composed by his clerk, one of the descriptions pleased Hawkins so much that he underlined the whole paragraph:

> In the passinge of theis greate thinges, thadversaries of the worke have contynewallye opposyd them selves against me & the servis so farr as they durst be seene in hit, So that emonge a nomber of trryfflinge crossings and slaunders, the verye wauls of the Realme have byne brought in questyon; and their slaunder hathe gone veryee farr and generall, to thincoraidgement of the Enemyes of god and or countrye. onlye to be avenged of me and this servis, wch dothe discover the coruptyon & ignoraunce of the tyme past.[43]

This was John Hawkins exasperated. The complaints he referred to were from William Winter and the other members of the Navy Board, from Baker and other shipwrights who had fallen out with Hawkins, and from contractors who objected to the tightfisted way Hawkins ran the office. He told Burghley that since Christmas of 1582 "the offycers have taken coorage and hardynes to oppose them selves agaynst me," and "dyvers matters have byne omytted, delayed, and hynderyd by many subtyle practyses." Criticisms of this sort were a normal part of life for men in public office, then and now, but the Hawkins critics were so persistent in their attacks that members of the Privy Council felt obliged to move very carefully in naval matters. In a case involving the use of a royal ship to thwart the activities of French pirates, Francis Walsingham told Lord Burghley that it would be wise to take special precautions about the transfer of funds in order "to remove all suspicion."[44]

Hoping to settle the Hawkins dispute without making matters worse, the queen appointed five members of the Privy Council to a special investigating commission. The members named by letter in the document were Lord Burghley, Lord Howard of Effingham (who was then the lord chamberlain), the earl of Lincoln (who was then the lord high admiral), Sir Walter Mildmay, and Sir Francis Walsingham. They were to be assisted by the four members of the Navy Board, Sir William Winter (who held appointment as surveyor of the ships), John Hawkins (treasurer), William Holstocke (comptroller of the ships), and William Borough (clerk of the ships). Finally, the master shipwrights, Peter Pett and Matthew Baker, were to join the group. The brief and carefully worded document still exists and is worth reading:

> Articles touching the survey of her ma^{ts} shipps, as allsoe for the inquirie of abuses heretofore committed, and to sett downe remedies for preventing of the same/
>
> that wheras it is given out, that her ma^{ts} shippes, be growne to very great decay, and that such charges as have of late yeares been bestowed (since the yeare 1579) for the repayringe of them, hath not been soe well imployed as appertayneth. Her ma^{tie} doth therefore thinke it very expedient, that her commissoner A B. C. D & L (whereof A. B. and C. & L be of the quorū) shall make choyce of persons of best skill to view and survey the sayd shippes.
>
> That the sayd persons soe authorised to take the sayd view, shall (for their better assistaunce) call unto them the most skillfull maisters and shipwrights, to be present at the sayd view and survey/
>
> That the sayde survey shalbe taken in the presence of her ma^{ts} officers, viz. Sr William Wynter, M^r. Hawkyns, William Holstocke, and William Borrough, Pett and Baker/
>
> that after the view and survey taken, the certificate be

made, under the handes and seales of such as shalbe appoynted to view them/

That whereas her ma^tie. hath allsoe be given to understand, that divers adbuxes (since her comminge to the crowne) have been committed by the officers them selves, especially in the imbeselinge away of both the lymber provided for the buyldings and repayringe shippes, as allsoe in imbeselinge of her ma^ts provision, out of her ma^ts storehouse/ To enquire therefore where the sayd abuses and spoyles have been soe committed/ and to devise some such orders and Rules. How the sayd abuses may be prevented. To cause a survey to be taken of the provisions in the storehouses, and to certifie, how the somme hath been encreasde since the yeare 1579 [45]

The queen had ordered all the aggrieved parties to meet with the commissioners, so she clearly wanted to resolve differences between the parties without finding fault on one side or another. The result was somewhat different from what she had hoped it would be.

On 25 January 1584 the commissioners inspected twenty-two of the ships (the *Achates* was on duty in Ireland) and declared most of them to be "in sufficyente and servisable state for eny sodaine service." A few of the ships were not in good condition, mostly because of poor work by the shipwrights before Hawkins took charge of the contracts in 1579. The *Philip and Mary* "was newe repayred in Depeforde docke in A° 1578 (by order of thofficers) and a greate chardge entred uppon her, and little worke don for the same wherby the shippe is nowe broughte into a drye docke at Depeforde to be newe repayred againe." The *Antelope* had received similar treatment but was repaired again at the expense of the shipwrights. Several others had been built with "unseasoned plankes" and were very expensive to maintain. Since 1578 all the ships had been put into good order, but an organized program was needed to see they remained that way. The inspectors suggested that for the next fifteen years one or two ships be rebuilt every year.[46]

All this was good news for John Hawkins. His own work was thoroughly vindicated, and any fault seemed to lie with his critics, particularly a certain shipwright at Deptford. There were no problems with the ships built or repaired at Woolwich, Chatham, or Portsmouth, and little but praise for the vessels of master shipwright Peter Pett, who joined Hawkins in signing the document. Pretty clearly, the faulty construction was to be blamed on Matthew Baker, though the inspectors were careful not to mention his name. Nonetheless, Baker did not sign the report, nor did Winter or the other members of the Navy Board.[47]

Brimming with confidence, Hawkins wrote to members of the Privy Council, suggesting a new plan that would give him full responsibility for naval repairs and construction. The current arrangement simply bred controversy about the difference between "ordinary" and "extraordinary" repairs. "The Shippwrightes," he said, "denye some matters to be ordinarie, and refuse to doe the service." This was bad enough, but there was more. "The officers," he said, "denye to give allowance for sundrye matters, alleadging them not to be extraordinarie, and by those meanes the strife continueth." Under his written contract of 1579, plus the verbal agreements made later with Burghley, Hawkins undertook to reduce the cost of "ordinary" repair and maintenance to £4,000 per year. The extra £1,714 was applied to the purchase of supplies, enough to provide "a doble furnyture of her highnes ships."[48]

In his new offer Hawkins said that he could do both the ordinary and the extraordinary work for a total cost of £5,714. This, he said, would save the royal treasury more than £3,200 annually, the average cost in previous years for the "extraordinary" work of repair and reconstruction. It was creative accounting at its finest. Just a year later Hawkins sent Lord Burghley a list of "Extraordynarye reparacons Since A° 1579." The total he gave then was £8,470, or about £1,700 per year. But in 1587 Hawkins said that the cost for such work had averaged £2,500 per year.[49] Obviously, Elizabethan bookkeeping allowed budget totals to be juggled to meet the needs of the moment.

Admittedly, the budget categories were difficult to deal with. Neither repairs to ships damaged in service nor new construction to expand the navy were to be included in the ordinary or the extraordinary expenses. In fact, the new proposal did not commit Hawkins to any new construction. He promised only to put the ships "in new making" one at a time, replacing old ships with new ships only when necessary. Seemingly, the necessity would not arise any time soon, for the Privy Council had just authorized another £1,480 worth of repairs on the ships to meet the concerns of the investigating committee. Thus all of the ships were to be in acceptable condition at the start of his contract. Recent repairs had even brought two old ships, the *Bull* and the *Tiger*, into good enough shape for another six or seven years of service.[50]

There was more. The new proposal did not include supplies. "The thowsand pownd, which ys to be sparyd yeerly for supplyes, I do not speke of, for that yt ys another matter, which I wyll speke of heerafter." When he did get back to it, Hawkins called the £1,714 currently spent on supplies "£2,000." Bragging about his great success in providing the "doble furnyture," Hawkins said the annual allowance could be safely reduced to £1,000.[51]

The new contract was eventually approved, to take effect at the beginning of 1585. The terms were somewhat different, but in the end more generous, than Hawkins had asked for. The first ten items briefly described what the Privy Council expected him to accomplish.

The Bargayne of John Hawkins for the Navye. Viz:
Condicōns in the behalfe of her ma^{tie}

1 ffirst all that wch was ordinarv in such tyme as it was v^{m li} vii^c xiiii^{li} yerelie John Hawkins shall p[er]forme

2 As first to pay and contynewe the same number of Shippe keep^{er}s that hath bene since the saide ordinarie was reduced to the saide some of 5714 li together wth the same nomber of gonne^rs in Upnor Castle the Clerkes &c: the Watchemen and Rent that is paied in the ordinarye.

3 It^m to kepe in repayer all hir ma^{ties} Shippes so as uppon A grounding may be readie to s^{er}ve at the Seas until some one of them come to be newe made in A drie docque./

4 It^m to moare the Navye sufficientlie so that the Shippes maye ride wthowt daunger.

5 It^m to repayer all manner of Storehouses and wharfes at Chatham Wolwich, Deptford and Portesrnouth until any of them shall fall into such decayie as they must be newe built./

6 It^m to contvnewe all hir ma^{ties} Navye in s^rviceable order and everie yere to doe such rēpacōns as shalbe nedefull either in makinge of A newe Shippe repayringe in drie docques or any way otherwyse that shalbe nedefull so that the full nomber be. as they are nowe at this p[re]sent yf any Sippe be decayed an nother to be put new in her place of like lengh and breadth sufficiently

builded./

7 It^m to grounde the Shippes uppon all occasions of Sea s^{er}vice, Leakes or other nedefull causes.

8 It^m all the Boates Cocks, Pynnasses and Lyghters shalbe kept in s^{er}viceable order, and as the olde doe decaye newe to be made in their places.

9 It^m he shall finde Norwaye mastes for all the smalle Shippes under the Ayde and the Toppe mastes and toppe Sayle yardes of all the Shippes./

10 It^m that at all Hallowtide everie yere there shalbe presented unto the Lorde Treasourer, the Lorde Chamblayne, Mr Secretarye and Sir Walter Mildmay the names of twentie skillfull men as Captaynes, Gonners, Shipwrights and masters of wch nomber the foresaide Cornissioñs shall appoynt such A nomber as they will to make report of the estate of the navye, and to showe their opynion what shalbe nedefull to he donne to the Navye and yere followinge wch shalbe likewise p[er]formed.[52]

The second part of the agreement detailed the advantages that Hawkins hoped to realize from the agreement.

Condicõns in the behalfe of John Hawkins.

1 ffirst the saide John Hawkins shall have paied hym for the s^{er}vice to be donne of thother side the olde ordinarie Warraunt of 5714^{li} - 2^s - 2^d monethlie as it was in Anno 1578./

2 It^m he shalbe holpen wth the cõmission as in Anno 1578.

3 It^m it shalbe Lawfull for hym to entertayne as many

Shipwrightes as he will and as fewe as he will and at all seasons and tymes as the s^{er}vice shall require and noe more.

4 yf any of the Shippes shall come to A mischaunce (as god forbidde) either by fier, wracke, spoyle in warre or such like or the Boates Cocks or Pynnasses then the saide John Hawkins shall have allowaunce for the sup-plie of S̶u̶ such Shippes Boates and Pynnasses as the Chardge shall require and be iudged by the Comrnis-sionrs or officers of the Navie.

5 It^m that yf the hole Navye shall goe to the Seas or A greate parte of them whatsoever provisions of tymber Borde and Plancke shalbe taken into them for Sea s^{er}v-ice, the saide John Hawkins shall not he Chardged wth above the value of xl^s. in such stuffe for everie Shippe to Saye Boardes, Plancke, ffysshers for mastes Spare mastes for Toppe mastes and such like./

6 It^m the saide John Hawkins shall have the Assistaunce of the Shippe keap[er]s for the helpe of groundinge of the Shippes Loadinge and unloadinge of provisions and such like, the use of the Whoey for cariadge Launchinge, tackles, and Crane Roopes &c. as hath bene in tymes past.

7 It^m he shall also have the use of the wharfes, Storehous-es, fforges and Lodginge at Chatham, Deptforde, Wol-wich and Portesmouth for those ministers that shalbe nedefull to attende this s^{er}vice, and for the Layinge of all manner of p[ro]visions readilie for the saide s^{er}vice./

8 It^m that yf the Shippes shall ride in any other place by

hir ma^{ties} order then by the discrēcon of the Cōmission-
^{er}s it maye be iudged what shalbe increased for the same
moaringe, callinge unto them Thofficers and masters of
the navye./

9 It^m that when A newe Shippe shalbe made and readie to
be Launched the saide John Hawkins shall make his
Comoditie of tholde./

10 It^m yf any ambiguitie or doubt shall happen of either
p[ar]tie that ought to be Considered in equitie and Conscience, be omitted in this bargayne and that the same
can not be agreed uppon amongst the officers, that then
the Cōmission^{er}s aftresaide shall by their discrēcons
moderate the doubte and order the same./[53]

The terms of the new contract were more detailed than the first,
but still capable of being interpreted differently by different people.
Early in 1585, when William Winter heard about the agreement, he
penned a long letter of complaint to Burghley. "There is nothinge in
it," he wrote, "but conninge and crafte to maynteine his pride and ambi-
tion, and for the better fillinge of his purse, and to kepe backe from dis-
cov^{er}inge the faultes that are lefte in her ma^{ties} shipps at this day." An
example of this "conninge and crafte" was the annual program devised
in January 1584 for building and rebuilding ships. The Privy Council
and Hawkins seem to have agreed that this expense was outside the
contract, and the council continued to provide funds annually for this
purpose. The most telling complaint by Winter was that Hawkins was
"an invisible partner" of the shipwrights Pett and Baker. Pett was still a
friend of Hawkins's, Winter said, because Hawkins allowed Pett to do
substandard work, even leaving rotten timbers in one ship, covered
with plaster. According to Winter, Holstock, Baker, and Borough all

were critical of the contract and the way Hawkins ran naval affairs.[54]

None of this seemed to bother Burghley, who, if anything, drew closer to John Hawkins, conferring with him ever more frequently about naval matters. One reason was that the alleged offenses were either trivial or totally imaginary. Everything had been discussed earlier, when Hawkins and Burghley met with the Navy Board, and everyone was satisfied with the answers Hawkins provided. Moreover, Baker, Holstock, and Winter slandered one another nearly as often as they did Hawkins, though all of them maintained a thin veneer of friendship to mask their mutual aversion.[55] A further reason for Burghley's support was a renewal of hostilities with Spain, increasing the demand for the serviceable ships that Hawkins had proven he could provide.

With his new contract safely in hand, Hawkins told Burghley that it would be possible to put the navy into proper shape without much trouble. "We shalbe able to go forward wth the works of those apt and nymble vessells wch shall myghtely strenthen the navy & be most ffytt and forscyble to offend thennymye." These, his first and last words on ship design, show that Hawkins understood the new building trends in English shipyards and had a real commitment to the race-built warship. Although there were no new ships in 1585, Hawkins could report that five ships had received major repairs in dry dock. The Privy Council had ordered a great chain to be stretched across the river at Upnor Castle to keep raiders from sailing into the anchorage. This had been done, but Hawkins agreed with his critics that it might not be worth the trouble and expense.[56]

The chain was a sign of the times. For a year or more relations had been worsening between England and Spain. In the summer of 1584 Hawkins gathered together his old proposals for a raid on the Spanish treasure fleets and put them into a new form. Because Dom

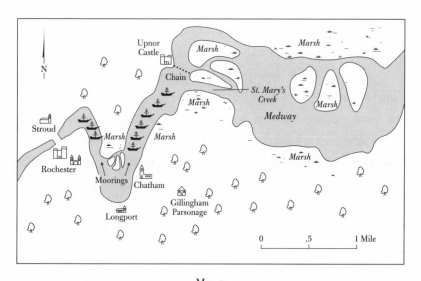

Map 9

In 1585 the Privy Council ordered Hawkins to install a great chain across the Medway at
Upnor Castle to protect the anchorage. Sketch from BL Cotton Augustus I.1.52.

Antonio still hoped to secure the throne of Portugal for himself,
Hawkins suggested that the government allow English ships to serve
under the Portuguese flag, paying "fyve or ten of the hondrethe" on
captured booty to Dom Antonio and a similar amount to the queen.
There would be no risk of war, for "french, f[l]emyngs, scotts and
soche lyke" would join the English sailors, making a force too great for
Philip to oppose. Moreover, the problem of piracy would be solved,
"for now ther can be none excuse but all Idell seamen may be
imployed." As with his earlier suggestions, this one was quietly put
aside. Once more Hawkins would stay home while other plans received
more serious consideration, including Ralegh's proposal to establish a
settlement near the Spanish forts in North America. In the final clause
to his own proposal Hawkins endorsed the plan just submitted by his
young cousin. "The voiage offered by S^r frauncys drake myght best be

made lawfull to go under this lycense allso, wch wold be secret tyll the tyme draw nere of their reddynes."[57]

Elizabeth had already decided to dispatch a new fleet, but Hawkins himself would not be part of it. Francis Drake had convinced the queen to name him as leader of a major expedition that would allegedly go to the Moluccas, where he had loaded spices on his earlier voyage around the world. The usual prominent officials and merchants were involved. Elizabeth herself became the major investor, with £10,000 in cash, plus two royal ships, for which she received an additional credit of several thousand pounds. Drake pledged £7,000, the earl of Leicester £3,000, John Hawkins £2,500, his brother another £1,000, and Sir Walter Ralegh £400. As usual, plans changed several times before the fleet left England. When Philip seized several English grain ships in the spring of 1585, the decision was made to drop the pretense of a voyage to the Moluccas and to authorize Drake to sail for Vigo, on the northwest coast of Spain, where the ships were interned. What he was supposed to do thereafter is unclear, perhaps seize the treasure fleet, perhaps raid the West Indies. As it turned out, Drake sacked Vigo, missed the treasure fleet, but went on to attack Spanish ports in the Canary Islands, the Cape Verde Islands, and the Caribbean. He captured Santo Domingo and Cartagena, then sailed north to destroy the Spanish fort at San Agustín.[58]

Richard Hawkins went with Drake, commanding a little oared pinnace called the *Duck*. Young, but a good sailor, he was the first one home, announcing the return of the fleet. On 22 July 1586 at three in the afternoon Richard brought his vessel into "the mounte." Securing a horse, he rode fourteen hours from Torrington to Exeter, where he gave news of Drake's imminent arrival and then collapsed in exhaustion. Some of his news was bad and some was good. Seven hundred and fifty of the 1,925 men were dead, and the considerable booty would not quite cover expenses.[59] But Drake's fleet had sailed at will through Spanish waters, and Philip was suddenly forced to admit that Elizabeth could be a powerful adversary.

While Drake and his fleet were at sea, John Hawkins continued to beg for a sea command. Fifteen years had passed since his connection with the Ridolfi plot, yet there were still rumblings about his loyalty. "The time beinge as it is," said one critic, "in reason he is not to be trusted, his for spanishe famyliarytie remembered." Nevertheless, Burghley trusted him, though not completely.[60]

During the early months of 1586 at Burghley's request Hawkins prepared a series of papers showing the condition of the navy. He listed all the ships available for service, both in the navy and from merchants, along with lists of needed mariners and gunners, and the names of men who could command the ships. In addition he supplied Burghley with an estimated cost for sending the fleet to sea for periods up to three months, about the length of time that ships could sail without resupply. From these studies it quickly became apparent that mobilization would involve huge difficulties and an enormous cost. In ordinary times only a few ships were sent out at once. The rest of the fleet stayed in port with skeleton crews on partial pay, while sails, rigging, and equipment were kept in storage. In a large-scale mobilization, three months of service at sea would cost twice the annual budget for the whole navy. It would mean summoning naval officers and seamen from all over the country, putting the ships back into service, and supplementing their numbers with merchant ships and merchant seamen. Most of these men would be reluctant to serve, because pay was so low. Reacting to this problem, Hawkins recommended a new pay scale, more than double the older rate, and it was quickly adopted.[61]

Hawkins also oversaw the construction of the first new ships added to the navy since he was appointed treasurer. These were the 350-ton *Rainbow* and the 450-ton *Vanguard,* built by Peter Pett and Matthew Baker, respectively. A third vessel, the 160-ton *Tremontana,* was the work of Robert Chapman, whose design was so successful that he was named royal shipwright in the following year. An older ship, the 1,100-ton *Victory,* built originally in 1562, was rebuilt "into the forme of a gallion" in 1586.[62] All of the new ships were constructed under special budget allowances, and thus were not charged to the Hawkins contract.

Drake's return home coincided with the discovery of what came to be called the Babington plot. It was another attempt to assassinate Queen Elizabeth and to put Mary on the English throne. As details of the scheme emerged, English attention turned once more toward Europe, particularly Spain and Catholic France. There was talk of sending Drake back to the West Indies with a new fleet, but it was just talk. In the end he was dispatched to Holland with funds and reinforcements for the troops Leicester had taken there a few months earlier. Beyond that, he was to meet with representatives of the States General and enlist them to help Dom Antonio in his campaign to win the throne of Portugal. Partly at Dom Antonio's urging, Hawkins was given command of a small fleet. His orders now are unclear. The Venetian ambassador said that he had been sent to keep track of a French fleet seen gathering near the coast of Brittany. The Spanish ambassador, recently relocated to France, thought his plans more sinister. "All the Hawkinses are born pirates," he said. "When I was in England they fitted out ships to plunder even in sight of land."[63] Perhaps both views were correct.

Early in August, Hawkins took command of his fleet, five royal ships, plus sufficient armed merchant ships and pinnaces to make a fleet of fifteen vessels. For his flagship he took the 500-ton *Nonpareil,* the former *Philip and Mary,* rebuilt in 1584 and rechristened so as not to honor the king of Spain. The vice admiral was William Borough, commanding the 500-ton *Lion.* The other royal vessels were the 600-ton *Hope,* commanded by Thomas Fenner; the 500-ton *Revenge,* commanded by Edward Berkeley; and the brand new 150-ton *Tramontana,* commanded by Benjamin Gonson, brother-in-law of Hawkins. Fenner was just back from the West Indies expedition, where he had commanded Drake's flagship.[64] Two were associated with the Navy Board. Borough was clerk of the ships and one of those Navy Board members hostile to Hawkins. Benjamin Gonson had served under Borough in 1583 and in 1589 was to succeed him as clerk of ships.

By late August, Hawkins was ready to depart. His movements are not well known from English records, but Spanish accounts help to fill the gaps. The Privy Council, assuming that Hawkins was already at sea, sent new orders on 30 August, instructing him to keep watch for French ships trying to land on the English coast. Pedro Sarmiento de Gamboa, taken prisoner and held for a time in Plymouth, said that he saw Hawkins with a fleet of twenty-two ships in the harbor there on the first of September. If so, Hawkins must have left there almost immediately, for a few days later near Cape St. Vincent he took a 150-ton ship returning from America. This was probably one of the four ships from Brazil that Hawkins captured on that day.[65] On 30 September, while sailing north of the Canary Islands under a Flemish flag, Hawkins took two more ships coming home from Brazil, the *Buen Jesus* and the *San Juan.* Never shy with his prisoners, Hawkins entertained Manuel Blanco, the master of the *Buen Jesus,* aboard his flagship. A few days later this mariner reported what took place, providing an outsider's description of the new English ship design. He said the *Nonpareil* looked just like the great Spanish galleons. The ship was clean and fast, equipped

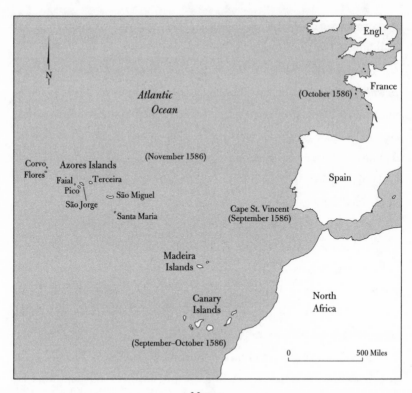

Map 10
The Hawkins raid on Spanish shipping, September to November 1586.

with new sails, and well supplied with food, including live animals and fresh fruit. Blanco counted forty-four bronze guns and estimated that the crew amounted to three hundred men, both sailors and soldiers. Hawkins told Blanco that Queen Elizabeth was about to join Dom Antonio in an expedition to invade Portugal, partly in order to forestall a Spanish attempt to invade England. As Blanco remembered the conversation, Hawkins said that he had not really wanted a sea command. "He came unwillingly," said Blanco. "He was tired of seafaring." From listening to the conversations of the crewmen, Blanco learned that the ships were headed for São Miguel in the Azores, where they would try to intercept the West Indies fleet.[66]

Another captive, Christopher Martin, master of the *San Juan,* was interviewed by Fenner aboard the *Lion.* Impressed with the size of the ship, Martin reported that Fenner's vessel was even larger than the *Nonpareil,* perhaps as big as the *San Martín,* a 1,000-ton Spanish galleon. He said that the ship carried fifty-four bronze guns and 350 men. Describing ornamentation of the ships, he said, "The outside of the poop of the vessel was much gilded with the queen of England's arms thereon, the other three great galleons being similarly decorated."[67]

After seizing the vessels, Hawkins may have returned to England with the captured ships and other booty. Reports surfacing in Paris had him departing once more from Southampton at the beginning of October, heading this time for the coast of France. One of his first captures was a French ship coming from Lisbon. Hawkins boasted to the captain of this vessel that he was heading for the Azores, where he hoped to capture the Spanish treasure ships.[68]

In the end, Hawkins did not manage to take his fleet to São Miguel. As he sailed in that direction, his ships were scattered in a great storm. Late in November the vessels limped home a few at a time, badly battered, provisions nearly gone. The total booty consisted of two ships from Santo Domingo and two from Brazil. Captured cargoes were mostly sugar and dye wood—valuable, but not worth the money spent preparing the fleet. Everyone was disappointed. Everyone but Hawkins. During the voyage Hawkins and Borough became great friends, a development that caused one critic to observe that the two "might have don greate *service* which was by them omitted."[69]

This was the only positive aspect of a voyage that was a personal setback for Hawkins. His critics argued that he had not made the sort of effort required to redeem himself from the taint of treason. John Hawkins had spent more than a dozen years trying to restore his reputation but had been only partly successful. One of the most influential men in the Elizabethan naval organization, he had the heart of a seaman but the soul of a businessman. While building a navy, he kept one eye on personal profit. In the process he made new enemies, who refused to let anyone forget his earlier shortcomings. The disappointing results of his recent voyage made it possible for enemies to continue saying that Hawkins could not be trusted.

8

War with Spain

This shalbe a thinge most manyfest to yor Lship and the hole woreled,
that the navye ys in good & stronge estate.

John Hawkins

Home once more from his disappointing foray at sea,
Hawkins tried to catch up with his work as treasurer of the navy. There were construction projects to
inspect and reports to write, but progress was slow,
and Hawkins was ill. "I have byne very syke," he
told Burghley in late January, "and contynew weake styll." Despite his
slow recovery, Hawkins managed to put some of his accounts in order
and send a report to Lord Burghley.[1]

Ever since Ridolfi had urged the king of Spain to burn the ships
moored near Rochester, the Privy Council had worried about the safety
of the moorings.[2] To allay their fears, Hawkins and other members of
the Navy Board told Burghley what they had done to protect the
anchorage. First, there was a huge chain, made in London and stretched
across the river at Chatham, at a cost of £290. Costly enough itself, the
chain was not the most expensive item. There were timber pilings to
hold the chain and a wheel house where machinery could pull the chain
taut across the channel, plus anchors, buoys, cables, and lighters to help
in moving the chain from one position to another. To keep enemy vessels from going around the chain, workmen had raised earthen barriers
across Saint Mary Creek and other channels. For added protection new
earthworks were dug around Upnor Castle, and new gun platforms
were built in the castle itself. Supplementing these efforts, Hawkins
established a system of warning beacons, with watchmen stationed at

various places, along with small boats patrolling the approaches. The cost for installing the chain and operating the defenses during the past year amounted to £1,500. Defense, it seemed, was complicated and expensive.[3]

To offset some of these costs the Privy Council appointed a commission to investigate Drake's recent voyage to the West Indies and try to extract a little profit from the enterprise. John Hawkins and William Winter were both members of the commission, as were Thomas Smythe (farmer of the London Customs), Alderman Richard Martyn (master of the mint), and Alderman John Harte (director of the Muscovy Company). Two of the commanders who had been with Drake on the voyage, Martin Frobisher and Christopher Carleill, joined this group and tried to reconstruct Drake's chaotic financial records. After "sundry meetings and divers considerations," the commissioners reluctantly decided to accept Drake's jottings as "an honest and true accompte." Investors would receive fifteen shillings for every pound invested in the voyage, a net loss of 25 percent. Not wanting to haggle with their sovereign, the commissioners decided to allow the queen a total of £15,350, slightly more than the amount due on her £20,000 investment.[4]

None of the discussions seemed to bother Drake, who involved himself in preparing another fleet to sail for the coast of Spain. Little is known about his original plans, which typically were not very detailed. Spanish informants thought for a time that he was going to the West Indies again. But as the Babington plot continued to unravel, all English ships were ordered to patrol the channel or sail along the coasts of Portugal and Spain.[5]

As spring approached, it became apparent that King Philip was proceeding with invasion plans, and Drake was given a deadline of 20

March to assemble his ships. On 15 March, Elizabeth signed his commission, and three days later Drake inked his own agreement with the London merchants who were to supply many of the vessels. By this agreement, "whatsoever pillage shall be had by sea or land" would be divided equally, half to the crown and half to the investors.[6]

The royal contribution was made in the form of four ships of war. Drake's flagship was again the *Elizabeth Bonaventure,* 550 tons. Other royal ships were the *Golden Lion,* 550 tons; the *Rainbow,* 500 tons; and the *Dreadnaught,* 400 tons. In addition, the 50-ton *Spy* went along to serve the larger ships. Drake added three or four ships of his own. These included the 80-ton *Drake,* the 200-ton *Thomas,* and the 70-ton *Elizabeth.* The lord admiral sent two ships that he owned, the 150-ton *White Lion,* and the 25-ton *Cygnet.* John Hawkins sent at least one ship, the 130-ton bark *Hawkins.* William Winter probably owned the 200-ton *Minion.* The London merchants had a fleet of ten ships they had originally hoped to send in pursuit of the East India fleet. These included some large vessels, the 400-ton *Merchant Royal,* the 350-ton *Susan,* the 300-ton *Edward Bonaventure,* three others ranging from 150 to 200 tons, and several pinnaces. As usual, Elizabeth remained indecisive about dispatching the fleet. Drake did not receive his sailing orders until 27 March. He immediately left for Plymouth, where the fleet assembled two days later. In all there were sixteen ships and seven pinnaces.[7]

Hawkins found the increased naval activity a nearly unbearable burden. Once he had Drake and his fleet safely out of port, he wrote a new report on the problem of maintaining the royal navy. A natural bureaucrat, Hawkins had mastered the art of exaggerating his work and understating his budget.

The state and manner how her ma^{ts} shipps have byn cōtynt-
ed & orderyd synce the eleventhe yere of her ma^{ts}
raigne

Howe it was in tyme past

ffirst. There was allowed and payde by warraunte dormant
5714 ^{li} yerlye

ffor wch some their was performyd theis thinges ffollowinge:

The Wages of Shypkepers

The Ransakinge and kepenge of the shippes in Harborowe
till they com to be new buylte or drye docked

The Groundinge of the saide shipps as was fytt for them,
and as there tyme came aboute to contynew them in harborowe, some in thre yeres some in two yeres, and others of the Lesser sorte once a yere,/

ffor this servis aforesaide all kinde of Irone worke and stuff
was provydyd

The wearinge of the shippes in harborowe

The wages of the Gonners in Upnor Castell

The wage of clarks &c. kepers of the plaggs at Chatham,
Depford, wollw^{ch} And Portesmouthe,

The ffees of shippwrights, Porters, messingers, and suche
lyke

The Rentt for storehouses

ffees for kepeinge of Houses att Wollw^{ch} and Portesmouthe

Repayringe of houses att Depforde, Woll^{ch} Chatham, and
Portesmouthe

The watche att chatham and Depford

All this aforesaide hathe byn borne uppon the olde ordy-
narye warraunte abovesaide of 5714^{li} yerlye

Their was also besydes this (Comñibus annis) an Extra ordinarye chardge wch past by warraunte from her ma^ti for the new buyldinge & repayringe of shipps in drye docke. To the some of 2500^li yerlye

Howe it is now

Then followed the agreement wth John Hawkins in a° 1579. And synce that tyme thordinary above saide, and thextraordinarye chardge of repayringe and new reforminge of the shippes in Drye docks hathe byn mayntaynyd onlye upon the chardge of the first ordinary warraunt of 5714^li yerlye

The Navye is now greatlye increasyd, ffor whiche it is fytt an ordinarye be consydered of for their mayntenaunce

The sea servis by meane of this troublesome tyme dothe greatlye increase chardge and busynes. So as yt is impossyble for any one man to answere the offyce of Tresourer and to take thys care.

Sir William Wynter and the rest of the offycers of the navy having substantyallye consyderyd wth my Lord Admyral, doe and will endevour them selves and are most desyerous to ease her maiests chardge, and to doe it in suche sorte as the Navy and provycyons thereunto belonginge be surely andsufficiently provyded for all servis. And w^thall to take soche substancyall care as her ma^ti be nott overchardged, Wherby her highnes shalbe incouraged to contyneue and mayntayne the saide Navy in fforcyble and reddy order for the defence of her maiestie and our Countrye.

Therfore myne oppyneyon ys as followeth

that it maye please her ma^{ti} to apoynte certaine of her coun-
sell and some others to Joyne wth my Lorde Admyrall in
Comyssyon to see how this chardge maye be settlyd,
and a new warraunte dormante made for such a some as
shulde be by them determyned,

In the ende of wch warraunte their wolde be suche a clause
made, as was in the Last bargaine wth mr Bashe, that
whate chardge shulde excede\ above the warraunte dormante (and reason showed under the hands of the Lord
Admiral and three others of thoffycers of the Lo Tresourer) that th[torn]

thereupon at the yers end, suche overplus shuld be payde to
the Tresoure[r] of the Navye wthout any other warraunte to be procured from her ma^{ti} for the same,

And for that dyvers disorders have byn in the carpentry, the
provisions apertayninge to the riggingee, and the powder and furniture of artillerye had out of the Tower,
wher by the great purloyninge and wast of the provisions appertaining to those matters aforesaide Her ma^{ti}
hathe byn greatlye Burdenyd and over chardged, This,
in dutie. if it may stande with the consytheracyon and
liking of the Comyssyoners, Thatt duringe theis tymes
of servis, I thincke it wolde be mete their weare a
provost marshyall attendaunte upon th^e Lo. Admyrall
and offycers of the Navye, to doe suche present exe-
cusyon aboorde the shippes uppon the offenders, as
shulde be appoyntyd and adjudged by the saide Lorde
Admyrall and thoffycers of the Navye accordinge to the
qualletie of thoffence comytted

When it shall please god to sende a quiette tyme; then the
saide comyssyoners maye have order to compounde a
certentie of her maiests chardge of all manner of
expense belonginge to the Navye, And Soe Devyde it to
the chardge of ffewe or suche nomber of persons as
shalbe by them thought mete for her highnes proffytt
and saffetie[8]

It was a clever report. After claiming he had carried the entire
burden of naval maintenance for several years, Hawkins asked that the
annual allowances be increased as they had been for Baeshe the vict-
ualer. In the new arrangement with Baeshe overexpenditures were
automatically reimbursed by the treasury, without the need for royal
approval. Hawkins also asked for special provost marshals in the shipyards and on shipboard to prevent theft and misappropriation of supplies, something that might seem agreeable to all. But when his oppo-
nents got wind of the report, they began to organize their own
response, while most of the authorities had their minds on Drake.

Not everyone agreed either about the timing or the destination of
Drake's voyage. A plan, perhaps rightly attributed to John Hawkins,
had suggested that Drake should be kept at home until September.
That would be the proper time to send Drake to Cádiz and Puerto de
Santa María, because the defending galleys were always laid up during
the winter. "I know a waye to wynne the towne w[th]out any losse of
men," he wrote. "We shall be well able to kepe it forever."[9] Other than
the timing, the plan seems to outline the assault Drake actually made on
that port. If it was really devised by Hawkins, then he probably
deserves some credit for Drake's surprise attack on Cádiz.

Despite this advice, the London investors had urged Drake not to
tarry in Plymouth but to leave as soon as the fleet was assembled. Thus

he sailed from Plymouth harbor on 2 April 1587, and it was well he did. A few days later information arrived in London that made the authorities think the threat from Spain had diminished. Consequently, the Privy Council issued new orders forbidding such an attack. "You shall forbeare to enter forcibly into anie of the said Ks portes or havens or to offer violense to anie of his townes or shipping within harbouring or to do anie act of hostillity uppon the land." On the other hand, he might seize whatever Spanish ships he could find on the high seas, especially those going to or from the Indies. In order to avoid future arguments about just how much booty he might take, he was forbidden to offload any cargo or treasure, but was to bring captured ships into port with their cargoes intact.[10]

As it turned out, Drake did not receive the message. Richard Hawkins, who had been to the West Indies with Drake, was sent in a pinnace belonging to William Winter with new orders for Drake. Delayed by bad weather, Richard failed to rendezvous with Drake's fleet.[11] Perhaps this was what had been intended, for Drake was able to follow his original plans. If the attack went awry, the government could claim that Drake had acted against orders. In any case, young Hawkins in his first solitary command showed what he had learned from his father and his uncle. On the way back from his attempt to deliver the message Richard captured a merchant vessel containing £5,000 worth of sugar and dye wood. When he reached Plymouth the booty was parceled out among himself, his father, and Winter, with his father taking the greatest share.[12]

This was too much for the merchants who had invested in the voyage. They wanted a share of the £5,000. In midsummer Drake himself returned to Plymouth with shiploads of booty from Cádiz, plus a Spanish vessel from the East Indies carrying a cargo of porcelain, vel-

17
John Hawkins and his son Richard, from the
title page of Purchas, *Hakluytus Posthumus*.
This item is reproduced by permission of
the Huntington Library, San Marino,
California

vet, silk, gold, jewels, and black slaves. The merchants claimed a share
of this booty as well, but inventories were slow in coming, and nobody
could tell what the shares might be. On 1 July 1587 the Privy Council
named Hawkins and several others to a commission to inventory "all
such coffers and boxes as you maie judge or know to have in them anie
gold, stones, jewelles or other like precious thinges." Once this was
done, Hawkins was to accompany Drake to London with the "shipp

and her fraight." Drake objected strenuously to this arrangement, for it impugned his honesty. As a result, Hawkins was directed to "surrender the chardg of the said shipp and fraight." When the Privy Council met on 3 October 1587, Drake and Hawkins had still not accounted for their booty, though Burghley and the others remained determined that they should do so.[13]

In this they were encouraged by the Hawkins critics, who renewed the attacks on their favorite target. This time Lord Burghley began to believe the stories they told. To Walsingham, Burghley wrote that the navy was sadly deteriorated. "I am sorry to thynk th^t I heare of every daye th^t the Q. shipps ar in such decaye as they are not s[er]viseable untill great cost may be doone up them." Soon a long list of complaints against Hawkins appeared in a gossipy letter to Burghley from a nameless Hawkins associate. This tale bearer had been watching his quarry for four years, and was convinced that the treasurer of the navy was a man of "injust mynde and deciptfull dealinge." Yet despite his suspicious, the man could never quite put his hands on solid evidence of dishonesty. Instead, he found "shewes & shadowes wthout eny substance." Some people said that Hawkins purchased goods and invested in ships in his wife's name. Hawkins dismissed such stories. "My wife hathe purchased a little thinge," he said. "I meddle not wth it." There were also reports that Hawkins would sometimes purchase supplies on his own account, and then sell them to the queen at a markup. Hawkins replied that when prices were low and royal funds were not available, he bought goods with his own money, just so the queen could have them more cheaply. Most of the accusations against Hawkins were hearsay. The anonymous accuser claimed to have seen only one incident himself. He said that Hawkins had bought cheap Lynn and Boston cordage, then altered the invoices to show high-quality Dansk and Muscovy rope.[14]

At dinner one evening with Winter and others, the tale bearer heard one of the guests explain how Hawkins had convinced the shipwrights to accept the contract for the "ordinary" upkeep of Her Majesty's ships. "Mr Hawkins persuaded the shipwrites thereunto, by the recytinge of a tale of one th^t undertouke in .7. yeres to make an asse to speake." This story was one of Aesop's tales, then popular among the Elizabethan gentry, Lord Burghley in particular. In a popular version of the fable, there was a tyrannical master who gave his servant ten years to teach an ass his letters. The man's friends commiserated with him, saying the task was impossible. "'I am not afraid,' the servant replied. 'During this time, either I will die, or the ass will, or the master.'" There was a moral to the story: "A perilous enterprise can be safe if postponed and deferred for a long time."[15]

This was the most serious charge, that Hawkins had no intention of honoring the terms of his contract. The complainer declined to interpret the meaning of the parable, saying, "I leave it to th^e construction of the wise." Obviously, he hoped Burghley would think himself the butt of the joke and be offended. Burghley was disturbed, but not about the story. His concern, as he had mentioned to Walsingham, was the way the ships were being repaired and rebuilt. It was not good, according to the unnamed gossip. "Mr Hawkins and m^r Pett fell at varyance upon accompts," and the former friend began to provide information to the secret enemy. He said Hawkins had charged the queen £13,478 for repairing the ships Drake had brought back from the West Indies, padding the bill by £5,000. He accused Hawkins of buying timber at Her Majesty's contract price, then using it to repair the *Primrose* and the *Talbot,* his own ships. He said that Hawkins manipulated the books so that most of the repairs that should have been charged to his new contract were paid by special budget allowances. Finally, he charged that Hawkins failed to keep the ships in good repair. The navy had deteriorated under his supervision, and would be very expensive to maintain in the future. For this reason Hawkins wanted to cancel the contract. "He will not contynue his bargaine, he saith he will lye in prison rather."[16]

All these problems remained hidden, said the anonymous complainer, because the members of the Navy Board now supported Hawkins. Winter had become his great chum, and the two were "as fast as bockle and girdell." This became clear to the tale bearer when he met Hawkins and Winter walking one day in Greenwich. Hawkins confronted his adversary, calling him "a syfter & searcher." The man denied it, but admitted his interest in gossip. "If eny woulde tell me enythinge either of him or eny other," he admitted, "I would not stoppe myne eares." Borough had become a good friend of Hawkins's, the informant said, so much so that "one maynteneth anothers cause to th[e] uttermost." In addition Hawkins was a "partner wth Chapman," the newest master shipwright. In this way Hawkins had members of the Navy Board and others under his control. Besides, Hawkins was a liar and a traitor. "In reason, he is not to be trusted," said the gossip, "his for spanishe famyliarytie remembred, his tale of th[e] asse, and the manifest deceipt and decayinge of hir ma[tis] navye respected." In the opinion of the tale bearer, the only possible solution would be a special investigation by two members of the Privy Council, Sir Walter Mildmay and Sir Francis Walsingham.[17]

Faced with the charges, Burghley asked the master shipwrights, Baker and Pett, to report on the condition of Her Majesty's ships. In the meantime, the anonymous letter was summarized for him in a brief report, apparently prepared by Thomas Allen.[18] A one-time associate of Frobisher, Allen held an appointment as "Qu[een's] merchant for

Danske" and had been authorized since 1561 to import naval stores. His dislike for Hawkins had its origin in a commercial rivalry that dated from 1572. In that year Allen complained to Burghley that Hawkins was supplying cordage to the navy, supplanting the service that Allen himself was authorized to provide.[19]

Avoiding names but leaving no doubt about his meaning, Allen listed several ways in which he thought "her ma[ties] Treasurer" had failed in his duty. Six of his complaints also applied to the rest of "her highnes offycers," but in a marginal note Burghley interpreted the entire document as "Contra Jh. Hawkyns." In Allen's words the various abuses were "not convenyent," an Elizabethan phrase that meant at best something unethical, at worst something illegal. For one thing, Hawkins was buying things at a low price and reselling them to the crown at a profit:

> Ffyrst, that it is not convenyent tht he who is her maties Treasurer shuld buy or provide any comoditie, for her maties navye, wth her maties mony, nor play the mrchaunt to buy and sell to others. for by thys meanes her matie shall have the remainer when the best is sould and at a deere pryce.

Hawkins was not the only dishonest man in the naval service. Other members of the Navy Board were also corrupt. Shipbuilders or shipowners, as all of them were, they used their positions to their own advantage:

> Secondlye it is verye unmeet for her maties proffet that those her highnes offycers shalbe any buylders of shippes, or setters foorth of any shippes to sea, but only her maties shipps, or to provide any comoditie for them be cause all

her maties provision is at ther comandement, to delyver and
to send wher they will, & to whom.

Perhaps worse, the principal officers of the Navy Board were
often in partnership with contractors:

> Thirdlye it is not convenyent that her highnes offycers shall
> have any partnars wth any, and especyally not with hym
> who is appoynted to provide her maties provision, for ther is
> danger, &c.

Beyond this, Allen thought it unseemly that members of the
board should be directly involved in purchasing. Rather, they should
restore the old system. The queen should appoint special purveyors, as
Allen once had been. Board members should simply negotiate fair
prices and pay the bills:

> Ffourthly it is verye unconvnyent that her maties offycers
> sholde provyde all thyngs for her navye, because they are
> appoynted to geve order to them, who it shall please her
> matie to appoynte to make provision, and when it commeth
> they are to se whether it be good and sufficyent to serve her
> matie or no, or else to refuse it; and it be good then they are
> to set a reasonable pryce in conscyence, between her maties
> and her marchaunt, but yf it be their owne, and off ther
> owne provyding, they wyll hardly do, for there consyence
> wyll nott serve them.

Here was a major complaint: the members of the board sold
goods to the navy, set their own prices, and then approved payment to
themselves. No wonder they were so rich:

Ffiftly thys must needs be a very good offyce, & will quick-
lye make one ryche and there consyence be open, to have the
provyding of all thyngs, for her maties navye, then to make
hys owne pryce, be it good or badde, none to comptrowle
them, then to pay them selves, what can be more desyred of
hym tht is covetous, or doth not meane to deale trulye with
her matie.

A different complaint had to do with purchases made by royal
commission. Under this arrangement a royal official could make forced
purchases of goods in short supply and pay no more than the normal
price. Allen thought members of the navy board were using this system
for their own benefit. This was against the law, and the law ought to be
enforced:

> Sixthlye yf they neyther feare god nor meane not to do right
> to her matie, yet let them take heede of her maties lawes,
> that the cry of the poore, and ryche be not revenged by ~~of~~
> god, for there is a statute tht what offycer soevr he be that
> hath a comyssyon from her matie, to provide any thyng for
> her maties use, & do take it up by her maties comyssyon,
> and doth sell the same agayne, or any part thereof to hys
> own profett, it is fellony, This statute is in vayne, never exe-
> cuted.

To discourage misappropriation of goods, Allen made what he
thought was a novel suggestion: keep careful records. Once each year
the warehouse records should be compared with the records of the
vendors and the records of the users. Allen suggested a prototype for
double-entry bookkeeping:

Sevently & laste, & most to be regarded, that good order may be taken for it to have all yor provision to com first into yor maties storehouses, wher it ought to com, then he that hath the keping thereof to be charged there wth, and once a year, or more & need be, to geve accompt what he hath received and to whoom he hath deliyvred it, and howe much remayneth. Let the remayner be sene, wch remayner and that whych is delvred must agre wth yor marchaunt's booke who delyvred it fyrst into yor maties storehouse. so thus far yor matie can have no wrong yf they do agre.

Allen's "seventh and last" point was really not the last. There was one more, so scandalous that Allen dared not put it into print. What it might have been is anybody's guess, which may be just what he had in mind:

But yet ther is one thyng more to be consedered of, whereof I can not wryte.

Allen affixed two additional documents to his "Certayne articles." One was a fairly complete summary of the anonymous letter, including a few bits of gossip not found in that document. Two of the stories are worth mentioning. Matthew Baker seemingly had charged that Hawkins demanded half the proceeds of the contract between the shipwrights and the crown. "Matthew Baker sayeth that when Peter Pett and he dyd take the repayring of her ma^ties shippes Hawkyns would needes be halffe wth them," wrote Allen, who added that "the reste of the offycers did not knowe that Hawkyns had any pte wth them." The second accusation had to do with flags and pennants for the ships. "Hawkyns wyffe and maydes muste make them," he said, and thereby prevent poor flag and pennant makers from earning a living. In a final burst of generosity Allen offered to take over the supply service for the navy. Noting the need for "a specyall honeste and true offycer," Allen said, "If it be yo[r] ma[ties] pleasure . . . I shall provyde from hensforth those things of provision for yo[r] highnes navye."[20]

The final attachment to the report was a review of the various means by which Hawkins had enriched himself and left the navy poorer. The first item summarizes everything: "Ffirst his bargayne is not performed/ in buldinge her ma[ties] shipps, in tyme convenyent as their state requyred/ but hathe sparinglye passed them over/ ffrom yeare to yeare/ and so are they brought to there last ende/ and dangerous state/ and he nowe in revokinge his bargaine/ shall leave her ma[tie] a greate charge to renewe them/ and him selfe go a waye withe no small gaune." To settle the matter Allen suggested that Hawkins be required to put the ships "in suche order as he ffound them," even perhaps to build two or three new ones at his own expense. "This he may do and go a gayner awaye."[21]

More was about to come. On 12 October 1587 Peter Pett and Matthew Baker placed their report in Lord Burghley's hands. Their task had been difficult. Serious criticism of any of the ships would reflect on the shipwrights, for all work had been done in their yards. It is not clear how the inspection was made. Eighteen of the ships were at the anchorage near Chatham, and perhaps the shipwrights inspected these. In any case, Baker and Pett reported that many of these ships were old and decayed. Nine other vessels were either docked at Portsmouth or in service at sea. All of these were in good condition. They concluded that the fleet, though flawed, was ready for service, largely because of their own recent construction work.

On the surface, the report seemed to be a factual account, but anyone who knew the ships could see statements that were intentionally misleading. When Hawkins made his own written response, he had the reports both of the shipwrights and of Allen in mind. Far from profiting on the contract, Hawkins said, he had spent all surplus funds on ships and supplies. As a result of his careful stewardship, the royal store of canvas and cordage had tripled in value; there was a greater supply of anchors; pulleys and sheaves of brass had all been refurbished; and sails were mended and renewed. Beyond this, every ship had been reconditioned in dry dock; all the boats and pinnaces were "newmade"; and shops, storehouses, and wharves were repaired and enlarged. Even with the expansion of the naval service, special budget allowances had been necessary only for repairs on four vessels, the *Bonaventure,* the *Foresight,* the *Lion,* and the *Nonpareil.* Rather than squandering money, Hawkins claimed to have been most frugal, both in his personal life and in his work as treasurer of the navy. "I have lyved in a very meane estate synce I came to be an officer," wrote Hawkins." Neyther have I vaynely or sup[er]flously consumyd her ma^{ties} or myne owne substance, but ever byne dyllygently and carefully occupyed to prepare for the danger to come." With this he felt he had said enough. "I wyll speke lyttell in myne owne behallf," he said, adding, "I lay asyde the vanytye of the defendynge of every malycyous report." He asked to have the contract canceled by Christmas, just six weeks away. Perhaps to show his confidence in the fleet, Hawkins requested an appointment to a naval command. If he were given seven royal ships, along with a number of pinnaces and small merchant vessels, he could patrol the entire west coast and prevent an enemy attack.[22]

Ignoring his suggestions once more, Burghley instead asked Winter and Holstocke to report on the condition of the navy and to give their opinion of the manner in which Hawkins had fulfilled his contract.[23] Their report, submitted on 9 December 1587, completely contradicted the previous criticisms. The *Elizabeth Jonas,* the *Triumph,* and the *White Bear,* three old ships described by Pett and Baker as "decayed in the timbers," were actually being renovated in the drydock at Woolwich. Similarly, the *Swallow, Aide, Antelope,* and *Merlin* had all been extensively rebuilt in the dry dock at Deptford. The *Hope,* described by the shipwrights as "an ancient bottom and very near worn," had been "putt in verie good order with great charge at Portsmouthe" in the past two years. There had been complaints that Hawkins had skimped on that part of his contract that had to do with the mooring of ships. Specifically, he was said to be underpaying workmen and using inadequate mooring lines. Winter and Holstocke said this was simply untrue. So far as general maintenance of the vessels was concerned, they said Hawkins had spent "a farre greater somme" on carpentry than had been allowed for in the contract. The two men gave a positive report on the other provisions of the agreement, concluding that Hawkins "hath carefullie perfourmed the condicions of that offer in suche sorte as wee have no cause to complayne of him."[24]

This was not the final word, but it was nearly so. Late in January, Pett and Baker fired a final shot at Hawkins, a long report covering the same complaints as before. Only one difference is worth noting. "Fyve of the greater ships are dep[ar]ted from Chatham very fowle & not grownded," they wrote, "wch is both dangerous, & great hinder to their woorking & sailing." They were talking about the *Hope,* the *Nonpareil,* and the *Revenge,* which Hawkins had sent to Plymouth, along with the *Swiftsure* and the *Aid.* There William Hawkins was to have charge of grounding and tallowing the vessels. Aware of all the criticism directed at his brother, William wrote to say that the ships seemed so solid when he careened them that they might have been carved out of a single

18

Aboard the *Elizabeth Bonaventure,* Hawkins wrote his plan for the defense of the realm. Drawing from the map of Cartagena by Baptista Boazio. This item is reproduced by permission of the Huntington Library, San Marino, California

piece of wood. "The shypes syt agrounde so strongly, & are so stanche, as if they were mad of a holl tree."[25]

Sixteen other royal vessels were stationed at Queenborough under Lord Admiral Charles Howard. Faced with Burghley's growing hostility, and thinking he had been relieved of the contract, Hawkins left for Queenborough, where he took command of the 500-ton *Bonaventure.*[26] On 1 February, aboard his ship, Hawkins directed a letter to Secretary Walsingham, outlining a plan for defense of the realm. The letter is not in his hand nor even in his words, but it is easy to find the parts that represent his thinking. The unknown writer was almost certainly a cleric, perhaps the man who wrote similar letters for Francis Drake. This clerical amanuensis opened the Hawkins letter with a round condemnation of all things Catholic. He recalled for Walsingham "the malycious practises of thye Papistes combynded generally throughout Christendome to allter the governmente of this Reallme and to bring yt to Papistrie, and consequentlye to servitude, povertie and slaverye." Then, observing that good Christians seek peace, he noted that some Christians do not. Those people were interfering with trade and taking markets that ought to belong to English merchants.

The last sentence was surely a Hawkins idea, and some of the words may have been his as well. "Howe dead and uncertaine our Traffiques bee," he said in the letter, "moste men in povertie and discontented. Our navigãcon not sett on worke. But the Ffrenche and Skottes eatt us upp, and growe in wealth and ffraightes, and not assured to us in ffrend shippe." Then remarking that England ought to stop the aid to "forayne Countries," he came to the heart of his plan. A fleet of twelve ships, six small, six large, ought to be stationed on the Spanish coast, victualed for four months. At the end of that time a similar fleet would be sent to replace it. Each fleet would require about 1,800 men and cost no more than £2,700 per month. Like all Hawkins plans, this one would be a profit-making venture, aiming to recover costs, even make a profit, from captured ships and merchandise. "Yt wilbe a verye badde and an unluckie moneth that will not bringe in treble that charge."[27] It was a weakness Hawkins shared with Drake and their contemporaries. They could not see the point of warfare that excluded personal profit.

Naturally, profit was not all Hawkins had in mind. His secretary concluded the letter with another theological excursion:

> In open and lawfull warres god will helpe us for wee defende the chiefe cause, our religion, goddes owne cause; ffor yf wee wold leave our profession and tourne to serve Baal (as god forbidd, and rather to die a thousande deathes) wee might have peace but not with god. By open warres all the subiects of this Reallme sholde knowe what to doe, they

wold not onlye bee satisfied in conscience, but they wold every manne that loveth god, the Queene, and his countrey, contribute, sette forwarde, fighte, devise, and doe somewhat for the lybertye and freedome of this country. By open warres all the Jesuitts & ill affected persons wold be discerned and cutt of from the hope of their malycious practises: many thinges more/ might be said to the preferringe of open warre before a dissembled peace, wch god doth best allowe, and the well affected people of the Realme doe desire even to the spending of a great portion of their substaunce. And therefore I conclude that with gods blessinge and a lawfull open warre, the Lord shall bringe us a moste honourable and quiett peace, to the glorie of his churche, and to the honour of her matie and this Reallme of England, wch god for his mercie sake grant.[28]

Though a skillful businessman, Hawkins lacked a good understanding of the Spanish threat. In his opinion it scarcely mattered that his proposal would split and thus weaken the navy. "A sufficiente companye" would always be at home to thwart the landing of a Spanish army. Besides, Hawkins did not think the Spanish king could mount a successful invasion, "ffor an armye as he provideth cannot continewe eny longe time." As it turned out, no one in the Privy Council agreed with him. Not only was his advice ignored, Hawkins himself was recalled to London to render an account of his performance as treasurer of the navy.[29]

The impetus came from his friends Winter and Burrough, who were alarmed at the thought that no one was in charge of the shipyards. On 17 February they wrote to Lord Admiral Howard, "We know that it wear hard for him to continewe it [the bargain] naie, that he is not able to continewe yt." Even so, they were not sure he had been relieved of responsibility for the navy, and they felt certain the Privy Council did not realize he had relinquished his office. Equally worried, Howard told Borough to send Burghley a copy of the letter. As a result, an order arrived the next day for Hawkins to leave Queenborough. Sick at heart and in body as well, he returned to his home on London's Mincing Lane and stayed there recuperating for another week. While he recovered, the lord admiral wrote to Burghley, praising Hawkins for his work with the ships, and no doubt letting Hawkins have copies of the letters.[30]

By mutual understanding with Burghley, Hawkins resumed control of the ships in harbor. On 3 March he wrote that his health was much improved, and he enclosed copies of several letters attesting to his good work with the ships. He hoped this would contradict the "lewyd brewts" of those who said, "We wyll wery Hawkyns of his bargayne." To the contrary, he felt rejuvenated, for the navy was in good shape. "This shalbe a thinge most manyfest to yor Lship and the hole woreled, that the navye ys in good & stronge estate." Hawkins and Burghley agreed that the old contract was at an end. In its place Hawkins would submit new estimates for the operation of the navy.[31]

For the next several months Hawkins remained at his post, overseeing fleet maintenance and supply. Meanwhile, reports continued to arrive, some describing the unbelievably good condition of the ships, a few others saying they were a hazard to navigation. Howard was effusive in his praise for the ships and for Hawkins, who continued to remind Burghley that the ships were in good condition. With his own recent service in mind Hawkins said, "The Bonadventur, which was condempnyd before yo^{ur} Lship for a decayed ship dothe prove farr contrary." Even so, London gossips made some "hard speeches againste

Mr. Hawkins" when the *Hope* was forced to return because of a bad leak. Howard called it a matter of little consequence. "It was suche a leake that I durste have gon wth yt to Venice."[32]

As the new year opened, English defense plans began to take more definite shape. For some time a belief had flourished in Spain that Francis Drake was head of the English navy, though he was not. In December 1587 Charles Lord Howard of Effingham was confirmed as commander of the fleet, but Drake's name continued to dominate official Spanish reports. Little or nothing was done to counter such misconceptions. Instead, Drake received orders in the middle of March to prepare for a two-month voyage, starting the end of April 1588. Two weeks later he gave the Privy Council his own plan for conducting the war. Apparently written in the same hand as the plan Hawkins had submitted two months earlier and containing many of the same ideas, it was no doubt the product of discussions with Howard, Hawkins, and others. The new proposal was based on the assumption that a great psychological advantage might be gained from striking an early blow against the Spanish fleet. Lacking warships of his own, the duke of Parma could not bring an invasion force from Flanders without substantial help from the Armada then being assembled in Spain. Where Hawkins had suggested a dozen ships, Drake asked the queen for fifty, plus permission to attack the Armada while it was still on the coast of Spain. A blow struck in Spanish waters, if not decisive, would at the very least weaken the determination of Spanish forces and raise morale in England.[33]

Although Spanish agents in England were already saying that Drake had a roving commission and could go wherever and whenever he wished, this was not the case. Royal officials ordered him to keep his fleet at Plymouth while they considered his proposal. When an answer came, it was that he could take half the ships already assigned to him and attack the Spanish vessels sheltered in the harbor at Lisbon. This was not quite what Drake had in mind, and he said so in a letter to the queen. Further discussions followed. Finally, in the middle of May he was summoned to London. There he learned that Lord Admiral Howard would bring his own fleet to Plymouth, leaving Lord Henry Seymour to guard the channel coast where Parma's army was likely to appear. Howard would command the combined fleet at Plymouth, with Drake as vice admiral.[34]

Everyone expected the worst from Drake, but Howard handled the situation with his usual charm and grace and soon had Drake's complete confidence. During the same period Howard worked closely with Hawkins to keep the ships repaired and provisioned. When Howard sailed for Plymouth, Hawkins went along as commander of the *Victory*, leaving a deputy at London in his place.[35] Immediately upon arrival, Howard assembled a council of his most experienced commanders: Hawkins, Drake, Martin Frobisher, and Thomas Fenner. In the first meeting Drake explained his plan for sailing toward Lisbon, where the duke of Medina-Sidonia was gathering his Armada, and the other commanders backed his proposal. Howard quickly yielded to their superior experience.[36]

It was too late. The English fleet left port on 30 May, just as the Spanish Armada cleared Lisbon harbor and sailed away. Gale-force winds battered both fleets. The Armada took refuge in various ports along the coast of Galicia, Asturias, and Vizcaya, while the English ships headed back for Plymouth. Once his ships were resupplied, Howard divided the command. Drake, in the *Revenge*, had a squadron of twenty ships. Hawkins, in the *Victory*, had another twenty, and Howard, in the *Ark Royal*, kept the rest himself. On 19 June the English fleet left port once more, only to be driven back two days later. Again they set out, hearing that the Armada was gathered at La Coruña. Hoping to intercept the advance guard, Howard spread the ships widely but kept close contact between the three divisions. Drake's squadron was on the left, patrolling in the direction of Ushant. Howard kept his own force in midchannel and dispatched Hawkins toward the Scilly Isles.[37] Then the wind changed, and Howard feared his Spanish opponent might use it to reach the coast of England. Consequently, he headed once more for Plymouth. Arriving there on 12 July, he kept his fleet in port for the next few days, refitting and taking on supplies.[38]

While all this was going on, Burghley sent off a constant stream of letters to Plymouth, questioning expenditures, inquiring about the possibility of releasing some men from service, and asking whether all the ships were really seaworthy. Howard answered the accusation of extravagance by saying that Drake and Hawkins would "consider" the matter. But he warned Burghley that warfare was expensive. "Such an army dothe breade sondrie greate and extraordinarie charge." Hawkins wrote as well, boasting that the *Triumph, Elizabeth Jonas, Bear,* and *Victory*—the ships so roundly criticized a few months earlier—were in wonderful condition. "The four great shippes the Trehomphe, the elsabethe Jonas, the Bere, & the Victory are in most royall and p[er]fyctt estate." A minor leak in the *Bear* had stopped of its own accord. "I know ther wilbe reports," he said, "but this ys the trewthe." Along with the letter he sent a requisition for another £19,000 signed by himself and Howard.[39] Then suddenly, on 19 July, before another exasperated reply could come from London, a messenger arrived in Plymouth, saying that the Armada had arrived. The Spanish ships were poised off the Lizard, the southernmost tip of Cornwall, heading for Plymouth.[40]

The Spanish and English fleets were approximately equal in

effective strength. Medina-Sidonia had assembled about 130 ships for his Armada, while Howard and Seymour had about 120 ships between them. Of the total English fleet, Howard had about 90 ships at Plymouth. Many of these were small coasters; scarcely two dozen could be considered major ships of war. Nineteen were queen's ships and the rest armed merchantmen. Of the 30 ships in Seymour's fleet, about half were royal navy vessels. In the Spanish Armada there were about 23 fighting galleons and galleases, the latter heavily armed ships that supposedly combined the maneuverability of a galley with the armament of a galleon. Most of the others were merchant ships, only a few of which proved to be effective in battle. Others were urcas and hulks, transports carrying men and supplies for the invasion.[41]

Armada commanders had a slight advantage in experience. At Lepanto in 1571 and again in the Azores campaign of 1582–83, Spanish captains had worked with fleets of considerable size and armament. This was offset to a certain extent by a ponderous command system and a failure of strategic planning. The Armada was divided into provincial squadrons drawn from Portugal, Castile, Andalucía, Guipúzcoa, Vizcaya, and Levant. In addition, there were special units for hulks, pinnaces, galleases, and galleys.[42]

With orders from King Philip to head straight for the channel and to avoid fighting before then, Medina-Sidonia gave only passing consideration to an attack on Plymouth. Instead, he lay off the Lizard, sending out patrol vessels and assembling his fleet for an advance toward the Isle of Wight. What he intended to do there is not exactly clear, though Wight had been suggested to him as a possible assembly point for the Armada and a possible place to meet Parma's invasion force.[43] With the decision to bypass Plymouth the Spanish commander lost a wonderful opportunity to catch the English fleet while it lay bottled up in the harbor, facing contrary winds and currents.

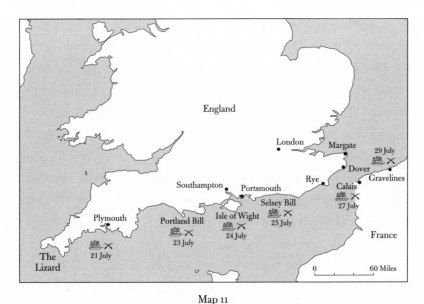

Map 11

Dates for the Armada battles are shown in English style. Spain used the new Gregorian calendar, with corresponding dates from 31 July to 8 August.

Bringing the ships out of Plymouth was hard work. The English sailors took small boats out with their anchors and dropped them far ahead of the ships. The vessels were then drawn forward and the process repeated. By the afternoon of 20 July (30 July by Spanish calculation) little more than half of the English ships were out of port, gathered under the Eddystone, where the lookouts could see the Armada assembling under the Lizard. While the Spanish scouts sailed off to report their progress, the English ships began tacking inshore, working their way westward to meet the enemy. As dawn broke on 21 July the breeze shifted, and the English fleet gained the weather gage of the Armada.[44]

By this time Medina-Sidonia had his ships drawn up in an arc, with the heavily armed vessels in the center, the lighter and faster ships on the projecting ends, ready to envelop the enemy. When he discovered the English fleet coming up from the west, Medina-Sidonia immediately raised his battle flag and ordered the Armada to come about. Exactly who fired the first shot is unclear. Howard had a challenge fired at what he thought was the Spanish flagship, though it was probably the *Santa María* (called *Rata Encoronada*). For a time Hawkins, Frobisher, and Drake exchanged furious rounds of gunfire with a Spanish squadron led by Juan Martínez de Recalde's great galleon *San Juan de Portugal.* Still, the English refused to come in close enough for boarding, and Medina-Sidonia took this to mean that they did not want to fight. After some time spent trying to recover the weather gage, he ordered his fleet to break off and to continue sailing eastward up the channel.[45]

The fight had lasted for less than four hours, with very little damage on either side, except for a couple of shots lodged in the *San Juan*'s foremast. Writing to Burghley a few days later, Hawkins described the first battle as a "smale fight," though the men on both sides came away with new respect for their adversaries. The English commanders, expecting the underpowered artillery they had encountered at Cádiz, were impressed with the number and size of the heavy guns on the enemy ships. The Spanish, though forewarned, were still astonished at the firepower and maneuverability of the English ships.[46]

The most serious loss of the day occurred as the Armada turned about. At five in the evening an explosion reverberated through the fleets. The *San Salvador,* flagship of the Guipúzcoa squadron, had blown up. From survivors fished out of the water, men in both fleets soon learned that the explosion was caused by sabotage. A German artilleryman, angry at what he took to be mistreatment by the Spanish officers, had set a match to a barrel of gunpowder. Everything above decks was destroyed, and many men were killed or horribly burned. After seeing the damage, Medina-Sidonia ordered the able-bodied survivors taken off the ship and had the hulk set adrift, still loaded with an enormous quantity of guns, powder, and shot.[47]

As the *San Salvador* continued to smolder, another ship came to grief. Attempting to come about, the *Nuestra Señora del Rosario* of Don Pedro de Valdés collided with the *Santa Catalina* and lost its bowsprit. As a result, the foremast was loosened and came crashing down against the main yard. As strong westerly winds kept driving the Armada eastward, the *Rosario* began to fall astern. Rather than halt his advance and try to save the *Rosario*, Medina-Sidonia ordered a few ships to stay with the stricken vessel and attempt to take her in tow. It is difficult to understand why he felt obliged to abandon the *Rosario*. For several hours he had been skirmishing with the English ships, trying to force one of them to come to grips with his own ships. Here was another opportunity that he simply failed to recognize.[48]

It was also an opportunity that several English commanders recognized very clearly. Calling the English captains into council, Howard ordered them to follow the Armada at a distance, waiting for the rest of his ships to emerge from Plymouth harbor and come up with the fleet. During the meeting Drake received two assignments. First, he was ordered to send a caravel to Seymour off the coast of Dover, informing him of the arrival of the Spanish fleet. Secondly, he was assigned to lead the pursuit, his stern lantern acting as a marker for the rest of the fleet. Despite these clear orders, Drake had the lantern extinguished and sailed off in the darkness to capture the *Rosario*. As it turned out, an English privateer, the *Margaret and John*, had similar plans. Reaching the *Rosario* before Drake, the crew exchanged a few shots with the stricken vessel, then gave up, deciding their ship was no match for the much larger Spaniard.[49]

With Drake's *Revenge* nowhere in sight, the English fleet was left without a guide. Howard in the *Ark Royal* followed the Spanish fleet, along with the *Bear* and the *Mary Rose*. The other English ships remained behind, waiting for some signal to advance. Drake meanwhile came up to the *Rosario* after dawn and somehow persuaded the Spanish commander to surrender.[50] It was Monday, 1 August, the second day of the running battle.

While not exactly an act of cowardice, the surrender was a great blow to Spanish morale. Don Pedro de Valdés had nearly 350 men on board his heavily armed galleon. The ship was as large as any English galleon, carried nearly fifty great guns, and had a huge supply of ammunition. His capitulation without firing a shot must be seen as the act of a man not terribly eager to fight. Probably the only thing that can be said in his defense is that many in the Spanish fleet thought he had been abandoned without reason.[51]

Surprisingly, the capture of the Spanish ship caused nearly as much consternation in the English navy. The *Rosario* was one of the pay ships of the Armada. Just how much remained in her hold is unclear, though most sources said she had left port with 50,000 gold ducats.[52] Drake later surrendered about half this amount to Howard. Frobisher and others, who wanted a share in the booty, thought that Drake had kept much of the rest for himself, perhaps 15,000 ducats.[53] After removing the treasure and the important prisoners, Drake sent the *Rosario* under escort to Torbay. Although Howard was probably disappointed with his vice admiral, he took no action to censure him, probably thinking that he was acting very much as he had always done.

Unaware of the surrender of Valdés, but no doubt expecting

19

Charles Howard, lord high admiral and commander of the English fleet.
Granger, *Biographical History of England,* vol. 3, part 2, no. 107. This item is
reproduced by permission of the Huntington Library, San Marino, California.

some such development, Medina-Sidonia spent most of the morning revising the battle formation for the Armada. Still formed in the shape of a crescent, the right and left wings of the fleet became a rearguard of forty-three of the strongest galleons and galleasses. Medina-Sidonia with the rest of the fleet composed the vanguard. Once these arrangements were completed, the Spanish commander sent a message to Parma, warning him that the Armada was approaching the channel and asking for pilots to guide them along the Flemish coast.[54]

It was late Monday evening before the stragglers caught up with Howard, who with a few other ships trailed close behind the Spanish fleet. The English captains found that their admiral had not been idle. The *San Salvador,* heavily damaged by fire the day before, was abandoned by the able-bodied members of the Spanish crew, who went aboard other ships in the Armada. Howard sent John Hawkins and Lord Thomas Howard in a skiff from the *Victory* to inspect the derelict vessel. They found most of the superstructure gone, but the hull was still sound, as was much of the cargo of powder and shot. Many wounded men, horribly burned, for the most part, were still on the ship, which reeked with the stink of charred flesh. All of the wounded seem to have been left aboard a bit longer, while the vessel was towed into Weymouth the following day.[55]

The fleets lay becalmed that night, but on Tuesday morning, 23 July, the wind came up from the northeast, giving the Armada the weather gage. As the English fleet moved toward shore, the Spanish came down to intercept it. Several Spanish ships sailed in close to grapple. The *Regazona* came very near the *Ark Royal,* which quickly moved to leeward and out to sea. Hawkins on the *Victory,* along with the *Nonpareil* and the *Elizabeth Jonas,* immediately moved up to assist the *Ark Royal,* but help proved unnecessary, as the Spanish ships were forced south by the swift currents of the Portland Race and fell astern of the English vessels.[56]

Meanwhile, several other English ships came under threat off Portland Bill. Seeing that these vessels were separated from the main fleet, several Spanish galleasses moved in to attack. The battle lasted for about an hour and a half, but again the Spanish were unable to get close enough to board the English ships. At length the wind shifted once more, and Howard was able to bring up his larger galleons. Medina-Sidonia in the *San Martín* then moved in to grapple with Howard in the *Ark Royal*, but the heavier fire and the superior maneuverability of the English ship again drove the Spanish off. When the wind shifted once more to give the English ships the weather gage, the Spanish vessels broke off the fight and sailed east.[57]

As dawn broke on Wednesday, 24 July, the English ships could see an armed Spanish merchant vessel, the *Gran Grifón*, straggling behind the rest. With a light morning wind, the English galleons hastened to catch up with the wallowing ship. One heavily armed Englishman, unnamed in the reports, came swiftly across the beam of the *Gran Grifón* and loosed a broadside at her. Turning about, the English galleon then came across her stern and again raked the ship with heavy fire. Not wanting another *Rosario*, Medina-Sidonia quickly dispatched his galleasses to take the *Grifón* in tow. The Spanish admiral then tried to engage the English vessels in a general battle, but they withdrew out of range once more.[58]

It was a stunning maneuver at close range by a daring sea captain. The ship was almost certainly Drake's *Revenge*.[59] The Spanish relief forces, taking the attacker under heavy fire, managed to destroy the "entena del arbol mayor," either the main topmast or the main yard. A survey of the Queen's ships made in October 1588 found the mainmast of the *Revenge* "decayed & periyshed w^t shott."[60] It was not a crippling blow, but Drake found it necessary to take the *Revenge* out of action for a short time in order to make repairs.

While inflicting comparatively little real damage on either side, the heavy fire from the guns had cost both fleets an enormous amount of powder and shot. As a result Howard sent orders to have the powder and shot removed from the two prizes and parceled out among the ships of the fleet. Howard was also becoming aware of the tactical differences between his own disorganized fleet and the highly disciplined Armada. As his fleet was reassembled, Howard took the opportunity to organize it into four attack squadrons. The four commanders were Howard himself, Sir Francis Drake, John Hawkins, and Martin Frobisher.[61]

Medina-Sidonia also regrouped his fleet. Then, following another council with his captains, he decided to pause in the anchorage off the Isle of Wight until some word was received from Parma concerning the date and place for a meeting. In order to improve his own tactical mobility, he rearranged the rearguard of the Armada in two squadrons, adding Leyva's vanguard to the rearguard previously commanded by Recalde. With the rearguard sailing in a crescent formation and the other ships in an arc, English accounts described the new Armada formation as a roundel. Having accomplished this reorganization, Medina-Sidonia then proceeded with his Armada toward the eastern entrance of the Solent.[62]

On Thursday morning, 25 July (4 August in the Spanish accounts), Hawkins with his newly designated squadron sighted the Portuguese galleon *San Luís* and the Andalusian hulk *Duquesa Santa Ana* becalmed and lying somewhat to the rear of the rest of the Armada. With small boats he began to tow his galleons into firing range, pulling close enough to rake the *San Luís* with musket shot. It was a trap.[63] As soon as the English ships opened fire, three Spanish galleasses headed for the two threatened vessels. There was a furious exchange of gunfire, but Hawkins and his men managed to keep the Spanish relief vessels out of grappling distance. The English commanders thought the Spanish ships took heavy losses. However, the galleasses were able to take the *San Luís* and *Santa Ana* in tow, and none of the ships was badly damaged.[64]

Meanwhile, Frobisher used the currents to work his squadron around the landward end of the Armada, where his *Triumph* engaged Medina-Sidonia in a gun duel. For a time it looked as though his ship was disabled, when a shot knocked the rudder loose. Just as the Spanish ships closed in for boarding, the wind came up a bit, and Frobisher managed to pull away. Two Spanish vessels gave chase, and Frobisher led them clear around the Armada. With his extra speed he easily kept ahead of his pursuers and escaped with little permanent damage.[65]

The other action of the day occurred in the center of the Armada. There Howard's *Ark Royal* very nearly penetrated the Spanish line, forcing Medina-Sidonia to retreat to the east and abandon his attempt to enter the Solent. Having accomplished this, the English fleet broke off the battle, intending to save powder and shot for the expected fight near Dover. During the lull of the next two days Howard received "men, powder, shot, victuals, and ships" from forts along the coast. Still shadowing the Armada, he took advantage of the respite to call his principal officers into council. There he conferred the order of knighthood on Hawkins and Frobisher, as a reward for their gallant service the previous day.[66]

Medina-Sidonia was in a quandary. None of his messages to Parma had brought an answer. He had not the slightest idea what

Parma was doing or where he wanted to meet. Having failed to reach a haven at the Isle of Wight, Medina-Sidonia headed instead for Calais, where he could anchor and arrange a rendezvous with Parma. Some of his men were growing doubtful about the whole affair and were beginning to think the invasion plans ought to be abandoned. Faced with this uncertain future, the Spanish admiral asked Parma to send some fighting vessels and to embark his men in preparation for the channel crossing. A reply finally came. Parma said that he could not be ready for another week. Moreover, the anchorage at Calais was hazardous, but a move farther up the channel would be more so, for the winds could easily drive the Armada into the North Sea.[67]

On Saturday, 27 July (6 August in Spanish accounts), both fleets reached Calais. The Armada sighted the French coast about ten in the morning and anchored off Calais at about 6 P.M. The English fleet, reinforced by Seymour's squadron, reached Calais Cliffs at nearly the same time. With about 140 ships under his own command, Howard realized that the Armada was in a serious predicament. He summoned Sir William Winter, who commanded one of the newly arrived ships. According to his own account, Winter observed that the Armada was in a position where fire ships would be very effective. Howard was delighted with the idea, which promised to disperse the Spanish ships at the cost of only a few expendable English vessels. Medina-Sidonia's command was crowded into an open roadstead, with the treacherous Flemish shoals to the leeward. At a council of war on Sunday morning, 26 July, the English captains accepted Winter's suggestion and determined to send eight burning ships into the closely anchored Spanish fleet.[68]

Eight merchant vessels, one of them Drake's *Thomas,* were packed with combustibles, and their guns were loaded, ready to fire when the flames should reach the touch-holes. As it turned out there was no chance for secrecy. Medina-Sidonia knew about the "Hellburners of Antwerp" that had put fear into Parma's soldiers three years earlier, and he warned his captains to set out boats to take fire ships in tow and move them out of the way. Moreover, the English sailors were careless, setting two of the ships alight before they left the fleet and thus notifying the Spanish vessels that an attack was coming. Despite this warning, several of the English fire ships got through the Spanish picket boats. Medina-Sidonia ordered his captains to move out of the way, and in something approaching panic, the Spanish ships simply cut their mooring lines and sailed off.[69] It was the decisive moment in the running battle.

Every one of the fire ships drifted ashore without exploding or setting fire to a single Armada vessel. Even so, they accomplished their purpose. Once under way the fleeing Spanish ships fell into the grip of high winds and strong tides that forced them out of the anchorage. A few ships were able to turn about and reenter the anchorage, but most drifted off in the direction of Dunkirk. In the confusion the flag galleass *San Lorenzo* suffered a damaged rudder and mainmast and was forced to head for shore. Caught in a falling tide, the *San Lorenzo* ran aground at the entrance to Calais, where English gunboats promptly pounced on the luckless ship. With the vessel heeled over to one side, its guns were useless, and a boarding party from Admiral Howard's flagship sacked the vessel.[70]

On Monday morning, 29 July (8 August by Spanish calculation), Medina-Sidonia found himself out of the roadstead, a few miles off Calais, with four ships in his company and the English fleet bearing down for the attack. He fired a signal cannon to call the other ships to his assistance, and most of the fighting ships then turned about. Lord

Admiral Howard was still involved with the *San Lorenzo,* so Drake brought his squadron forward. His *Revenge* fired the first shot at the *San Martín,* opening the Battle of Gravelines. For nine hours the battle raged, while the fleets drifted between Gravelines and Ostend. Other ships soon closed in, firing so furiously that it was impossible to see more than one or two ships at a time through the smoke. Eventually as many as thirty-two of the Armada's fighting ships managed to join the formation, against a somewhat larger number of English ships. Fighting was done at a such a close range that men on opposing sides could shout and curse at one another and fire muskets between the ships.[71]

In the course of the battle both Spanish and English ships felt for the first time the real effect of the enemy artillery. The Spanish flagship *San Martín* took more than a hundred hits in her hull, masts, and sails, with several shots below the water line that caused serious leaks. Two Spanish galleons, *San Felipe* and *San Mateo,* hoping to grapple with the enemy, worked their way past the battle line and into a nest of ships from Frobisher's squadron. On the *San Felipe* five guns were out of action, decks very nearly destroyed, pumps broken, and rigging in shreds. Seeing this, her captain broke out the grappling hooks and challenged the English sailors to come alongside and fight hand-to-hand. When they would not, his crew shouted out that they were "Cowards" and "Lutheran chickens" and drove the English ships away with musket fire.[72]

Much of the action took place on the left and in the center, where the *San Mateo* was surrounded by English galleons and riddled with English shot. Her own cannons very nearly finished the work of the English gunners, as the recoil began to pull the hull apart. Unable to keep up with the Armada, both the *San Mateo* and the *San Felipe* were beached by their commanders between Nieuwpoort and Ostend. A third Spanish ship, the *María Juan,* was badly damaged during the fighting. As relief ships came up to take off the survivors, the ship suddenly sank with most of the crew. These are the losses that are known, but other ships may have been sunk or driven ashore. It is not clear which of the English ships inflicted the most damage. In Peter Pierson's reconstruction of the battle, the *San Mateo* and the *San Felipe* were surrounded by elements of Frobisher's, Seymour's, and Drake's squadrons. Hawkins and his squadron on the right flank of the fleet stayed in the battle all day. "In this fight," he reported in one of the great understatements of the campaign, "ther was some hurt done amonge the Spaniards." For reasons that are not entirely clear, Drake remained at Gravelines only for the first hour or so, then withdrew, probably to take his Spanish prisoners to the safety of an English port.[73]

By 31 July, when Hawkins penned his remarks, the English fleet was tracking the Armada in a heavy storm northward out of the channel and into the North Sea. From his own observations, together with information obtained from prisoners, Hawkins was able to construct one of the first accurate reports on the numbers of ships and men in the Armada. He also reported that the troops on Medina-Sidonia's ships were simply supplements to the actual invasion force that was to be supplied by Parma. The Spanish had left Lisbon on 19 May with six months' rations, so they probably had some supplies left. "This is the greatest and strongst cōbiñacōn to my understanding," he wrote to Walsingham, "that ever was gethered in christendome." Hawkins concluded that the Armada was still capable of a fight, and Medina-Sidonia might yet manage to carry Parma's army to the English coast.[74]

This is exactly what the Spanish commander proposed to do. During a council on 30 July, Medina-Sidonia determined that if he

IOANNES

HAWKINS

Aduancement by
diligence

Qui vicit toliens in fluctis classibus hostes
Ille vagis HAVKINS vitam relliquit in vndis

20

Engraved portrait of John Hawkins, from Holland's *Herωologia Anglica* (1620),
probably based on the Boissard engraving (1618), now in the Plymouth Museum.
Note the ring in his left ear. This item is reproduced by permission of the
Huntington Library, San Marino, California.

encountered favorable winds he would go back to Calais. Otherwise, he would sail north, around Scotland and Ireland, and return to Spain. With this in mind he made one more attempt to bring the English fleet into a close battle. On 31 July 1588 he turned his flagship about and ordered signal guns fired so the rest of his ships would join him. Perhaps a dozen responded. He fired another gun and still another with the same result.[75]

Although the English ships held back, lacking sufficient ammunition for another fight, Medina-Sidonia was in a rage. When he managed to gather the Armada once more, he convened a court-martial and sentenced twenty captains to hang. Only one was actually executed, but the others received a lesson in obedience. Two days later, with the wind still driving the Armada north, the English fleet broke off and headed for home. The Armada continued on its course around Scotland.[76]

This was the end of the invasion attempt. Though battle weary and weathered, the Armada was still in no worse shape than the English fleet. But Medina-Sidonia was unable to join Parma, so the great effort to invade England came to nothing. There were reasons for the Spanish failure, inadequate armament and outmoded ship design among them. But the most important reason was organization. The administrative processes of the sixteenth century were insufficient for such a complex undertaking, and this led to the eventual destruction of the Armada. In the ensuing weeks Medina-Sidonia sent his fleet along the coasts of Scotland and Ireland. Battered by storms, many ships were driven ashore, and only about half of them actually made port again in Spain.

The English were more effectively organized. With a relatively modest budget Hawkins had turned the naval ships of an island nation into a fighting force that could challenge the great Spanish empire. For a year or two Hawkins had toyed with Spanish offers to defect. Finally abandoning this attempt, he worked for years to restore his good name and show himself a loyal Englishman. His allegiance became clear in the Armada campaign, where he was knighted for bravery and leadership. Hawkins himself declined to write or speak about these accomplishments. Confident of his own bravery and seamanship, he assumed that they were equally obvious to others. He fought valiantly as one of the leading commanders in the fleet he had prepared for the queen. In the end this is what began to restore his reputation and silence his critics.

9

There Is No Other Hell

And so began to gather my companie aboord, which occupied
my good friends, and the Iustices of the Towne two dayes, and forced
vs to search all Lodgings, Tavernes, and Ale-houses. (For some would
ever be taking their leaue and never depart:) some drinke themselues
so drunke, that except they were carried aboord, they of themselues
were not able to goe one steppe: others knowing the necessitie of
the time, fayned themselues sicke; others, to be indebted to their
Hostes, and forced me to ransome them; one his Chest;
another, his Sword; another, his Shirts; another, his
Carde and Instruments for Sea.

Richard Hawkins

T he English fleet headed for home on 2 August (12
August by Spanish calculation), leaving some pinnaces to shadow the Armada as far as Fair Isle. The
plan was to land at Harwich, Margate, and Dover,
where the ships could be resupplied, and a lookout
could be kept for the reappearance of the Armada. By the time the fleet
reached port, most of the ships had exhausted their supplies. Then a
sort of plague swept through the ranks, and men died by the dozens.
On 22 August, Howard wrote to the Privy Council from Dover, saying
that so many men were sick that some ships could not weigh their
anchors. Whatever the disease, it spread quickly. "The Infecsion is
growne very great," Howard wrote to the queen. "Those that comme in
freshe are sonest infected they secken the one day and dy the nexte."[1]

Through all these troubles Hawkins continued to get letters from
London nagging him about expenditures. When he reached Harwich

on 8 August, he found food and everything else in short supply. There was no money to pay off the men, so they had to be kept in service. Meanwhile, Burghley asked why so much money was needed if so many men were dying. "I marvell th^t wher so many ar dead on th^e seas the paye is not dead wth them." With great patience Hawkins answered, explaining that it was necessary to give the back pay of dead men to their friends, who would deliver it to the families. At last Howard wrote to Burghley, suggesting an end to complaints. "My good lo[rd] this is as muche as is posyble for Mr Hawkynse to dow at this tyme."[2]

The lord treasurer's response was not good. Exactly what he had to say is unclear, but the general tenor can be seen in the reply by Hawkins. "I am sorry I do lyve so long as to reseave so sharp a letter from y^r Lship." Apparently the complaint was that Hawkins had simply asked for money without providing details, including names of ships, numbers of men, date and place of service, numbers discharged for illness, new recruits, and so forth. "Your Lship hathe many p[ar]tyculers of them and ther nombers," he answered. "Notw^{t}standyng I do send yor Lship all those agayne." Beyond this, Burghley objected to some of the payments customary in the navy. For example, officers were entitled to dead-shares for deceased members of their command. Hawkins insisted he did not take such payments. "I never yet knew any peny proffytt by sea books, nor know not what a ded pay meanethe."[3]

Most of the ships needed repairs. Some of them were close to sinking. The ordnance and ballast were taken out of the *Hope,* and the ship was grounded for major repairs. The *Bear* had a bad leak low in the hull. Even so, the lord admiral ordered Hawkins to bring his ships to Dover so that the fleet could send out patrols off Margate and the Downs. When the ships arrived, Howard went to London to report in person. Not yet convinced that the danger was past, Howard thought the fleet was being too swiftly demobilized. Lords Thomas Howard, Seymour, and Sheffield went with him to London, while Hawkins, Frobisher, and Winter were left in charge of the ships.[4] The main concerns were to discharge the men, pay the contractors, and put the ships into some sort of order for quick recall to sea duty.

There was no organizational structure in the Elizabethan navy to handle expenditures on such a vast scale, so Hawkins organized six "companyes" to pay the men. Holstock assigned two of his clerks, as did Burrough. William Winter and William Hawkins helped supervise payments. Sir Francis Drake had been sent to Plymouth with his fleet, so the officers of the navy appointed a special clerk to handle the books for Drake's ships. "I have six of mine own company that attend the pay," said Hawkins, "so I furnyshe vi companyes." Hawkins paid off those he could, and made special grants to the sick and needy. As the crews were paid off, he sent the ships to Chatham, but he ran out of money with many men still unpaid.[5]

For a few days bad weather kept Hawkins from going to the various ships to check the books and count the men still in service, as Burghley wanted. He could only guess at those who were still at sea. Finally on 4 September the entire fleet assembled in the Downs, and within a couple of hours Hawkins had a full report for Burghley. Of the great fleet assembled at Plymouth scarcely two months earlier, there remained only thirty-three ships and 4,453 men. Even these, Hawkins warned, were "utterly unfyttyd" for service "w^{t}out a thorrough new trymynge, refreshynge & new fornyshyng w^t provycons, growndyng, & freshe men."[6]

Casting about for a way to find the money she needed, the queen thought of Drake and his proven method for increasing the royal revenue. At her urging Walsingham asked Howard to consider sending Drake to the Azores to intercept the Spanish treasure ships coming from the West Indies. With some difficulty Howard explained that Drake was ill, that his ships were unfit for a long journey, and that going to the Azores was not the same as a day spent crossing the channel. Seeing that the authorities in London had little understanding of the real situation, Hawkins began once more to beg for release from the Navy Board. "I wold to god I were delyveryd of the deling for mony," he wrote to Walsingham. "God I trust wyll delyver me of it er[e] yt be long for ther ys no other helle." To Burghley he wrote, "Yf I had any enymy I wold wyshe hym no more harme then the course of my troblesome & paynfull lyffe."[7]

Despite these protests, Hawkins was not relieved from duty as treasurer of the navy. Instead he was told to prepare some of the royal ships for a raid on Spanish ports. The new expedition evolved from discussions between the queen and her counselors on the one hand and Drake, Sir John Norris, and Dom Antonio on the other. Numerous other men were involved, but these were the ones who ultimately took charge of things. As usual, it was to be a profit-making venture, with private investors and royal ships. The queen would contribute several thousand soldiers, half a dozen ships, and £20,000 in cash. Merchants and other investors would contribute twenty ships and £40,000 and would try to find additional support in the United Provinces of the Low Countries.[8] Drake and Norris were given a joint commission to "invade and destroy" those unnamed enemies who "this last year both by sea and by land with their hostile and warly powers sought and attempted the invasion of our realm of England." Authority was divided fairly evenly. Drake would command the navy, and Norris would lead the land forces.[9] Over the next few months, plans changed, and the fleet increased in size. At one point the Dutch decided not to participate, though they ultimately did help. Of more importance, objectives began to diverge. The queen began to see the expedition as a way to destroy the Armada survivors that had taken refuge in Spanish ports, even while Drake and Norris began planning to invade Portugal and put Dom Antonio on the throne. As it turned out, there was no attack on the Spanish fleet. Instead, Drake and Norris expended much time and effort in a pointless attack on La Coruña. The army then landed at Peniche and made an agonizing overland march to Lisbon. There was heavy fighting around Lisbon, but the city did not fall, largely because Drake either would not or could not bring his vessels upriver to support the attack. Upon their return the two commanders were summoned to London to face formal charges and a very angry queen.[10]

While Drake and Norris were at sea, great changes came to the Navy Board. William Winter died, and Sir Henry Palmer was appointed to his post as surveyor of the ships. Benjamin Gonson Junior took Borough's place as clerk of the ships. Hawkins continued as treasurer, while Borough assumed William Holstocke's post as comptroller of the ships.[11] Earlier Hawkins had asked for help to put his accounts into shape. Consequently, Edward Fenton, a relative of the Gonson family by marriage, was appointed as his deputy.[12] These changes indicate a marked improvement in Burghley's attitude toward his overworked naval treasurer. Recently Winter had submitted a letter of mild criticism about the expenditures made by Hawkins as treasurer of the navy, but the alleged abuses were negligible. Burghley gave it only a cursory review, then dropped the matter without any further action.[13]

As soon as Drake and Norris returned, Hawkins submitted his own plan to Lord Burghley, describing a way "to have peace (as it becomethe good Christians)." This was not evidence of John Hawkins converted. The plan was the same one he had sent to Walsingham a year and a half earlier—same ships, same men, and the same objectives. Moreover, the proposal was not especially peaceable. In his original submission Hawkins had said the best course would be "to seke our pece by a determynyd and resolute warre." In his new letter Hawkins predicted that an aggressive attitude on the part of England would eventually move Spain to sue for peace.[14]

The letter that accompanied his proposal was probably a draft. It was poorly developed and in part contradictory, though some of the fault may lie with the clerk who wrote it out for Hawkins. In one sentence he offered to lead the fleet himself and perhaps to die in the service of God, the queen, and England. "I shall never be abell to end my dayes in a more godly cawse for the churche of god, a more dewtyfull service to her ma^tie, or a more p[ro]fytable service for our contry." Still, Hawkins was sure his offer would bring others of greater ability to volunteer for command in his place. This would not really disappoint him, he claimed, since he held no grudge against Spain and no longer wanted to avenge the loss at San Juan de Ulúa. "Tyme hathe made me to forgett yt, & refferre yt to god who ys the avenger of wronges."[15]

As if this were not contradiction enough, Hawkins ended the letter with a humble offer to lead the fleet anyway, if this should be Her Majesty's wish. Besides, his accounts would be up to date by the end of July, so he would then be free to go to sea. "And tochyng myne owne contentacon, in my wyffe, my frynds, or any other wordly matter, as well pleasyd & contentyd as I desyre, all wch I lay a syde & forgoe, yf yt shalbe thought welle by her ma^tie that I shall provyde in this service; wch I doupt not but our good god shall blesse w^t a happy successe, beyng intendyd cheffly for his glory."[16]

The draft was penned so nicely that Hawkins did not trouble to have it recopied. Instead, he sent it along to the lord treasurer, unsigned but with an attached note initialed "J.H." Burghley probably surprised Hawkins by treating this casual offer seriously. Other English fleets were already at sea, or nearly so. The earl of Cumberland had the *Victory* and a few armed merchant ships searching for the Indies fleet. Cumberland found the fleet, but not quickly enough. The Spanish ships ran for cover under the guns of Angra in the island of Terceira. There they unloaded the treasure, then waited until near-starvation forced Cumberland to sail for home. Frobisher took a similar voyage in the fall of 1589 with a slightly larger fleet and slightly more success, capturing a few ships and coming home with a profit. A Hawkins ship, the 300- or 400-ton *Repentance,* was part of this fleet and managed to capture ships loaded with valuable cargoes of clapboards and iron. The owners claimed neutrality, and after action in admiralty court, Hawkins was directed to restore everything to them. With years of experience in taking ships at sea, Hawkins knew how to delay and proceeded to do just that. Finally exasperated, the Privy Council ordered him to return the goods or their value forthwith, "all other excuses layd a parte."[17]

Late in September 1589 Hawkins finished assembling the accounts of his expenditures for the past eleven years. These went to Burghley, along with a projection of expenditures for the rest of 1589. Several new ships were under construction, but with the account problem nearing solution and a newly pliable Navy Board installed, Hawkins suddenly seemed to have naval matters well in hand.[18] With verbal approval from Burghley, Hawkins began to get six warships and four pinnaces ready for the sea. The work had hardly started, however, when another personal blow landed on Hawkins. His brother William, visiting in the Hawkins home at Chatham, sickened and died on 7

October 1589. He was buried in the chancel of the church at Deptford, and Hawkins erected a monument there with this inscription:

Sacræ perpetuæq; Memoriæ Gulielmi
Haukyns, de Plymouth
Armigeri
Qui veræ Religionis verus cultor, Pauperibus Præcipue
Nauiculariis Munificus, Rerum Nauticarum studiosis-
simus, longinquas instituit sæpe Nauigationes; Arbiter in
causis difficilimis Æquisimus, Fide, Probitate & Prudentia
singulari. Duas duxit Vxores, e quarum una 4. ex altera 7.
suscepit liberos.
Johannes Haukyns Eques Auratus, Classis Regiae Quæstor,
Frater Mœstissimus posuit.
Obiit Spe certa Resurgendi 7. die mensis
Octobris, An. Dom. 1589.

Hawkins could not read this himself, but he knew what it said: "Sacred to the eternal memory of William Hawkins of Plymouth, gentleman. A true believer in the true religion, especially generous to poor seamen, learned in things of the sea, often away on lengthy voyages, the fairest judge in the most difficult causes, standing alone in faith, honesty, and prudence. He had two wives, by one of whom he had four children and by the other seven."[19]

Still intent on the voyage, within a month Hawkins had the vessels at Chatham undergoing repairs. Their names were the *Ark Royal,* 800 tons; the *Mary Rose,* 600 tons; the *Nonpareil,* 500 tons; the *Swiftsure,* 400 tons; and the *Foresight,* 300 tons.[20] The work was finished by the first of the year. Supposing that a quick thrust at Angra might drop the offloaded Spanish treasure into his hands, Hawkins urged the Privy

Council once more to approve his voyage. On 23 February 1590 the council debated his request but decided that it would be "unmeet for him to goe." The main reason was uncertainty about Spanish intentions, as Burghley's notes make clear.

1   The tyme far spent to goe out now
2   The nombre to fewe to acheve any thing to the annoyance of the armye of Spayne
3   The Shipps will growe fowle and subiect to other accidents
4   The shipps may misse the spa. armye

Dissatisfaction with rising naval costs was an added factor.[21] There were anchors, cables, cordage, dozens of new sails, hundreds of mariners, sailors, gunners, carpenters, provisions for six months, and a host of other things, all of which would have to come from royal stores.[22]

The reports Hawkins submitted in September were approved by Burghley, who assured Hawkins that he was completely satisfied. But Queen Elizabeth was not pleased. Increasingly irascible as she got older, the queen vented her wrath at Hawkins. Apparently in his presence, she complained about the money he demanded for the navy and said that someone ought to audit his accounts. Burghley assured her that the records had already been checked and approved, but she was not appeased. Her outburst was probably nothing more than Queen Elizabeth keeping one of her officers on his toes, but Hawkins was thoroughly shaken. "I thynke ther ys no man lyvinge that hathe so carefull, so myserable so unfortunate, and so dangerous a lyfe," he told Burghley later. He could almost see himself in prison, were it not for Burghley's renewed support. "I wold even playnely gyve over my place, and submyt myselfe to her mat^ies mercye, though I lyvid in pryson all the dayes of my lyffe." Still, he did not want to leave office under a cloud. He would rather prove to the queen that he had done his work honestly and efficiently; then he could let someone else take the job. "My onely desyre ys that yt may please hir Maiestie some course may be taken wherein hir Maiestie may be sattysfied that a playne and honest course hathe byne taken and caryed in thoffice and then to dyspose of my place to whome yt shall please hir Highnes."[23] For her own part, the queen probably wanted nothing more than to convince Hawkins that he should keep working and watch expenses.

A false alarm finally brought the approval Hawkins wanted. Late in April reports reached London that a great Spanish fleet was assembling off Cape Finisterre. In urgent meetings the Privy Council ordered a general mobilization.[24] During the first few days of May 1590 Elizabeth signed an order sending Hawkins to sea for six months, issuing a similar order to Martin Frobisher at the same time.[25] They would command fleets of approximately equal strength. The six ships and two pinnaces in Frobisher's command carried 1,230 men. The six ships commanded by Hawkins had a complement of 1,340 men. Frobisher was probably given the pinnaces because he was heading for the shallow ports in the Azores. Hawkins was to sail near Cape Finisterre and watch for a new armada heading for England, France, Ireland, or Scotland. If he found such a fleet, he was to send a message back immediately. But if nothing appeared after "some reasonable time," then Hawkins might go off on the sort of raid he had originally proposed. "Yo^w maye Raunge the Coaste of Spaine where yo^w shall thinke fitteste, to Impeache such as traffique in and oute uppon that Coaste." Perhaps with Drake in mind, the queen directed Hawkins to follow the orders strictly "untill yo^w shalbe putte at libertie by writinge from us to followe your owne Adventure."[26]

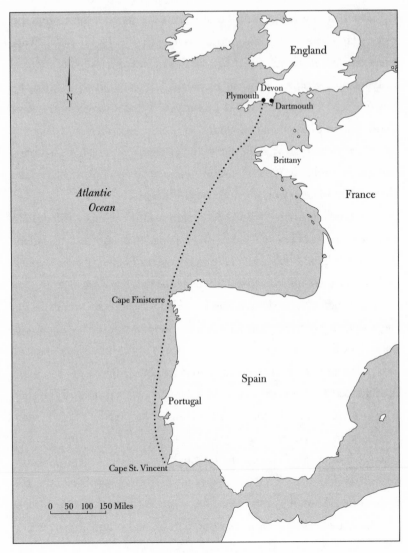

Map 12
The area where Hawkins sailed in 1590.

With the addition of Frobisher's squadron, there was a reshuf-
fling of ships. Frobisher would have the *Revenge,* which Richard
Hawkins called an "unfortunate" ship, though it had been Frobisher's

flagship for a time in 1589. Along with this he took the *Golden Lion,* the *Elizabeth Bonaventure,* the *Dreadnought,* the *Crane,* and the *Quittance,* as well as the pinnaces *Moon* and *Marlin.* Hawkins had the *Mary Rose* for his flagship, plus the *Hope,* in place of the *Revenge,* and the *Ark Royal.* He also had the *Nonpareil,* the *Rainbow,* the *Swiftsure,* and the *Foresight,* as originally planned.[27]

The fleets assembled as usual in Plymouth, where they took on provisions for four months, no doubt at some profit for the Hawkins family. The seamen boarded ship on 25 May, and both fleets left port immediately thereafter.[28] On orders from the Privy Council, Hawkins and Frobisher scouted the seas close to Plymouth. At first the orders extended until 10 June, later until the fifteenth, and finally until the end of the month, just in case the expected invasion fleet should appear.[29]

One part of the instructions called for the interdiction of naval stores coming to Spain from the Baltic and elsewhere. Hawkins and Frobisher interpreted this as a license to seize any merchant ships from the Netherlands, France, or the Hanseatic ports. Late in June on the coast of Portugal, the *Swiftsure* took three ships loaded with spices, cochineal, iron, and wine. On 3 July, Hawkins brought them into Plymouth, saying that he had found incriminating letters on board proving that the vessels were in the service of Spain.[30] For several months the Privy Council fielded protests from the owners of these ships and other irate and perhaps innocent merchants. Safely at sea most of the time, the two commanders remained oblivious to the whole matter, while their agents at Plymouth disposed of the ships and cargoes in complete defiance of the council's orders.[31]

Other cargoes were captured by private merchant ships making their customary forays into the channel. Merchant investors were not directly involved in the two expeditions, but Hawkins, Frobisher, and others had their own ships raiding under the protection of the royal fleets. One of the Hawkins ships was the *Dainty*, a ship of 300 to 400 tons built late in 1588 in a shipyard on the Thames. The vessel was at Deptford the following spring when the queen saw it from her barge. After being told that it was called the *Repentance*, she insisted that the ship looked much too graceful for such a ponderous name, and she immediately rechristened it *Dainty*.[32]

By the middle of summer the Spanish threat seemed to be over, but October brought news of another Spanish fleet assembling on the coast of Brittany. The council therefore ordered Hawkins back to the coast of Devon, extended the term of service by two months, and provided additional supplies.[33] Nothing much came of this, except that Hawkins was home in Plymouth when another blistering letter came from the lords of the Privy Council. He had confiscated a cargo of cochineal and some leather hangings. After protests were lodged, the lords ordered Hawkins to restore it all to the owners. He did as he was ordered, then seized the ship once more, as soon as it put to sea. He then wrote to Burghley, explaining that there were so many conflicting orders, he was not certain what to do. The lords directed Hawkins to give it back once more "without any further delaie or excuse." They added a solemn warning, "You will answere the contrarie at your per- ill." Even so, Hawkins kept the cochineal for another month in his ware- house at Plymouth. There he had some of it mixed with cheaper dyes and repacked in the original cases. What the owners got back in December was an adulterated shipment of the same size, and Hawkins had some cochineal for sale.[34]

The Hawkins voyage of summer 1590 was generally regarded as a failure, because both Hawkins and Frobisher failed to capture ships from the Indies. A contemporary document reported erroneously, "They could not possesse themselves of one shipp," and Hawkins himself reported to Burghley much the same thing. "I dyd refrayne to wryt to yor Lship, for that I ever hopyd upon some notable thynge to come into our hands, but this yt hathe pleasyd god to delle w^t us that we mett w^t nothynge."[35] This was only partially correct. For Hawkins personally the venture was a great commercial success, because his *Dainty* and several other privately owned ships brought in rich cargoes. Part of this was shared with the queen, though only after great arguments. Having contributed heavily to finance the fleet that fought the Armada, the coastal merchants were not in a mood to share their wealth again.

In this as in his other sea voyages, Hawkins apparently had the services of a chaplain, who also acted as his secretary. In a formal report on the voyage, he elaborated somewhat on his lack of success. "Gods infallyble word ys p[re]servyd," he wrote, "in that the holy gost sayd paule dothe plant, appollo dothe waster, but god gyvethe the increase." According to one popular story, probably not true, Queen Elizabeth was as disgusted with the letter as she was with the voyage. "God's death," she exclaimed. "This fool went out a soldier and is come home a divine."[36] In fact, the gloomy report Hawkins had submitted was a little premature.

Only a few days after confessing failure Hawkins wrote once more to Burghley, crowing about success. The *Dainty* had just come into Dartmouth harbor with a huge Spanish ship taken off Cape St. Vincent. The cargo was oil, wine, iron, velvet, and silk, plus ten bags and a barrel of silver reals worth £1,500. "When man is weakest god is strongest," he reported piously to the lord treasurer, enclosing a description of the rich cargo. Perhaps of equal value were the hundred or so Portuguese and Spanish prisoners. "Nowe at last god hathe done somewhat for us," Hawkins told the lord admiral, noting that the prisoners would be kept in Plymouth castle until he could exchange them for Englishmen held captive in Spain. He also suggested that it might be best to discharge the captured cargo at Plymouth, where he could keep the goods safe in his cellars until proper division could be made. Hawkins did not say, though the lord admiral knew it, that it would be much easier to put the greatest share of the spoils into the hands of the officers and men if the cargo were kept away from the queen's agents in London.[37]

The happy turn of events did not bring Hawkins the sort of tranquility he sought. The prize ship was not brought to Plymouth, where Hawkins could easily supervise things. Instead, an inventory was taken in Dartmouth under the supervision of agents of the crown. Moreover, Hawkins was low on cash, having been forced to pay for repairs to many of his ships, including a mast and rigging for the *Rainbow,* which collided with the *Foresight* in a storm.[38] Then came news that his wife had taken sick. Hawkins hurried back to his house at Deptford, where she lay at the point of death. In the midst of all these troubles came rumors that the queen was most annoyed with him. Huge sums had been spent on the fleets, but nothing had been accomplished.[39] Could Hawkins possibly be in the pay of the king of Spain? Again? According to court gossip, the queen thought he was.[40]

Deeply discouraged, Hawkins felt helpless. His wife remained sick, and on 4 July 1590 she died. "It hath pleased God to take my wife to his mercy," he wrote to Burghley, "godly in her life and godly in her death." She was in fact a good woman, loved by her husband and by her stepson as well. Richard Hawkins later described her fondly as "a religious and most vertuous Lady." It was she who named his ship the *Repentance,* for that was "the safest ship we could sayle in, to purchase the haven of Heaven." Distracted by grief, Hawkins managed to be standing in the wrong place at a ship launching. The *Swiftsure,* built originally in 1573, was totally rebuilt in 1592. At the launching a tackle gave way, whipped against his legs, and, as he wrote, "hurt me in vi places." He begged once more to be released from his work as treasurer of the navy. "Be a meane to her matie that some dyscret and able man may be thought uppon to supply my place."[41] As always, his request was ignored.

Introspective when depressed, Hawkins also became more sensitive to the suffering of others. Together with Howard and Drake he is said to have organized a collection of funds levied on seamen's wages to help relieve men who had suffered debilitating injuries in naval service. A large iron chest with multiple locks was provided to safeguard the money, and the fund thereupon became known as "The Chest at Chatham." In 1592 the fund proved insufficient to meet all the needs, and Parliament then passed a relief act for soldiers and mariners.[42]

After a time loneliness overcame grief, and Hawkins married once more. His new wife was Margaret Vaughan, daughter of Charles Vaughan and his wife, the former Elizabeth Baskerville. Margaret had been lady of the queen's bedchamber.[43] The union was apparently satisfactory for Hawkins, but not for his son, who had a distinctly cool relationship with the new stepmother.

During these years English piracy enjoyed a remarkable resurgence, as Queen Elizabeth and her ministers turned the West Country pirates into privateers. Professional pirates and adventurous merchants could purchase letters of marque and reprisal from the lord admiral, thus turning an odious business into an act of patriotism. Many commanders preferred to keep costs to a minimum and operated without such letters. Even with documents the legal distinction was probably lost on foreign merchants whose ships and cargoes were seized by Englishmen who looked and acted like pirates. As a rule Hawkins and the other English privateers were not greatly concerned with nationality. If a cargo was rich and the ship foreign, it was likely to be seized. When neutral merchants asked the Privy Council to intervene, the lords appointed Sir Francis Drake as "Commyssyoner for the Causes of Reprysall." Assigned to settle disputes between the privateer captains and the merchants who owned the ships and cargoes, Drake somehow managed to let his friends keep their booty, or so the owners said. There were rules, of course, one of which was that the cargoes had to be inventoried by royal officials, for piracy was not just an instrument of war in Elizabethan England. It was also an important source of revenue.[44]

The prime example lies in the capture of a Portuguese carrack named the *Madre de Dios,* said to be the largest ship afloat. This vessel was part of a fleet of four or five carracks returning from the East Indies, their cabins and holds crammed full of gold, diamonds, rubies, silks, musk, ambergris, and pepper. News of their arrival in European waters drew an array of merchant vessels, privateers, and royal ships, all going in search of the carracks. One of these fleets had originally been organized by Sir Walter Ralegh to go to the West Indies. When the carracks reached the north Atlantic, Ralegh changed his plans. Then he found himself in trouble for a liaison with Elizabeth Throckmorton, a lady of the queen's bedchamber, and Martin Frobisher took his command. The earl of Cumberland had five of his own ships at sea, and these soon joined the pursuit. John Hawkins sent the *Dainty,* and a group of London merchants provided funds in the amount of £6,000. The royal contribution to the chase came in the form of two ships, the *Garland* and the *Foresight,* for which the queen later took a major share of the profit.[45]

The English ships headed for the Azores to intercept the Portuguese fleet. Almost immediately a carrack was sighted. After a hard chase the ship ran aground at Flores and was burned by the crew. There was very little plunder, but the purser was taken prisoner. Without much coaxing he revealed the whereabouts of another vessel, the *Madre de Dios,* sailing nearby. With this information the English ships set out in pursuit. The *Dainty* was the first to reach the *Madre de Dios,* about noon on 3 August, and for a time she fought all alone against the giant carrack. Another ship, the *Dragon,* soon arrived and joined the battle, but not before the *Dainty* lost her mast and started to burn. As the *Dainty* dropped away, Ralegh's *Roebuck* and the royal warship *Foresight* arrived to join the battle, followed by the earl of Cumberland's *Samson* and the *Tiger.* The fight lasted past midnight, and the Englishmen boarded the Portuguese ship several times, only to be driven away. When it was all over, the soldiers and seamen began to plunder the ship, fighting among themselves for the richest pieces. No one knows now what the total spoil might have been. One report held it at £1 million. Sir John Burgh, captain of the *Roebuck,* said the *Madre de Dios* was richer than "any shypp that ever came into England."[46]

Some order was restored the following day, but not before the seamen managed to scour the vessel thoroughly. Once this was accomplished, the ships of the fleet scattered to Plymouth and other ports along the channel coast, leaving the *Roebuck* alone to escort the *Madre de Dios* into Dartmouth harbor. The prize was so rich that various special commissioners were sent to help with the inventory. At first Hawkins was named as the queen's representative, but that changed after someone realized that he had his own interests to protect. Even then no clear accounting could be made. Finally, Hawkins dispatched an urgent request to Burghley, and Sir Walter Ralegh was released from jail to give a hand. Before commissioners arrived at the various ports, the seamen removed whatever they could carry, and merchants came down from London to purchase their booty. After all this the commissioners still counted more than £150,000 as the value of the cargo.[47]

Obviously someone had gotten away with a great deal of booty, and the queen was determined to have her share. Knowing that suspicion would fall upon him as well as on other investors and shipowners, John Hawkins stayed safely in Deptford, informing Burghley that he would keep a careful watch for purloined riches from that vantage point. After two weeks he reported the seizure of fourteen bags of spices, thirteen bags of anil, and a puncheon of cloves and cinnamon on a ship just arrived from Plymouth. His own ship *Dainty* came home empty, or so he said, sending along a letter from the captain to verify the matter. According to Captain Thompson, the *Dainty* drifted at sea for five days while he struggled to fit a jury-mast. When he returned to the scene, all the booty had been divided. "Ys there never a chaine of gold left?" he asked Sir John Burrough. "I have some thinge for you said he because you weare awaie." Thereupon he gave Thompson "a common sailers cheste wch had byn broken upp before."[48]

While this may have been true, it was certainly misleading, and Hawkins probably knew it. Nonetheless, he sent the letter on to Burghley, noting that he had carefully refrained from meeting the captain of the *Dainty*, lest he be suspected of removing something of value. Whatever was in the chest, it was not an ordinary sea chest. Surgeon John Pawson told an investigating commission that the chest was "as hye as the table wch these comisshoners sate at and halfe as longe" and presumably full of valuables. Boatswain John Rogers reported that he had demanded to be told what was in the chest. "Some skenes of silke, a few books of Calicos and certen spice," Captain Thompson had replied. This was an understatement. A merchant named Richard Goodwyn bought £500 worth of silk, calico, and spices from the *Dainty* and did not take it all. The chest was just the captain's share. Every seaman and soldier had loot of greater or lesser value.[49]

What Hawkins received out of all this is not clear, but it was enough to restore his flagging spirits and make him forget his recent offer to resign. After conferring with Burghley, Hawkins sent word to his son Richard to meet the *Madre de Dios* at Dartmouth dock and take charge of the plunder. Richard went to Dartmouth as instructed but found that much of the booty had already been sold or hidden away. Merchants came from London and bought whatever they could find. Sir Robert Cecil, sent to Dartmouth by his father, wrote that the men he passed on the road carried so much amber and musk he "could well smell them almost."[50]

At Gravesend the sergeant of the admiralty and his "tow wayters" searched the *Dainty*, but by that time Thompson had been in English waters for some weeks, and the officials found nothing. Claiming a larger share of the plunder, Hawkins said that the crew of the *Dainty* had boarded the Portuguese vessel three times before any other English ship came on the scene.[51] A few days later he raised the total to four times, and said that what little spoil the *Dainty* got was spent for repairs when the ship came home. According to Hawkins's account, the men from the *Dainty* had killed both the captain and the master of the other ship during the fierce two-hour fight. In the process they had kept the vessel from being beached and burned at Flores:

> By meane of the dayntyes dystresse in the fight w^t the carrake they came to have lyttell of the spoyle & that was consumyd at harwyche
>
> I most Humbly desyre yor honours the good service of

the daynty may be declaryd to her ma^{tie}, she bordyd the carrake foure tymes before any ship cold come by to her,
savyng the dragon wch wold not bord w^t her when she came
by; yf the daynty had not bordyd so often & so desperately,
the carrack had recoveryd the Ilond of flores & biene burnt
as thother carrake was

They report yt for trothe that the daynty in her bordyng
slew bothe the captayne & master of the carrake wch were
sworen to the kynge never to yeld the ship to ynglyshe men
but to fyre her rather what so ev^r this or any other service
done or to be done by me or by my meane I accompt yt but
my bounden deuty to her ma^{tie}, wch shalbe all wayes thus
(w^t godes favour) to my lyves end.[52]

At the end of October the queen named a special commission to
divide the spoils. Members were Lord Burghley, his son Sir Robert
Cecil, Chancellor of the Exchequer Sir John Fortesque, and four London merchants (for the queen); Sir John Hawkins representing his own
interests; and four others to represent the lord admiral, Sir Walter
Ralegh, and other merchants, soldiers, and mariners. The goods were
inventoried at Leaden Hall in December for a total of more than
£140,000, exclusive of the jewels, gold, and silver. Of this amount
Hawkins was allotted £14,225, "according to the custom of the sea,
After the rate of tonne for tonne, and man for man." In addition
Hawkins received £2,000 for various expenses. The earl of Cumberland received £36,000, and the London merchants £12,000, plus additional amounts for expenses. The queen herself received £23,000, plus
another £20,000 for expenses.[53] Of course, ship owners had to share
the spoils with officers and crew, but it is not exactly clear how the division was accomplished in this case.[54] Ralegh thought his share should

have been £36,000, for an apparent profit of £2,000. But various charges were levied against this amount, and his profit quickly turned into a loss. Ralegh complained bitterly about this arrangement, though Hawkins did not, so far as the record shows. Hawkins probably had other income from the voyage. During the previous October he certainly had felt rich, for he bought Drake's reversionary rights to the manor of Sydbery, Devon, for his son Richard.[55]

Continued hostilities meant continued need to help sick and injured soldiers and seamen. When Parliament met in February 1593, Sir Robert Cecil spoke about the whole question of relief, not just for soldiers and seamen but for the poor in general. This might have seemed like a proposal that no one could oppose, but members complained that assistance of this sort could only increase the numbers of louts and laggards who loafed about the countryside. Cecil withdrew his proposal, but a relief act was passed anyway, and members were required to contribute to the relief fund. Members of the Privy Council gave thirty shillings each, knights twenty shillings, and burgesses five shillings. A committee was then named to dispense the money, and Hawkins was required to certify the need in each case. At about the same time Hawkins saw to the construction of a hospital for seamen at Chatham. The institution received a royal charter in 1594 as the Hospital of Sir John Hawkins. This charitable work may have helped Hawkins achieve election to the Honourable Society of the Middle Temple in February 1594.[56]

While this business was being settled, Richard Hawkins came forward with a plan to sail around the world, repeating the journeys of Drake in 1577–80 and Thomas Cavendish in 1586–88. Both commanders had returned with their ships fairly wallowing in the sea from the heavy loads of treasure they carried. For John Hawkins it seemed like the opportune time to introduce his thirty-year-old son to the family business of raiding Spanish colonial ports. He therefore sold the *Dainty* back to Richard for use as a flagship. Nearly new and fully reconditioned after the fight with the Portuguese carrack, the *Dainty* was "pleasing to the eye, profitable for Stowage, good of Sail, and well conditioned."[57]

To make up his fleet Richard planned to take another ship of 100 tons and a 60-ton pinnace, called the *Fancy*. Working quickly and with much help from his father, he was ready to sail at the end of March 1593, having spent less than a month in preparation. The voyage began with a near-disaster, as so many long voyages seemed to do in those days. Coming out of the river near Barking, the *Dainty* began to heel, taking water into the ports, which had been left open and uncaulked. It was a narrow escape and delayed the sailing another two weeks. The fleet sailed once more on 13 April, reaching Plymouth on the twenty-sixth. There was more delay when the *Dainty* was cast up on the rocks and damaged, and the third ship failed to arrive in port. Finally, with more financial help from his father, Richard loaded provisions on a ship called the *Hawk* and repaired the other two vessels. The little fleet left Plymouth on 12 June 1593, with much ceremony. First the ship's trumpeters sounded a call, then the other musicians joined. Finally the guns fired a salute as a sign of "the love and zeale which I, my Father, and Predecessors, have ever borne to that place as to our naturall and mother Towne." The crowd on shore raised a cheer, and the salute was returned from the fort, "which with the fayre evening and silence of the night, were heard a great distance off."[58]

The start was not auspicious. Caulkers in Plymouth had left an open seam, and as soon as the wind came up, the *Hawk* began taking on water. The ships returned to port once more, where the leak was repaired, and the fleet left again the following day. Sailing down the coast of Portugal, the fleet passed the Madeiras and stopped for water in the Canaries. After several days spent fishing in the Cape Verde Islands, the fleet headed for Guinea, where Hawkins tried to land but failed to find a mooring. At last the fleet sailed west, reaching the coast of Brazil on 18 October 1593.[59]

At Santos Richard used the usual Hawkins excuse in his bid for supplies of water and food: he had been blown off course. He was allowed to buy some oranges and lemons for scurvy, and a few hens, but the governor forbade any further aid to the English enemy. The expedition stopped for a time near the Rio de Janeiro to nurse the men back to health. Then, with the crew reduced by sickness, Hawkins abandoned the *Hawk,* setting it afire, as Drake had done with the *Swan.* Leaving Rio de Janeiro on 10 December they reached the Straits of Magellan on 10 February, having suffered through various incidents of illness, accident, and insubordination.[60]

The expedition passed into the Pacific Ocean, reaching the island of Mocha on 19 April 1594. Finding Valparaiso undefended, Richard entered the port and captured four ships, letting three go back for a hefty ransom. Then, with a small store of treasure, he sailed on up the coast. Determined not to be caught again by English raiders, the Spanish authorities were ready. Ports were deserted and ships gave Hawkins a wide berth. The ship taken at Valparaiso began to leak, so it was stripped and burned. Then about the middle of May the English fleet was attacked by a six-ship armada under Don Beltrán de Castro. The attackers were beaten off, but the fight was renewed farther up the coast. The new battle lasted for three days, at the end of which Hawkins and his men surrendered. The survivors were taken to Panama and then to Lima. Some of the men gained their freedom quickly, but Richard Hawkins remained a captive for eight years.[61]

In fall 1593 Francis Drake met with other royal officials who were in Plymouth to round up the spoils from the Portuguese carrack. Forever brimming with confidence, Drake passed his free time by outlining another raid on the West Indies. In an unaccustomed burst of enthusiasm Hawkins put his name to the proposal as well, and it was sent off to the queen. The exact details are unclear, but it was probably much like the one Ambassador Mendoza received and forwarded to King Philip. Translated twice, this document is murky in parts, but the purpose is clearly stated: "a voyage to ruin the Spanish entirely." With twelve warships and six pinnaces the two men said they could take every port in the West Indies, plus Panama, sack the towns, rob the treasure ships, and perhaps even sell a few slaves to eager customers. The document contains several firsthand references to Drake's 1585 raid on the Indies, but both the title and a final note credit the document to Hawkins as well. Early in 1594 Elizabeth issued a warrant permitting Drake and Hawkins to prepare for the journey, taking three of her ships, plus twenty others owned by merchant-investors. For both men it was to be another joint command, this time with Drake and Hawkins together.[62]

Almost as soon as the warrant was issued, hostilities in France grew more complicated, and plans were suspended for a few months. Frobisher, Norris, and others took English ships and soldiers to lift the Spanish siege of Brest. After a final furious assault on the Spanish position English troops won the day, but Frobisher was mortally wounded in the attack. The result was a temporary end to the Spanish threat to France and to the English navy. Before the end of 1594 the Drake-Hawkins plan was dusted off, with Panama as the final objective.[63] But a few months made a lot of difference. With time to think it over,

Hawkins was reluctant to go. And that was not all. He asked again to be relieved of his responsibilities on the Navy Board.

In February 1594 he wrote to Lord Burghley saying his wife was sick, he was unwell, and he wanted to resign. "I humbly pray yor Loship to favour me to be delyveryd from this contynewall throwldome." As usual, he was ignored. Caught up in the work of preparing ships for the war in France, he forgot his problems for a time. Then in August 1594 he wrote to Lord Burghley once more. Citing age and health, he asked to have someone appointed to take his place on the Navy Board, "so that with a quiet mind he may leave the cares of this world and prepare himself for the time to come." These are not the thoughts of a man eager to challenge the Spanish empire. Rather, Hawkins wanted to put his affairs in order, for he was sixty-two and feeling every year. Once willing to take a big chance for a bigger profit, Hawkins now wanted to know exactly what the future held. A man who was close to Hawkins said he had become "ould and warie entringe into matters with so laden a foote that the others meate would be eaten before his spit could come to the fire."[64] Nevertheless, his request for retirement was ignored, and arrangements for the journey continued.

So many people with conflicting aims were involved in the voyage that it is difficult now to know exactly what the ultimate objectives might have been. Queen Elizabeth doubtless hoped that Drake and Hawkins together might be able to tap the Spanish treasure fleet one more time for the funds she needed to support her increasingly active navy. There was always a thought of capturing Panama, which sat astride the treasure route from the Pacific, but it is difficult to imagine that either Drake or Hawkins thought the isthmus could be held permanently. Although the Drake-Hawkins plan confidently declared that

Panama could be taken with five hundred men, others knew better. A large land army would be needed, and the earl of Essex used his influence to help recruit proper commanders for the force.[65]

With the navy draining her treasury, the queen could not afford to pay for such an army, so the expedition became another joint-stock venture. The queen contributed £30,000. Drake and Hawkins each invested £10,000. Soldiers and sailors were to receive shares of the plunder instead of salaries, and few men wanted to enlist under such conditions. Private ship owners received credit in shares for their own vessels, but the total amount invested in cash and ships was probably not much more than £60,000. In a commission dated 29 January 1594, but 1595 by the current calendar, Queen Elizabeth assigned six of her own ships to the expedition. The *Garland* at 660 tons became the flagship of Sir John Hawkins. The *Defiance* at 550 tons was Drake's flagship. The other royal ships were the *Hope*, the *Bonaventure*, the *Adventure*, and the *Foresight*.[66]

By this time it was obvious that voluntary enlistments would not be sufficient to support the new expedition. For this reason the commission included the authority to impress sailors, carpenters, gunners, soldiers, "and other artificers and seafaringe men as shalle be sufficiente to furnishe all the shippes." In the end some 2,500 men joined the expedition to the Indies, about a thousand of them soldiers, surely more than enough to capture Panama.[67]

There was almost no attempt to keep the plans confidential. Don Pedro de Valdés, Drake's prisoner from the Armada campaign, gave a detailed outline of the plan to King Philip as early as March 1593. At first it seemed that the commanders wanted to capture Puerto Rico and to establish a base there for further attacks on Havana and San Juan de Ulúa. Then plans changed to allow for occupation of the Island of

Curaçao. Valdés reported this as well, for a base there would command the route between Nombre de Dios and Cartagena and imperil the Spanish fleets coming from New Spain and Tierra Firme. In the winter of 1594, when the English commanders decided to march across the isthmus and capture Panama, a warning was issued to the governors of Santo Domingo, Havana, and Panama.[68]

There was a new mood in Spain, a determination to do whatever might be necessary to defend the Indies. The raids by Hawkins and Drake from the 1560s to the mid-1580s had finally registered on the Spanish bureaucracy, and new money was made available for defense of the colonies. More than this, there were discussions about building and maintaining a special fleet just to defend the Indies from pirates. Spanish officials began building and equipping defensive installations in all the places that had proven vulnerable to attack. They also began to carry the war to the shores of England. Before the English fleet was ready to depart, a Spanish landing force descended on Cornwall, burning Penzance and other towns, then leaving.[69] Rumors said another fleet was headed for Ireland, and still another would come to England the following year.

Grown old and quarrelsome, Queen Elizabeth berated her commanders for this development, citing their procrastination and lack of secrecy. "Yo^r own delayes hath made yor iorney and purposes now so notorious (yea in particular to the Spaniard) as they have sufficent warning to provide for y^r discent." Thinking that the money spent to equip the fleet was probably wasted, she ordered Hawkins and Drake to try to intercept the Spanish treasure fleet heading home from the West Indies. For good measure, they were to look for any Spanish fleet that might be going in the direction of Ireland and destroy it. Then she said the fleet had to be home by next May.[70]

Stung by the unjust accusations, Drake and Hawkins immediately fired off messages of protest. The queen was ready to reply in kind, refusing to let them leave at all. A letter to this effect was drafted and ready to go, but it was not sent.[71] Not that Elizabeth thought she was wrong. Rather, she was intrigued by news from Hawkins and Drake that a Spanish treasure galleon was sitting in the harbor at San Juan de Puerto Rico, dismasted and rudderless, with all the guns put ashore. The partners offered to capture this ship on their way to Panama. "It lyeth in our way," they said, "& wyll no way impoache us." This was what Elizabeth wanted to hear. As the lord treasurer reported to his son, "Th^e plymouth Generalls do cōtent hir Ma^{ty}."[72]

While the queen may have been pleased, the officers and men of the expedition were not. The problem was the system of joint command. They saw Hawkins and Drake as men of conflicting temperaments, both used to command but having incompatible styles. According to Thomas Maynarde, Drake was "a man of greate spirit," but he lacked some essential leadership qualities and was not able to bring a project to conclusion. "His selfe willed and peremptorie command was doubted." Hawkins was a competent administrator, but he was just too old. Beyond this, the two argued incessantly. "What the one desireth the other would commonly oppose."[73]

Before leaving Plymouth both men prepared detailed wills. Hawkins left £2,000 as a dower to his wife, Margaret, plus an additional thousand as a sign of his "good will and affection towardes her." He also left her plate, jewels, and household goods. She was to have the use of the house on London's Mincing Lane for life, and the houses and outbuildings at Deptford as well. Upon her death they would go to his son Richard Hawkins. In addition to this, he gave Richard his half-interest in the house where Richard's family lived in Plymouth, along

21

Hawkins's will begins with a declaration of faith. Public Record Office, PROB 11/94.

with its garden, stables, wharf, and forge. He left good sums to his in-laws, nephews, and granddaughter, to charity, and to his friends. Among the bequests were instructions to his executors "to goe throughe with the erection of my hospital at Chatham." A few days after the will was finished, word arrived that Richard Hawkins had been captured and was a Spanish prisoner. Hawkins thereupon added a codicil, leaving £3,000 for his ransom.[74]

The Hawkins will reveals the thoughts of a man concerned about the condition of his immortal soul. In Elizabethan times it was common to begin a will with some sort of declaration of faith, usually intended to convince authorities that the testator was a firm adherent of the established religion. In this regard the declaration of John Hawkins was completely orthodox. "I beleeve in God the Father, god the Sonne & God the holie Ghoste three persons, one God. I beleeve all the articles of the faithe wh[ch] are mayntayned by the bookes of the ould and newe Testament." Pretty general thoughts, but Hawkins went further:

Prostrating my selfe before the Maiestie of the Omnipotent God/ confessing my selfe from my youthe uppe a most greivous synner; never hable to p[er]forme any good acte/ have thereby fallne into the wrathe of the Allmightie, and worthely deserved the paines of hell fier; for the whch I doe most earnestly repent me from the bottome of my harte, and in the most humblest manner that can be expressed, or devised wth teares doe crave pardon, at the handes of God throughe the Love of my Lorde & Savyr Jesus Christ.

These are the thoughts of a soul in anguish. Hawkins may not have composed these words himself, and probably did not, but subscribe to them he did.[75]

The fleet left Plymouth harbor on 28 August 1595. There were twenty-seven ships in two squadrons. Following the customary route south to the Canaries, Hawkins and Drake called their first conference on 3 September just off Cabo San Vicente. Drake as usual had sailed without sufficient victuals for all the men in his fleet. Some said he had skimped on expenditures. When he asked Hawkins to relieve him of some of his men, Hawkins refused. Some said Hawkins had skimped as well; in any case, there were hard words between the two. Hawkins said he would not take any men "unles he were entreated," and Drake refused to do this. In a later meeting Drake suggested an attack on one of the Madeiras or Gran Canaria, where they could get more supplies, and plunder as well. The army commander, Sir Thomas Baskerville, seconded his proposal. Hawkins said that they must stick to the original plan, and Sir Nicholas Clifford supported his view. There were reasons for this. Hawkins felt that there was no need to resupply the ships, considering the short time they had been at sea. In addition, he thought the fortress at Las Palmas was too strong. It would be impossible "to cary yt wthout hazerding all." Finally, they were on a tight schedule,

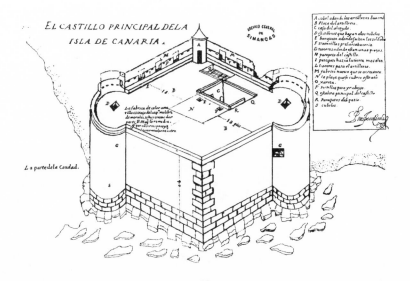

22

The principal castle at Gran Canaria, sketched by engineer Prospero Casola the year after the battle. España, Ministerio de Educación, Cultura, y Deporte, Archivo General de Simancas, GA 460, no. 296.

and he hated to lose the time. At first neither side would relent, and the arguments became so heated that it seemed for a time Drake might go to the Canaries alone. In the end Hawkins relented, but he was not happy.[76]

On 25 September the fleet was at Las Palmas in the island of Gran Canaria. Intending to land his troops from the pinnaces, Drake first fussed around in the bay for several hours, placing markers where the boats should go ashore. When Baskerville finally took the troops to land, he found the surf too high. In the meantime artillerymen from the shore began firing into the boats, and other men gathered onshore to oppose the landing. Faced with such unexpected opposition, the attempt was abandoned, with four men lost to hostile fire. Disgusted with the proceedings, Hawkins wrote a brief account and sent it to his wife, asking her to tell Burghley, Howard, and Robert Cecil exactly

There Is No Other Hell

what had transpired. Margaret made a copy and sent it to Robert Cecil, asking him whether she should also send a copy to the queen. There it stopped, or so it seems. Margaret thought that the queen might be angry if she heard that Lady Hawkins had a letter and she had none. What happened to the letter from Hawkins is not known. Apparently the news was not all bad. "Although it be not as good as I wish and daily pray for," she wrote, "I thank God it is not very ill."[77]

Next day the fleet sailed to the other side of the island, where the ships took on water for the next two days. On 28 September, Captain Grimstone took one of the shore parties to a nearby hill, presumably for a better view. There the soldiers were set upon by shepherds armed with clubs. They killed several Englishmen, wounded all the rest, and took the survivors into custody. One of the prisoners was the surgeon from the ship *Solomon*. He revealed the whole plan of the voyage to his captors, though it was already well known from other information sent out of England. This was not an auspicious beginning. The Spanish authorities immediately dispatched a fast ship to alert the treasure fleet in Puerto Rico. Other vessels were sent to Spain carrying the same warning, and after some delay a fleet was dispatched from Lisbon to intercept the English ships.[78]

After the dismal interlude at Gran Canaria, Drake and Hawkins took their fleet directly to the West Indies. They reached the Lesser Antilles on 26 October and came to anchor at Guadalupe on 29 October. Hawkins immediately became ill, perhaps from the water, though everyone thought it was just general debility. "Sr John Hawkins not hable to bear his grifes one [day] longer, Sickned." The next day two small English barks, the *Delight* and the *Francis,* lagging behind the rest of the ships, sighted the fleet of Don Pedro Tello de Guzmán in the distance and mistook the Spanish ships for the English fleet. By the time they realized their error, it was too late. The Spanish ships gave chase and captured the *Francis,* but the other ship escaped. The Spanish captors took the crew off the *Francis* and left the little ship "driving in the sea."[79]

Questioning the captives, Tello de Guzmán quickly determined that the destination of the fleet was Puerto Rico, and he hastened there to give the warning. The *Delight* meanwhile sailed off to warn Drake and Hawkins. There are two versions of what happened next. According to one, Drake suggested sailing immediately for San Juan and trying to capture the port before the news arrived. Hawkins thought that they should spend a few more days putting the fleet in order. Drake and the others did not argue the point, because Hawkins was so obviously ill. This is the version recorded by Thomas Maynard. The other version comes from Spanish prisoners captured by Drake and released later. Their story came secondhand from other members of Drake's expedition, who said that Drake wanted to capture the *fragatas*—small dispatch boats—before Tello could reach Puerto Rico. Hawkins, they said, "did not want to go after the fragatas from Guadalupe, though he knew that they had captured the ship and were headed for Puerto Rico."[80]

In fact, both versions may be mistaken. The English fleet was in no condition for a fight. All the guns were stowed below decks, and it was probably not possible to chase Tello's fragatas and bring up the guns at the same time. In any case, Drake and Hawkins spent ten days in Guadalupe, bringing the guns up on deck and preparing their pinnaces for the attack on San Juan. On 3 November, Tello reached the island with the news that the English fleet had arrived. Already alerted, the military authorities began a new round of preparations. San Juan was situated on an island at the mouth of the bay. During the previous decade extensive work had been carried out to protect the entrance to the harbor. The fortifications were far from complete, but work had progressed sufficiently that with everyone mobilized the island people could put up a stout defense.[81]

The English fleet was also ready for war. The pinnaces were launched the same day Tello reached Puerto Rico, and the next day the soldiers and seamen boarded the ships. On the fifth of the month the fleet set sail but was becalmed within sight of land. Next morning the wind blew up a gale, and the fleet had good sailing for another three days. On the afternoon of 8 November they anchored "in a sounde in the Virgines northe northeaste from Santa Cruse." Hawkins knew he was close to death, so he called his "good frend Mr John Troughton" and a few others to his side. Then he dictated a codicil, affirming the will he had left at home with his wife. As sometimes happens, approaching death brought clarity of mind and lifted his deep depression. In the will, he said, "I made declarãcon of my fayth and hope of my salvation in Jesus Christe nothinge doubtinge but the Lord of his mercy will axcepte me into everlastinge life amonge his Saintes." Apparently he had been thinking of debts unpaid, for he added a curious clause to the will:

> I doe will there shalbe knowledge given by the space of one whole yeare and a day where I have had most conversation and habitaon that is to say, in Plymouth in London, in Saincte Dunstones in the East and at Debtford Strond in East Greenwch the mynisters of those places shall publishe that my will is that whatsoever wronge I have done any man if their shalbe shewed any just any honest or conscionable cause/ that he shalbe restored whatsoever it be, And if I have taken any interest of any man wherin he doth fynde

him selfe agreved my mynd is he shalbe restored to his contentment./ For the faultes or offences which I have or might have comitted against her matie I doe geve unto her Twoe Thousand poundes (yf shee will take it) for that shee hath in her possession of myne a far greater some wch I doe release unto her This I meane with godes grace to p[er]forme my selfe if he of his mercye send me home.[82]

Next morning bright and early the men were mustered on shore and then boarded again. The captains were called into conference, and afterward the fleet set sail. On Monday morning, 11 November, they anchored off Puerto Rico, where John Hawkins died. The loss was felt immediately, for no one was left to counter the rashness of Drake.[83]

From this point the enterprise took a distinct turn for the worse. Several important officers and many good men were lost in an unsuccessful attempt to take San Juan. When that attack had to be abandoned, Drake took the fleet to a series of other ports where he had found easy victories in earlier years. Now everything was changed. Towns were deserted, treasure almost nonexistent. After brief stops at Cabo de Vela, Santa Marta, and Nombre de Dios, the army began the long-delayed march to Panama in late December. It was the worst season of the year. Rain, mud, bad roads, and sickness took their toll, and the attack was soon called off. With his whole project in ruins, Drake ordered the ships to sail toward Porto Bello. On the way a bloody dysentery swept through the fleet, and this time the commander was stricken. Francis Drake died off Porto Bello on 28 January 1596 and was buried at sea, just as Hawkins had been a few weeks earlier. With both commanders dead, the men sick and discouraged, the expedition was quickly abandoned. Late in the spring the survivors arrived home in England with little or nothing to show for their efforts.

There were a few encomiums for Hawkins and Drake, but not many. The men who wrote about their experiences did not hesitate to express frank opinions about both of them. Thomas Maynarde thought Hawkins was old and slow. He was tight-fisted in providing victuals and discussed his plans too freely in front of the men. An anonymous letter writer whom Samuel Purchas called "R.M." said more about Hawkins, most of it unflattering. He was slow, jealous, and indecisive. In arguments he would simply oppose everything, implying that he had good reasons but refusing to explain them. And he preferred the company of "the common sort" rather than "his equals." He was overambitious, but not so much as Drake. With all this he had a few of the more admirable virtues. He was patient, tough, knowledgeable, and brave. Above all, "Sir Iohn Hawkins had in him mercie and aptnesse to forgive, and true of word; . . . he was withall severe and courteous, magnanimious and liberall." Not so bad, if R.M. had only left it there, but he added, "Sir Iohn Hawkins had in him malice with dissimulation, rudenesse in behaviour, and passing sparing, indeed miserable." Was there a final word? Yes. Hawkins was one of the "Great Commanders," but Drake was greater.[84]

John Troughton would not let R.M. have the last word. As soon as he arrived in England, Troughton wrote to the queen, explaining what had happened to his friend. "Through the perverse and crosse dealinges of some in that Jeorney, whoe preferringe their owne fancye before his skill, wolde never yelde but rather overrule him, whereby he was so dyscouraged, and as himsellfe then sayde his harte even broken, that he sawe no other but danger of ruyne lyklye to ensue of the whole voiage."[85]

From a more distant vantage point it is possible to say a few more things about John Hawkins as a navy man. He was a proven success in a job he had come to detest, treasurer of the navy. He was a fine administrator. Queen Elizabeth and Lord Burghley valued his services, though they did not always trust him, and they often let his shortcomings cloud their appreciation of his virtues.

10

Weighing Hawkins

At so great a Distance of Time, it may seem strange to enter
into, or at least to enter minutely into, the Character of this famous
Seaman; but as we have good Authorities, and such Reflections,
may be of Use to Posterity, we think it not amiss to undertake
this Task; in performing which, we shall use all the Care
and Impartiality that can be expected.

John Campbell

The earliest published record about John Hawkins
came from his own hand, no doubt with some considerable secretarial assistance. As soon as he arrived
in London after the disastrous battle at San Juan de
Ulúa he gave an account of the entire voyage to the
printer. This soon emerged as a twenty-eight-page pamphlet entitled *A
True Declaration of the troublesome voyadge of M. John Haukins to the
parties of Guynea and the west Indies, in the yeares of our Lord 1567.
and 1568.* In this account Hawkins describes his own "honest behaviour towards the inhabitants" of the various Spanish towns he had
attacked and sometimes set afire, contrasting it with the "treason" of
the Spanish viceroy. There is no sign of compassion for the "Negrose"
he enslaved or for the death and destruction he caused in Guinea and
the Indies. If the story reveals any hint of sensitivity in Hawkins, it is
for his own "miseries and troublesome affayres of this sorowefull voyadge." This was a persistent theme for Hawkins, who saw life as a constant struggle to escape overwhelming problems. A few years later
Richard Hakluyt adapted the *True Declaration* for his book on *The
Principall Navigations, Voiages and Discoveries of the English Nation,*

which he published for the first time in 1589. To the original material provided by John Hawkins, Hakluyt added an account of a trip made by his father, William Hawkins, plus much information about the two voyages that Hawkins made in 1562 and 1564. These stories provide the earliest published glimpses into the character of the Englishman who decided "that Negroes were very good marchandise."[1]

A Spanish account of the "Troublesome Voyage," takes a different and not very flattering perspective. "This renegade Don Juan," was the villain in a narrative poem published in 1570 by Alvaro Flores. "Don Juan Hawkins," he said, was "the enemy of God and our Christians."[2]

English writers soon began to cite the adventures of Hawkins and other captains to enhance their own accounts of voyages to the New World. One of the first was George Peckham, who published *A True Report* in 1583 to promote a trip to America by Sir Humphrey Gilbert. In the style of the time Peckham included several pages of bad verse credited to Hawkins, Drake, Frobisher, and others. Filled with references to heroes of ancient Greece and Rome, these verses implied a classical education that Hawkins did not have. A similar pamphlet by John Davis appeared in 1595. It was entitled *The Worldes Hydrographical Discription,* and recounted Davis's own voyages to North America. In addition, there was a brief description of Drake's voyages, plus a few references to Hawkins. "The first Englishman that gaue any attempt upon the coastes of West India being parte of America was Syr Iohn Hawkins knight: who there and in that attempt as in many others sichins did and hath prooued himselfe to be a man of excellent capacity, great gouernment, and perfect resolucion. For before he attempted the same it was a matter doubtfull and reported the extremest lymit of danger to sayle upon those coastes." His comments do not contain much of substance, but they show Hawkins as a man with a reputation for success. "Howe then may Syr Iohn Haukins bee esteemed who being a man of good account in his Country, of wealth and great imployment, did notwithstanding for the good of his Country, to procure trade, giue that notable and resolute attempt. Whose steps many hundreds following sichins haue made themselues men of good esteeme, and fit for the seruice of her sacrid maiestie."[3]

In 1595, when Hawkins and Drake were having problems with enlistments for their voyage, Henry Roberts tried to help them with a nine-page pamphlet in verse called *The Trumpet of Fame: Or Sir Fraunces Drakes and Sir Iohn Hawkins Farewell: with an encouragement to all Sailers and Souldiers that are minded to go in this worthie enterprise. VVith the names of many Ships, and what they have done against our foes*. A brief section compares Hawkins to Drake, but manages to do so without saying anything of substance.

> And Hawkins in this action his compere,
> Full well is knowne a famous Cauilere.
> whose valure showne, and service often done,
> with good successe, immortall fame hath wonne.
> In India land, he Englands cullours spread,
> where Spanish Powers he brauely vanquished.
> The French and other Nations far and neare,
> Hath felt the force of this stout Cauilere.
> To English Queene and officer long beene,
> which place of trust, he did full well beseeme.
> For which his seruice, as due deserts and right,
> he honored is, with title of Knight.[4]

In 1598 Emanuel van Meteren, a successful Belgian merchant who had lived for years in London, published his own view of recent history, *Historica Belgica*. Meteren, who knew Hawkins well, described English adventurers in a way that could well be a portrait of the man. "This is a nation of overwhelming audacity, courageous, impetuous, unmerciful in war, warm on first acquaintance, sneering at death, but boastful about it, cunning, and completely given to dissimulation, whether in word or deed; above all they possess prudence, but with great eloquence and hospitality."[5]

Early in the seventeenth century there was a resurgence of interest in Elizabethan seamen. John Howes and other English chroniclers began to write about Hawkins as part of a larger chronicle of Elizabethan history. In his 1615 *Annales, or Generall Chronicle of England,* Howes devoted a page or so to Hawkins, calling him "the first Englishman, that discovered and taught the way" to Guinea and the West Indies. He also gave Hawkins credit for reorganizing the navy, for inventing the chain pump, and for "the cunning stratagem of fals netings for ships in fighting." Beyond this, he said that Hawkins was the first to bring tobacco to England, an accomplishment that now seems less beneficial than was previously supposed.[6]

The admiring glimpses in Howes were followed by Henry Holland, whose *Herωologia Anglica* (1620) established a pantheon of English heroes. It is a beautiful volume, with full-page portraits and three or four pages of text about each man. Hawkins merited a four-page biography, but no epitaph, as there were for Drake, Frobisher, and Cavendish. On his engraved portrait was the motto: "Advauncement by dilligence." Howes said nothing derogatory about Hawkins, but nothing laudatory, either. In fact, he made no comment on the man's character, except for a phrase from the first sentence: "Most accomplished in naval affairs" *(Rei Nautica Expertissimus);* and the last: "His body was honorably committed to the deep" *(corpus ejus honorifice oceano mandatum fuit).*[7] The influence of Holland's work was limited by its having been written in Latin. Even so, it placed Hawkins squarely in the company of England's famous admirals.

Two years later John's son Richard Hawkins published his *Observations,* thereby rescuing himself from obscurity and providing some interesting glimpses of his father and other prominent Elizabethans. Many of the facts he gives about his father are recorded nowhere else, and at least one seems to be at odds with his father's own testimony: the occasion in 1567 when Hawkins fired on a Spanish fleet and chased it from Plymouth harbor. John Hawkins said that he did so because he thought the fleet was hostile. Richard said that he did so because the Spaniard had not saluted the royal ensign. By restating facts in this way, Richard began to refurbish the reputation of John Hawkins, who still suffered from the taint of treason. Although Richard's book had a limited distribution, his ideas gained a much wider circulation in 1625, when Samuel Purchas included a condensed form of the book in *Purchas his Pilgrimes*. Purchas also reprinted Hakluyt's accounts of the voyages and added as well a transcription of the 1571 pardon from King Philip and the comments of R.M.[8]

Publishing at about the same time, William Camden took note of the various Hawkins voyages and credited Hawkins with teaching Drake the principles of seamanship, but he was put off by the man's association with slavery. Still, he felt there was an excuse. Englishmen took up this ghastly business only because the Spanish had shown them how. Hawkins may have been the first Englishman to do so, and he was certainly the most prominent. In Camden's opinion, it was nothing to be proud of. Several years later he added three pages in his book recounting the voyage of Richard Hawkins, but he said nothing more about John Hawkins except that he was a famous seaman who shared a command with Drake on his last voyage.[9]

One of the most important published contributions to the

Hawkins biography appeared in the 1633 edition of John Stow's *Survey of London*. This included a Latin inscription from the Hawkins monument in the Church of St. Dunstan-in-the-East, plus a narrative poem by Margaret Hawkins. Beginning with a reference to her own good self, "Dame Margaret" proclaimed her late husband to be

> One fearing God
> and Loyal to his Queen,
> True to the State
> by trial ever seen.

Thus she sought to clear away any trace of treason from his name, and hers as well. Among other details, she established his year of birth with these lines:

> His Yeeres to six times
> ten and three amounting,
> The ninth, the seventh
> Climacterick by counting.

He was sixty-three years old when he died in 1595, his climacteric being nine times seven. Check and double check.[10]

None of these publications brought Hawkins great fame. He was always overshadowed by his protégé Francis Drake, who lacked the taints of slave trading and treason. By the turn of the following century this began to change. John Prince compiled a volume of biographical sketches of *The Worthies of Devon,* among whom both John Hawkins and his son Richard had prominent positions. Prince quoted R.M. for an assessment of Hawkins, but he also gave the man credit for the defeat of the Spanish Armada, "his greatest glory." Prince felt certain that there were other achievements that might have been recounted, had someone only thought to record them. Since that had not been done, he said, "many of them are buried in oblivion."[11]

Some years later, perhaps inspired by Prince, John Campbell published a fourteen-page sketch of Hawkins, based on numerous manuscript and printed sources. He described the Hawkins character in two ways. First Campbell summarized the opinion of R.M. Then he made his own assessment, based largely on the description given a century earlier by Howes. "In spite of his Imperfections, he was always esteemed one of the ablest of his Profession; of which these are no inconsiderable Proofs, that he was a noted Commander at Sea forty-eight Years, and Treasurer of the Navy two and twenty. He and his elder brother *William* were Owners at once of thirty Saill of good Ships, and it was generally owned, that *Sir John Hawkins* was the Author of more useful Inventions, and introduced into the Navy better Regulations than any Officer who had Command therein before his Time."[12]

When Spanish historians began investigating their own archival sources for the history of this period, they were understandably less impressed by the man's achievements and strength of character. In 1832 Tomás González published a documentary study of relations between Spain and England during the first two decades of Elizabeth's reign. He not only described the details of the Hawkins offer "to enter the service of Philip," he also published some of the documents to prove it.[13]

This led to a careful and somewhat tentative revision of English attitudes toward Hawkins. In his ten-volume *History of England* John Lingard remarked that "this singular transaction" raised suspicions in the Privy Council. However, Hawkins presented excuses "such that the lords were, or pretended to be, satisfied." His contemporary Sir Clements

Markham called Lingard's words an "absurd calumny." In Markham's opinion, Hawkins may not have been terribly honest, perhaps, or very gentlemanly, but he was a patriot. "It was not very clean work and it ended in failure," wrote Markham, "but it is false that Hawkins was ever untrue to his country."[14]

Looking more closely at the Spanish documents, James Anthony Froude came up with an interpretation that has become standard for English historians. Hawkins simply wanted to free his men from Spanish captivity. Originally, he intended to free them by force, but he was not allowed to do so. "Hawkins, since he was forbidden to use force, determined to try what he could do by cunning." With the queen's permission and the help of Cecil, he proceeded to trick the Spanish ambassador and ultimately the Spanish king. As a result his men were released, and Hawkins received £40,000 or £50,000, plus a grant of nobility from the Spanish king. Recognizing inconsistencies in his story, Froude said that the definitive Spanish documents had been destroyed. "The King did not care to leave on record an account of the trick by which he had been taken in." With this problem settled, Froude called Hawkins Queen Elizabeth's "ablest commander," but admitted he may have lacked some qualities of a gentleman. "Sir John was not a virtuous man in the clerical sense of the word, but he had the affection of a brave man for the comrades who had fought at his side."[15]

A few refused to enter the controversy about treason. Among them was W. H. Smith, who published important British Museum documents about Hawkins in 1849. These helped to reinforce the idea that Hawkins had done much to modernize the English navy before the Armada campaign. Unfortunately for the Hawkins reputation, Smith also helped to reinvigorate the slave-trade controversy, referring to the popular conception of Hawkins as "the first proposer and actual founder of the odious Slave Trade."[16]

These charges struck too close to home for the comfort of a group of Plymouth historians. In 1883 R. N. Worth defended Hawkins in a lengthy and well-documented article. He said that Hawkins was not the "founder of the slave trade," though he was involved in that "horrible traffic." Worth then compared men of Elizabethan times, who thought "God had given [them] the heathen for an inheritance," with Englishmen of his own day, who were "content with the heathen land," said Worth. "I cannot see much difference." In summing up, Worth called Hawkins "not only the ablest seaman of this day, but the best shipwright that England had ever seen; often entering upon what in modern eyes are questionable ways, but never false to his own conscience." Worth was the first biographer to sketch the entire life of John Hawkins and to place him in a family setting. Sir Clements Markham had published a very brief sketch some years earlier, but for all practical purposes, Worth was correct in saying, "Their story remains untold."[17]

Inspired by his remark, Mary W. S. Hawkins prepared the first book-length account of the Hawkins family. Published in 1888 under the title *Plymouth Armada Heroes,* this carefully documented work included material not only on John Hawkins, but on his father, his brother William, his wives and his son, and a few other Hawkinses besides. She found her presumed ancestor to have been a marvelous seaman, courageous, pious, skilled in mathematics, a shrewd tactician, an able administrator with a boundless capacity for work. "He was not without failings," she said, "but these were exaggerated by such people as found it easy to censure a man whom it would have been difficult to imitate."[18]

When the first *Dictionary of National Biography* was published in 1891, John Knox Laughton contributed a number of lengthy sketches of prominent Elizabethan seamen. His sketch of Hawkins in volume 25 is still worth reading, as is his conclusion: "Whatever his faults, history has condoned them, rightly considering him one of the great men who broke the power of Spain, and established England's maritime supremacy."[19]

In 1927 James A. Williamson published the first scholarly biography, *Sir John Hawkins: The Time and the Man*. The book was the fruit of Williamson's painstaking research. Among the Cottonian manuscripts in the British Museum, which also earned him the 1926 Julian Corbett Prize of the Institute of Historical Research, Williamson found a long but incomplete account of the 1568 voyage. Both the beginning and ending pages were missing, and the tops of all pages were burned away. Intrigued by what still remained, Williamson transcribed the document, made careful guesses at missing words and phrases, and wrote an extensive introduction. Williamson admired Hawkins and said so. He thought it unfortunate that others did not. "In the popular mind he remains to this day only as the man who began the slave trade." Even so, he said the stamp of Hawkins and men of his kind was visible in the national character. "Many who have never heard their names may be moulded in their likeness." Williamson's Hawkins was an outstanding seaman, a clever administrator, loyal to queen and country, honest, religious, and in his last days something of a Puritan. Williamson's unique contribution was to document the immense importance of Hawkins in building a formidable English navy.[20]

A few years after the biography appeared, in 1933, Williamson published an edition of *The Observations of Sir Richard Hawkins*. Although this work had been reprinted earlier, Williamson's edition corrected errors and added much introductory information.[21] As he had done with the biography of the illustrious father, Williamson also added unpublished documents that gave important details about the family. A revised edition of Williamson's biography of John Hawkins appeared in 1949 under a new title and including corrections from documents published by Irene A. Wright and Antonio Rumeu de Armas. *Hawkins of Plymouth* included more on other family members and less documentation than the first edition.[22]

In both his editions Williamson made use of materials gathered in the Mexican archives by G. R. G. Conway, who deposited copies and translations in various libraries, including the University Library (Cambridge) and the Library of Congress. Conway also published his own brief book on the men taken prisoner in Mexico, *An Englishman and the Mexican Inquisition*. These new sources soon came to the attention of Rayner Unwin, who mined them for a popular work he titled *The Defeat of John Hawkins*. According to Unwin, "Hawkins' third expedition to the Slave Coast and the Spanish Main marked a turning-point in naval strategy, and established between England and Spain the future pattern of their political destiny."[23] Long on gripping narrative but short on documentation, Unwin's account became very popular. Perhaps because the author was also the publisher, the book has apparently never been out of print.

Several important Spanish assessments of Hawkins appeared in the twentieth century. In 1913 the Instituto de Estudios Americanistas in Seville published a study of the four Hawkins voyages to America. Written by C. Sanz Arismendi, a professor at the University of Seville, this was the first scholarly work on Hawkins based entirely on material from the Archivo General de Indias. Sanz concluded that the documents showed Hawkins to have been a very different man from the cruel and grasping pirate presented in Spanish histories. Rather, he was "loyal to his word, magnanimous in returning treasure to Spaniards, generous in indemnifying damage he had caused, and with regard to his personal ability, a very accomplished seaman and more than a pirate."[24] No doubt this served as an inspiration to Rumeu de Armas. In 1947 the Escuela de Estudios Hispano-Americanos published his study, *Los Viajes de John Hawkins a America, 1562–1595*. The work was based almost entirely on archival sources, some of which had been published in earlier decades by Irene A. Wright. While her work was concentrated in the archives of Seville, Rumeu de Armas worked through the archives in Simancas and the hitherto unexplored archives in his native Canary Islands. He also included an extensive appendix with transcriptions of important documents from all three archival collections. In his opinion Hawkins was a man caught between two nations, sometimes more Spanish than English, sometimes not. Rumeu said the negotiations with Philip were genuine efforts to join with Spain. This was not a character flaw, in his opinion. Hawkins was one of the greatest seaman England ever produced. "The English cannot fail to recognize that Hawkins placed the first stone in the colossal edifice that in time would become the British Empire."[25]

Other books about John Hawkins have appeared from time to time, none of them adding much to the basic facts assembled by Williamson. In 1969, for example, Michael Lewis published *The Hawkins Dynasty*. This work summarized previous publications about the Hawkins family, at times without attribution. In the life of his illustrious ancestor Lewis saw the triumph of a brave and honest Englishman over a perfidious but gullible Spain. For him it was a story of national character and national religion, with the English brand of each a clear winner.[26]

During the past century or so various documentary collections have been published, adding considerably to the sources for a life of John Hawkins. The earliest, and in some ways the best, were the volumes of documents translated by Irene A. Wright from the massive collections at the Archivo General de Indias in Seville. Of particular interest for the life of John Hawkins are the volumes issued by the Hakluyt Society in 1929 and 1932, which cover the voyages to America to the year 1569. A related volume by Mary Frear Keeler and published by the Hakluyt Society in 1981 is useful for documenting the work done by Hawkins on the ships used in Drake's voyage to the West Indies in 1585–86.[27]

Other documentary collections, while very useful, do not match the meticulous standards set by these two scholars. In 1894 the Navy Records Society published two volumes of documents transcribed at the Public Records Office by John K. Laughton. These cover naval operations during 1588 and provide a clear view of the role played by Hawkins in building and later commanding ships of Her Majesty's navy. Four years later the Navy Records Society issued a companion volume by Julian S. Corbett, covering the naval war with Spain from 1585 through 1587.[28] In both of these collections the editors made the unfortunate decision to modernize spelling, punctuation, and in some cases sentence structure, all of which detract from the value of these works as sources of scholarly investigation.

Several Spanish collections are of interest for the life of John Hawkins. Four volumes in the massive *Colección de documentos inéditos para la historia de España* were issued between 1888 and 1892. Edited by José Sancho Rayon and Francisco de Zabálburu, these works provide a fairly accurate Spanish text of many of the documents summarized in the *Calendar of State Papers, Spanish*. A more recent Spanish collection edited by Jorge Calvar Gross and others provides a Spanish text of documents relating to the naval war between Spain and England. In addition, the work includes bibliographical information and excerpts from documents published elsewhere.[29] In all of these volumes grammar, spelling, and punctuation are modernized. Anyone interested in the actual words must consult the original copies in the archives at Simancas.

A related work, issued by the Hakluyt Society, was done with meticulous attention to detail. In 1972 Kenneth R. Andrews added a final volume to his earlier book on *English Privateering Voyages, 1588–1595*. Once again using Spanish manuscripts provided by Irene A. Wright, Andrews assembled a collection of documents from various European libraries and archives, describing *The Last Voyage of Drake and Hawkins*. While stating that he wants to avoid drawing any conclusions about the expedition, Andrews still manages to show that the whole enterprise was badly planned, carelessly organized, and "a miserable failure," without much actual effect on the continuing contest between England and Spain. He believes that both Hawkins and Drake were too old to have command, much less to share command when they were so different in temperament. Beyond this, he finds both to have been eager for the chance to prove themselves one last time, which for Hawkins, at least, was probably untrue.[30]

In each of these studies John Hawkins appears first as one sort of man, then as another. Where is the true John Hawkins? He is somewhere in between. He was smart, literate, good with numbers, but he was not well educated, and he was not in any sense a scholar. He was an outstanding seaman, and he understood ships, but he was not a shipwright. He was a born merchant and trader, and he was not afraid to go far afield for a profit. He had a quick temper, but he was equally quick to forgive, and as time passed he overcame the tendency to anger. He was reserved and quiet, and his friends were mostly members of his immediate family. He understood loyalty, but he understood that there were limits. This is why he was able to forgive Drake for desertion at San Juan de Ulúa. It was also why he could deal secretly with the king of Spain and not feel like a traitor. He was brave but not foolhardy. He preferred advance preparation to audacity. These were qualities that made him the perfect choice for the job of treasurer of the navy. He could deal effectively with merchants and bureaucrats. He could recognize good ship construction, and he was aware of the ways of contractors. He knew how to equip a navy at a price England could afford. His greatest achievement was the preparation of the naval force that made it possible for England to resist the Spanish Armada and send it to its doom.

Appendix 1

Latin Text of Hawkins's Damage Claim
for Losses at San Juan de Ulúa

Scedula continens species bonorum, etrerum, cum valore, et estima-
cione earundem monete Anglie; quibus Johannes Hawkins spoliatus
fuit, in portu Sancti Johannis de lowe per vim armatam, vice regis Mexi-
cæ Regionis Admiralli classis, articulate, aliorumque hispanorum./

1   Imprimis Navis articulata vocata le Jesus de Lubecke
    cum apparatu, et ornamente suis ex Anglia emissa.   5000^{li} ster

2   Item bellica tormenta, sive bombarde æneæ, et ferrae,
    que fuerunt, de ornamentis, apparatu et munimentis
    eiusdem Navis, vocat le Jesus in eadem navi reposite,
    et ex Anglia exportato   2000^{li}

3   Item pulvis bombardicus, pile ferreæ, arma, et alia
    tormenta, sive bombarde in eadem Navi reposita, et ex
    anglia exportato   1000^{li}

4   Item due anchore, et tres funes anchorarii vocato cables,
    de apparato navis articulate vocate le Mynnion, qui
    deperditi fuerunt dum dicta navis a vi hispanorum se
    raptum expediret   200^{li}

5   Item navis articulata vocata le Swallowe cum apparatu,
    ornamentis, et munimentis suis, ex Anglia emissa, victualia
    et nautarum bona, in eadem reposita   850^{li}

6 Item navis articulata, vocata le Angell cum apparatu,
   ornamentis, et munimentis eiusdem ex anglia emissa,
   necnon victualia et nautarum bona, in eadem reposita   180^{li}

7 Item navis articulata vocat le gracia dei, cum apparatu,
   ornamentis, et munimentis eiusdem necnon victualia, et
   nautarum bona in eadem imposita   400^{li}

8 Item in navi articulata vocat le Jesus, aliisque tribus
   navibus, predictis, aut eorum aliquibus 57. Nigri
   Æthiopes, vulgo dicto negros optimi generis, et stature,
   quorum singuli valebant in regionibus Indie occidentalis
   400 pesos auri   9120^{li}

9 Item in dc̃a navi vocata le Jesus, aliisque tribus navibus
   predc̃is, vel earum aliquibus 30 bale panni linei quorum
   singule valebant 3000 Rs   2250^{li}

10 Item in dc̃is quatuor navibus, vel earum aliquibus, 1000
   panni tincti vulgo dicto pintados quorum singuli valebant
   15^{s} ster   750^{li}

11 Item in dc̃is quatuor navibus, vel earũ aliquibus 400 libre
   eius generis m^{er}cium que vulgo dicuntur margaritas,
   quarum singule libre valebant v^{s} ster   100^{li}

12 Item in dictis quatuor navibus vel earum aliquibus,
   300^{li} stanni, quarũ singule valebant ii^{s} ster   30^{li}

13 Item bala bisso vulgo dicto taffata continens 40 vares   40^{li}

14 Item quatuor balas pannorũ laneorũ dicto hamsheres et
   northens quorũ singuli valebant viii^{li} ster   340^{li}

15 Item sex bale cottonorum   90^{li}

16 Item cista continens 30 gladios deauratos   120^{li}

17 Item 12 klo cere   120^{li}

18 Item septem dolia manilior̃u vulgo vii tonnes of manilios
   quarum singula valebant 50^{li} 350^{li}
19 Item in d̃ca navi vocato le Jesus, sacculus auri et argenti
   continens 6000 pesos auri et argenti   2400^{li}
20 Item in d̃ca navi, cista continens diversas species argenti
   facti vulgo dicto silver plate   200^{li}
21 Item in dicta navi argentum dicto coriente   500^{li}
22 Item in d̃cis quatuor navibus, vel earum aliquibus; viginti
   dolia vini cretici et hispanici vulgo xx butts of malmseys
   & stecks   300^{li}
23 Item in dictis quatuor navibus vel earum aliquibus 36
   vascule farine, vulgo xxxvi barrells meale, quor̃u singule
   valebant 4^{li} 144^{li}
24 Item in d̃cis quatuor navibus vel earum aliquibus, alia
   victualia et necessaria ad valor^{em} 150li^{li}
25 Item in dicta navi vocato le Jesus bestitus dicti Johannis
   Hawkins, aliaque in eius proprium usum comparata   300^{li}
26 Item in d̃ca navi vocato le Jesus ciste et sarcine nautarum   900^{li}
27 Item in d̃ca navi vocato le Jesus bale 20 mantellorum vulgo
   dicto a packe of xx clokes, quorum singuli valebant 4^{li} 80^{li} [1]

Appendix 2

Account of the Battle at San Juan de Ulúa

ALVARO DE FLORES

Obra nueuamēte compuesta so
bre vna admirable victoria que bono Don
Francisco Luxan
contra don Juã d Acle lutherano capitan de
la
Reyna de Inglaterra. Compuesto por
Aluaro
de Flores natural de Malaga y vecino de
Sebilla. V[i]sta y examinada por el do
ctor millan, y con licēcia impreša
en Burgos por Pedro de
Sātillana impressor.
Año.M.D.LXX.

A work newly composed
about the admirable victory won by Don
Francisco Luxan
against Don Juan Hawkins, Lutheran,
captain for
the Queen of England. Composed by
Alvaro
de Flores, native of Malaga and citizen of
Seville. Seen and examined by Doctor
Millan, and printed with license
in Burgos by Pedro de
Santillan, printer.
In the Year 1570.

Comiença la obra.

The work begins.

Emperadora del cielo
Rosa fresco linda aurora
pues que soys nuestro cõsuelo
alcançame en este suelo
de la gracia que en vos mora,
Sagrada virgen Maria
madre de mi redemptor
dame gracia en este dia
porque cõ la historia mia
diga con vuestro fauor.

Oh Empress of heaven
Blooming rose, Glowing dawn,
Thou who art our consolation,
Grant me while in this vale
the grace that dwells in thee.
Holy Virgin Mary,
Mother of my Redeemer
Give me grace this day
So that my history
May be told with thy approval.

¶ Porӄ todos los christianos
que en el mundo son nascidos
dexen los vicios mundanos
que los ciegos lutheranos
vean como descreydos
Porque tengan en memoria
lo que ahora acontescio
contare en aquella h[i]storia
la gran batalla y victoria.
que ahora en Indias subcedio,

¶ De Sebilla se partio
una poderosa armada
a Sant Lucar allego
y luego de alli salto
un juebes de madrugada,
A seys de Julio fue el dia
quando la armada que cuento
de Sant Lucar se Partia
llena segun convenio
de vizcocho y bastimē̃to,

¶ Y llevan por general
vn hombre muy esforçado
mas valiente que vn Roldan
por nombre Francisco Luxan
en guerra hombre auisado
con buen viento y temporal
a Canaria han arribado
mando luego el general
hagan salua principal
assi como es obligado.

¶ Las ancoras han hechado
en el puerto a do llego
y el general esforçado
con seys hō̃bres bien armado
en vn esquilfe salto,
Al tiempo ӄ el sol se encierra

So that all Christians
Who are born into the world
Might abandon worldly vices,
So that the blinded Lutherans
Might be seen as unbelievers,
So that they might remember
What I am now undertaking
To tell in that history
About the great battle and victory
That has already happened in the Indies.

From Seville there set out
A powerful armada.
It arrived at San Lucar,
And then left that place
One Thursday at dawn.
The sixth of July was the day
When the armada that I am telling about
Departed from San Lucar,
Filled as it should have been
With biscuit and provisions.

And they had as their general
A very brave man,
More valiant than Roland,
called Francisco Luxan.
A man trained in warfare,
With good wind and weather
At the Canaries he arrived,
Then the general told them
They should salute the governor
According to the standards of courtesy.

The anchors were dropped
In the port where they arrived,
And the brave general
With six well-armed men
Got into his skiff
At the hour of sundown.

para refrescos tomar	To renew their provisions,
fueron a saltar en tierra	They were going to land,
mas los isleños con guerra	But the armed islanders
no les dexarian entrar	Would not allow them to enter.
¶ Y la gente de Castilla	And the men from Castille
se lo ruega con prudencia	Asked with moderation
que les de entrada en la villa	To be allowed to enter the town.
ellos dizen q̃ en Sebilla	Those people replied that in Seville
ay fama de pestilencia,	The pestilence is said to be widespread,
y por ser mal peligroso	And since it is such a dangerous curse,
no les dexarian llegar	They would not let them disembark
a tomar algun reposo	To renew their supplies,
porque el mal es contagioso	Because the plague is contagious
y se les puede pegar.	And could spread among them.
¶ El general ques prudente	The general, who is reasonable,
desta suerte respondio	Answered thus forcefully:
por cierto en toda mi gente	In truth, among all my men
hombre de tal acidente	A man of such description
en mis naos no se embarco,	Has not embarked on my ships.
Los de la isla dexaron	Then the men of the island allowed
a todos desembarcar	All to disembark,
y ellos en tierra saltaron	And they went on land
donde refrescos tomarõ	Where they took soft drinks
para lleuar por la mar	To take to sea.
¶ A diez y siete contados	On the seventeenth day
de Julio de alli partio	Of July they departed therefrom,
el armada y los soldados	The armada and the soldiers,
apercebidos y armados	Ready and armed,
porque assi me escriuio,	Just as he wrote to me.
La capitana y las otras	La Capitana and the others
con las demas nauegaron	Sailed with the rest,
La admiranta y la falcona	La Almiranta and La Falcona,
a la isla de La mona	At the island of Mona,
puerto de indias allegaron.	A port of the Indies, arrived.
¶ Al puerto nr̃os christianos	In the harbor our Christians

dieron ferros a la mar	Dropped their anchors in the sea.
y a los indios comarcanos	And in the Indies nearby
doze naos de lutheranos	Twelve ships of Lutherans
vinieron a conquistar	Came to conquer,
y la ciudad les quemaron	And they burned the city,
estos falsos lutheranos	These false Lutherans,
y los templos derribaron	And they destroyed the temples,
y en ellos se aposentaron	And they lodged themselves there,
matando muchos Christianos	Killing many Christians.
¶ Luego el sargento mayor	Then the sergeant major
en vn esquilfe ha saltado	Jumped into a skiff,
perdiendo todo temor	Abandoning all fear,
como fuerte guerreador	As a brave warrior,
con dos hombres a su lado	With two men at his side.
y los indios con plazer	And the Indians, with pleasure,
los reciben y contento	Greeted and welcomed them.
y luego sin detener	And then without hesitation
los traxeron de comer	They brought food
de su pobre bastimento	From their scant supply.
¶ Y luego sin mas tardar	And then without much delay,
vieron vn baxel venir	They noticed a vessel coming
por la parte de alta mar	From the high seas,
nabegando a mas andar	Sailing as though to anchorage.
que el puerto viene a surgir	As the boat approached the port
Desputa q̃ en el puerto entro	Uncertain about entering the port
bieron que era de Christianos	They saw that it belonged to Christians.
y el sargento pregunto	And the sergeant asked
si porventura topo	Whether they happened to meet
nauios de lutheranos.	Some ships of the Lutherans.
¶ El patron le respondio	The patron answered him
que punto no se dilata	Without belaboring the point,
como aquel que los conto	As one who told,
que ocho nauios vio	The eight ships he saw,
junto al puerto de la plata,	were near the Puerto de la Plata.
El sargento se bolvio	The sergeant sailed
con el esqilfe a su armada	With his skiff to his armada,

Battle at San Juan de Ulúa
{289}

y a su general conto	And he reported to his general
todo lo que le passo	All that had happened,
sin que le mintiesse nada	Omitting nothing.
¶ y luego sin mas tardar	And so without delay
las ancoras han sacado	The anchors were raised
del profundo de la mar	From out of the deep,
comiençan a nauegar	And they began to sail
con biento fresco templado	With a fair wind.
a Sant Juan de Lua llegaron	They arrived at San Juan de Ulúa
vn juebes por la mañana	On a Thursday morning,
y antes q̃ en el puerto entraron	And before they entered the port
ocho nauios hallaron	Eight ships appeared,
de la gente lutherana.	Belonging to the nation of the Lutherans.
¶ Antes q̃ e al puerto entrarõ	Before they moored,
de la ciudad vera cruz	From the city of Vera Cruz
vna barquilla embiaron	There came a small boat,
con la qual les auissaron	By which they advised
los amigos de Jesus,	The friends of Jesus,
Diziendo que esta ganada	Saying they had occupied
la ciudad y destruyda	The city and destroyed it,
de Sant Juã de Lua nõbrada	The one named San Juan de Ulúa,
de ocho nauios de armada	With eight ships of the armada
desta gente descreyda.	Of this unbelieving nation.
¶ Y el buen Francisco Luxan	And the good Francisco Luxan
mando apercebir su gente	Ordered his men to prepare,
como fuerte capitan	As a strong captain,
porque estaua alli don Juan	Because here was Don Juan,
vn lutherano valiente,	A valiant Lutheran.
Todos en la capitana	Everyone in La Capitana
fueron juntos en vn hora	Was ready in an hour,
con voluntad limpia y sana	With a fair and healthy will,
pretendiendo muy de gana	Considering it an honor
morir por nuestra señora.	To die for Our Lady.
¶ Y a grandes bozes dezia	And in a loud voice spoke
el buen Francisco Luxan	The good Francisco Luxan,

que su gente bien te oya
hermanos oy es el dia
que saldremos bien de affan,
Oy henchiremos las manos
en sangre del antechristo
muriendo como Rornanos
y como fieles Christianos
por la fe de Jesu Christo.

¶ Apercebios y entende
que saldremos con victoria
segun tenemos porfe
y al capitan vencere
quedando de nos memoria,
Por sus estancias mando
ordenar bien sus trincheras
y ansi los apercibio
y luego se obedescio
puestos en sus ballesteras.

¶ Dõ Juã de acle el enemigo
de dios y nuestros christianos
se quiso dar por amigo
del general como digo
con todos sus lutheranos,
En vna barca embio
el renegado don Juan
vn mensajero y entro
en la nao donde hablo
a Francisco de Luxan.

¶ Diziẽdo el Rey desta tierra
manda que luego a la hora
obedezcays sin dar guerra

¶ la Reyna de Inglaterra
Ysabella mi señora
El general como oyo
lo que el hereje dezia

So that his men might hear him well:
Brothers, today is the day
That we may well put aside fear.
Today we will cover our hands
With the blood of the Antichrist,
Dying like Romans
And as faithful Christians
For the faith of Jesus Christ.

Be ready and understand
That we shall emerge with victory
Just as we cling to the faith.
And I will vanquish that captain,
Giving him something to remember us by.
To your stations I order you.
Prepare well your defensive walls.
And so he prepared them
And he was obeyed,
And they set their crossbows in the portholes.

Don Juan Hawkins, the enemy
Of God and our Christians,
Wished to present himself as a friend
Of the general, as I say,
With all his Lutherans.
In a small boat he sent,
This renegade Don Juan,
A messenger, and he entered
In the ship where he talked
To Francisco de Luxan,

Saying the sovereign of this land
Orders that forthwith
You should obey without hostilities

The Queen of England,
Isabella my Lady.
The general, upon hearing
What the heretic said,

desta suerte respondio,	Replied to his challenge,
dezia quien os embio	Saying, whoever sends you
con esta mensajeria.	With this dispatch,
¶ Que quiẽ a Dios a negado	He who has denied God,
tambien su Rey negara	His king also denies,
y que este bien auisado	And he should be forewarned,
el lutherano maluado	This wicked Lutheran,
porque presto morira,	For I am about to kill him,
y su sangre en este dia	And his blood on this day,
derramare con crudeza	To pour out savagely,
dando fin a su porfia	And bring an end to his obstinacy,
dezepando su heregia	Uprooting his heresy
cortandose la cabeça.	Cutting off his head.
¶ El mensajero boluio	The messenger returned
al hereje capitan	To the heretic captain
y todo se lo conto	And told him all.
y el hereje se espanto	And the heretic began to fear
de Francisco de Luxan,	Francisco de Luxan.
Luego el lutherano entro	Then the Lutheran sailed
en su esquilfe en la mar	In his skiff into the sea.
de fuertes armas se armo	He armed himself heavily
y a los nauios se llego	And he approached the ships,
el qual le mando llamar.	Calling as he came.
¶ Francisco Luxan salto	Francisco Luxan leapt
en otro baxel armado	Into another armed vessel
y al contrario se allego	And he approached the enemy
con dos hombres que lleuo	With two men that he brought
que alli estaua concertado	Of those who were gathered there.
Como el tirano a su lado	Then the tyrant by his side
vio a Francisco de Luxan	Saw that Francisco de Luxan
todo se ha temorizado.	Made everyone fearful,
y con soberuia ha hablado	And he was overcome with arrogance,
diziendo buen capitan.	Saying, this good captain,
¶ Mucho he desseado ver	I have longed to challenge
tu persona con la mia	You face to face

por solo ver tu poder	Simply to test your strength,
para te poder vencer	So that I can overcome
tu gran soberuia y porfia,	Your enduring presumption.
Mas yo quiero paz contigo	But I want peace with you.
aunque podiera vencerte	Even though I could defeat you,
tu te muestras mi enemigo	You show yourself to be my enemy.
de oy demas sere tu amigo	From today I will ever be your friend,
si quieres hasta la muerte.	If you wish, to the death.
¶ Para que con mas verdad	In order to confirm
pazes seguras esten	This arrangement,
darete mi voluntad	I will give of my free will
diez hombres de calidad	Ten men of quality,
trueque por por [*sic*] trueq̃ en rebẽ	One for one in exchange.
Con animo coraçon	With a stout heart
el general ha hablado	The general replied:
no me espanta tu blason	Your blustering does not frighten me.
que a muchos de tu opinion	So much for your opinion
he muerto mas de tu grado.	I prefer death to your esteem.
¶ Y si es que en ti se hallo	If there is within you
tanta fuerça y valentia	Such strength and bravery,
luego puedes aceralla	Then you can find it out.
hagamos nuestra batalla	We will do battle,
de tu persona a la mia	Just you and me.
El tirano acabardado	The tyrant, intimidated,
no se la quiso aceptar	Did not wish to accept it.
mas la respuesta que ha dado	But this reply was given,
que aũque a pesar de su grado	To his offer,
que la guerra sea en la mar.	That there should be war at sea.
¶ El general ques prudente	The general, who is prudent,
la palabra le acepto	Accepted the words,
y en aquel dia presente	And that very day
mando apercebir su gente	Ordered his men to make ready,
y en la capitana entro,	And entered into La Capitana.
La tierra mando tomar	He ordered that the land be guarded
con dos naos bien armadas	With two well-armed ships,
y el con tres tomo la mar	And with three he took the sea

| que no puedan escapar | So that none should be able to escape |
| las ocho ya estan cercadas. | Of the eight that were already surrounded. |

¶ Un Juebes por la mañana
se les bio la bateria
llamando de buena gana
a la virgen soberana
sacratissima Maria,
Ciento y treynta lutheranos
murieron sin los heridos
y solos veynte Christianos
fuerõ muertos por las manos
de las perros descreydos.

¶ La capitana tomaron
con otros quatro baxeles
y otra nao grãde quemaron
y dos se les escaparon
destos perros infieles
El capitan sementido
en la miñona escapo
en vna pierna herido
y el thesoro recogio
que en esta nao se lleuo.

¶ Treynta caxas de oro fino
que en la mar auia robado
Se las lleva de camino
el lutherano maligno
sin thesoro que ha dexado,
Con voz que al cielo subia
y ansias de su caraçan
sus bistiduras rompia
con el dolor que sentia
dize el perro esta razon.

¶ No con muy pequeña saña
los defuntos desentierra
diziendo por fuerça, o maña

One Thursday morning
The army began the fight,
Calling willingly
To the sovereign Virgin
Mary most holy.
A hundred and thirty Lutherans
Died, not counting the wounded,
And only twenty Christians
Were dead at the hands
Of those unbelieving dogs.

They captured La Capitana,
Along with four other vessels,
And they burned another great ship,
And two made their escape.
Of those infidel dogs.
The disappointed captain
Escaped in the Minion
With a wounded leg.
But the treasure he had amassed,
Which he carried in this ship,

Thirty cases of refined gold
That he had stolen on the sea,
He left them on the road,
That malignant Lutheran.
Without his treasure, which he abandoned,
With a voice raised to heaven,
And heavy of heart,
He ripped his garments,
Because of the sorrow he felt.
The dog gives this reason.

With no little fury
He exhumes the dead,
Crying aloud, O cunning

a Phelippe rey de España	Philip, king of Spain.
no le dare cruda guerra,	I shall not make such savage war.
Cinco oras y mas duro	Five hours and more went
la batalla en este dia	The battle on this day
y nuestra gente vencio	And our men conquered
y el despojo se partio	And divided the plunder
que se gano en aquel dia.	That they took on that day.

¶ Antonio de Delgadillo	Antonio de Delgadillo
teniente del contador	Lieutenant of the contador
ve hallado en un castillo	Was ensconced in a castle,
tan flaco y tan amarillo	So weak and so sickly
que era de velle dolor,	That he was *de velle dolor.*
Villanueua y Bustamante	Villanueva and Bustamante,
teniente del thesorero	Lieutenant of the treasurer,
hombre rico y muy pujante	That rich and powerful man,
le lleuaron por delante	He was carried off with
muy gran suma de dinero.	A very great sum of money.

¶ Aqui fueron rescatados	Here they were rescued,
librandolos de la muerte	Freeing them from death,
nuestros valientes soldados	Our valiant soldiers,
como hōbres muy esforçados	Such brave men,
dando por buena su suerte	Happy with their good fortune.
en sant Juan de Lua entrado	Into San Juan de Ulúa entered
el general y christianos	The general and the Christians,
y contigo habian lleuado	And with him he brought,
de los que hauian captiuado	Of those captured,
cinquenta y dos lutheranos	Fifty-two Lutherans.

¶ Roberto Enrrique y tomas	Roberto Enrique and Tomas
y Alexandre de caçalla	And Alexandre de Caçalla
con Gregorio de Gormaz	With Gregorio de Gormaz
y otro Fernando de paz	And another, Fernando de Paz,
prendieron en la batalla,	Were captured in the battle,
y el general pregano	And the general ordered
que los pressos embarcassen	The prisoners to go on board ship,
y despues desto mando	And afterward he ordered

a cien hombres que dexo	A hundred men should be left
que la ciudad amparassen	To protect the city.
¶ Acabada esta victoria	With the victory won,
saca del puerto su armada	He took his armada out of the port.
este digno de memoria	This battle is worthy of memory
con el triumpho de la gloria	With the triumph of glory
que alli gano por su espada,	Gained here by the sword.
Y luego los marineros	And afterward the seamen
las belas fueron a alçar	Raised their sails,
con todos los prisioneros	With all their prisoners
y gran sumo de dineros	Along with the great treasure
que tomaron en la mar	That they took at sea.
¶ Y con aquesta pujança	And with that vigor
nauego con su cõpaña	He sailed with his company
con buena mar de bonança	With fine sailing weather.
y con aquesta esperança	And with this hope
llegaron a nuestra España,	They arrived in our Spain.
de oy de mas nr̃os christianos	And so today Christians
tengan gozo y alegria	Are filled with joy and gladness,
pues q̃ ya los Lutheranos	For now the Lutherans
y los moros comarcanos	And the neighboring Moors
los vencemos cada dia.	Are conquered every day.
¶ Y a vos Virgen soberana	And to thee Oh Sovereign Virgin,
principio de nuestra gloria	The origin of our glory,
Maria do siempre magna	The ever great Mary,
nuestra intercessiõ Christiana	Our Christian intercession.
dadle a nuestro rey victoria,	Grant victory to our king
y al moro que en nuestra tierra	And over the Moor in our land
se ha coronado por rey	May he be crowned king
por darnos trabajo y guerra	For leading us in work and warfare
con los moros de la tierra	With the Moors of the land,
confundio su secta y grey	Confounding their religion and race.

¶ *Villancico*

¶ Si en la mas fuerte batalla
buelue Christo por su fe
patentemente se vee
que impossible es derriballa.

¶ Los moros y lutheranos
no se procuren cansar
pues no pueden derribar
a los patentes Christianos,
No basta fuerça de manos
ni todo humano saber
para los poder vencer
un fuerte cota de malla.

¶ De continuo ha de tomar
reino pues es nuestro padre
por la yglesia nuestra madre
ques su esposa singular.
y en esto no ay que dubdar
segun en sancta escriptura
patentemente se halla.

¶ Nuestra fe ques infalible
siempre ha de preualecer
porque no puede caer
pues a Dios todo es posible
La maldad incorregible
esta es la que caera
y nuestra fe durara
imposible es conquistalla.

¶ *Otra villancico*

Rey Philipe con la espada
venceras tan cruda guerra

Carol

If, in the fiercest battle
Christ returns for his Faith.
Overwhelmed, one sees
How impossible it is to defeat it.

The Moors and the Lutherans
Never cease trying,
But they cannot destroy
Convinced Christians.
Human force does not suffice
Nor does man know how
To be able to conquer
A heavy coat of mail.

Everlasting is
The reign of Our Father
Through our Mother the Church
Which is his only spouse.
And in her without doubt
The truth, perfect and pure,
According to Sacred Scripture,
Is made manifest.

Our faith that is infallible,
Will always prevail,
For she cannot fail.
For God everything is possible.
Incorrigible evil
Will fail,
And our faith will endure.
It is impossible to conquer her.

Other carol

King Philip with your sword
You will win the savage war

al reyno de Inglaterra
y a los moros de Granada.

Cõ tu espada y fuerte escudo
se que tienes de vencer
al gran Turco y su poder
los del Meco y Tartamudo
y al falso rey de la tierra
daras muerte desastrada

¶ Los imperios affricanos
benceras con braço armado
con todo lo ques poblado
de Turcos y Lutheranos
coronandote en su tierra
con tu persona ganada
al reyno de Inglaterra
y a las moros de Granada.[1]

Laus Deo.

Against the kingdom of England
And the Moors of Granada.

With your sword and strong shield
I know you must defeat
The Great Turk and his power,
Those of Mecca and the netherworld,
And on the false king of that land
Inflict a violent death.

The African empires
Conquer with your armed might,
Along with all the people on earth,
Turks and Lutherans,
Crowning yourself in their land
Conquered by your own hand
The kingdom of England
And the Kingdom of Granada.

Praise God.

Appendix 3

Inscription on the Memorial to Hawkins
at St. Dunstan in the East

Johannes Hawkins; *Eques auratus, clariss. Reginae clariss.*
Reginae Marinarum causarum Thesaurarius. Qui cum
XLIII annos muniis bellicis, & longis periculosis naviga-
tionibus, detengendis novis regionibus, ad Patriae utili-
tatem, & suam ipsius gloriam, strenuam & egregiam oper-
am navasset, in expeditione, cui Generalis praefuit ad
Indiam occidentalem dum in Anchoris ad poitnin S. Joan-
nis in insula Beriquena staret, placide in Domino ad
coelestem patriam emigravit, 12 die Novembris anno salutis
1595. In cujus memoriam ob virtutem & res gestas Domina
Margareta Hawkins *vxor moestissima, hoc monumentum*
cum lachrymis posuit.

By the tomb hangs a fair table, fastened in the Wall, with these verses in
English:

Dame Margaret;

A widow well affected
This monument
Of memory erected,

Deciphering
Unto the viewer's sight
The life and death
Of Sir John Hawkins, Knight
One fearing God
And loyal to his Queen,
True to the State
By trial ever seen,
Kind to his wives,
Both gentlewomen born
Whose counterfeits
With grace this work adorn.
Dame Katharine,
The first, of rare report,
Dame Margaret
The last, of Court consort,
Attendant on
The chamber and the bed
Of England's Queen
Elizabeth, our head
Next unto Christ,
Of whom all princes hold
Their scepters, States,
And diadems of gold.
Free to their friends
On either side his kin
Careful to keep
The credit he was in.
Unto the seamen
Beneficial,

As testifieth
Chatham hospital.
The poor of Plymouth
And of Deptford town
Have had, now have,
And shall have, many a crown.
Proceeding from
His liberality
By way of great
And gracious legacy,
This parish of
St. Dunstan standing east
(Wherein he dwelt
full thirty years at least)
Hath of the springs
Of his good will a part
Derived from
The fountain of his heart,
All which bequests,
With many more unsaid,
Dame Margaret
Hath bountifully paid.
Deep of conceit,
In speaking grave and wise,
Endighting swift
And pregnant to devise,
In conference
Revealing haughty skill
In all affairs
Having a worthie's will

Inscription on the Memorial to Hawkins

On sea and land,
Spending his course and time
By steps of yeeres
As he to age did climb.
God hath his soul,
The sea his body keeps,
Where (for a while)
As Jonas now he sleeps;
Till He which said
To Lazarus, Come forth,
Awakes this knight,
And gives to him his worth.
In Christian faith
And faithful penitence,
In quickening hope
And constant patience,
He running ran
A faithful pilgrim's race,
God giving him
The guiding of His grace,
Ending his life
With his experience
By deep decree
Of God's high providence.
His Yeeres to six times
ten and three amounting,
The ninth, the seventh
Climacterick by counting.
Dame Katharine,
His first religious wife,

Saw yeeres thrice tenne
And two of mortall life,
Leaving the world the sixth,
The seventh ascending.
Thus he and she
Alike their compasse ending,
Asunder both
By death and flesh alone,
Together both in soul,
Two making one,
Among the saints above,
From troubles free,
Where two in one shall meet
And make up three.
The Christian knight
And his good ladies twain,
Flesh, soul, and spirit
United once again;
Beholding Christ,
Who comfortably saith,
Come, mine elect,
receive the crown of faith.[1]

Appendix 4

Portraits of Hawkins

Three or four times during his life John Hawkins seems to have sat for a portrait artist. Exactly when and where this took place is now uncertain, as is the authenticity of one or two of the portraits. The earliest is a miniature said to have been done by Peter Oliver. The subject has a full beard and a distinctly receding hairline. The picture is said to have a blue background and to be framed in ivory, the size about two inches by an inch and a half. It bears no more resemblance to the other portraits of John Hawkins than the Isaac Oliver miniature does to other portraits of Francis Drake.[1]

Another portrait has a problematical inscription but is almost certainly John Hawkins. This is a large oil on panel now in the collection of the National Maritime Museum at Greenwich (BHC 2755). There are three inscriptions in the top corners of the painting: (1) "Ann$^{o.}$ Dñi 1581." (2) "Ætatis suæ 44." and (3) "Sr Iohn Hawkins." The problem is twofold. Hawkins did not spell his name as it is shown on the painting, and he was forty-nine years old in 1581. At one time the painting belonged to the Sir John Hawkins Hospital at Chatham, where it had been from the beginning, so far as anyone could determine.[2]

Another painting of less certain provenance but more appropriate inscription is one by Federigo Zuccaro, now in the Plymouth City

23

Engraved portrait of John Hawkins by Robert Boissard (1618). Note the ring in his right ear. Granger, *Biographical History of England*, vol. 3, part 2, no. 111. This item is reproduced by permission of the Huntington Library, San Marino, California.

Museum and Art Gallery. The inscription in the upper right corner of that work is impeccable: "ÆTATIS SUÆ LVIII / Anno Dñi 1591." There is also an accurate representation of the subject's coat of arms in the upper left corner of the canvas. In the Zuccaro portrait Hawkins is wearing a hat, perhaps to hide his receding hairline.

Two or three engravings of John Hawkins appeared in the first quarter of the seventeenth century, probably copied from the portraits. The earliest (1618), by Robert Boissard, shows Hawkins with a full beard, wearing a hat, and holding a staff. His coat of arms, with augmentation, is in the upper right corner of the picture, along with the motto: "Advauncement by Dillige[nce]." A brief poem at the bottom asserts among other things "that Indians in their barbarous tongues do praise him." The Hawkins picture, along with four other engravings by Boissard, is among the rarest of the various portraits that appeared in Holland's *Bazileωlogia*.[3]

A new engraving, evidently based on Boissard, but with the subject facing the opposite way, appeared in Holland's *Herωologia* in 1620.[4] The engravings seem to have been based on the Zuccaro portrait, with which they share some important details. Various similar likenesses, based on these originals, were produced in succeeding years.

A third drawing, almost a cartoon, appeared in the title page of *Purchas His Pilgrimes* in 1624, along with portraits of Richard Hawkins, Drake, Cavendish, and others. All of them seem to have been based on Boissard portraits, but the portrait of John Hawkins is not well done. The subject has a full beard and a hat perched squarely on his head. The collar and coat are the same as shown by Boissard, but the face is too round.[5] As in the Oliver portrait, John Hawkins seems to have been too large a figure to be done in miniature.

Notes

1
The Uses of Duplicity

1. DRO, W/46, Black Book, in Worth, *Plymouth Municipal Records,* 43.
2. John Elyot and William Hawkins to Thomas Cromwell, 1 January 1536, in Gairdner, *Letters and Papers of Henry VIII,* 10:19; Piers Eggecomb et al. to the Council, 25 July 1536, ibid., 11:73; Star Chamber Proceedings, Henry VIII, bundle 25, no. 323, in Williamson, *Sir John Hawkins,* 21–24.
3. DRO, W/130, Old Audit Book, in Worth, *Plymouth Municipal Records,* 107.
4. Hakluyt, *Principall Navigations,* 520–21. His information was from John Hawkins, who, as will be seen, was not born until about 1532.
5. Hakluyt, *Third and Last Volume of Voyages,* 700–701. Hakluyt also changed the name of the ship: the *Paule of Plymouthe.*
6. "Como no sabia leer no la vide." Testimony of Ginés Navarro, 19 November 1528 [actually 1527], AGI Patronato 265, ramo 1, no. 1. See also AGI Santo Domingo 9, no. 21, ramo 1, testimony of Antonio Martin (fols. 6–7), Pedro Montiel (fols. 7–8v), 26 November 1527; Francisco de Prado (fols. 11–12v); Alonso de Avila (fols. 12v–15v); Diego Martel (fols. 15v–17v); Juan Garcia Caballero (fols. 17v–19); Juan de Loaysa (fols. 19–22); and Juan Jimenez (fols. 22–23v), 9 December 1527.
7. AGI Indiferente General 421, libro 13, fols. 260v–61, king to Audiencia of Santo Domingo, 27 March 1528. There is a good translation of the greater part of the original documents in Wright, *Spanish Documents,* 29–56. The printed versions are translated in part in Biggar, *Precursors of Jacques Cartier,* 165–77. An early account by the official chronicler of the Indies can be found in Oviedo, *Coronica de las Indias,* lib. xix, cap. 13, fols. clxi–clxii.
8. Devon Record Office, W/46, Black Book, in Worth, *Calendar of Plymouth Municipal Records,* 16.
9. BL Stowe 1047, fol. 266v.
10. John Stow, *The Survey of London,* ed. A.M. and H.D. (London: Elizabeth Purslow for Nicholas Bourne, 1633), book II, pp. 139–41. See also John Strype, ed., *A Survey of the Cities of London and Westminster . . . Written at First by John Stow . . . from the Year 1633 . . .* (2 vols.; London: A. Churchill et al., 1720), 2:44–45. A memorial composed by Hawkins's wife said that his age when he died in 1595 was "six times ten and three."

11. William Hawkins as mayor: DRO, W/46, Black Book, in Worth, *Plymouth Municipal Records,* 16.

12. Devon Record Office, 710/674, 710/675, grant and quitclaim from John Pers to William Hawkins, 20 October 1538; 710/676, quitclaim from Nicholas and Alyce Hynyston to John Elyott, 24 June 1546.

13. Gill, *New History of Plymouth,* 196–99; Pounds, *Culture of the English People,* 141–43, 161–65, 319.

14. DRO, W/48, White Book, in Worth, *Plymouth Municipal Records,* 52–54.

15. Howes, *Annales or Generall Chronicle of England,* 807.

16. Indenture signed by Thomas Clowteynge and William Hawkins, 19 September 1538, no. 384, in Gairdner, *Letters and Papers of Henry VIII,* 13:150–51.

17. DRO, W/130, Old Audit Book, in Worth, *Plymouth Municipal Records,* 110–14, 116.

18. Privy Council to Lord Russell, 28 July 1549, Inner Temple Library, Petyt ms. no. 538, vol. 46, fols. 439–41, in Pocock, *Troubles Connected with the Prayer Book of 1549,* 30–33. Rose-Troup, *The Western Rebellion of 1549,* 159, 251, 359–60.

19. DRO, W/361, no. 10, in Worth, *Plymouth Municipal Records,* 230.

20. DRO, W/360, no. 9, in Worth, *Plymouth Municipal Records,* 230.

21. John Elyot and William Hawkins to Thomas Cromwell, 1 January 1536; Piers Edgecombe et al. to the Council, 25 July 1536; in Gairdner, *Letters and Papers of Henry VIII,* 10:19, 11:73. PRO, Privy Council, 21 May 1545, 31 May 1545, 17 July 1545, 27 July 1545, fols. 15, 29, 78, 92, in Dasent, *Acts of the Privy Council,* n.s. 1:167, 177–78, 210, 220–21.

22. "Et non feloniter aut p[er] malitiam suam precogitatam." PRO, C66/850, membrane 15, pardon issued to John Hawkins, 12 July 1553.

23. The date of William's death is unknown. His will was seemingly signed on 13 July 1554, and distribution was made in October. DRO 710/678, quitclaim from Henry Hawkins to William Hawkins, 31 October 1554. For the location of the house see DRO B/46, Black Book, fol. 83v, in Worth, *Plymouth Municipal Records,* 40. The Canary connection is described in Rumeu de Armas, *Viajes de John Hawkins,* 41–46. For early voyages see Hakluyt, *Principall Navigations,* 521.

24. Dr. Wotton to the Council, 12 December 1556, in Turnbull, *State Papers Foreign 1553–1558,* 280.

25. It was either the French ship or possibly a Hanse vessel of the same name seized by the Hawkins brothers in 1558. Rumeu de Armas, *Viajes de John Hawkins,* 70–76.

26. Museo Canarias, Inquisición, Signatura LIII-5, fol. liiii. See also Rumeu de Armas, *Viajes de John Hawkins a America,* 76.

27. Confiss^{on} de gen^{al} richarte aquynes ynleses [sic] la qual le fue tomada por el sr g^{al} don Beltrán de castro g^{al} desta mar del sur, 10 July 1594, AGI Patronato 265, ramo 54, fol. 1. "Dixo que se llama Richarte aquines y ques yngles segun tiene declarado y de hedad de treinta y quatro años poco mas o m^{o}s y q̃ benia por g^{al} del galeon que se dize la linda en Lengua de castilla que le fue tomado por el dho s^r g^{al} don Beltrán de castro y que es hijo de juan aquines y de catalina quinza sus p^{es} yngleses de londres y plemua." In the translation by Williamson the name is written as "Catalina Quinzu." See his *Observations of Sir Richard Hawkins,* pp. 169–77.

28. "Artycles of discov^{r}y of the injust mynde and deciptfull dealinge of m^r John Hawkyns," 1587, BL Lansdowne ms. 52, no. 43, fol. 118.

29. White Book, memorandum establishing the Grammar School, 14 July 1561, fol. 4, in Worth, *Plymouth Municipal Records,* 50.

30. Guzmán de Silva to the king, 21 July 1567, AGS Estado 819, fol. 107.

31. Hakluyt, *Principall Navigations,* 522.

32. *Recopilación de leyes de los reynos de las Indias,* vol. 3, fol. 84v; vol. 4, fol. 1.

33. Andrews, *Drake's Voyages,* 16–17.

34. Hakluyt, *Principall Navigations,* 522. The tonnage estimates given by Hakluyt need some interpretation. He has the *Swallow* confused with its later namesake. Moreover, he lists the *Salomon* as 120 tons, while the bounty records list it as 160, no doubt reflecting the difference between the merchant system of measuring capacity and the admiralty system of "ton and tonnage." I have accepted the figure of "7 score" given by John Sparke, which fits neatly between the two extremes. See his account "The Voyage Made by the Worshipful M. John Hawkins Esquire," ibid., 523. For the bounty figures see Dietz, "Royal Bounty," 77:5–20.

35. Kelsey, *Sir Francis Drake,* 16. This conclusion is based on Drake's birth in January or February 1540 and the information from Howes that Drake took his first trip to the Guinea Coast at the age of twenty. See Howes, *Annales or Generall Chronicles of England,* 807.

36. Guzmán de Silva to the king, 21 July 1567, AGS Estado 819, fol. 107, 2. Information that Martínez could speak English because of his residence in Cádiz is from Cristóbal Bernáldez to the king, AGI Santo Domingo 71, quoted in Rumeu de Armas, *Viajes de John Hawkins,* 116.

37. Hakluyt, *Principall Navigations,* 522. The usual assumption is that Hakluyt had his information from Hawkins himself.

38. The Portuguese claims are detailed in *Processo agitatus coram prestantissimum dño doctore Symone Cabral,* 8 July 1568, PRO, SP 70/99, fols. 1–4. According to a summary document compiled by Contador Ortega de Melgosa, in Seville, 4 March 1566, AGI Justicia 92, no. 2, fol. 5v, Hawkins seized

more than a dozen Portuguese ships and five hundred slaves, which is far more than the Portuguese themselves claimed.

39. Stow, *Annales or Generall Chronicle of England,* ed. Edmund Howes (London: Thomas Adams, 1615), 807.

40. In a statement of surprising frankness, Hakluyt called the Hawkins cargo "his Praye." See Hakluyt, *Principall Navigations,* 522.

41. Lorenzo Bernáldez to the king, August 1563, AGI Santo Domingo 71, fols. 280–81v.

42. "En tanto quanto yo puedo e de derecho devo e no mas." License from Lorenzo Bernáldez to John Hawkins, 19 April 1563, AGI Santo Domingo 71, no. 51, no folio numbers. Copy dated 12 March 1564, from other copy dated 7 May 1563. Another copy of the license may be found in AGI Patronato 265, ramo 10.

43. "Acorde engañalles ofreciendoles la licencia que me pedian y dandosela de suerte que no obrasse efecto alguno . . . no valia cossa alguna." Lorenzo Bernáldez to the king, August 1563, AGI Santo Domingo 71, fol. 281–v.

44. The trade relationships are described in Ortega de Melgosa to the king, 4 March 1566, AGI Justicia 92, no. 2, fol. 5v. Licenciado Echegoyan to the king, 28 July 1563, AGI Santo Domingo 71, fol. 274. See also the Melgosa summary, 4 March 1566, AGI Justicia 92, no. 2, fol. 5v, which apparently summarizes several reports from Echegoyan; and Guzmán de Silva to the king, 21 July 1567, AGS Estado 819, fol. 107, in which the Spanish ambassador reported the results of his investigation into the trip Hawkins made in 1562 and 1563. See also the testimony of Hugo Johnson, 17 November 1575, PRO, HCA 13/21, fols. 300v–301, and the testimony of Thomas Hampton, 24 November 1575, ibid., fols. 301v–2. Both men said the hides were worth thirteen shillings, fourpence each.

45. Williamson, *Sir John Hawkins,* 87–91; Andrews, *Spanish Caribbean,* 114–15.

46. Translated in Wright, *Spanish Documents,* 65. Licenciado Echegoyan to the king, 28 July 1563 and 4 November 1563, AGI Santo Domingo 71, fols. 273–74v. "Una grande burlería . . . mañana sera toda esta tierra inglaterra si no se remedia." Ibid., fols. 286–89.

47. Hugh Tipton to Challoner, 8 December 1563, PRO, SP 70/66, fols. 43–44; 70/73/461, fols. 6–7v. Challoner to John Hawkins, 5 July 1564, PRO, SP 70/73/461, fols. 6–7v. Testimony of Hugo Johnson, 17 November 1575, PRO, HCA 13/21, fols. 300v–301. Testimony of Thomas Hampton, 24 November 1575, PRO, HCA 13/21, fols. 301v–2. At that time Tipton thought Hawkins was with Challoner at the Spanish court to plead his own case, but this seems unlikely.

48. Hakluyt, *Principall Navigations,* 522, says that Hawkins arrived home in September 1563. If so, it must have been early September, because Queen Elizabeth wrote to the king of Spain on 8 September, asking for a favorable decision in the claim for the return of the confiscated cargoes. PRO, SP 70/63/176, fol. 37v. Although this letter implies that Hawkins intended to go personally to Spain to plead his case, he did not do so, as is clear from the letters from Tipton to Challoner, 8 December 1563, PRO, SP 70/66/205, fol. 39; and Challoner to Hawkins, 5 July 1564, SP 70/73/461, fols. 6–7v.

49. Rumeu de Armas, *Viajes de John Hawkins,* 121–25.

50. See the testimony of Cristóbal Nuñez Vela, 8 July 1563; Juan Prieto, 3 July 1563; Francisco Hernández, 3 July 1563; Bernardino Justiniano, 8 July 1563; Pedro Lorenço, 8 July 1563; in Museo Canarias, Inquisición, LXXX-12, fols. 871v–74v.

51. Rumeu de Armas, *Viajes de John Hawkins,* 144–45. Guzmán de Silva to the king, 21 July 1567, AGS Estado 819, fol. 107.

52. Original purchase: Seymour to the Council, 15 November 1544, in Gairdner (ed.), *Letters and Papers of Henry VIII,* vol. 19, part 2, p. 369.

53. John Sparke, "The Voyage Made by the Worshipful M. John Haukins Esquire," in Hakluyt, *Principall Navigations,* 523–43. Guzmán de Silva to the king, 31 July 1564, AGS Estado 817, fol. 65.

54. Guzmán de Silva to the king, 2 July 1564, AGS Estado 817, fol. 47; 31 July 1564, AGS Estado 817, fol. 65; 19 August 1564, AGS Estado 817, fol. 81; Guzmán de Silva to the queen, 22 August 1564, PRO, SP 70/73/537, fols. 199–200; "lo que escrive el s⁰ siçel [Cecil] al embax^or de Inglat^a," 27 August 1564, AGS Estado 817, fol. 84; Chilton to Challoner, 2 September 1564, PRO, SP 70/74/556, fol. 30v; "relación de lo que tracto luís de paz en la corte de la Rey^a de Inglat^a por p^te del embax^or guzmán de Silva," no date, AGS Estado 817, fol. 103; king to Guzmán de Silva, 7 October 1564, AGS Estado 817, fol. 107.

55. Howes, *Annales or Generall Chronicles of England,* 807. It is not possible to reconcile all the dates and times in the various accounts of Drake's early life. In this case, Howes says that at age twenty-two Drake was "made captain of the Judith at San Juan de Ulloa," an apparent reference to the trip he made with Hawkins in 1568. Howes is confused. Drake was captain of the *Judith* some months before arrival at San Juan de Ulúa in 1568, and he was certainly older than twenty-two. On the other hand, he was quite likely in the Indies at age twenty-two, just as he was on several other occasions.

56. Sparke, "Voyage Made by the Worshipful I. Haukins," Hakluyt, *Principall Navigations,* 523.

57. Ibid.

58. Ibid.

59. MC, Inquisición, LXXX-12, quoted in Rumeu de Armas, *Viajes de John Hawkins*, 145.

60. Sparke, "Voyage Made by the Worshipful I. Haukins," Hakluyt, *Principall Navigations*, 523.

61. Ibid.

62. Andrea de Estévez and Juan Váez, MC, Inquisición LXXX-12, quoted in Rumeu de Armas, *Viajes de John Hawkins*, 145-46. Sparke seemed to think the battle was not worth a mention, though he did note the lack of fortifications and weapons. See his "Voyage Made by the Worshipful I. Haukins," Hakluyt, *Principall Navigations*, 523.

63. Sparke, "Voyage Made by the Worshipful I. Haukins," Hakluyt, *Principall Navigations*, 523.

64. *Processo agitatus coram prestantissimum dño doctore Symone Cabral*, 8 July 1568, PRO, SP 70/99, fols. 4-5v.

65. Sparke, "Voyage Made by the Worshipful I. Haukins," Hakluyt, *Principall Navigations*, 523. Guzmán de Silva to the king, 5 November 1565, AGS Estado 818, fol. 85.

66. Sparke, "Voyage Made by the Worshipful I. Haukins," Hakluyt, *Principall Navigations*, 523. Guzmán de Silva to the king, 5 November 1565, AGS Estado 818, fol. 85.

67. John Hawkins to Alonso Bernáldez, 16 April 1565, AGI Justicia 93, fol. 88v.

68. Sparke, "Voyage Made by the Worshipful I. Haukins," Hakluyt, *Principall Navigations*, 523. Testimony of Juan Pacheco, 16 April 1565, AGI Justicia 93, fols. 99v-101; testimony of Alonso Bernáldez, 18 April 1565, AGI Justicia 93, fol. 111; official report, AGI Justicia 93, fols. 112-14. Wright thinks that Hawkins's refusal to pay the thirty-ducat license fee to the royal treasury, while agreeing to the 7.5 percent customs duty to the local treasury, was a protest for the previous confiscation of his cargo in Seville. See *Spanish Documents*, 14-15.

69. Sparke, "Voyage Made by the Worshipful I. Haukins," Hakluyt, *Principall Navigations*, 523. Guzmán de Silva to the king, 5 November 1565, AGS Estado 818, fol. 85.

70. Sparke, "Voyage Made by the Worshipful I. Haukins," Hakluyt, *Principall Navigations*, 523. Diego Ruiz de Vallejo to the king, 21 April 1568, AGI Santo Domingo 78, fol. 1.

71. "Muy buen cavallero servidor de su magestad cuyo criado avia sido siendo su rey de Ingalaterra." Testimony of Juan Pacheco, 16 April 1565, AGI Justicia 93.

72. "Yo soy grande servidor de la magestad real del rey don Felipe a quien e

servido siendo rey de Ingalaterra." Hawkins to Bernáldez, 16 April 1565, AGI Justicia 93, fols. 88v–89.

73. AGI Justicia 902, p. 577.

74. Sparke, "Voyage Made by the Worshipful I. Haukins," Hakluyt, *Principall Navigations,* 523. Trade license, 21 May 1565, AGI Patronato 265, ramo 10, no. 5. Interrogatories by Santiago de Riego, c. 1567, AGI Justicia 38, fols. 1–4.

75. Guzmán de Silva to the king, 5 November 1565, AGS Estado 818, fol. 85. Sparke, "Voyage Made by the Worshipful I. Haukins," Hakluyt, *Principall Navigations,* 523.

76. Lázaro Peserano to John Hawkins, 13 May 1565, AGI Patronato 265, ramo 9, no. 2. "Recibio del señor lazaro de peserano de la ysla de curasau .978. queros a Razon de 10 Reales de plata de cada cuero por la qual apagado yo a artur moios seis piezas desclauos dos honbres dos mugeres & dos muchachos & 344 varas de Ruan & por ques verdad quel dho artur a Resçebido la paga afirmado esto de su nonbre. 13 de mayo de 1565 años artur mue laçaro peseraro Mas Riº mi paga de 707 cueros quatro esclauos 214 baras de Ruan & 30 varas de telillas 15 de mayo 1565 años artur mue."

77. Peserano to Hawkins, 13 May 1565, AGI Patronato 265, ramo 9, no. 4.

78. The Jamaican is a somewhat mysterious person. Juan Pacheco, who talked to the man, gave his name as Llerena and said he was a Castilian and a citizen of Jamaica. See his testimony in AGI Justicia 93, fol. 99. He was very likely the Cristóbal Lerena who represented Hawkins in his negotiations with Bernáldez on 16 April. See AGI Justicia 93, fol. 100. Ambassador Guzmán de Silva, who later questioned Hawkins about him, reported that the man was a captive negro servant from Portugal, freed by Hawkins in Guinea and taken along as an interpreter. Guzmán de Silva to the king, 4 February 1566, AGS Estado 819, fols. 66–67. Sharpe, who sailed with the man, called him "a merchant, and inhabitant in Jamaica." In another place he seemed to refer to the same man as a pilot. See "Voyage Made by the Worshipful I. Haukins," Hakluyt, *Principall Navigations,* 536.

79. Guzmán de Silva to the king, 5 November 1565, AGS Estado 818, fol. 85. Sparke, "Voyage Made by the Worshipful I. Haukins," Hakluyt, *Principall Navigations,* 523.

80. Laudonnière, *L'Histoire notable de la Floride,* fols. 94v–98. Guzmán de Silva to the king, 22 October 1565, AGS Estado 818, fol. 78; 5 November 1565, AGS Estado 818, fol. 85.

81. Sparke, "Voyage Made by the Worshipful I. Haukins," Hakluyt, *Principall Navigations,* 523. Hawkins to the queen, 20 September 1565, Pepys mss., Magdalen College, Cambridge, quoted in Froude, *History of England,* 8:64n.

82. License to trade at Río de la Hacha, 21 May 1565, AGI Patronato 265, ramo 9, fol. 1. Certificate from Hernando de Heredia, 30 May 1565, AGI Patronato 265, ramo 9, fol. 3.

83. Sparke, "Voyage Made by the Worshipful I. Haukins," Hakluyt, *Principall Navigations,* 523, 527, 528, 533, 543.

84. Ibid., 541. Howes, *Annales or generall chronicle of England,* 948, credits both Hawkins and Ralegh at different dates on the same page. The difficulty of crediting Hawkins, Drake, Ralegh, or anyone else with the introduction of these plants is well covered by Salaman, *History and Social Influence of the Potato,* 144–58; and Dickson, *Tobacco in Sixteenth Century Literature,* 78–79, 129–38.

85. Guzmán de Silva to the king, 1 October 1565, AGS Estado 818, fol. 68; 5 November 1565, AGS Estado 818, fol. 85.

86. "Sa[ble] ore a pointe wavie a lyone passant golde in cheife the besantes his crest ore a wrethe argent and azure a demye moore in his proper coolor bounde in a corde as captyve with amulette ore his armes and in his eares." BL Stowe 1047, fol. 266v. *Barnstaple Records,* 2:258–59. Smyth, "Certain Passages," 205–6.

87. Guzmán de Silva to the king, 22 October 1565, AGS Estado 818, fol. 78; 5 November 1565, AGS Estado 818, fol. 85; 4 February 1566, AGS Estado 819, fols. 66–67.

2
Robbing Portugal and Selling to Spain

1. Guzmán de Silva to the king, 22 October 1565, AGS Estado 818, fol. 78; Guzmán de Silva to the king, 5 November 1565, AGS Estado 818, fol. 85. "E assí vino á platica en secreto con el Gouer^or. y q̃ entre ellos se auia conçertado que otro dia echase gente en tierra, y començasse á querer yr al lugar y q̃ hacer daño, y q̃ el saldria, y q̃ por q̃ no lo hiziesse, le dexariã hazer su Contrataçion, lo qual se hizo assí."

2. Guzmán de Silva to the king, 4 February 1566, AGS Estado 819, fols. 66–67. "Tienenle por buen piloto, y él parece hombre de ingenio. no esta satisfecho de lo de aquí he le dicho que no es hombre para esta tierra que mejor haria en ir á servir á V. M^d que tendria enque occuparse, como lo han hecho otros Ingleses."

3. AGI Patronato 265, ramo 9, nos. 2, 3, 4, 5. A copy of Guzmán de Silva's covering letter of 11 February 1566 is in no. 1 of the same ramo.

4. Guzmán de Silva to the king, 11 February 1566, AGS Estado 819, fol. 82. "Podria seruir a su costa con tres nauios de a dozientos toneles y algo mas y

con uno de trezientos muy buenos. en los cuales lleuaria quinientos hombres muy escogidos y que se contentaria por premio de su seruiçio con que quedando çiento y tantos esclauos .o. el Valor dellos a .V. M^d. que quedaron en sancto domingo en poder de los ministros de .V. M^d. se les diese cierto deposito de dinero que se hizo de Unos cueros que el Envio en vna urca a sevilla. Guzmán de Silva to the king, 23 March 1566, AGS Estado 819, fol. 71; 30 March 1566, AGS Estado 819, fol. 75.

5. Guzmán de Silva to the king, 4 May 1566, AGS Estado 819, fol. 97; 18 May 1566, AGS Estado 819, fol. 1*; 4 June 1566, AGS Estado 819, fol 98; 3 August 1566, AGS Estado 819, fol. 125. King to Guzmán de Silva, 12 August 1566, AGS Estado 819, fol. 114.

6. Guzmán de Silva to the king, 4 October 1566, AGS Estado 819, fol. 210; 12 October 1566, AGS Estado 819, fol. 47; "Relación de los Nauios que dizen q̃ van a las Indias," AGS Estado 819, fol. 48.

7. David Lewes to William Cecil, 13 October 1566, PRO 12/40/84, fol. 182. Guzmán de Silva to the king, 19 October 1566, AGS Estado 819, fol. 7. Lewes to Cecil, 28 October 1566, PRO 12/40/95, fol 204.

8. Lewes to Cecil, 31 October 1566, PRO 12/40/99, fol. 211; bond, 12/40/99, fol. 213.

9. There is no record of the date of Katherine's birth, but she was forty-two when she died in 1591, according to a metaphysical poem on the Hawkins monument at St. Dunstan in the East. The inscription has puzzled biographers for years, but W. N. Gunson seems to have worked out the meaning. He showed that the verse "should be read as a conundrum. . . . Ten and two make 12, 3 times 12 = 36 and another 6 years to the time of her death = 42. This is balanced in the last line by the equation 6 times 7 = 42, ascending implying multiplication as well as ascension to heaven in the year of death." See Gunson, "Who Was Sir Richard Hawkins?" 72. For the original verse, see the epigraph of this chapter.

10. London Guildhall Library, Parish Register of St. Dunstan in the East, ms. 7857, no page numbers. Hawkins still lived in Plymouth in October 1566. See the commission dated 8 October 1566, PRO 70/288.

11. Guzmán de Silva to the king, 23 March 1566, AGS Estado 819, fol. 71. "Tiene diez .o. doce criados entienden la navegaçion de aquellas partes tan bien como el."

12. Plymouth Port Book, PRO E 190/1010/18, 9 November 1566, cited in Williamson, *Sir John Hawkins,* pp. 122–23. The *Paul* and the *Salomon* are listed as 160 tons in the bounty records consulted by Dietz, "The Royal Bounty," *Mariner's Mirror,* 77:7, 14.

13. See the description of the *Pascoe* in "The Numbre of Shippes and vessells

and the masters names being within all the Portes and Creekes as with in the Realme of England, and tradinge the ware of merchandize as appearith by the Customes Accomptes, from the Feaste of St. Michaell Tharchangel anno 1571 unto the same Feaste anno 1572, Collected by Thomas Colbin Surveior of the Port of London," PRO SP 15/22, fol. 21v. The *Pascoe* is described in Nichols, *Sir Francis Drake Revived*, 2, as a 70-ton ship.

The *Swallow* is not the same vessel as the 30-ton ship of the same name that went on the 1562 voyage. See the testimony of Tomás Fuller, 2 November 1569, AGI Justicia 902, p. 50. See also Christóval Roberson, 23 November 1569, AGI Justicia 902, p. 72, who thinks it was about 100 tons. Dietz, "The Royal Bounty," *Mariner's Mirror*, 77:14, lists the *Swallow* as 180 tons. The *Swallow* is listed elsewhere as 120 and 140 tons. Hakluyt, *Principall Navigations*, 522–23.

14. PRO Plymouth Port Book 1010/18, 9 November 1566, cited in Williamson, *John Hawkins*, 123.

15. Testimony of Miguel Morgan (Morgan Tillert), 7 February 1573, AGN Inquisición, tomo 55, exp. 1, fols. 25v–26.

16. "Dixo que botava a Dios que avia de venir a estas islas y que aquella Nuestra Señora que esta en Candelaria avia de quemar y a su lumbre avia de asar un cabrito." AHN Inquisición 1824, ramo 1. Testimony of Juan de Arcaya, 1 July 1568, transcribed in Rumeu de Armas, *Viajes de John Hawkins*, 428.

17. "Se lo dezia Frances Drac, Ingles gran luterano que venia en el navio y le convertia en su ley . . . y que en qualquiera de las dos leyes de la de Roma o de la de Ingalaterr recivia dios el bien que se hazia y que la verdadera y mejor ley era la de Ingalaterra . . . cada dia el enseñava y tratava dello." Testimony of Miguel Morgan (Morgan Tillert), 14 January 1574, AGN Inquisición, tomo 75, fol. 115-v, photostat in the George R. G. Conway Collection, Library of Congress.

18. "Joannes Cobel sub belli pretextū . . . ad conspectū insulae Sancti Jacobi quandam nav magnam Sacharo, Aethiopibusque oneratam rapuit. . . . Cuius navis capitanius, & reliqui Lusitani gravissime lesi sunt, & in terram eiecti, exceptis nonullis Lusitanis, quitum temporis crudeliter ab Anglis interfecti sunt." PRO SP 70/99, *Processo Agitatus coram prestantissimo dño doctore Symone Cabral*, 8 July 1575, fols. 5v–6v. In the documents Lovell is called Cobel, and Hawkins is called Canes.

19. Testimony of Diego Ruiz de Vallejo, 21 April 1568, AGI Santo Domingo 78, no. 62, fol. 1v.

20. Ibid.

21. Ibid.

22. "Los unos a los otros se encubren." Ibid. "Tenemos gran escrupulo de con-

sçiencia, nosotros los oficiales de vuestra magestad por los juramentos que les hazemos tomar. pues dello no se puede averiguar otra cosa sino que crehemos que se perjuran."

23. Several *cedulas* (royal orders) had been issued on this matter. Two laws dated at Valladolid on 16 April 1550 declared all unmanifested goods and slaves forfeit; a third dated at Toledo on 22 September 1560 forbade anyone, native or foreigner, to go to the Indies without a license. *Recopilación de leyes de los reinos de las Indias* (2d ed.; Madrid: Antonio Babas, 1756), Libro ix, titulo 26, leyes I and II (vol. 3, fol. 84v); Libro viii, titulo 17, ley I (vol. 4, fol. 1).

24. Baltasar de Castellanos and others to the king, 23 June 1567, AGI Santo Domingo 202, ramo 1, no. 13, fol. 2. The reference to his abandonment of the slaves is in AGI Santo Domingo 202, ramo 1, no. 14, 10 July 1567, fol. 2. Both letters are transcribed in Rumeu de Armas, *Viajes de John Hawkins,* 416.

25. "Vuestro general le embio a desir que viniese a tierra que se queria ver con el." Diego Herrero et al. to the king, 8 January 1568, AGI Santo Domingo 202, ramo 1, no. 15, fol. 1v. The letter is transcribed in Rumeu de Armas, *Viajes de John Hawkins,* 422–23. Miguel de Castellanos to the king, 1 January 1568, AGI Santo Domingo 78, fol. 1.

26. "Echo en tierra algo lexos del pueblo noventa e seys esclavos que de viejos e flacos y enfermos se le morian." Ibid., fols. 1–2.

27. Williamson thinks that Lovell was somehow tricked into bringing the slaves ashore and that the Spanish colonists treacherously refused to pay for them. He cites in proof a later reference in an anonymous manuscript that he attributed to George Fitzwilliams or "more probably" Balentine Ber or Beerd (Beard?). BL Cotton, Otho E VIII, fol. 32. See *Sir John Hawkins,* 125, 144, 520. The attribution to Balentine Beerd is based partly on the supposed similarity of this passage to statements in Beerd's testimony before a Spanish notary on 5 October 1568, AGI Patronato 265, ramo. 11, fols. 1–3. In both of these stories the slaves left by Lovell at Río de la Hacha are of almost no interest to Hawkins. Another possible author for the Cotton manuscript is Micael Soole, who "went with John Hawkins as a gentleman companion" (El bino en la dha armada por gentil hombre a acompañar al dho Jnº aquines) and was so well educated that he testified in Latin. See his testimony, 6 October 1568, AGI Patronato 265, ramo 11, fols. 5v–6.

28. "Ansi se fue y atraveso a la ysla española donde dizen que hizo mucho estrago y daño." Diego Herrero et al. to the king, 8 January 1568, AGI Santo Domingo 202, ramo 1, fol. 1v.

29. BL Cotton, Otho E VIII, fol. 32. The word *deputies* was supplied by

Williamson, who has edited and transcribed the manuscript in his *Sir John Hawkins*, 520.

30. The losses also involved battles at San Juan de Ulúa, as will be seen. Nichols, *Sir Francis Drake Revived*, 2.

31. PRO C 66/1038, 2 June 1567, in *Calendar of Patent Rolls, 1566–69*, 4.

32. Hawkins to ???, 24 June 1567, PRO 12/43/12, fol. 34.

33. Guzmán de Silva to the king, 21 July 1567, AGS Estado 819, fol. 107. "El secretario en su presençia con gran juramento me a firma lo mesmo." BL Cotton, Otho E, VIII, fol. 17. The names of the Portuguese adventurers have been given in various forms. According to the Spanish ambassador, they were Anton Luís (also known as Pedro Vásquez Francisco), Diego Home, and a third man named Gaspar Caldera, though some of the names are interchanged in the documents. Guzmán de Silva to the king, 9 August 1567, AGS Estado 819, fol. 62; 27 September 1567, AGS Estado 819, fol. 199. The latter manuscript bears two dates, 27 September and 28 September, the first appearing twice. See also the testimony of Guillermo de Oclando, 24 November 1569, AGI Justicia 902, p. 324.

34. Hawkins to Cecil, 28 September 1567, PRO 12/44/13, fol. 29–v. BL Cotton, Otho E, VIII, fols. 17v–18. Guzmán de Silva to the king, 6 October 1567, PRO 70/94/1746, fol. 94. De Wachen to Guzmán de Silva (extract), 23 October 1567, PRO 70/94/1384, fol. 157. DeWachen to Guzmán de Silva, 24 October 1567, PRO 70/94/1386, fol. 159.

35. Hawkins to Cecil, 28 September 1567, PRO 12/44/13, fol. 29–v.

36. See *Observations of Sir Richard Hawkins*, p. 118. Richard Hawkins's account is followed by most English historians, even though the author was then admittedly of "tender yeares"—actually, about two years old. See Corbett, *Drake and the Tudor Navy*, 1:97; Williamson, *Hawkins of Plymouth*, 107–8; Andrews, *Spanish Caribbean*, 123; and Andrews, *Trade, Plunder, and Settlement*, 126.

37. Hawkins to Cecil, 28 September 1567, PRO 12/44/13, fol. 29v. BL Cotton, Otho E. VIII, fol. 18.

38. Hawkins to the queen, 16 September 1567, PRO 12/44/7, fol. 15; Hawkins to Cecil, 28 September 1567, PRO 12/44/13, fol. 29; Clifton to Cecil, 30 September 1567, Hatfield ms., Cecil Papers, 155:57–58; BL Cotton, Otho E. VIII, fol. 18v.

39. "Se dize ser general de seis nauios . . . sin saber (segun dice) para donde por que la Reyna nolo auia declarado." DeWachen to the king, 23 September 1567, AGS Estado 819, fol. 202. Spanish translation of French original. BL Cotton, Otho E. VIII, fol. 18v.

40. Richard Hawkins always considered his home to be Plymouth (see *Obser-*

vations of Sir Richard Hawkins, p. 118), where his name appears with reasonable frequency in the municipal records. PRO W132, Widey Court Book, reprinted in Worth, *Plymouth Municipal Records,* 128–32.

3
Slave Trading

1. Testimony of Tomás Fuller, 2 November 1569, AGI Justicia 902, p. 51.
2. Testimony of John Hawkins, 10 March 1568(69), PRO, SP 12/53, fol. 34.
3. Admiralty inquiry, 23 March 1568(69), PRO, SP 12/53, fol. 4.
4. Testimony of Antonio Godard, 2 November 1569, AGI Justicia 902, pp. 22, 30, 34. Godard was mayor of Plymouth in 1587–88, PRO, Widey Court Book, W/132, transcribed in Worth, *Plymouth Records,* 127.
5. Testimony of Tomás Nyculas, 7 November 1570, AGI Justicia 902, pp. 595–96.
6. Testimony of Tomás Fuller, 2 November 1569, AGI Justicia 902, pp. 47, 67. Testimony of Christóval Bingan, 1 December 1569, AGI Justicia 902, pp. 170–71, 187. The signatures of Fitzwilliams, Verde, and others are copied in the Spanish style, implying that they used these signatures to accommodate their Spanish hosts. AGI Justicia 902, pp. 324, 372. Testimony of Ricardo Tempul, 28 November 1569, AGI Justicia 902, pp. 373, 506. Testimony of Enrique Quince, 6 December 1569, AGI Justicia 902, pp. 450, 514.
7. Bennet's signature was copied by the notary as Thomas Benot. See his testimony of 6 December 1569, AGI Justicia 902, p. 200. For the testimony of the second, dated 18 October 1568, see AGI Justicia 902, p. 267.
8. *A true declaration of the troublesome voyadge of M. John Haukins to the parties of guynea and the west Indies, in the yeares of our Lord 1567. and 1568.* (London: 1569). The manuscript is in BL Cotton, Otho E VIII, fols. 17–41v. A reasonably accurate transcription was made by Williamson in his *Sir John Hawkins,* 491–534. After seeing G. R. G. Conway's translations of testimony taken in Mexico, Williamson concluded the author was "George Fitzwilliams or more probably Valentine Verde."
9. Dietz, "The Royal Bounty," *Mariner's Mirror,* 77:14. Some of the crew called the flagship the *Great Jesus*—see, for example, Antonio Godard, 2 November 1569, AGI Patronato 265, p. 22.
10. BL Cotton, Otho E. VIII, fol. 18v. As usual, the sources differ in listing tonnage for the ships. The Spanish ambassador in London said the two largest ships belonging to the queen were 800 tons and 300 tons, respectively. Of the four ships in Plymouth, one was 150 tons, one 100 tons, and one 80 tons.

See the letter from Guzmán de Silva to the king, 2 August 1567, AGS Estado 819, fol. 61. Tomás Fuller gave the ship sizes in toneladas as follows: 700, 300, 150, 80, 40, and 30. See his testimony of 2 November 1569, AGI Justicia 902, p. 50. *Swallow*'s refitting: testimony of Robert Barrett, 8 October 1568, AGI Patronato 265, ramo 11, fol. 16. Drake's captaincy: Miles Phillips, "A Discourse Written by Miles Phillips Englishman," in Hakluyt, *Principall Navigations,* 562.

11. Testimony of Antonio Godard, 2 November 1569, AGI Justicia 902, pp. 24–25. Testimony of Tomás Fuller, 2 November 1569, AGI Justicia 902, p. 47. Testimony of Christóval Roberson, 23 November 1569, AGI Justicia 902, p. 72. Guillermo Oclando said there were "a hundred persons more or less" on the *Minion*. See his testimony of 24 November 1569, AGI Justicia 902, p. 325. There were exactly 408 men and boys on the ships, according to BL Cotton, Otho E. VIII, fol. 18v. Other sources give various figures, all near the 400 mark. Guater Joanes reported that he saw the slaves being loaded at the Plymouth docks. See his testimony, 6 December 1569, AGI Justicia 902, p. 984. Juan Truslon said that he saw 40 slaves loaded in Plymouth; testimony of 6 December 1569, AGI Justicia 902, p. 1006. Barrett said they "brought fifty blacks from England." See his testimony of 8 October 1568, AGI Patronato 265, ramo 11, fol. 16. Mycael Sol said 60 slaves were loaded in England; testimony of 26 November 1569, AGI Justicia 902, p. 343. Fleet ready to sail: Guzmán de Silva to the king of Spain, 13 October 1567, AGS Estado 819, fol. 207.

12. Juan Hol was one volunteer. See his testimony of 6 December 1569, AGI Justicia 902, p. 465.

13. "Lo resçibio por su criado el dho Juº aquines e para ello le hizo fuerça diziendo lo hazia por myedo de la Reyna de Yngalaterra." Testimony of Juan Brun, musician, 26 November 1569, AGI Justicia 902, p. 166. "Dixo que no ganava sueldo ninguno por que por comysion de la Reyna de Yngalaterra fue tomado y conpelido para yr por fuerça." Testimony of Christóval Bingham, gentleman, 1 December 1569, AGI Justicia 902, p. 172. "Fue tomado por fuerça por mandado de la Reyna de Yngalaterra." Testimony of Enrique More, seaman, 9 December 1569, AGI Justicia 902, p. 211. "Fue tomado por fuerça para el dho Juan aquines para fue se con el el dho viaje por virtud de çierta probision que tenya de la Reyna de Yngalaterra para hazer çiertos hombres que llevo consigo la jornada." Testimony of Juan Cornyl, 6 November 1569, AGI Justicia 902, pp. 129–30.

14. "Servia de Jentilhombre y soldado de la nao Capitana del dho Juan aquines e q̃ no le pago por ello cosa ninguna ny llevava sueldo señalado syno q̃ bolviendo de tornaviaje a yngalaterra selo pagaria el dho Juan

aquines como meresçia la calidad de su persona." Testimony of Juan Cornyl, 26 November 1569, AGI Justicia 902, p. 128.

15. "A not of the places aryved at & tymes in the voiag made wt the Ihs & the mynn 1567 & 68," dated 20 January 1568(69), PRO, SP 12/49/40.1, fol. 85. This seems to have been the source used by the author of the *Troublesome voyadge,* fol. A.ii. Miles Phillips, who wrote fifteen years later (in Hakluyt, *Principall Navigations,* 562), also specifies 2 October, but his dates may be based on those in the *Troublesome voyadge.* On 8 October 1568 Robert Barrett testified that it had been a year and six days since the fleet left Plymouth. AGI Patronato 265, ramo 11, fol. 1.

16. BL Cotton, Otho E. VIII, fol. 18v. This first part of the account was probably written during the stay at Santa Cruz in Tenerife. Testimony of Mycael Sol, 26 November 1569, AGI Justicia 902, p. 339.

17. BL Cotton, Otho E. VIII, fols. 18v–19v. The date appears as "th^e ii. daie of the same moneth" in the *Troublesome voyadge,* fol. A.ii, an obvious typographical error for 11.

18. Testimony of Juan de Valverde, 16 May 1568, Museo Canaria de las Palmas, Inquisición LIII-5, fol. 48v. The Cotton manuscript says that a new Spanish governor made secret preparations to fire on the fleet but Hawkins discovered the plan and moved his ships out of range. BL Cotton, Otho E. VIII, fols. 20–21v. Testimony of Gregorio Esteban, 8 October 1568, AGI Patronato 265, ramo 11, fol. 3v. Testimony of Thomas Fuller, AGI Justicia 902, p. 52. Testimony of Noe Sarjen, AGI Justicia 902, p. 94.

19. Testimony of Juan de Venero, 7 May 1568, and of Juan de Valverde, 16 May 1568, MCP, Inquisición LIII-5, fol. 48-v.

20. BL Cotton, Otho E. VIII, fols. 20v–21. Pedro de Soler, *Interrogatorio de preguntas para los testigos,* MCP, quoted in Rumeu de Armas, *Viajes de John Hawkins,* 217–18.

21. Testimony of Roger Armar, 2 March 1573, AGN, Inquisición 1A, fol. 276. The vicar in question was probably Matheo de Torres.

22. There is some uncertainty about the exact sequence of events. The Cotton manuscript says Hawkins left Santa Cruz for Adeje (Adessia) and remained there for a day before receiving word that the three ships were at Gomera; Hawkins then sent the *Judith* to tell them he was on his way. BL Cotton, Otho E. VIII, fol. 21v. However, Tomás Venito in his testimony said that Hawkins sent the *Judith* to Gomera to see whether the others had arrived; when she did not return in three days, he took that as a sign the lost ships were indeed at Gomera. See his testimony of 18 September 1568, AGI Patronato 265, ramo 12, fol. 3v. Both the Cotton manuscript (fol. 18v) and the *Rare Travailes* of Job Hortop (first page of text) agree that the ships

were supposed to meet in Tenerife, though the *Troublesome voyadge* (fol. A.ii. verso) says that they were supposed to meet in Gomera.

23. Testimony of Juan de Venero, 7 May 1568; Juan de Valverde, 16 May 1568; MCP, Inquisición LIII-5, fol. 48–v. According to Josepe Prieto, "Muchas personas dezian que tiro a la yglesia porq por aquel derecho pasó la pelota." Josepe Prieto, 25 May 1568; MCP, Inquisición LIII-5, fol. 49.

24. Testimony of Robert Barrett, 6 October 1568, AGI Patronato 265, ramo 11, fol. 15v. Testimony of Guillermo de Oclando, 24 November 1569, AGI Justicia 902, pp. 327–29.

25. Testimony of Juan de Venero, 7 May 1568, MCP, Inquisición LIII-5, fol. 48. Testimony of Tomás Benito, 18 September 1568, AGI Patronato 265, ramo 12, fol. 3v. MCP, Inquisición LIII-5, fol. 52v. Rumeu de Armas quotes Baltasar Zamora, a local merchant, as saying that "un hermano de la condesa de Soria [Feria] que iva con ellos y que era católico y mostro recaudos y fué a missa en la dicha isla." The only man on the voyage known to be a relative of the Condesa de Feria (Lady Jane Dormer) was George Fitzwilliams. MCP, Inquisición LXX-15, quoted in his *Viajes de John Hawkins,* 224.

26. Testimony of Robert Barrett, 8 October 1568, AGI Patronato 265, ramo 11, fol. 15v. Rumeu de Armas suggests that the supplies could have come from no other place than the Canaries. Once the supplies were loaded, Nuñez returned to England though Stevens remained with the fleet. *Viajes de John Hawkins,* 231.

27. Testimony of Valentín Verde, 3 November 1569, AGI Justicia 902, p. 316. Testimony of Guillermo de Oclando, 24 November 1569, AGI Justicia 902, p. 329.

28. "Çinco Françeses que heran capitanes y maestres que trayan liçençias del almyrante de françia pa hir donde quisiesen." Testimony of Antonio Godard, 2 November 1569, AGI Justicia 902, p. 28.

29. Testimony of Guillermo Oclando, 24 November 1569, AGI Justicia 902, p. 329. His account is supported by the testimony of Roger Armar, 2 March 1573, AGN, Inquisición 1A, fol. 276v. Testimony of Ricardo Tempul, 28 November 1569, AGI Justicia 902, p. 955.

30. One English witness later said that the French and Portuguese ships were taken at Cabo Verde, but others disagreed with this account. Testimony by Tomás Venito, 18 September 1568, and by Guillermo Sanda, 19 October 1568, AGI Patronato 265, ramo 12, fol. 11–v. BL Cotton, Otho E. VIII, fols. 22–23v. Testimony of Tomás Fuller, 2 November 1569, AGI Justicia 902, p. 54. Testimony of Juan Cornyl, 26 November 1569, AGI Justicia 902, p. 134.

31. Hortop, "Travailes," in Hakluyt, *Third and Last Volume of the Voyages,* 487.

Testimony of Gregorio Estevan, 6 October 1568, AGI Patronato 265, ramo 11, fol. 3v. Testimony of Rodrigo Caro, 23 July 1572, AGI Patronato 267, ramo 54, fols. 1v–3. Testimony of Ricardo Tempul, 28 November 1569, AGI Justicia 902, p. 955. Testimony of Gregorio Simon, 24 November 1569, AGI Justicia 902, p. 127. Testimony of Antonio Godard, 2 November 1569, AGI Justicia 902, p. 28.

32. Hawkins, *Troublesome voyadge,* fol. A.iii. Miles Phillips, "Discourse," in Hakluyt, *Principall Navigations,* 563. Testimony of Valentín Verde, 5 October 1568, of Gregorio Estévan, 6 October 1568, and of Robert Barrett, 8 October 1568, AGI Patronato 265, ramo 11, fols. 1–3, 3v, 15–18v. Hortop, "Travailes," in Hakluyt, *Third and Last Volume of the Voyages,* 488.

33. Testimony of Valentín Verde, 5 October 1568, AGI Patronato 265, ramo 11, fol. 1v. "Fueron al rrio grande a contratar con los portugueses los quales no quisyeron contrataçion con ellos."

34. Portuguese ambassador to Queen Elizabeth, December 1568, PRO, SP 70/104A/2702, fols. 89–90. In this letter the ambassador gives the total as 70,000 ducados, though the figures actually amount to 74,000 ducados. Queen Elizabeth to the ambassador of Portugal, 23 May 1568, PRO, SP 70/98/2224, fols. 74–78v. The full Portuguese account is contained in a Latin book of testimony taken at Lisbon, 8–13 July 1568, PRO, SP 70/99/2314.

35. Portuguese ambassador to Queen Elizabeth, December 1568, PRO, SP 70/104A/2702, fols. 89–90.

36. Testimony of Tomás Benito, 18 September 1568, AGI Patronato 265, ramo 12, fol. 3. "Para hazer gerra a los portugueses que topasen."

37. BL Cotton, Otho E. VIII, fol. 24. The name of the place is missing from this page of the manuscript, but the identity can be established from the testimony of Noysa Jen, 2 November 1568, AGI Patronato 265, ramo 12, fol. 17. Portuguese ambassador to Queen Elizabeth, December 1568, PRO, SP 70/104A/2702, fols. 89–90.

38. BL Cotton, Otho E. VIII, fol. 25.

39. Ibid., fol. 26–v.

40. Ibid., fols. 27–28v. Hortop, "Travailes," in Hakluyt, *Third and Last Volume of the Voyages,* 488. Hawkins, *Troublesome voyadge,* fol. A.iiii. The anonymous narrative dates this battle on 27 January, which does not seem to fit the chronology of the journey; BL Cotton, Otho E. VIII, fols. 27. Phillips, "Discourse," in Hakluyt, *Principall Navigations,* 563. The account by John Hawkins consolidates this battle with the previous fight at the Río Santo Domingo but has Hawkins personally coming to the aid of his beleagured lieutenants. For this and other reasons I have concluded that the story was

composed by another writer from information related verbally by Hawkins. The anonymous narrative has the appearance of an account written during the voyage, while records now missing were still available and the events were still fresh in the mind of the author.

41. BL Cotton, Otho E. VIII, fols. 25, 26, 28v.

42. Robert Barrett in his testimony of 8 October 1568, said that Hawkins's men got 220 captives in battle and traded for another hundred; AGI Patronato 265, ramo 11, fol. 16. Tomás Benito said in his testimony of 7 September 1568 that they had 400 slaves, almost all taken at Río Tagarín; AGI Patronato 265, ramo 12, fol. 4v. William Saunders (called Guillermo Sanda or Santa in the manuscript), in his testimony of 19 October 1568, AGI Patronato 265, ramo 12, fol. 11v, said that they had between 500 and 600 slaves, almost all captured at Río Tagarín, for which Hawkins gave his allies some cloth and linens. Hawkins said in his published account that he had "betwene 4 & 500. Negrose" and that they received nothing from the kings with whom they were allied. See his *Troublesome voyadge,* fol. A.iiii. The anonymous narrative says Hawkins captured 260 in battle, bought some, and received others from his allies, for a total of about 470 slaves. See BL Cotton, Otho E. VIII, fol. 28v. Mycael Sol says they brought 60 slaves from England, purchased another 12 from Portuguese merchants, and had a total of 445 when they set out from the Río Tagarín. See his testimony of 26 November 1569, AGI Justicia 902, p. 343.

43. Testimony of Thomas Bennett (Tomás Benito), 18 September 1568, AGI Patronato 265, ramo 12, fols. 2–9. Hortop, "Travailes," in Hakluyt, *Third and Last Volume of Voyages,* 488.

44. Hawkins gives the departure date as 3 February in his *Troublesome voyadge,* fol. A.iiii. The date is given as 9 February in BL Cotton, Otho E. VIII, fol. 29.

45. For information about conditions during later periods see Hugh Thomas, *The Slave Trade: The Story of the Atlantic Slave Trade, 1440–1870* (New York: Simon and Schuster, 1997), 410–25; Colin Palmer, *Human Cargoes: The British Slave Trade to Spanish America, 1700–1739* (Urbana: University of Illinois Press, 1981), 42–56.

46. There is a record of some of the furnishings left on the flagship by Hawkins in the "Relación del suceso acaecido entre el general inglés Juan de Aquins," AGI Patronato 265, ramo 11, transcribed in Rumeu de Armas, *Viajes de John Hawkins,* 484. See also the testimony of William Collins (Guillermo Calens), 20 November 1572, AGN Inquisición, tomo 52, fols. 68–74. Low was twenty-four in 1572, though the friars where he lived seemingly thought he was no more than seven or eight years old. His testimony is

in AGN Inquisición, tomo 56, exp. 5, fols. 73–99.

47. Testimony of Morgan Tillert (Miguel Morgan), 10 January 1573, 7 February 1573, and 2 March 1573; testimony of William Collins (Guillermo Calens), 17 November 1572, AGN Inquisición, tomo 52, exp. 3, fols. 68–80; tomo 55, exp. 1.

48. Testimony of Morgan Tillert (Miguel Morgan), 7 February 1573, AGN Inquisición, tomo 55, fols. 25–27.

49. Testimony of William Collins (Guillermo Calens), 19 November 1572, AGN Inquisición, tomo 52, exp. 3, fols. 73–75.

50. Hawkins, *Troublesome voyadge,* fol. A.iiii.

4
San Juan de Ulúa

1. BL Cotton, Otho E. VIII, fol. 29–v.

2. Testimony of Henry Keene, 6 December 1569, AGI Justicia 902, pp. 458–59.

3. BL Cotton, Otho E. VIII, fol. 29. Strikethroughs indicate manuscript deletions, and bracketed words have been added where pieces are missing from the edges of the manuscript.

4. Ibid., fol. 29v.

5. Testimony of Mycael Sol, 26 November 1569, AGI Justicia 902, p. 344. BL Cotton, Otho E. VIII, fol. 29–v.

6. Antonio Godard, 2 November 1569, AGI Patronato 265, p. 30. "Andando por el dho pueblo de la margarita con algunos v°s della hallo unas letras questavan escritos en la muralla de una casa que dezian en letra Françeza que este testigo entiende muy bien Vengança de la Florida."

7. BL Cotton, Otho E. VIII, fols. 30v–32. Spanish records show the arrival as 14 April; see the letter from Diego Ruiz de Vallejo to the king, 21 April 1568, transcribed in Rumeu de Armas, *Viajes de John Hawkins,* 426.

8. "Le oyo dezir muchas vezes al dho ju° aquines . . . que el primer cavallero que el rey don Phelipe su senor avia armado en yngalaterra asydo el." Testimony dated 30 October 1570, AGI Justicia 902, p. 577.

9. "Instruction de lo que vos don Guerau Despes cavallero de la orden de Calatraua, haueis de hazer, y del modo con que os haueis de hauer y gouernar en la corte de Ingalaterra, donde os embiamos a residir por ñro Embaxador ordinario," 28 June 1568, AGS Estado, Libro 109, fols. xxiii–xxxiii verso. "Entre otros es muy nombrado un Cossario Ingles, llamado Juan Achines, que he andado en las Indias con quatro nauios de armada, haziendo robos y daños harto grandes a mis subditos . . . para que

comunicandolo con Diego de Guzmán, que tiene mucha noticia deste pirata . . . para que sea castigado tan exemplarmente como sus delictos lo merescen."

10. BL Cotton, Otho E. VIII, fol. 30v.

11. Ibid., fol. 31.

12. Ibid., fol. 31–v.

13. Testimony of George Fitzwilliams, 28 November 1569, AGI Justicia 902, p. 933. BL Cotton, Otho E. VIII, fols. 30v–32.

14. Hortop, *Rare Trauailes*, fol. B. Testimony of William Collins, AGN Inquisición, tomo 52, exp. 3, fol. 75.

15. Castellanos to the king, 26 September 1568, AGI Santo Domingo 206, ramo 1, no. 19, fol. 1.

16. BL Cotton, Otho E. VIII, fol. 32.

17. These figures are the ones given by the respective commanders. Hawkins said Castellanos had 20 horsemen and 100 other troops. See his *Troublesome Voyadge*, fol. A.v. Castellanos said Hawkins had 600 armed men. See his letter to the king, 26 September 1568, AGI Santo Domingo, ramo 1, no. 19, fol. 1. The anonymous manuscript also mentions armed Indian and black auxiliaries, both of which seem unlikely to have been highly motivated. BL Cotton, Otho E. VIII, fol. 32v.

18. Antonio Godard, 2 November 1569, AGI Justicia 902, p. 32. The anonymous narrative says two men died later. BL Cotton, Otho E. VIII, fol. 33.

19. BL Cotton, Otho E. VIII, fol. 33.

20. Testimony of Christóval Roberson, 20 November 1569, AGI Justicia 902, p. 79. Testimony of Noe Sarjen, 23 November 1569, AGI Justicia 902, p. 99. Testimony of Juan Cornyll, 26 November 1569, AGI Justicia 902, p. 138. Testimony of Juan Brun, 26 November 1569, AGI Justicia 902, p. 157.

21. Testimony of Guillermo Calens [William Collins], 10 December 1572, AGN Inquisición 1A, fol. 256v. Testimony of Roger Armar, 2 March 1573, AGN Inquisición 1A, fol. 277. Hawkins, *Troublesome voyadge*, fol. A.v verso. Phillips, "Discourse," in Hakluyt, *Principall Navigations,* 563. Testimony of Christóval Roberson, 20 November 1569, AGI Justicia 902, p. 79.

22. Hawkins, *Troublesome Voyadge,* fol. A.v verso. Testimony of Juan Brun, 26 November 1569, AGI Justicia 902, p. 149. Testimony of Guillermo Calens, 10 December 1572, AGN Inquisición 1A, fol. 256v. Tomás Benito says Hawkins sold 214 slaves here and left another sixty to cover damages and royal levies. See his testimony of 18 September 1568, AGI Patronato 265, ramo 12, fol. 6.

23. Castellanos to the king, 26 September 1568, AGI Santo Domingo 206, ramo

1, no. 19, fol. 1v. See also Antonio Godard, 2 November 1569, AGI Justicia 902, p. 33, who said Castellanos paid Hawkins 5,000 pesos in exchange for 60 slaves. Testimony of Christóval Roberson, 20 November 1569, AGI Justicia 902, p. 79.

24. Testimony of Robert Barrett, 8 October 1568, AGI Patronato 265, ramo 11, fols. 16–17. Hawkins, *Unfortunate Voyage,* fol. A.v. Phillips, "Discourse," in Hakluyt, *Principall Navigations,* 563. BL Cotton, Otho E. VIII, fols. 32v–35v. Prince, *Worthies of Devon,* 472. Testimony of Thomas Fuller, 2 November 1569, AGI Justicia 902, p. 60. The value of a ducado was generally taken to be five shillings, sixpence, which is the value stated in Bigges, *Summarie and True Discourse,* 38.

25. "Places aryved at & tymes," PRO, 12/49/40.1, fol. 85. BL Cotton, Otho E. VIII, fol. 35v.

26. Testimony of Tomás Benito, 8 September 1568, AGI Patronato 265, ramo 12, fol. 6v.

27. "Places aryved at & tymes," PRO, 12/49/40.1, fol. 85. According to BL Cotton, Otho E. VIII, fol. 36v, the fleet left Santa Marta on 26 July and arrived in Cartagena on 1 August. This would mean a three-week stay in Santa Marta, though the English witnesses agree they stayed in Santa Marta only about two weeks. See for example the testimony of Tomás Fuller, 2 November 1569, AGI Justicia 902, p. 61. Testimony of Miguel Sol, 26 November 1569, AGI Justicia 902, p. 351. Antonio Godard, 2 November 1569, AGI Justicia 902, p. 34.

28. Testimony of Guillermo Oclando, 24 November 1569, AGI Justicia 902, p. 333. Testimony of Tomás Fowler, 2 November 1569, AGI Justicia 902, p. 63. "Places aryved at & tymes," PRO, 12/49/40.1, fol. 85. According to the *Troublesome Voyadge,* fol. A.v. verso, the fleet left on 24 July.

29. Testimony of Robert Barrett, 8 October 1568, AGI Patronato 265, ramo 11, fol. 17. BL Cotton, Otho E. VIII, fols. 37–38v. Testimony of Tomás Benito, 8 September 1568, AGI Patronato 265, ramo 12, fols. 6–7v. Letter from Martín de Alas to the king, 30 September 1568, AGI Santa Fe 62, transcribed in Rumeu de Armas, *Viajes de John Hawkins,* 441–43. Hawkins, *Troublesome Voyadge,* fol. A.v.

30. Testimony of Ricardo Tempul, 28 November 1569, AGI Justicia 902, pp. 389–90. Testimony of Tomás Fuller, 2 November 1569, AGI Justicia 902, p. 63. BL Cotton, Otho E. VIII, fols. 38v–39.

31. Testimony of Antonio Godard, 2 November 1569, AGI Justicia 902, p. 35. BL Cotton, Otho E. VIII, fols. 38v–39. Testimony of Francisco Maldonado, 27 September 1568, AGI Justicia 1000, no. 2, ramo 3, fols. 118v–22. Testimony of Robert Barrett, 28 October 1568, AGI Patronato 265, ramo 11, fol. 17v.

32. English sailors were astonished at the lack of protection. See the accounts by Henry Hawkes, "A Relation of the Commodities of Nova Hispania and of the Inhabitants," and Robert Tomson, "The Voyage of Robert Tomson Marchant, into Nova Hispania in the yeere 1555," in Hakluyt, *Principall Navigations*, 545, 586. Hawkins, *Troublesome voyadge,* fol. A.vi.

33. Testimony of Enrique Mores, 10 November 1568, AGI Patronato 265, ramo 12, fol. 27. Testimony of Noysa Jen, 2 November 1568, AGI Patronato 265, ramo 12, fol. 20–v. Testimony of Guillermo Sanda, 19 October 1568, fol. 13–v. Testimony of Robert Barrett, 28 October 1568, AGI Patronato 265, ramo 11, fol. 17v. Antonio Godard, 2 November 1579, AGI Justicia 902, p. 46.

34. BL Cotton, Otho E. VIII, fols. 39v–40. Luís Zegri to the king, 18 September 1568, AGI Patronato 265, ramo 12, fol. 3. Testimony of Antonio Delgadillo, 28 September 1568, AGI Justicia 1000, fol. 122–v.

35. Testimony of Tomás Fuller, 2 November 1569, AGI Justicia 902, p. 64. In Barrett's words "en una casa grande que dizen de las mentiras." Testimony of 28 October 1568, AGI Patronato 265, ramo 11, fol. 18. Irene Wright writes that the name came from the fraud involved in its construction. See *Spanish Documents,* 132. Balentin Beerd [Valentín Verde] remembered the greeting this way: "Entrad señores que el S^{or} general os quiere hablar." Testimony given October 1568, AGI Patronato 265, ramo. 11, fol. 3.

36. Antonio Delgadillo said that they fled to the mainland. See his testimony of 28 September 1568, AGI Justicia 1000, fol. 123. Tomás Fuller said Delgadillo took them to the mainland himself. See his testimony of 2 November 1569, AGI Justicia 902, p. 65.

37. Testimony of Antonio Delgadillo, 28 September 1568, AGI Justicia 1000, fol. 123. Testimony of Juan Benito, AGI Patronato 265, ramo 12, fol. 8–v; and Guillermo Sanda, 19 October 1568, AGI Patronato 265, ramo 12, fols. 13v–14. According to Sanda "sienpre estuvo en su nao salvo una o dos vezes que salio a beber." Hawkins, *Troublesome voyadge,* fol. [A.vi verso].

38. BL Cotton, Otho E. VIII, fols. 39v–40. Luís Zegri to the king, 18 September 1568, AGI Patronato 265, ramo 12, fol. 3. Testimony of Ricardo Tempul, 28 November 1569, AGI Justicia 902, p. 391. Testimony of George Fitzwilliams, 28 November 1569, AGI Justicia 902, p. 391. Testimony of Noe Sarjen, 23 November 1569, AGI Justicia 902, p. 105.

39. Testimony of Antonio Delgadillo, 28 September 1568, AGI Justicia 1000, fol. 123–v.

40. The contents of the letter are summarized in the brief message from Martín Enríquez to John Hawkins, 18 September 1568, AGI Indiferente General 858. BL Cotton Otho E. VIII, fol. 41v.

41. Martín Enríquez to John Hawkins, 18 September 1568, AGI Indiferente General 858. Luís Zegri to Audiencia, 18 September 1568, Patronato 265 (4), fols. 5v–6. Testimony of Francisco de Bustamante, 30 September 1568, AGI Justicia 1000, fols. 151–52. Fear of the storm was not imaginary. Hawkins recognized the perilous position of the Spanish fleet as well, saying that if he had not allowed the ships into port, they could have been damaged or sunk with a loss of nearly two million pounds. Hawkins, *Troublesome voyadge*, fol. A.vi.

42. Martín Enríquez to John Hawkins, 18 September 1568, AGI Indiferente General 858. Hawkins claimed in the *Troublesome voyadge*, fol. B.i. and verso, that the viceroy agreed to let him keep possession of the island, but this is contradicted in the letter of 18 September, which clearly encompasses the final terms, including a change from twelve hostages to ten. On the other hand, Francisco de Bustamante, who was a prisoner of Hawkins's, said that Hawkins insisted on retaining possession of the fortifications. No doubt there was a grave misunderstanding on both sides.

43. Testimony of Guillermo de Oclando, 24 November 1569, AGI Justicia 902, p. 334. "Syendo el dho General Fran^{co} de luxan a desembarcar de un barco se topo con el dho Juan aquines el qual le dixo que estubiese tan seguro como sy estuvyera en su Casa." Testimony of Martin Enríquez, 27 September 1568, AGI Justicia 1000, fol. 116–v. Testimony of Antonio Delgadillo, 28 September 1568, AGI Justicia 1000, fol. 122v. Testimony of Juan de Ubilla, 29 September 1568, AGI Justicia 1000, fol. 143v.

44. Testimony of George Fitzwilliams, 28 November 1569, AGI Justicia 902, p. 941. Testimony of Gregorio Simon, 24 November 1569, AGI Justicia 902, p. 113. Testimony of Guillermo Oclando, 24 November 1569, AGI Justicia 902, p. 334. Testimony of Anthony Godard, 2 November 1569, AGI Justicia 902, p. 647.

45. Testimony of Martín Enríquez, 27 September 1568, AGI Justicia 1000, fol. 117–v.

46. Testimony of Robert Barrett, 28 October 1568, AGI Patronato 265, ramo 11, fol. 18.

47. Hortop, *Rare Travailes,* fol. B2 verso. Among the most imaginative enhancements to the story are the challenges Francisco de Luxan supposedly gave, with corresponding replies from Hawkins in a poetic narrative by Alvaro de Flores, *Obra nueuamte compuesta,* fols. 2v–3v. Flores was the nephew of Diego Flores Valdés, capitán general of the fleets going to and from the Indies. Although it is not clear that Flores was a witness to the battle, he was certainly there a few months later. He apparently had access to the participants and their reports, but he did not allow the facts to hinder the development of his story.

48. Testimony of Juan de Ubilla, 29 September 1568, AGI Justicia 1000, fol. 144–v. Hortop, *Rare Trauailes*, fol. B2 verso.

49. Testimony of Francisco Maldonado, 27 September 1568, AGI Justicia 1000, fols. 120v–121. Testimony of Antonio Delgadillo, 28 September 1568, AGI Justicia 1000, fol. 125. Testimony of Francisco de Bustamante, 30 September 1568, fol. 153v.

50. Testimony of Henry Keene, 6 December 1569, AGI Justicia 902, p. 460. "Se començo a alborotar la gente ynglesa diziendo a vozes traiçion trayçion despararon alguna artilleria a los españoles." Testimony of Antonio Godard, 2 November 1569, AGI Justicia 902, p. 43.

51. Testimony of Robert Barrett, 8 October 1568, AGI Patronato 265, ramo 11, fols. 17–18. Testimony of Martín Enríquez, 27 September 1568, and of Juan de Ubilla, 29 September 1568, AGI Justicia 1000, fols. 117–v, 144–45v. Testimony of Francisco Maldonaldo, 27 September 1568, and of Francisco de Bustamante, 30 September 1568, AGI Justicia 1000, fols. 121–22, 153v–55. Testimony of Antonio Godard, 2 November 1579, AGI Justicia 902, pp. 44–45. "Les avia dado palabra de les dexar en paz en su tierra." Testimony of Henry Keene, 6 December 1569, AGI Justicia 902, p. 461.

52. The remark about Drake did not appear in Hortop's original 1591 account, but was added for a second edition, published the same year and later reprinted by Hakluyt in his *Third and Last Volume of Voyages,* 490. The addition was very possibly suggested by Francis Drake to counteract the severe criticism of his actions made by John Hawkins, which dogged Drake all of his life. The critical phrase is found in Hawkins, *Unfortunate Voyage,* fol. B.v.

53. The number of ships at various stages of the voyage is unclear. According to English sources Hawkins left the African coast with nine vessels, left one at Cartagena (a Portuguese ship), and parted from the *William and John* in the storm off the coast of Cuba. The Spanish reports usually credit him with ten ships on his arrival in Borburata and seven at San Juan de Ulúa. BL Cotton, Otho E. VIII, fol. 32v. Testimony of Robert Barrett, 8 October 1568, AGI Patronato 265, ramo 11, fols. 17–18. Testimony of Diego Ruiz de Vallejo to the king, 21 April 1568, AGI Santo Domingo 78, no. 62, fol. 1v. Testimony of Antonio Delgadillo, 28 September 1568, AGI Justicia 1000, fol. 125v. Testimony of Francisco Maldonado, 27 September 1568, AGI Justicia 1000, fol. 119.

54. Testimony of Francisco de Bustamante, 30 September 1568, AGI Justicia 1000, fol. 154–v. "Relación del suceso entre Juan de Aquins y la armada de la Nueva España en el puerto de San Juan de lua," 1568, AGI Patronato 265, ramo 12, no. 3, fols. 1–2v. Testimony of Francisco Maldonado, September 1568, AGI Justicia 1000, fol. 121v.

55. "Los que tenian poco quisieron ayudar a los que tenian algo par salbar lo segun paresçe pusieron lo en cobo para si." Luís Zegri to the Audiencia y Chancilleria de Nueva España, 18 September 1568, AGI Patronato 265, ramo 12, no. 4, fol. 6.

56. "Todo el oro e plata e perlas que traya el dho Juan Aquines el dya de la batalla qelo tomaron los españoles que les dieron la batalla." Testimony of Henry Keene, 6 December 1569, AGI Justicia 902, p. 473.

57. "Juan Aquines se fue huyendo con las dhas naos y dexo en las que dexo mucho oro e plata esclavos y mercadurias y otras cosas." Testimony of Tomás Ellines, 28 August 1570, AGI Justicia 902, p. 553.

58. Testimony of Martín Enríquez, 27 September 1568, AGI Justicia 1000, fol. 118. "La mayor parte de su hazienda y robos."

59. Testimony of Tomás Fuller, 2 November 1568, AGI Justicia 902, p. 50. The guns, slaves, and other materials are listed in some detail in the letter from Juan de Ubilla to the king, 16 December 1569, AGI Mexico 168, no folio numbers. A reasonable approximation of the contents can be found in Lewis, "Guns of the Jesus of Lubeck," *Mariner's Mirror* 22 (January 1936):324-45; and Lewis, "Fresh Light on San Juan de Ulúa," *Mariner's Mirror* 23 (January 1937):295-315.

60. Testimony of Christóval Roberson, 23 November 1568, AGI Justicia 902, p. 69. Testimony of Ricardo Matheo, 9 December 1568, AGI Justicia 902, p. 208. Roberson said a bit more than seventy men were put ashore; Matheo said there were about ninety, and Antonio Goddard confirmed this figure in his own testimony, AGI Justicia 902, 2 November 1569, p. 22. As time passed, the figure grew larger. Hortop, perhaps taking a cue from others who reached England, gave the total as 96. Hawkins said there were a hundred, and Phillips said 114. Hawkins, "Unfortunate Voyage," and Phillips, "Discourse," in Hakluyt *Principall Navigations,* 456, 468. Hortop, "Travailes," in Hakluyt, *Third and Last Volume of the Voyages,* 490. Job Hortop, *Rare Trauailes,* fol. B3 verso.

61. See the statement of William Borough, c. 1587, BL Lansdowne ms. 52, no. 39, fol. 108v.

5
Counting the Cost

1. Hawkins, *Troublesome voyadge,* fols. B.vi-vii. Testimony of Fernando de Sçia, 24 February 1569, AGI Patronato 265, ramo 13, fol. 11v.

2. Testimony of Antonio Pita, 23 February 1569, AGI Patronato 265, ramo 13, fol. 7. This is thirdhand testimony; Pita apparently heard it from a woman

named Blanca Díaz, who operated an inn at Vigo. One of her guests, "a merchant from the region of Valençia," had bought the slave from Hawkins and told her the story.

3. Testimony of Gregorio de Sias, 28 February 1569, AGI Patronato 265, ramo 13, fol. 25v. Testimony of Antonio Pita, 23 February 1569, AGI Patronato 265, ramo 13, fol. 5–v. "Traya bistido una rropa aherrada en martas con unos pasamanos de seda negra y un sayo colorado de grana con unos pasamanos de plata y unos guardamuslos de lo mesmo y una m^a de seda y una cadena grande de oro al pescueço." Testimony of Juan de la Torre, 28 February 1569, AGI Patronato 265, ramo 13, fol. 28.

4. Testimony of Antonio Sarmiento de Montenegro, 27 February 1569, AGI Patronato 265, ramo 13, fols 23v–24. Testimony of Antonio Pita, 23 February 1569, AGI Patronato 265, ramo 13, fol. 5v.

5. Hawkins, *Troublesome voyadge,* fol. B.vii.

6. Testimony of Gregorio de Sias, 28 February 1569, AGI Patronato 265, ramo 13, fols. 25v–27. Interestingly enough, the Hawkins account insists that none of the men went ashore at Pontevedra. *Troublesome voyadge,* fol. B.vii.

7. Testimony of Tomás Olanda, 26 February 1569, AGI Patronato 265, ramo 13, fols. 21v–23.

8. William Hawkins to Cecil, 3 December 1568, PRO SP 12/48/50, fols. 119–20. Williams received confident assertions of his brother's safety from Gregorio Sarmiento de Valladares (24 February 1569) and Tomás Olanda (26 February 1569), who said later that John was accompanied home by a small ship sent specifically for that purpose. AGI Patronato 265, ramo 13, fols. 13–14, 22.

9. William Hawkins to Cecil, 22 January 1568 (1569), PRO SP 12/49/37, fol. 77; and 20 January 1568 (1569), PRO SP 12/49/36, fol. 75. The dates of these letters are uncertain. The one marked 22 January asserts that Drake arrived "this p[re]sent nyght." The other, dated 20 January, says he arrived "this p[re]sent oure." William Hawkins to Cecil, 27 January 1568 (1569), PRO SP 12/49/42, fol. 88.

10. Gregorio Sarmiento de Valladares thought that this assistance had been sent by the queen of England. See his testimony of 24 February 1569, AGI Patronato 265, ramo 13, fol. 14. It is likely that this was the aid William Hawkins referred to in his letter to Cecil of 27 January 1568 (1569), PRO SP 12/49/42, fol. 88. The fact that such aid arrived from England was affirmed by Spanish, Portuguese, and English merchants in Vigo a month later to Spanish officials investigating the matter. Testimony of Antonio Pita, 23 February 1569, AGI Patronato 265, ramo 13, fol. 6; of Alonso

Sanchez, 23 February 1569, fol. 8v; of Rafael Coton, 25 February 1569, fol. 19; and of Pedro Ramos 25 February 1569, fol. 21.

11. Testimony of Pedro Ramos, 25 February 1569, AGI Patronato 265, ramo 13, fol. 21. Testimony of Antonio Pita, 23 February 1569, AGI, Patronato 265, ramo 13, fols. 6, 7. Testimony of Simón Vásquez, 24 February 1569, AGI Patronato 265, ramo 13, fol. 9v. Testimony of Juan de la Torre, 28 February 1569, AGI Patronato 265, ramo 13, fol. 28v. One merchant said that Hawkins sold two slaves and 1,200 varas of cloth, receiving in exchange "fine silk and taffeta" (sedas de tercio pelo y tafetan). Testimony of Fernando de Sçia, 24 February 1569, AGI Patronato 265, ramo 13, fol. 11.

12. "Vio otro onbre yngles moço bien tratado con unas calças de trciopelo carmisi y medias de aguja y una cuera de scarlata guarnescida de franjas de plata / y de mediana estatura algo moreno de rostro y aquel dezian que se llamaba el capitán Juan aquines." Testimony of Gregorio Sarmiento de Valladares, 24 February 1569, AGI Patronato 265, Ramo 13, fol. 13v.

13. Hawkins, *Troublesome voyadge*, fol. B.vii. Testimony of Gregorio Sarmiento de Valladares, 24 February 1569, AGI Patronato 265, ramo 13, fol. 14. Testimony of Tomás Olanda, 26 February 1569, AGI Patronato, ramo 13, fol. 22. Testimony of Antonio Pita, 23 February 1569, AGI Patronato 265, ramo 13, fol. 6-v. William Hawkins to Cecil, 27 January 1568 (1569), PRO SP 12/49/42, fol. 88. The exact date of John Hawkins's arrival is unclear. In a letter to Cecil dated 25 January 1568 (1569), John Hawkins said that he had arrived on 24 January. PRO SP12/49/40, fol. 83. However, the summary log attached to that letter (fol. 84) indicates that he arrived on 25 January, as does the *Troublesome voyadge*, fol. B.vii.

14. John Hawkins to Cecil, 25 January 1568 (1569), PRO SP 12/49/40, fol. 83. Guerau de Spes to the king, 12 March 1569, AGS Estado 821, fols. 25-26. The French ambassador told his own monarch that Hawkins came home with thirty men, but perhaps this figure included the slaves. Fénélon to the king, 6 February 1569, *Correspondance Diplomatique*, 1:179. William Hawkins to Cecil, 27 January 1568 (1569), PRO SP 12/49/42, fol. 88.

15. John Hawkins to Cecil, 25 January 1568 (1569), PRO 12/49/40, fol. 83. John Hawkins to Cecil, 6 March 1568 (1569), PRO 12/49/57, fol. 116.

16. Guerau de Spes to the king, [January 1569] AGS Estado 820, fol. 28. "Nota de lo que pasó en el tomar de las 13 ulcas que ultima venieron a plemua," 25 April 1569, AGS Estado 826, fol. 56.

17. The sequence of events from the end of December through the first week of January is outlined in the queen's proclamation of 6 January 1568 (1569), PRO SP 12/53, fols. 58-62v. William Hawkins to Cecil, 3 December 1568, PRO SP 12/48/50, fol. 119; 20 January 1568 (1569), PRO SP 12/49/36, fol.

75; 22 January 1568 (1569), PRO SP 12/49/37, fol. 77; 27 January 1568 (1569), PRO SP 12/49/42, fol. 88.

18. "Ynformaçion q̃ se saco por el regente de galiçia de su mag^d en el neg^o de un Juan aquyns yngles," 30 January 1569, AGI Patronato 265, ramo 13. Testimony of William Harrys, John Caige, William Harebrowne, and Giles Fluyde, 2 July 1569, PRO SP 12/53, fols. 63–66v.

19. PRO SP 12/53, fols. 1v–7. Material from this manuscript, rearranged and summarized, can be found in *An English Garner,* 104–26.

20. PRO SP 12/53, fols. 8, 14, 22, 42v, 48.

21. Herrera, *Primera parte de la historia,* tomo I, libro 15, capitulo 18, p. 720. Irene Wright outlines the argument for this alternative explanation in her *Documents Concerning English Voyages to the Spanish Main,* xxi–xxiv.

22. Initial estimate: William Hawkins to Cecil, 22 January 1568 (1569), PRO SP 12/49/37, fol. 77. Claim for *Angel:* PRO SP 12/53, fols. 6v–7. For the earlier valuation of the *Jesus* see the warrant to the Earl of Pembroke et al., 8 March 1563, PRO SP 12/28/2 and the certificate by William Winter et al., 23 October 1565, PRO SP12/37/61. Juan de Ubilla later said he thought the *Jesus* might have been worth about 3,000 ducados, or about £540. See his letter to the king, 16 December 1569, AGI Mexico 168, no folio numbers.

23. William Hawkins to Cecil, 22 January 1568 (1569), PRO SP 12/49/37, fol. 77. The valuation of the slaves amounts to £160 each. Hawkins had paid twenty ducados (about £3) apiece for slaves on the Río Tagarín. Testimony of Christopher Bingham, 1 December 1579, AGI Justicia 902, pp. 176–77. He sold slaves for about £18 apiece at Río de la Hacha. Testimony of Tomás Fuller, 2 November 1569, AGI Justicia 902, p. 60.

24. Guerau de Spes to the duke of Alba, 15 April, 1569, AGS Estado 822, fol. 43.

25. "No dubdamos que ay se interpretara muy a su modo lo que ha sucedido en la nuevua españa y el castigo que Don Martin Enrríquez mi visorey ha dado al Capitán Juan de Aquines Cossario natural de esse Reyno que hauia ydo allo [*sic*] con siete nauios de guerra." King to de Spes, 18 February 1569, AGS Estado 821, fols. 14–15.

26. The king had left the matter to Alba's discretion; see his letter of 18 February 1569, AGS Estado, libro 104, fols. 116v–17. See also duke of Alba to the king, 4 April 1569, in Hume, *Calendar of English Papers at Simancas,* 2:141.

27. Pro parte Catholici Regis oratoris ad Dños Consiliaros Ser^mæ Angliae Reginae secretioris consilii, Responsio, presented by Sir George Speake, 13 April 1569, BL Add. 48023, fols. 323–24. "Non absimilis iniuria a Joannæ Akins Catholici Regis amicitiæ est inflicta, quæ Regia classe, aliquõrque ut dicitur Consiliariõr ope atque hortatu, quartam iam ad occidentales Regis potentis-

simi ditiones (quae Indiarum nomine appellantur[)] expeditionem suscepit, contra foedera ac Regias leges, naves obvias diripiens, oppida expilans et incendens, homines tam indigenas quam hispanos, inter quos est nobilis Joannes Mendossa nunc in hybernia asservatus, captivans. Quem quidem Ackins oportet tandem punire, aurumque omne atque argentum, cum unionibus atque hominibus, restituere, deque aliis etiam depredationibus a pyratis Anglis et Gallis ex Angliae portibus exeuntibus factis, integre omnino satisfacere, mare liberum reddere. Protestante in his omnibus praefato oratore, prout ei licet decet, in superioribus etiam protestationibus persistente." Mendoza, as we shall see, had been captured by the *William and John* en route back to England.

28. Guerau de Spes to duke of Alba, 15 May 1569, AGS Estado 822, fol. 61.

29. The first English edition of *Actes and Monuments of Martyrs* was published by John Daye in 1563; the revised edition appeared in two volumes in 1570.

30. Guerau de Spes to duke of Alba, 15 May 1569, AGS Estado 822, fol. 61. "Despues de haver publicado el dicho libro andan recogiendo los que allan, mostrando pesarles havello hecho." *Principall Navigations,* 553–57. Guerau de Spes to duke of Alba, 15 May 1569, AGS Estado 822, fol. 61.

31. PRO SP 12/53, fol. 56v.

32. Antonio de Guaras to duke of Alba, 18 September 1569, in Hume, *Calendar of English Papers at Simancas,* 2:193–95. Interestingly enough, the original of this letter is missing from the legajo in Simancas, and the P.R.O. does not have a copy of the Hume transcript.

33. Fénélon to the King, 8 October 1569 and 12 November 1569, *Correspondance Diplomatique,* 2:275, 330.

34. Marginal note in the hand of Philip II on his letter to Guerau de Spes, 26 December 1569, AGS Estado 821, fol. 186. Guerau de Spes to the king, 25 February 1570, AGS Estado 822, fol. 65a.

35. Testimony of Vicente Romano, 19 January 1569, AGI Indiferente General 738, no. 116, ramo 3. The incident was said to have taken place on the previous day. The captain was "an old man of about fifty years" (un hombre viejo de çinq^{ta} años).

36. Juan de Mendoza to the king, 6 March 1570, AGI Indiferente General 738, no. 117, ramo 3. Juan de Abalia to the king, 6 March 1570, AGI Indiferente General 738, no. 116, ramo 4. There are several other reports in this legajo, plus testimony from sailors who claimed to have been robbed or to have known those who had been robbed by Hawkins in January.

37. Guerau de Spes to the king, 25 February 1570, AGS Estado 822, fol. 65. When the Portuguese ambassador heard that Hawkins was in town, he wrote to Cecil [February 1569 (1570), SP 12/70/105, fol. 82] that this would

be a propitious time to discuss reimbursement for the damage Hawkins had inflicted on Portuguese shipping.

38. "I was the prime mover in getting him and his ships to serve Your Majesty" (Yo fui el primer autor para que se rreduxesse con sus naues al serviço de .V.M^d.). Stucley to Philip II, 15 March 1570 (1571), AHN Ordenes Militares 3511/10. Obviously Stucley was used to the English system of dating which began the year on 25 March.

39. Juan de Mendoza to Cecil, 26 January 1569 (1570), PRO SP 63/27/7, fol. 12. Guerau de Spes to the king, 2 April 1569, AGS Estado 821, fols. 37–38. Juan de Mendoza to Cecil, 1 July 1569, Hatfield mss., Cecil Papers, vol. 156, fols. 38–39. Copy on microfilm, M485/41, British Library. Mendoza to the duke of Alba, 30 April 1570, PRO SP 70/111/658, fol. 100. "Fui preso da inglesi, stando nella isola di ucatan." It is not clear who translated the letter into Italian. Stucley's release is in "Acts of the Privy Council in Ireland, 1556–1571," *HMC Fifteenth Report,* Appendix, Part III, *The Manuscripts of Charles Haliday, Esq., of Dublin* (London: HMSO, 1897), pp. 232–33 (ms. fols. 319–20). Stucley's offer was first made to Philip in June 1569. Guerau de Spes to the king, 14 June 1569, AGS Estado 821, fols. 78–79.

40. George Fitzwilliams et al. to Cecil, 25 February 1569 (1570), PRO SP 70/110/7, fol. 87. "Aquí guardan los prisioneros muy estrechamente allende que a los españoles tractan muy mal y a muchos dellos tienen en cadenas." De Spes to the king, 2 April 1569, AGS Estado 821, fols. 37–38.

41. Antonio Godard (Tejeda) said that Hawkins had "eighty men more or less," when he left them at Panuco, including "about sixteen slaves more or less." See his testimony of 15 October 1569, AGI Patronato 265, ramo 12, fol. 5.

42. Flores, *Obra nueuamẽte compuesta,* fol. 3. The hostage Micael Sol said, "There were thirty-six prisoners with the nine [others?] given as hostages" (Quedaron en poder del dho gen^l de españa treinta y seis ingleses con los nueveque fueron dados en rehenes). Testimony given 24 November 1569, AGI Justicia 902, p. 354.

43. In his greatly exaggerated claim for damages Hawkins claimed that there were fifty-seven slaves. PRO SP 12/53, fol. 7. Juan de Ubilla said that there were fifty slaves on the *Jesus of Lubeck* and the other English vessels abandoned in the harbor, but he probably exaggerated in order to place greater blame on the local citizens who carried them away. See his letter to the king, 16 December 1568, AGI Mexico 168, no folio numbers. What happened to them became a matter of great dispute between Ubilla and Maldonado, but it seems clear that a huge quantity of gold and silver and seventeen slaves disappeared after the battle into the possession of merchant Agustín Villanueva. See the letters and testimony of Ubilla and other cap-

tains, 5 September 1568–19 December 1569, AGI Justicia 1000, no. 2, ramo 3, part 1.

44. It is not possible to be more specific about the numbers of men involved. Godard said that "ninety persons more or less" went ashore. See his testimony of 2 November 1569, AGI Justicia 902, p. 22. Phillips said 110 were put ashore, of whom half went north. Half of those returned, and only three of the others reached England. See his "Discourse," in Hakluyt, *Principall Navigations,* 567. Phillips wrote his story after talking to other survivors, but some years after the event. Ingram said that a hundred were set on land. See his account in BL Sloane 1447, fols. 1–11, "The Relacon of Davyd Ingram of Barkinge in the Couñ of Essex, beinge nowe about the age of fortye yeares of sundrye thinges wch he wth others did see in Travelinge by lande for the most northerlie p[ar]te of the Baye of mezico where he wth many others weare sett on shoare by Mr Hawkyns throughe agreate p[ar]te of Ameryca untill they came w^thin fivetye leagues or theraboute of Cape Britton wch he reported unto S^r ffrauncys Walsingeh^am knight her ma^ts principall Secretarye and to Sr George Peckh^am knight and dyv^es others of good iudgment and credditt in August and September A^o Dni 1582./" This tale is so fantastic that little can be taken for fact, except that Ingram's fellow escapees were Richard Browne and Richard Twide, a fact confirmed by Phillips. Nevertheless, Ingram's story had such currency that in 1582 Francis Walsingham summoned him to explain himself. See "Certeyne questions to be demaunded of Davyd Ingram, saylor, dwellinge at Barkinge in the countye of Essex./ what he observed in his travels one the northe side of the ryver of May where he remayned three moneths or there abouts," [probably November–December 1582, though a notation of the back of the manuscript says "abt 1584"] PRO SP 12/175/95, fols. 163–64. Hakluyt published the story with minor changes in 1589 in the "Relation of David Ingram," *Principall Navigations,* 557–62. Both manuscripts were published by Quinn in *The Voyages and Colonising Enterprises of Sir Humphrey Gilbert,* series II, 84:281–96.

45. Seventy-seven is the total in the Spanish report of 8 October 1568, AGI Patronato 265, ramo 12, fols. 1–9. Some were not English. There were four French sailors, apparently from the crew of Captain Bland. Godard managed at first to pass himself off as Antonio de Texera, a Portuguese from the Island of San Miguel in the Azores, but his real identity soon became known.

46. See the orders of 8–18 October, 1568, in Patronato 265, ramo 12, no. 2, fols. 1–9v. Medina, *Inquisición en México,* 321, says that a total of fourteen died between the time of leaving the *Minion* and arriving in the city of Mexico.

Christopher Robertson testified, "They took them overland to Mexico and fifteen or sixteen died there" (Los llevaron por tierra a mexico y alli fallesçieron los quinze o dies y seis dellos). Both accounts may be describing the same losses. See Robertson's testimony of 23 November 1569, AGI Justicia 902, p. 70.

47. Phillips, "Discourse," in Hakluyt, *Principall Navigations*, 569, 571–72. Testimony of Enrique More, 9 December 1569, AGI Justicia 902, p. 218.

48. Their testimony is in AGI Patronato 265, ramo 11, Valentín Verde, fols. 1–3; Gregorio Estevan, fols. 3v–5; Micael Sol (Soole), fols. 5v–8; Richart Red, fols. 8–10v; Juan Hol, fols. 10v–12v; and Tomás Estevan, fol. 12v–15. They were moved to Vera Cruz on 23 September, and the interrogation was held 4–6 October. On 9 October they were apparently in Xalapa, where Robert Barrett, master of the *Jesus of Lubeck,* was interrogated (fols. 14v–18v). Phillips, "Discourse," in Hakluyt, *Principall Navigations,* 570–71.

49. Their testimony is in AGI Patronato 265, ramo 12, no. 1; Thomas Benot (Tomás Benito), 18 September 1568, fols. 1v–9; Guillermo Sanda, 19 September 1568, fols. 9–14v; Noe Sarjen (Noysajen), 2 November 1568; Enrique Mores, 10 November 1568, 21v–28.

50. Testimony of Christopher Robertson, 23 November 1569, AGI Justicia 902, p. 70. Robert Bell and a French prisoner named Claudio died in the fall of 1569. Ricardo Tempal, Christopher Bingham, Guillermo Calan, and Henry Keene died in early 1570. AGI Justicia 902, pp. 246, 251, 506, 509, 514. Claudio, captured at Nombre de Dios, was perhaps from the French pirate vessel released by Hawkins at the end of July near Cartagena.

51. "Las bienes de Ingleses arrestados en españa," AGS Estado 822, fol. 23. Although Fitzwilliams is usually given credit for assisting the other English prisoners, he can hardly have been of much help, as his goods were already sequestered to cover his debts. Clifford, *Life of Jane Dormer*, 175. Fitzwilliams et al. to Cecil, 25 February 1569 (1570), PRO SP 70/110/7. fol. 87.

52. Guerau de Spes to the king, 12 June 1570, AGS Estado 822, fol. 110a; 18 June 1570, AGS Estado 822, fol. 117; 22 June 1570, AGS Estado 822, fol. 119; 1 July 1570, AGS Estado 822, fol. 124. Antonio de Guaras to Zayas, 30 June 1570, AGS Estado 821, fols. 126b, 126d; 1 August 1570, AGS Estado 822, fol. 137; 7 August 1570, AGS Estado 822, fol. 140a.

53. Guerau de Spes to the king 12 August 1570, AGS Estado 822, fol. 124; Guaras to Zayas, 12 August 1570, AGS Estado 822, fol. 143b; 20 August, 1570, AGS Estado 822, fol. 152. Guerau de Spes to the King, 19 August 1570, AGS Estado 822, fol. 151.

54. Guerau de Spes to the duke of Alba, 21 August 1570, AGS Estado 822, fol. 154. "Bastaria libertarle sus hombres."

55. Guzmán de Silva to the king, 4 February 1566, AGS, Estado 819, fols. 66–67. Guzmán de Silva to the king, 23 March 1566, AGS, Estado 819, fol. 71. Mendoza to the king, 6 March 1570, AGI Indiferente General 738, no. 117, ramo 3. Stucley to the king, 15 March 1570 (1571) AHN OM 3511/10, summarizing his negotiations with Hawkins.

56. Francis Edwards, *The Marvellous Chance: Thomas Howard, Fourth Duke of Norfold, and the Ridolfi Plot, 1570–1572* (London: Rupert Hart-Davis, 1968), 90–116.

57. Robert Hogan to Henry Norris, 12 August 1570, SP 70/113/807. Stucley to the king, 15 March 1570 (1572) AHN OM 3511/10. "Esto podra ser Aquines que como .V.M^d. Sabe es muy grande amigo mio, y yo fui el primer autor para que se rreduxesse con sus naues Al serviçio de .V.M^d."

58. AGI Justicia 902, no. 1, pp. 516–17. The computer copy of this document now provided at the Archivo General de Indias includes several pages of introductory documents. Because the folio numbers in the document are not continuous, I have used the page numbers on the electronic copy, which add about fifteen numbers to the pagination. Guerau de Spes to the king, 3 September 1570, AGS Estado 822, fol. 161.

6
Turning Defeat into Victory

1. See the royal cedula of 17 April 1570 for the release of Christopher Bingham and Tomás Fuller, AGI Justicia 902, p. 534. Unfortunately, Bingham died before the cedula was prepared, and this created problems for Fuller, who had to submit a separate request for release. The cedula and accompanying papers for Berin and Fitzwilliams are in AGI Justicia 902, pp. 241–43, 516–17. Bingham was one of several Hawkins prisoners who died of "the fever" in February 1570. The others were Ricardo Temple, Henry Keene, and Guillermo Calan. AGI Justicia 902, pp. 506–14. Another prisoner, Robert Bell, who may also have been one of the ten hostages, died on 9 September 1569. One of the French sailors, named Claudio, died a day earlier. AGI Justicia 902, pp. 246–51.

2. Guerau de Spes to the king, 2 September 1570, AGS Estado 822, fol. 159d. "Del Capitán Aquines ya he dado auiso a .V.Mag^d. como me ha offresçido desarmar, y dexar los viages de Indias, lo qual yo no acabo de creer."

3. Guerau de Spes to the king, 12, 18, 22 June 1570, AGS Estado 822, fols. 110a, 117, 119. Antonio de Guaras to Çayas, 30 June–1 July, 1, 7, 12, 19, 20, 22 August 1570, AGS Estado 822, fols. 126b and d, 137c, 140a, 143b, 151, 152,

153. Fénélon to the king, 27 April, 11, 21 August, 10 September 1570, *Correspondance Diplomatique,* 3:132, 269–70, 285, 303.

4. Privy Council to John and William Hawkins, 5 October 1570, Hatfield ms., Cecil Papers, B.L. Microfilm, reel M485/56.

5. The accusations are in AGI Justicia 902, pp. 517–19. Testimony of Richard Guest, 25 October 1570; Jorge Ellis, 26 October 1570; Juan Gilefort, 27 October 1570; and Juan de Urquiza, 30 October 1570; AGI Justicia 902, pp. 569–80.

6. Testimony of Juan de Urquiza and Alonso de Palomares, 30 October 1570, AGI Justicia 902, pp. 576–84. Not everyone agreed. One Spanish merchant who was aboard one of the ships said that he was unsure who was at fault, because he could not hear very well. Testimony of Rodrigo Sanz de Santiago, 7 November 1570, AGI Justicia 902, p. 600. "*Como este tet*$^{\underline{o}}$ *no oye muy bien no supo ny entendio quien tubo la culpa en el dicho negoçio.*"

7. The sentence, dated 19 December 1570, is in AGI Justicia 902, pp. 609–10. The appeal and accompanying papers, dated 20, 21, 22 December 1570, are in AGI Justicia 902, pp. 610–14.

8. A summary account, signed "I. H. January 1576," says, "George fytzwyllm̄s was sent by me into Spayne to obtayne lybertye for for soche men as I had in captyvytye." The queen apparently found out about the offer of service after Fitzwilliams returned, and thereafter Hawkins asked for specific royal approval for such visits. See BL Cotton Galba C, v, fol. 263. In a claim for reimbursement submitted in 1577 Hawkins implied that the queen had approved of both visits, without saying that she approved the first visit in advance. "I was at the sole charge of sendynge fytzwyllm̄s into spayne twyse for intellygence w^t her ma^{ties} consent." "S^{r}vice done by Jo^n Hawkyns unrecompensyd," 14 February 1577, PRO SP12/111/33, fol. 74.

9. Thomas Stucley's Proposal, *State Papers Rome,* 1:374, citing Vat. Arch. Misc. Arm. ii. vol. 100. (Polit. 99.), fol. 199. BL Cotton Galba, C, vi, part 1, fols. 5–8. Robert Hugins to Walsingham, 25 January [1570/1], PRO SP 70/116/101; M. T. Kelly, "A Knight of the Road and Sea," Cork Historical and Archaeological Society *Journal,* series 2, 1:498–513.

10. Robert Hugins to Henry Norris, 12 August 1570, PRO SP 70/113/807, fol. 101v. Hugins also sent his servant Matthew to London to make a personal report to Cecil. See Daniel A. Binchy, "An Irish Ambassador at the Spanish Court, 1569–1574, Part II," *Studies: An Irish Quarterly Review of Letters, Philosophy, and Science* 10 (December 1921):573.

11. Guerau de Spes to the king, 3 September 1570, AGS Estado 822, fol. 161. "*Un pariente de la Duquesa de Feria que me trujo cartas del Duque.*"

12. King to duke of Alba, 4 August 1571, AGS, E-Flandes, Leg. 547-2, tran-

scribed in Jorge Calvar Gross, *La Batalla del Mar Océano* (5 vols., Madrid: Ministerio de Defensa, Armada Española, Ediciones Turner, 1988–93), 1:57–59. "Lo que Jorge FitzVillams Gentilhombre Ingles, embiado por el Capitán Juan Aquines, refiere de parte del dicho Capitán. Traducido de Ingles," undated, AGS Estado 824, fol. 26. "El Capitán Juan Aquines, viendo la gran ruina de su tierra natural, acresçentandose cada dia por las heregias que en ella tiranicam^{te}. esta sembrada, es desseoso para ensalçamiento de la gloria de Dios servir al Rey cath^{co}. en favor de la Reyna Maria de Escoçia, ayudandola a la Justa possession y dignidad del Reyno de Inglaterra por donde Dios pueda ser servido y glorificado en aquella tierra como solia/ . . . Item el dicho Capitán oyendo la llegada de Estucley a esos Reynos de España y la buena acogida que por fama alla le ha dado la M^d. Cath^{ca}. ha sido parte de induzille a poner su designo por effecto y mostrar al Rey Cath^{co}. el desseo que tiene de Juntarse con el dicho Estucley en esta tan Justa demanda por el grande amor q̃ siempre ha sido muy unidos entre los dos. . . . Item el dicho Capitán traera para effectuar esto una armada de viente y cinco navios por lo menos muy buenos y basteçidos de todo lo necess^o. excepto solamente la paga de la gente y costas en adelante hasta q̃ se concluya esta empresa la qual con el ayuda de dios no estara mucho en hazerse. . . . Que le sea señalada la mr̃d de alguna pension honrrada y bastante por el año mientras durare la ampresa / o / sino prevalesciesse (lo qual Dios no quiera) y el creo ser impossible, que entonçes la tal merçedle sea otorgada mientras biviere, y si por caso el muriere en la demanda, q̃ luego le sucçeda en la dicha pension y en la misma forma su hermano Guillermo Haquines, que tambien le acompañara en este viage / . . . . Que el Duque y Duquesa de Feria sean obligados debaxo de sus palabras y firmas que todo lo aquí contenido sera guardado y salgan por fiadores que le sera hecho a el y a los suyos ningũ agravio sino el acogimiento liberal y benigno segun que del poderossissimo Rey sera concedido /."

13. "Lo que propone Jorge Fitzwilliams," undated, AGS Estado 824, fol. 29. Thomas Fuller is identified in the Ferias' (?) undated notes in AGS Estado 824, fol. 28 (margin). Leonardo Donado to the Signoury, 19 February 1571, in Brown and Bentinck (eds.), *State Papers Venice*, 7:464.

14. "Lo que Jorge FitzVillams . . .," undated, AGS Estado 824, fol. 26. "El Ju^o. Haquins y su her^{mo}. . . . erã Catho^{cos}. y tenian por su Rey^a. verdadera la deScoçia, y con la ysabel estavan oppresos y maltratados."

15. Thomas Stucley to the king, 15 March 1570 (1571), AHN Ordenes Militares 3511/10. A reference to the duke is followed by the phrase "que Dios tenga," no doubt because the Duke was sick.

16. AGS Estado 824, fol. 28. "Si tiene alguna intelligen^a. con la rey^a. deScoçia /

respondio q̃ entre el y uno de los ~~presos~~ tres q̃ se libertarõ en Sevilla, q̃ este es mucho de la deScoçia / llamase Thomas Fuller. . . . vii .o/ viii. de 25. 28. toneladas / otros de .150 . 130. y otras de no mas q̃ .30. y son de Jnº Haquines y Guillermo su herº."

17. This "preamble" was translated by or for Hawkins in a letter he wrote to Burghley in January 1576 (1577). See BL Cotton Galba C, v, fols. 263–64. "Beinge so that the pryncypall end wch ys p[re]tended in theis thyngs that be treatyd of, ys the service of god, and the restytucon of the catholyk faythe in the reallme [margin: preamble] of Ingland, and to delyver yt to quene mary of Scottland, to whom of ryght it dothe appertayne; Jon hawkyns must se what way he thynketh best that he may and ought to take to attayne this and putt yt in execucõn."

18. Feria's notes about the conversation and a final copy of his list of questions are contained in AGS Estado 824, fols. 27, 28. Another copy in AGS Estado 823, fol. 111, carries the date April 1571 and thus makes it possible to date the accompanying documents with considerable certainty.

19. "Lo que propone Jorge Fitzwilliams," undated, AGS Estado 824, fol. 30. BL Cotton Galba C, v, fols. 263–64.

20. John Leslie, bishop of Ross, to Burghley, 9 November 1571, BL Cotton Caligula III, fols. 228–229v. The bishop, writing from a faulty memory, placed the visit earlier in the year.

21. Hawkins to Burghley, 13 May 1571, PRO SP 49/6/61, transcribed in James A. Froude, *History of England, from the Fall of Wolsey to the Defeat of the Spanish Armada* (12 vols.; London: Longman, Green, 1870), 9:513.

22. Shrewsbury to Burghley, 3 June 1571, in Boyd, *State Papers, Scotland,* 3:595. De Spes to the king, 15 June 1571, AGS Estado 823, fol. 139. In his later summary Hawkins said the gifts were from the king of Spain and the duke of Feria and included a third ring for Hawkins himself. BL Cotton Galba C, v, fol. 263. Queen of Scotland to Philip, 3 June 1571, AGS Estado 820, fol. 135; and to duke of Feria, 4 June 1571, fol. 136. Both letters are in Spanish, translated from French.

23. "Far be it from us to boast, except in the Lord Jesus Christ." Hawkins to Burghley, 7 June 1571, PRO SP 49/6/73, quoted in Boyd, *State Papers, Scotland* 3:598. Several years later Hawkins recalled the start of the phrase as "Absit mihi," which is the way it appears in the Vulgate version of St. Paul's letter to the Galatians. On that later date he also thought the book was intended as a gift for the king. BL Cotton Galba, C, v, fol. 263.

24. Hawkins to Burghley, 7 June 1571, PRO SP 49/6/73, quoted in Boyd, *State Papers, Scotland* 3:598. As Hawkins noted in his summary, he again received specific royal approval. "By her ma^ties consent I sent fytzwyllm̃s to the kinge." BL Cotton Galba, C, v, fol. 263.

25. Doctor Velasco to Diego de Espinosa, 27 July 1571, BL Additional 28,336, fol. 70. "The Hawkins negotiations ought to be held somewhat suspect because he has met often with Lord Burghley" (Que el negoçio de Haquins se puede tener alguna sospecha por haver communicado muchas vezes el y Fitzuilliams con Milord Burle). Guerau de Spes, Puntos de cartas, 12, 14, and 19 July 1571, AGS Estado 823, fol. 167b.

26. "Haquins que haze? Donde esta? Quantos nauios tiene, y de que qualidad y portada, y si se ha abierto con vos de manera que nos podamos assegurar que recogiendo y fauores çiendole yo, me seruia lealmente/." King to Guerau de Spes, 13 July 1571, AGS Estado 823, fol. 170.

27. Velasco to Espinosa, 23 July 1571, and 27 July 1571, BL Additional 28, 336, fols. 64-v, 70-v. Feria to Zayas, 26 July 1571, AGS Estado 153, fol. 95. Parker, *Grand Strategy of Philip II,* p. 161. Feria to Zayas, 9 August 1571, AGS Estado 153, fol. 103.

28. Unsigned letter to Robert Hogan, 8 July 1571, SP 70/119/3, fols. 5-6. Edwards thinks that this mysterious stranger might have been Roberto Ridolfi, but Ridolfi could scarcely have been mistaken for an Englishman. *The Marvellous Chance,* 303. On the other hand, Fitzwilliams may not have arrived in Madrid before late July, well after these meetings were over.

29. "Lo que se platico en consº. sobre las cosas de Inglaterra," 7 July 1571, AGS Estado 823, fol. 152b. For news of the arrival of Fitzwilliams see Velasco to Espinosa, 27 July 1571, BL Additional 28, 336, fol. 70-v.

30. "Aquí ha llegado Fitzvilliams con la respuesta de los artículos q̃ habia llevado á Juan Haquins, sobre la qual se va tratando con el, para sacar en claro si trae cosa de substançia/ que si la trae, y el dicho Haquins camina de buen pie, no hay dubda, sino que seria de seruiçio/ mas para creer esto, son menester muchas comprobaçiones." King to Guerau de Spes, 5 August 1571, AGS Estado 824, fol. 17.

31. "Memoriale di Roberto Ridolfi sopra la Petitione d'Achins," AGS Estado 824, fol. 24, July–August 1571 (?); "Apuntamentos que ha dado Roberto Ridolfi sobre el negocio de Inglaterra," July–August 1571 (?), AGS Estado 824, fols. 188–89. Guerau de Spes to the king, 8 August 1571, AGS Estado 824, fols. 13–14.

32. "Por donde ellos no solamente quedaran obligados a V. Exª. / En todo lo de mas q̃ tocare al resto de mis negocios me remito a la relación del portador, a quien creera como si yo presente estuviera." AGS Estado 824, fol. 33. The copy in the file is not in the hand of John Hawkins, though it may have been signed by him as "Juan Haquines." It is part of a group of papers in the hand of George Fitzwilliams, some of which bear his signature.

33. "La respuesta q̃ dio Jorge Fitzwilliams en nombre de Juan Haquins," AGS Estado 824, fol. 25. "Los perticulares de quy .G.F. a de trayr relación

ample," AGS Estado 826, no folio number or date. "Repoisto al .11. Articoles . Per .I.H." and "Los navios de I H sus portaio y quantos Hombres poidon levar con el carga de dos meses," AGS Estado 826, no folio number or date. The first appears to be in the hand of George Fitzwilliams, the other three in the hand of John Hawkins.

34. "Los navios de I H sus portaio y quantos Hombres poidon levar con el carga de dos meses," AGS Estado 826, no folio number or date.

35. AGS Estado 824, fol. 25. "En respuesta de lo contenido en el decimo capitulo escrive al duque de Feria y embia un anillo por contraseño y remitese enteramente a Jorje Fitzvilliams, assegurando q̃ cumplira lo q̃ por el en su nombre cerca deste particular fuere prometido / q̃ sera todo lo a el posible / advirtiendo q̃ no se le escriva ni embia a dezir cosa alguna sino fuere por el mismo Jorje Fitzvilliams / o / por medio del embaxador don Guerau."

36. Ibid. "Seria lo mejor darles libertad, para q̃ cada uno se baya a su ventura : por q̃ no balen el gasto q̃ con ellos se haze y q̃ sola la charidad le ha movido a favorescerlos y ayudarlos, y lo mismo pide para los q̃ eran de la misma compañia en las yndias."

37. "Informaçion dado por don guerau despes, acerca dloqe podria servir Joan Aquins Ingles asu M^d." AGS Estado 826, fol. 38. "Memoria de los navios de Juan Haquins y de que toneladas son quanta gente pueden traer y que pieças de artilleria tienen, y lo que montara el gasto de dos meses." AGS Estado 824, fol. 184. "Apuntamientos que ha dado Roberto Ridolfi sobre el negocio de Inglaterra," AGS Estado 824, fol. 189. See also the letter from Hawkins to Burghley, 4 September 1571, PRO SP 12/81/167a, in which Hawkins reports that it is his job to burn the ships in the Medway. The final agreed costs were expressed in ducados, rather than pounds. Memoria de los navios con q̃ Juan Haquins offresce servir a su Mag^d. y de q̃ toneladas son / quanta gente pueden traer / y q̃ pieças de artillria tienen y lo q̃ montara el gasto de dos meses./ AGS Estado 824, fol. 34. "Las naos pertenescientes a Juan Aquins," AGS Estado 824, fol. 23. Many of the discussion papers were bundled up and sent to the king in September 1571 by the duchess of Feria. See her undated letter in AGS Estado 826.

38. "Sy poido ser es necessario quy vine el .D.de.F. por el governador en Flandres o en esto feto, por ser amystad y moian passaremos meior en esta negocia," AGS Estado 826. "Lo q̃ se ha tratado y assentado entre don Gomez Suarez de Figueroa Duque de Feria, del consejo de estado de su M^d. Y su capitán de la Guarda / y Jorge Fitvilliams en nombre de Juan Haquins Yngles,"AGS Estado 824, fol. 35. "Seguira la orden que su mag^d. le mandaredar / o / el lugarteniente suyo en los estados de flandes que a la sazon fuere." "Porque el dho Juan Aquins y Jorge Fitzuilliams pretenden averseles

hecho daño y agravio en el caso succedido en el puerto de Sanct Juan de Ulúa de la nueva España el año passado de M.D.lxviii. que en esto su Md. mandara sean oydos a justicia, y sean desagraviados si la tuvieren."

39. "Lo que se ha tractado y assentado entre Don Gomez de figueroa duque de feria, del consejo destado de su Mt y su capitán de la de la guarda y Jorge FitzVilliams en nombre de Juan Aquins Ingles y en virtud de la orden y comission que del tiene," Biblioteca de Zabálburu, Colección Altamira, carpeta 153, doc. 153. Because Feria kept the signed copies in his own files, it is possible that the unsigned copy in AGS Estado 826, fol. 54 (included with the papers the duchess later sent to the king), is the one originally intended for Fitzwilliams. See also the letter from Hawkins to Burghley, 4 September 1571, PRO SP 12/81/167a, in which Hawkins says that his copy of the agreement is to be delivered later.

40. AGS Estado 824, fol. 35.

41. AGS Estado 824, fol. 32. AGI Justicia 908, no. 2, fols. 8v–10. Velasco to Espinosa, 14 August 1571, BL Additional 28,336, fol. 279. "Si nos engaña no nos sacara mucha sangre."

42. Antonio Gracian to Çayas, 6 August 1571, BL Egerton 2047, fol. 280. Copies of the release documents can be found in several places, among them, AGI Justicia 908, no. 2, fols. 1–23v. "La çerenysima rreyna descoçia ñra muy cara y muy amada her^{na} nos a escripto y embiado a pedir y rrogar que a los v^{te} yngleses questan presos en esa casa y se truxeron de la nueva españa los mandamos soltar y dar por libres." The cedula is on fol. 2–v.

43. BL Egerton 2047, fols. 279–81. AGI Justicia 908, no. 2, fols. 5–23v.

44. Hortop, *Rare Trauailes,* fols. B4–C1. Phillips, "Discourse," in Hakluyt, *Principall Navigations,* 565–78. The Inquisition's treatment of the English is described in copious detail in the proceedings against David Alexander (Alejandre) and William Collins (Calens) in *Corsarios Franceses e Ingleses,* 231–510.

45. Hortop, *Rare Trauailes,* fols. C2–C4. Phillips, "Discourse," in Hakluyt, *Principall Navigations,* 580.

46. Stucley as double agent: Edwards, *Marvellous Chance,* 303–4. Mendoza to Stucley, 11 January 1572, AGS Estado 550, fol. 81. "Yo fui rrobado delos françeses de gran suma de dinero y despues preso de yngleses y estando en poder dellos El capitán del nabio luego que tomo ñra nao hablando con el me dixo que abia tenido un amigo que se llama Juan de mendoça que abia tenido pensionero del rrey Enrríquez y muy querido del y como yo soy aquello pareciome que hera tpo de aprobecharse el hombre de ardides y asi dixe que hera mi padre." Phillips, "Discourse," in Hakluyt, *Principall Navigations,* 580.

47. Feria to Hawkins, 11 August 1571, PRO SP 70/119, fol. 86–v.
48. Hawkins to Burghley, 4 September 1571, PRO SP 12/81/167a.
49. Guerau de Spes to the king, 7 September 1571, AGS Estado 824, fol. 57. King to Guerau de Spes, 14 September 1571, AGS Estado 825, fol. 65. King to duke of Alba 14 September 1571, AGS E-Flandes 547–3, quoted in J. Calvar Gross, *Batalla del Mar Océano*, 1:62–64. King to Guerau de Spes, 15 October 1571, AGS Estado 824, fol. 85; 31 October 1571, fol. 96; 12 December 1571, fols. 111–12.
50. Guerau de Spes to the king, AGS Estado 825, fols. 1–2.
51. Guerau de Spes to the king, 20 September 1571, AGS Estado 824, fol. 67; 15 October 1571, fol. 85; 21 October 1571, fol. 87; 20 November 1571, fol. 102; 12 December 1571, fol. 111.
52. Burghley to Thomas Smith, 28 December 1571, in Digges, *Compleat Ambassador,* p. 161. "Informacion dada por don guerau despes, acerca dloque podria servir Joan Aquins Ingles a su M^d." AGS Estado 826 fol. 38. Undated. "Parecer acerca las cosas de Irlanda y Inglat." (Notes of a conversation with Guerau de Spes), 11 October 1572, AGS Estado 830, fol. 1.
53. Hawkins to Burghley, 4 September 1571, PRO SP 12/81/167A.
54. Smyth, "Certain Passages," 206.
55. BL Cotton Galba, C, v, fol. 163. "Don Guerau de Spes the imbasador laft me at his departynge a syphere to wrytt allways upon eny occasyon." "S^rvice done by Jon Hawkyns unrecompensyd," 14 February 1576 (1577), PRO SP 12/111/33, fol. 74.

7
Changing Course

1. Discursos sobre los disinios de la Reyna de ynglattr^a, 1572 (?), AGS Estado 830, fols. 156–59. Guerau de Spes to the king, 3 April 1572, AGS Estado 825, fol. 50; 3 July 1572, AGS Estado 827, fol. 107. Guerau de Spes, "Parecer a cerca las cosas de Irlanda y Inglat," AGS Estado, 830, 11 October 1572. Juan de Mendoça, Brussels, to Tomás Estucli, 11 January 1572, AGS Estado 550, fol. 81.
2. *Journals of the House of Commons,* 1:91, 105.
3. William, Count De la Marck to Privy Council, 25 January 1572, PRO SP 70/122/51. Charles IX to la Mothe Fénélon, 23 February 1573, PRO SP 70/126/429. Antonio Fogaça to Ruy Gomez, 16 September 1572, AGS Estado 825, fol. 107b. Letter of Thomas Stucley, [July 1572], Vatican Archives, Misc. Arm. II, vol. 100, Polit. (99), fols. 203<th>ff., summarized in Rigg, *State Papers, Rome,* p. 22. Antonio de Guaras to the king, 17 January 1573,

AGS Estado 827, fol. 8c. Relaçión de cartas de Antonio Fogaça a Çayas, 26, 30 January 1573, AGS Estado 827, fol. 10. Fogaça to Gabriel Çayas, 30 January 1573, fols. 22–23. Relaçión de lo que contiene los avisos embiados de Londres al rey de Portugal, 7 February 1573, AGS Estado 827, fol. 14. Guaras to duke of Alba 17 March 1573, AGS Estado 827, fol. 45. In fact, Hawkins seems to have done no more than send a single ship to relieve the besieged troops taken there by Sir Humphrey Gilbert and Sir Arthur Champernowne. See his "S^{r}vice done by Jo^n Hawkyns unrecompensyd," 14 February 1576 (1577), PRO SP 12/111/33.

4. Richard Bagwell, *Ireland Under the Tudors: With a Succinct Account of the Earlier History* (London: Longmans, Green, 1885), 2:299–301.

5. Ellis, *Tudor Ireland*, 267. Edwards, *Ireland in the Age of the Tudors*, 134. "Reduction of Rathlin in 1575," *Notes and Queries*, Third Series (January 1864), 90.

6. O'Donovan, *Annals of the Kingdom of Ireland*, 5:1677. Ellis, *Tudor Ireland*, 267. Bagwell, *Ireland Under the Tudors*, 2:259, 301. "S^{r}vice done by Jo^n Hawkyns unrecompensyd," 14 February 1576 (1577), PRO SP 12/111/33.

7. Strype, *Life and Acts of Matthew Parker*, 327, 328.

8. Guaras to duke of Alba, 31 October 1573, AGS Estado 827, fol. 141b. Queen Elizabeth quoted in Brooks, *Sir Christopher Hatton*, 102.

9. Thomas Smith to Burghley, 15 October 1573, BL Harley 6991, no. 34. Guaras to duke of Alba, 15 November 1573, AGS Estado 827, fol. 144b.

10. Antonio Fogaça to Çayas, 30 January 1573 (1574), AGS Estado 827, fols. 22–23.

11. Worth, *Plymouth Municipal Records*, 54, 122. Will of John Hawkins, 6 June 1595, and codicil, 16 June 1595, PRO Prob 11/94, fols. 100–105. Examination of Peter Fisher, 12 July 1574, Boyd, *State Papers, Scotland*, 5:24. Smith to Guaras, 3 January 1574 (1575), AGS Estado 829, fol. 4; Elizabeth to Philip 3 January 1574 (1575), fol. 7 (Latin); fol. 8 (Spanish); Guaras to Smith, 7 and 21 January 1575, fol. 9. Dale to Burghley, 3 November 1575, PRO SP 70/136/371, 70/136/448.

12. By all appearances Fitzwilliams completely misunderstood the arrangement. He fully expected to arrive home and find the Spanish ambassador waiting with money in hand, while the Spanish documents showed that Hawkins was still expected to supply guarantees. Guerau de Spes to the king, 7 September 1571, AGS Estado 824, fol. 57.

13. For information on these voyages see Kelsey, *Sir Francis Drake*, 44–64.

14. Acerbo Velutelli, "Answere and replye touchinge the priviledge of currants," BL Cotton Vespasian F.IX.220–21. "Lo que en sustançia contienen las cartas de Antonio de Guaras de Londres a viii xi xv xxi y xxviii de enero

1575," AGS Estado 829, fols. 11e–f. "Relación de las cartas de Antonio de Guaras a Çayas de 28 de junio 4 11 18 y 25 de julio 1575," AGS Estado 829, fol. 20d. Antonio de Guaras to Çayas 18 July 1575, AGS Estado 829, fol. 22c. "Relación de robos hechos por yngleses," 30 November 1575, AGS Estado 829, fol. 111 (draft); and other copies of the same in fol. 51 and (with a date of 30 November) fol. 127.

15. See the king's memorandum of 26 October 1575, in *CDIE* 91:102. See also Parker, *Grand Strategy*, 123, 143–46, 163–64.

16. See the letter from the queen to William Holstock, 3 November 1575, PRO SP 12/105/68, fol. 148; and the draft proclamation of November 1575, PRO/SP/83, fols. 177–78. Guaras to Çayas 8 October 1575, and king to Guaras, 11 October 1575, in *CDIE* 91:98, 101.

17. "Hawkyns 1576, touchinge his intelligence," BL Cotton Galba, C.V.263–64.

18. "S^{r}vice done by Jo^n Hawkyns unrecompensyd," 14 February 1576 (1577), PRO SP 12/111/33.

19. "Abuses in the Admiraltie touching hir Maties Navie exhibited by m^r Hawkins," undated (1577?), BL Lansdowne 113, no. 14, fols. 45–47. Simon Adams places the date of this manuscript in 1579, arguing that it referred to ship repairs made in 1578. See his "New Light on the 'Reformation' of John Hawkins: The Ellesmere Naval Survey of January 1584," *English Historical Review* 105 (January 1990):100. Actually, Hawkins was describing repairs made in 1577; they were not yet finished and would have to be completed in 1578.

20. See the order dated 18 July 1577, Hatfield mss., Cecil Papers, 160:136, BL microfilm M.485/42.

21. BL Cotton Otho E.VIII.9. "The determynacōn of a voiage to be made wth the Swallow of 300 tons & the pellycan of 120 ton to alexandria Tripoly constantynnople &c. June 1577," PRO 12/114/44, fol. 84. PRO Patent Rolls, C.66/1172. Hawkins to Burghley, February 1593, PRO SP 12/247/27, fol. 45. [Day left blank in letter.] Warrant dated 31 December 1578, PRO SP 12/127/33, fol. 59.

22. Robert Petre to Burghley, 16 October 1578, Hatfield mss., Cecil Papers, 10:66, BL microfilm M.485/3. Rodger, *Safeguard of the Sea*, 335. Loades, *Tudor Navy*, 189. Merino, "Graving Docks," 35–37.

23. See the warrant dated 31 December 1578, PRO SP 12/127/33, fol. 59. This document describes Hawkins as "tresurer of our marine causes," an indication that the title of his position was not firmly set.

24. Some of the expenses are described in general terms in Loades, *Tudor Navy*, 189–90. The most dependable budget totals for the Hawkins years are found in Parker, "Dreadnought Revolution," 289–90.

25. Robert Petre to Burghley, 16 October 1578, Hatfield mss., Cecil Papers, 10:66, BL microfilm M.485/3. "A note to shewe the state and sufficyenscye of her ma^ties shippes for eny p^resente service, and to shewe at what tyme they have ben repaired and newe builded," Huntington Library, Ellesmere ms. 1679, which says these ships were repaired in 1578 "by order of thoffi-cers." The seventh ship was the *Elizabeth Jonas,* finished in 1577.

26. Rodger, *Safeguard of the Sea,* 234–35. "Articles of ordence and agreements made & taken by the most myghty Princesse Elizabeth by the grace of God . . . w^t her Maties humble servant John Hawkins esqr. tresorer of her high-nes navye," 10 October 1579, PRO SP 12/132/41, fol. 89. Hawkins to Burgh-ley, 28 October 1579, PRO SP 12/132/51, fol. 131.

27. "Articles of ordence and agreements made & taken by the most myghty Princesse Elizabeth by the grace of God . . . w^t her Maties humble servant John Hawkins esqr. Tresorer of her highnes navye," 10 October 1579, PRO SP 12/132/41–42, fols. 89–90. BL Lansdowne 113, fol. 45. The plan was to keep in warehouse sufficient stock for "a doble furnyture of her highnes ships." Hawkins thought this could be done over a period of three and a half years. Hawkins to Burghley 24 December 1579, PRO SP 12/133/7, fol. 11.

28. "A proporcyon of the charge of iiii shipes of her ma^ties & other joyned wth them, & what ys nedefull to be dysbursyd in reddy mony," 12 August 1579, PRO, SP 12/131/64, fol. 189. Robert Petre to Burghley, Hatfield mss., Cecil Papers, 161:124, BL microfilm M. 485/42.

29. Pepys Library, Magdalene College, Cambridge ms. 2820. The development of the race-built ship is described in Margaret Blatcher, "Chatham Dock-yard and a Little-known Shipwright, Matthew Baker (1530–1613)," *Archae-ologia Cantiana* 107 (1990):155–59. Williamson, *Hawkins of Plymouth,* 24–50.

30. "Algunas se ponen en el astillero para pequeñas y despues salen grandes y otras para grandes y salen pequeñas." Biblioteca Nacional, Madrid, Juan Escalante de Mendoza, "Ytinerario de navegación de los mares y tierras occidentales," fol. 36. The manuscript was written in 1575. Michael Barkham, "Rival Fleets," in Rodríguez-Salgado, *Armada,* 152–53, 163.

31. Hawkins, *Observations,* 139, 152.

32. The launch date given in the Huntington Library, Ellesmere ms. 1679, is 1575, but the treasurer's accounts show that the work was not completed until 1577. Adams, "New Light," 99. The *Victory* may have been built in the older style. A report of 1586 said that the ship was changed into a galleon during that year. Glasgow, "Royal Ship *Victory.*"

33. BL Lansdowne 113, no. 14, fol. 45. Glasgow, "Royal Ship *Victory.*" Hawkins,

Observations, 139. As Geoffrey Parker shows, the reconstruction of these three vessels did not substantially increase their capacity to carry heavy artillery. See his "Dreadnought Revolution," 271.

34. Hawkins, *Observations,* 78–80. Ralegh, *Works,* 7:323, 345.

35. Loades, *Tudor Navy,* 189. Quinn and Ryan, *England's Sea Empire,* 52–53. The buildings at Deptford are mentioned in the will of John Hawkins, 6 June 1595, and codicil, 16 June 1595, PRO Prob 11/94, fols. 100–105; they are also mentioned in his correspondence.

36. Testimony of Thomas Rock, 15 September 1608, and Henry Palmer, 6 September 1608, transcribed in McGowan, *Jacobean Commissions,* 180–81, 216–17. According to Peter Buck, the practice may not have started until 1590, ibid., 173.

37. Hawkins to Burghley, 27 August 1580, Hatfield Manuscripts, Cecil Papers, 162:11, BL microfilm M.485/43. Morton, *Calendar of Patent Rolls, 1580–1582,* 9:288.

38. See, for example, Hawkins to Walsingham, 27 September 1580, PRO SP 12/142/29, fol. 87; Hawkins to Walsingham, December 1582, PRO SP 12/156/34, fol. 56-v; and Walsingham to Burghley, 30 August 1583, in Boyd, *State Papers, Scotland,* 6:595.

39. "A note of the cawse between Oratio Palavisina and william and John Hawkins," 14 April 1581, PRO SP 12/148/53, fol. 23; John Helle to Francis Walsingham, 14 April 1581, 12/148/54, fols. 215–16v.

40. Cobham to Burghley, 28 August 1581, Hatfield mss., Cecil Papers, 11:115–16, BL Microfilm M.485/1. Mendoza to the king, 16 April 1581, 14 July 1581, AGS Estado 835, fols. 60, 179; 4 July 1581, AGS Estado 833, fols. 64–66. Donno, *An Elizabethan in 1582,* 18–19. Digges, *Compleat Ambassador,* 379. Kelsey, *Sir Francis Drake,* 233–35.

41. See the undated commission, PRO SP 12/142/44, fol. 149. Mendoza to the king, 10 November 1582, AGS Estado 836, fol. 194. Diego Meléndez to the king, 30 July 1583, AGI Santo Domingo 169; Juan Melgarejo to the king, 30 July 1583, AGI Indiferente General 1887; Juan Sarmiento to the king, 20 October 1583, AGI Santo Domingo 184; translated in Wright, *Further English Voyages,* 1–5.

42. Mendoza to the king, 26 November 1583, AGS Estado 838, fol. 103, transcribed in Calvar Gross, *Batalla del Mar Océano,* 1:418. See also Burnand (Burnham) to Walsingham, 30 November 1583, Lomas, *State Papers, Foreign, 1583–84,* 246.

43. Naval Affairs, 1583–84, F.J. Savile Foljambe mss., in HMC *Fifteenth Annual Report,* Appendix, 5:106. Hawkins to Burghley, April 1584, PRO SP 12/170/57, fols. 86–87v.

44. Walsingham to Burghley, 30 August 1583, in Boyd, *State Papers, Scotland,* 6:595.

45. Undated but probably late 1583, PRO SP 12/186/47, fol. 92–v. Shipwright Richard Chapman and chief masters Thomas Gray and William Barnes were later added to the group. PRO SP 12/162/50, September 1583, fols. 168–69v. See also Donno, *Diary of Richard Madox,* 104, where Grey is called "the chief of the 4 masters of the queenes shyps."

46. John Hawkins, Peter Pett, Thomas Graye, and William Barnes. "A note to shewe the state and sufficyenscye of her majesties shippes for eny presente service, and to shewe at what tyme they have ben repaired and newe build-ed," 25 January 1583 (1584), Huntington Library, Ellesmere ms. 1679.

47. Ibid.

48. Hawkins to Mildmay, Lord Burghley, and the lord high admiral, 14 March 1583 (1584), BL Egerton 2603, fols. 39–41, transcribed in *Archaeologia,* 33:192–94. Hawkins to Burghley 24 December 1579, PRO SP 12/133/7, fol. 11.

49. Hawkins to Mildmay, Lord Burghley, and the lord high admiral, 14 March 1583 (1584), (1584), BL Egerton 2603, fols. 39–41, transcribed in *Archaeolo-gia, 33*:192–94. [Hawkins] to Burghley, 8 April 1585, PRO SP 12/178/12, fol. 21–v. John Hawkins, "The state and manner how her ma[ts] shipps have byn cotynted[?] & orderyd synce the eleventhe yere of her ma[ts] raigne," PRO SP 12/202/35, fols. 45–46.

50. Hawkins to Mildmay, Lord Burghley, and the Lord High Admiral, 14 March 1583 (1584), BL Egerton 2603, fols. 39–41, transcribed in *Archaeologia,* 33:192–94. [Hawkins] to Burghley, April 1584, PRO SP 12/170/57, fols. 86–87v.

51. Hawkins to Mildmay, Lord Burghley, and the Lord High Admiral, 14 March 1583 (1584), BL Egerton 2603, fols. 39–41, transcribed in *Archaeologia,* 33:192–94. [Hawkins] to Burghley, April 1584, PRO SP 12/170/57, fols. 86–87v.

52. "The Bargayne of John Hawkins for the navye," [1585] PRO SP 12/208/17, fols. 45v–46.

53. Ibid.

54. Borough composed and sent a scathing report on the Hawkins proposal in February 1584 (1585); BL Lansdowne 43, no. 33, fols. 74–75. Winter to Burghley, 8 April 1585, BL Add. 9294, fol. 60–v.

55. [Hawkins] to Burghley, April 1584, PRO SP 12/170/57, fols. 86–87v. See also the letter of Thomas Alleyn [?] to Burghley, 1587 [?], BL Lansdowne ms. 52. Art. 43, fols. 117–19, which summarizes gossip about the various men from 1583 to 1587.

56. Hawkins to Burghley, 19 December 1585, BL Additional 9294, fols. 58–59.

Glasgow names one ship constructed in 1585, the 30-ton *Cygnet,* but Hawkins considered it too small to list. See his "List of Ships," 306. No doubt the *Cygnet* was one of the ten unnamed pinnaces Hawkins reported in the enclosure to his letter to Burghley, 28 December 1585, PRO SP 12/185/33, fols. 70–72.

57. BL Lansdowne 43, no. 11, fol. 21v. The proposal was written by Hawkins, although the covering letter, signed by him, was not; too bad, in a way, considering the wonderful literary flourishes and religious allusions it contains.

58. Kelsey, *Sir Francis Drake,* 240–79. An undated commentary on Drake's plans, now attached to the Hawkins letter of 6 July 1589, may actually refer to this voyage. See PRO SP 12/225/14.II, fol. 25.

59. John Fitz and John Haele to Burghley, 22 July 1586, Hatfield Manuscripts, Cecil Papers, 14:77, BL microfilm M.485/4. BL Harley 366, fols. 146–47 gives the total as 1,922. The higher figure is from Folger Library ms. L.b. 344, cited in Keeler, *Drake's West Indian Voyage,* 46.

60. "Artycles of discov^{r}y of the injust mynde and deciptfull dealinge of m^r John Hawkins," BL Lansdowne 52, fols. 117–19. Two undated memoranda, apparently by Burghley and filed with papers of 1584 and 1586, refer to Hawkins, Fitzwilliams, and the queen of Scotland. "Matters in conference for the Low Countries and the King of Spain," 10 October 1584, Lomas and Hinds, *State Papers, Foreign, 1584–85,* 19:95. "Points arguing the King of Spain's ill-affection to her Majesty," Lomas, *State Papers, Foreign, 1586–88,* 21, part 1, 177–78. Both are very likely notes for meetings of the Privy Council, where Lord Burghley reviewed the earlier hostile actions by Philip. Read, *Lord Burghley and Queen Elizabeth,* 307.

61. Hawkins estimated the cost for three months at full mobilization to be £24,996, 1 shilling, eightpence. See his letter to Burghley 28 December 1585, PRO SP 12/185/33, fols. 68–79. Using PRO E 351/2213–2221 Adams concluded that the total expended by Hawkins in 1585 was £12,908. See Adams, "New Light on the 'Reformation' of John Hawkins," 103. This did not include money spent on Drake's expedition, which brought the total to £17,908. Parker, "Dreadnought Revolution," 289–91. Hawkins to Burghley, 28 December 1585, PRO SP 12/185/33, fols. 73 ff.

62. PRO AO 1, 1685/21; notes kindly supplied by Geoffrey Parker. See also Glasgow, "Shape of Ships," 185–86; Glasgow, "First Royal ship *Victory,*" 184–86.

63. Giovanni Dolfin to doge and Senate, 24 October 1586, in Brown, *State Papers, Venice,* 8:214–15. Mendoza to the king, 7 August 1586, AGS Estado K.1564, fol. 144, translated in Hume, *State Papers,* 3:601.

64. By order of the Privy Council, dated 6 August 1586, Hawkins was

"appointed to repaire to the seas with fower of her Majesties shippes and two pinasses." Dasent, *Acts of the Privy Council,* 14:207. Hawkins later claimed reimbursement for sea expenses for the period 1 August to 31 October 1586; PRO AO 1, 1685/21. The reconstruction and renaming of the *Philip and Mary* can be found in PRO AO 1, 1685/19. Information from the Audit Office accounts was kindly supplied by Geoffrey Parker. Keeler, *Drake's West Indian Voyage,* 293.

65. "Sumaria Relación," in Torres de Mendoza, *Documentos Inéditos,* 5:410. Testimony of Francisco de Valverde, transcribed in Fernández Duro, *Armada Invencible,* 1:508–12. Testimony of Benito Martin, 11 October 1586, AGS Estado K.1448, fol. 73, translated in Hume, *State Papers, Spanish,* 632–33. There is some confusion of dates in the accounts, doubtless arising from the fact that Spain adopted the Gregorian calendar in 1582 and England did not.

66. Testimony of Manuel Blanco, 11 October 1586, ibid. The date of capture was 30 September according to the Gregorian calendar.

67. Testimony of Christopher Martin, 11 October 1586, ibid.

68. Mendoza to the king, 20 October 1586, AGS Estado K.1564, fols. 193–96. Mendoza to the king, 24 October 1586, AGS Estado K.1564, fol. 209, translated in Hume, *State Papers, Spanish,* 643–44.

69. Mendoza to the king, 19 November 1586, AGS Estado K.1564, fol. 224; 28 November 1586, AGS Estado 1564, fol. 234; 17 December 1586, AGS Estado K. 1564, fol. 245; translated in Hume, *State Papers, Spanish,* 661, 666, 677–78. "Artycles of discov^{r}y of the injust mynde and deciptfull dealinge of m^r John Hawkyns," 1587, BL Lansdowne 52, fol. 118.

8
War with Spain

1. Hawkins to Burghley, 25 January 1586, PRO SP 12/186/34, fol. 76.

2. "Apuntamientos que ha dado Roberto Ridolfi sobre el negocio de Inglaterra," AGS Estado 824, fol. 189. Hawkins to Burghley, 4 September 1571, PRO SP 12/81/167a.

3. Hawkins, Winter, and Holstok, "A note of charges susteyned and paied for the guarding of her ma^{tis} navye royall," January 1586 (1587), PRO SP 12/186/44.

4. BL Lansdowne 52, fols. 92–93, in Keeler, *Drake's West Indian Voyage,* 60–62. Another version of the same document appears in Corbett, *Spanish War,* 86–92.

5. Mendoza to the king, 26 September 1586, AGS Estado K.1564, B 57, nos. 160–61.

6. Royal letters patent from Queen Elizabeth to Francis Drake, 15 March 1587, Plymouth City Museum, on display at Buckland Abbey. See Francis Drake's agreement with Thomas Cordell, John Watte, and others, 18 March 1586, BL Lansdowne 56, no 52, fol. 175, in Corbett, *Spanish War*, 105–6.

7. Thomas Fenner to Walsingham, 1 March/April 1587, PRO SP 12/200/1, fol. 1–v. The manuscript bears the name of both months, but April is probably intended. For ownership of the vessels I have relied on Keeler, *Drake's West Indian Voyage*, 282–89.

8. "The state and manner how her ma^ts shipps have byn cõtynted & orderyd synce the eleventhe yere of her ma^ts raigne," 27 June 1587, PRO SP 12/202/35, fols. 45–46.

9. "Concerninge Sr Francis Drakes voyage," 12/225/14.II, fol. 125–v. Williamson, *Sir John Hawkins*, 450–51, noted that this was "wrongly placed" with the Hawkins letter of 6 July 1589.

10. Council to Drake, 9 April 1587, PRO SP 12/200/17, fols. 25–26.

11. Burghley to Andreas de Looe, 28 July 1587, PRO SP Flanders No. 32, in Corbett, *Spanish War*, 148. Lansdowne ms. 52, art. 43, fol. 118.

12. Request of the Merchant Adventurers, 15 June 1587, PRO SP 12/202/27, fol. 38. Dasent, *Acts of the Privy Council*, 15:142, 191–92. "To be Considered," 3 October 1587, PRO SP 12/204/2, fol. 4.

13. Burghley to Walsingham, 13 September 1587, PRO SP 12/203/42, fol. 71. Lansdowne ms. 52, art. 43, fol. 117–v. From internal evidence it appears that this letter was written about the end of September or the first of October 1587.

14. Lansdowne ms. 52, art. 43, fol. 117v. Perry, *Aesopica*, 710–11. "'Nil timeo' inquit; 'nam interim aut ego moriar, aut asinus, aut dominus.' Quibus verbis ostendit salutare esse rem difficilem in longum protrahi ac differri."

15. Lansdowne 52, art. 43, fols. 117v–118v.

16. Ibid., fol. 118–v.

17. "Certayne articles to be delyvered to her ma^tie verye good to be amended by her ma^tie." 10 October 1587, PRO SP 12/204/16, fols. 26–27. Corbett reports that this document was "endorsed in Burghley's hand 'by Thos. Alleyn.'" See his *Spanish War*, 216. While this endorsement actually appears on 12/204/18, internal evidence supports the conclusion that he was the author of both manuscripts. On the other hand, Allen did not write the anonymous letter in Lansdowne 52, art. 43. Rather, he is one of several sources of information named in that letter.

18. Thomas Allen to Lord Burghley, undated 1572. Hatfield MSS, Cecil Papers, vol. 159, p. 67, B.L. Microfilm, M.485/42. Where Allen had been making and selling rope to the navy, others were providing "such stuffe and other

provision, wch I maye not disprayse; but yet not worthye to come into that house for the Quenes Maties service, delyvered by Mr. Hawkyns and the Muscovia House and they well lyking of it./" See also "The Names of the Officers of the Navy," [1583–1588,] Foljambe mss., F. 294, HMC, *Fifteenth Report,* appendix, part 5, 106. Zins, *England and the Baltic,* 101–2. Grant to Thomas Allen as "queen's merchant in the East parts," 20 June 1561, *Calendar of Patent Rolls, Elizabeth, 1560–1563,* 2:127.

19. This and subsequent quotations are from PRO SP 12/204/16, fols. 26–27.

20. "Certayne artycles and orders meete to be used and ordered touchinge the Queenes Maiestyes navye benefycial for her majestye," 10 [?] October 1587, PRO SP 12/204/18, fols. 29–30.

21. "Articles wherein may appeare her ma^{tie} to be abused and Mr Hawkyns greatlye enriched," PRO SP 12/204/17, fol. 28.

22. Hawkins to Burghley, 13 November 1587, PRO SP 12/205/22, fols. 41–42.

23. Burghley to [Winter and Holstocke, 7 December 1587?, draft], PRO SP 12/205/71, fol. 134. Corbett, *Spanish War,* 235, 238, said that this draft was an enclosure in the letter from Hawkins to Burghley, 13 November 1587, which seems unlikely for a number of reasons involving content and style. In fact, this letter or one very much like it is mentioned in the letter from Winter and Holstocke to Burghley, 9 December 1587, PRO SP 12/206/15, fol. 28.

24. Pett and Baker to Burghley, 12 October 1587, PRO SP 12/204/20, fols. 32–33. Winter and Holstocke to Burghley, 9 December 1587, PRO SP 12/206/15, fol. 28. BL Lansdowne 113, no. 15, fol. 48.

25. "An opiniō of peter pett and Mathew bak^r th^e shipwryghts uppon certen articles of Mr Jh Haukȳs," 22 January 1587 (1588), PRO SP 12/208/18, fol. 21-A. John Hawkins to Burghley, 18 January 1588, PRO SP 12/208/14, fol. 18. William Hawkins to John Hawkins, 17 February 1587 (1588), PRO SP 12/208/72, fol. 112.

26. "Shippes to remayne at Quborowe wth theire numbers diminished in the charg of th^e Admyrall," 5 January 1587 (1588), PRO SP 12/208/6, fol. 13A.

27. Hawkins to Walsingham, 1 February 1588, PRO SP 12/208/47, fols. 60–61.

28. Ibid. Compare the handwriting in this letter with that in Drake to the Privy Council, 30 March 1588, PRO SP 12/209/40, fol. 77. See also similar words and phrases in the letters from Drake to Walsingham, 2 April 1587, and Drake to Fox, 27 April 1587, both of which are discussed in Kelsey, *Sir Francis Drake,* 302–4.

29. Hawkins to Walsingham, 1 February 1587 (1588), PRO SP 12/208/47, fols. 60–61. Howard to Burghley, 22 February 1587 (1588), PRO SP 12/208/79, fol. 181.

30. Winter and Burough to Burghley, 17 February 1587 (1588), PRO SP 12/208/77.I, fol. 126; Borough to Burghley, 21 February 1587, PRO SP 12/208/77, fol. 124-v. Howard to Burghley, 29 February 1587 (1588), PRO SP 12/208/87, fol. 201v.

31. Hawkins to Burghley, 3 March 1587 (1588), PRO SP 12/209/5, fols 10–11.

32. Hawkins to Burghley, 12 March 1587 (1588), PRO SP 12/209/18, fol. 30. Howard to Walsingham, 17 July 1588, PRO SP 12/212/60, fol. 100.

33. Drake to Privy Council, 30 March 1588, PRO SP 12/209/40, fol. 58-v.

34. Mendoza to the king, 6 January 1588, AGS Estado K.1567, B 60, no. 12. Ubaldino, "Comentario della Impresa Fatta Contra il Regno D'Inghilterra del Re Catholica L'Anno 1588," BL Royal 14. A. XI, fols. 15–16, translated in Waters, *Elizabethan Navy,* 85–87. Drake to the queen, 13 April 1588, PRO SP 12/209/89, fol. 134. Howard to Burghley, 17 April 1588, PRO SP 12/209/99, fol. 146. Kelsey, *Sir Francis Drake,* 319.

35. Ubaldino, "Comentario della Impresa Fatta Contra il Regno D'Inghilterra del Re Catholica L'Anno 1588," BL Royal 14. A. XI, fols. 15v–16, translated in Waters, *Elizabethan Navy,* 87. Burghley "Memoryall at Rychmo[nd]," 25 July 1588, PRO SP 12/213/34, fol. 60.

36. Howard to Walsingham, 14 June 1588, PRO SP 12/211/18, fol. 29; 15 June 1588, PRO SP 12/211/26, 41. A few days later he expanded the group to include Lord Thomas Howard, Lord Sheffield, and Sir Roger Williams. Howard to Walsingham, 19 June 1588, fols. 56–57.

37. Howard to Walsingham, 6 July 1588, PRO SP 12/212/18, fol. 31. The captains of the royal vessels are named in lists prepared in July 1588, PRO SP 12/213/91, fol. 150. Drake's merchant ships and their commanders are ibid., fol. 151.

38. Rodríguez-Salgado, *Armada,* 30–32. Drake to Burghley, 6 June 1588, HMC, Manuscripts of the marquis of Bath, 2:28. Ubaldino, "Comentario della Impresa Fatta Contra il Regno D'Inghilterra del Re Catholica L'Anno 1588," BL Royal 14. A. XI, fol. 16-v, translated in Waters, *Elizabethan Navy,* 88.

39. Howard to Burghley, 17 July 1588, PRO SP 12/212/59, fol. 99. Hawkins to Burghley, 17 July 1588, PRO SP 12/212/61, fol. 102; "An Estimate of the chrge of the wages growinge for the companyes servinge under the charge of the Lo. Highe Admyrall of Englande," 17 July 1588, PRO SP 12/212/61.I, fols. 103–4. Burghley to Walsingham, 19 July 1588, PRO SP 12/212/66, fol. 113.

40. Ubaldino, "Comentario della Impresa Fatta Contra il Regno D'Inghilterra del Re Catholica L'Anno 1588," BL Royal 14. A. XI, fol. 16-v, translated in Waters, *Elizabethan Navy,* 88.

41. Waters, *Elizabethan Navy*, 28. Adams, *Armada Campaign of 1588*, 14, 18. Fernández-Armesto, *Spanish Armada*, 18.
42. Michael Barkham, "The Spanish Fleet," 154–55. M. J. Rodríguez-Salgado, "Spanish Commanders," in *Armada*, 219–20.
43. "Instrucción de lo que vos Don Alonso de Guzmán el Bueno habéis de hacer," 1 April 1588, in Fernández Duro, *Armada Invencible*, 2:7 Pierson, *Commander of the Armada*, 129–30. King to Medina-Sidonia, 1 April 1588, in Fernández Duro, *Armada Invencible*, 2:14.
44. Rodríguez-Salgado and Friel, "Battle at Sea," 237.
45. Pierson, *Commander of the Armada*, 141.
46. Hawkins to Burghley, 31 July 1588, PRO SP 12/213/71, fol. 164. Rodríguez-Salgado and Friel, "Battle at Sea," 237.
47. Pedro Coco Calderón, "Relación de lo suçedido a la real armada del Rei nuestro señor de que es capitán general el duque de medina sidonia, desde que salio de la coruña a donde se recojio despues que salio de Lisboa con el Tenporalque le dio," AGS Guerra Marina 221, fol. 190. 1° verso. The translation in Hume, *State Papers, Spanish*, 4:441–50, bears the date 24 September 1588, but the original manuscript is undated. Ubaldino, "Comentario della Impresa Fatta Contra il Regno D'Inghilterra del Re Catholica L'Anno 1588," BL Royal 14. A. XI, fol. 16–v, translated in Waters, *Elizabethan Navy*, 88. Rodríguez-Salgado and Friel, "Battle at Sea," 238.
48. Pierson, *Commander of the Armada*, 135–41. Recalde blamed Diego Flores de Valdés for the loss of the *Rosario*. Parker, "Testamento politico," 30.
49. Drake to Seymour, 21 July 1588, PRO SP Domestic 12/212/82, fol. 135. Rodríguez-Salgado and Friel, "Battle at Sea," 238. The *Margaret and John* was one of those sent under contract by the city of London. PRO SP 12/215/76, fol. 143.
50. BL Cotton Julius F.X.97v–98. Rodríguez-Salgado and Friel, "Battle at Sea," 238. Deposition of James Baron, 7 October 1605, PRO E133/47/3, typescript copy in DRO Drake Papers 346M/F534, 3 pp.
51. Michael Barkham, "Rival Fleets," in *Armada*, 154. Fernández-Armesto, *Spanish Armada*, 174–75. Pierson, *Commander of the Armada*, 144.
52. See the testimony of Juan Gaietan, 12 August 1588, PRO SP 12/214/18, fols. 59–60v.
53. Howard to Walsingham, 27 August 1588, PRO SP 12/215/59, fol. 104; Drake's endorsement, with listing of amount of treasure, PRO SP 12/215/59i, fol. 105. Deposition of Matthew Starke, "A note of certaine speaches spoken by Sir Martyn Frobisher," 11 August 1588, PRO SP 12/214/63; also PRO SP 12/214/64, fols. 139–40v, 141–42.
54. Medina-Sidonia to Hugo de Moncada, 2 August 1588, PRO SP Spanish,

quoted in *CSP Spanish, Elizabeth,* 4:359. Rodríguez-Salgado and Friel, "Battle at Sea," 238.

55. BL Cotton Julius F.X.97v–98. Ubaldino, "Comentario della Impresa Fatta Contra il Regno D'Inghilterra del Re Catholica L'Anno 1588," BL Royal 14. A. XI, fols. 17–18, translated in Waters, *Elizabethan Navy,* 92.

56. BL Cotton Julius F.X.98. Rodríguez-Salgado and Friel, "Battle at Sea," 239.

57. Ubaldino, "Comentario della Impresa Fatta Contra il Regno D'Inghilterra del Re Catholica L'Anno 1588," BL Royal 14. A. XI, fol. 98–v, translated in Waters, *Elizabethan Navy,* 92–93. Rodríguez-Salgado and Friel, "Battle at Sea," 239.

58. Martin and Parker, *Spanish Armada,* 176.

59. So identified by Corbett, *Drake and the Tudor Navy,* 2:247.

60. "Relación de lo subcedido a la Armada de su Magestad desde los 22 de Jullio hasta 21 de Agosto de 1588," Vatican Library, Urbinates Latini 1115, fol. 228. Pierson, *Commander of the Armada,* 151, 271. "The state of her ma^{ts} Shypps Shyp Botts and Pynesss examyned & grevyed by the mr shypwryts & other the masters attendant at Chatham, accordyng to the Direccone & order geven unto them from her ma^{ts} offycers of the navie," 28 September 1588, PRO SP 12/216/40.

61. Ubaldino, "Comentario della Impresa Fatta Contra il Regno D'Inghilterra del Re Catholica L'Anno 1588," BL Royal 14. A. XI, fol. 99, translated in Waters, *Elizabethan Navy,* 93. Rodríguez-Salgado and Friel, "Battle at Sea," 239.

62. Medina-Sidonia to Hugo de Moncada, 2 August 1588, in Hume, *State Papers,* 4:359. Pierson, *Commander of the Armada,* 145. Martin and Parker, *Spanish Armada,* 176–77.

63. B.M. Cotton Julius, F.X.99. Ubaldino, "Comentario della Impresa Fatta Contra il Regno D'Inghilterra del Re Catholica L'Anno 1588," BL Royal 14. A. XI, fol. 99–v, translated in Waters, *Elizabethan Navy,* 94. Pierson, *Commander of the Armada,* 151–52.

64. Jorge Manrique to the king, 11 August 1588, AGS Estado 594, in *CSP Spanish, Elizabeth,* 4:374. "Aviso de las armadas de Roan," 11 August 1588, AGS Estado K.1567, B 60, no. 102. Martin and Parker, *Spanish Armada,* 177. Rodríguez-Salgado and Friel, *Armada,* 239.

65. Pierson, *Commander of the Armada,* 153. Parker, "Testamento politico," 32.

66. Ibid., 153–55, 271. BL Cotton Julius F.X.99–v.

67. Pierson, *Commander of the Armada,* 156–59. Martin and Parker, *Spanish Armada,* 181. "Relación de lo subcedido a la Armada de su Magestad desde los 22 de Jullio hasta 21 de Agosto de 1588," Vatican Library, Urbinates Latini 1115, fol. 229. Rodríguez-Salgado and Friel, "Battle at Sea," 240.

68. Rodríguez-Salgado and Friel, "Battle at Sea," 240. Winter to Walsingham, 10 August 1588, PRO SP 12/214/7, fol. 11–v. Martin and Parker, *Spanish Armada*, 186.

69. Corbett, *Drake and the Tudor Navy*, 251. Pierson, *Commander of the Armada*, 162.

70. Martin and Parker, *Spanish Armada*, 187–88. Pierson, *Commander of the Armada*, 162.

71. "Relación de lo subcedido a la Armada de su Magestad desde los 22 de Jullio hasta 21 de Agosto de 1588," Vatican Library, Urbinates Latini 1115, fols. 229v–30. Ubaldino, "Comentario della Impresa Fatta Contra il Regno D'Inghilterra del Re Catholica L'Anno 1588," BL Royal 14. A. XI, fols. 99v–100, translated in Waters, *Elizabethan Navy*, 96. Pierson, *Commander of the Armada*, 164. Martin and Parker, *Spanish Armada*, 187–88.

72. "Tras esto el maestre de campo mando disparar la mosqueteria y arcabuseria. Lo que por los enemigos visto se retiraron. Y los nuestros llamandoles covardes y intimando con palabras feas su poco animo llamandolas de gallinas Luteranos." Pedro Coco Calderón, "Relación," AGS Guerra Marina 221, fol. 190, 3°–v.

73. Pedro Coco Calderón, "Relación," AGS Guerra Marina 221, fol. 190, 3°–v. Martin and Parker, *Spanish Armada*, 192–93. Pierson, *Commander of the Armada*, 165. Rodríguez-Salgado and Friel, "Battle at Sea," 241. Hawkins to Walsingham, 31 July 1588, PRO SP 12/213/71, fol. 119–v. Kelsey, *Sir Francis Drake*, 335–36.

74. Hawkins to Walsingham, 31 July 1588, PRO SP 12/213/71, fol. 120.

75. "Relación de lo subcedido a la Armada de su Magestad desde los 22 de Jullio hasta 21 de Agosto de 1588," Vatican Library, Urbinates Latini 1115, fol. 231. Pierson, *Commander of the Armada*, 167.

76. Howard had his principal captains cosign a memorandum signifying their agreement to end the pursuit. 1 August 1588, BL Add. 33,740, fol. 6. "Relación de lo subcedido a la Armada de su Magestad desde los 22 de Jullio hasta 21 de Agosto de 1588," Vatican Library, Urbinates Latini 1115, fol. 231. Pierson, *Commander of the Armada*, 167.

9
There Is No Other Hell

1. Rodger, *The Armada in the Public Records*, 24. Howard to Elizabeth, 22 August 1588, PRO SP 12/215/40, fol. 71.

2. Hawkins to Howard, 8 August 1588, PRO SP 12/214/46, fols. 106–7. Burghley to Walsingham, 24 July 1588, PRO SP 12/212/66, fol. 113. Hawkins to

Burghley, 26 August 1588, PRO SP 12/215/56, fols. 99–100, with endorsement by Howard.

3. Hawkins to Burghley, 26 August 1588, PRO SP 12/215/56, fols. 99–100; 28 August 1588, PRO SP 12/215/63, fols. 110–11.

4. Hawkins to Howard, 8 August 1588, PRO SP 12/214/46, fol. 106. Howard to Walsingham, 28 August 1588, PRO SP 12/215/66, fol. 115-v.

5. Hawkins to Burghley, 28 August 1588, PRO SP 12/215/63, fol. 110-v. See also Howard to Burghley, 22 August 1588, PRO SP 12/215/41, fol. 72-v, explaining his plan to keep as many ships as possible at Margate and the Downs, ready to rejoin the fleet on a day's notice. Also Hawkins to Burghley, PRO SP 26 August 1588, 12/215/56, fols. 99–100, where Hawkins reported "My lord was somewhat dyspleasyd" to find so many ships sent away.

6. Hawkins to Burghley, 4 September 1588, PRO SP 12/216/3, fol. 4. Hawkins to Walsingham, 5 September 1588, PRO SP 12/216/4, fol. 5.

7. Howard to Walsingham, 27 August 1588, 12/215/59, fol. 104. Hawkins to Walsingham, 5 September 1588, 12/216/4, fol. 5. Hawkins to Burghley, 28 August 1588, PRO SP 12/215/63, fol. 110v.

8. Memorandum of c. 17 September 1588, PRO SP 12/217/79, fols. 136–37; unsigned note of John Norris, 19 September 1588, PRO SP 12/216/32, fol. 58; note by Burghley, 20 September 1588, PRO SP 12/216/33, fol. 59.

9. See the queen's commission to Norris and Drake, 11 October 1588, Patent Roll, 30 Elizabeth, part 4, transcribed in Wernham, *Expedition of Norris and Drake*, 12–14.

10. Kelsey, *Sir Francis Drake*, 346–64.

11. This is based on the lists in Rodger, *Safeguard of the Sea*, 508–9. Oppenheim, *Administration of the Royal Navy*, 148–49, citing various patent rolls, says that William Winter was surveyor and master of ordnance until his death in 1589, when he was succeeded by Sir Henry Palmer. William Borough was clerk of ships until the end of 1588, when he was succeeded by Benjamin Gonson. Borough became comptroller in 1589. These dates seem to be at variance with the actual situation on the Navy Board. See, for example, the "Answers to my lord tresorers demaunds," 28 April 1589, signed by Hawkins, Palmer, Holstock, and Borough, PRO SP 12/223/105, fol. 175; and "A note of suche Provysyons as shalbe necessarye to ffurnishe the vii new shippes, and all the reste of her maiesties navy for settinge forthe to the seas," 9 February 1589 (1590), signed by Hawkins, Palmer, and Gonson, PRO SP 12/230/66, fol. 101-v.

12. Unsigned copy of a petition from Hawkins to Burghley and Howard, 14 December 1588, PRO SP 12/219/28, fols. 109-10, with autograph note on

front: "14.Dec. 1588. That Yo^rL. would be pleased to move hir ma^tie to allowe Mr. Ed: Fenton to serve as his deputy for one yeare, whereby he maie the better attend his accompts for th^e services past to perfect th^e same." See also the attached undated copy of the royal warrant authorizing Fenner's appointment, PRO SP 12/219/29, fol. 111.

13. See the unsigned note, "A Comparison betwixt th^e expences for .v. yeres afor Mr Hawk͞ys barg͞ay, and th^e .v. yeres sence th^e barg͞ay of Mr Hawk͞ys; Sr wm. W͞yters declarati͞o," 8 October 1588, with notes and endorsements by Burghley, PRO SP 12/217/12, fol. 21-v.

14. Hawkins to Burghley, 6 July 1589, PRO SP 12/225/14, fol. 22.

15. Ibid.

16. Ibid., fol. 22-v.

17. Oppenheim, *Monson's Naval Tracts*, 1:238-39. McDermott, 378-79. Minutes, 18 January 1589 (1590), 23 February 1589 (1590), *Acts of the Privy Council*, 18:315-16, 384. Hawkins, *Observations*, 2.

18. Hawkins to Burghley, 12 September 1589, 12/226/30, fol. 34. Hawkins and Borough, "A note of such anckers, Cables, wth other Cordinge and Sayle Canvas as shalbe needfull for the rigging and furnishing for Sea Service, the fyve shyppes, and two crompters, nowe in building at Debtford and woolew^ch," 4 October 1589, PRO SP 12/227/7, fol. 12; the estimate actually lists three ships (one each by Baker, Pett, and Chapman) and four crompters. See also the "Extraordinarie Estimate of monie demaunded by Sr John Hawkyns," 10 October 1589, PRO SP 12/227/16, fol. 22-v. Hawkins, Borough, and Gonson, "A note of th^e charge for newe buyldinge Anno 1589," 10 November 1589, PRO SP 12/228/6, fol. 56.

19. Stow, *Survey of London* (1633), 605.

20. "Abstracte of the p[ro]visions that are to be supplyed for the furnishynge of the syxe ships appointed to the Seas under the charge of Sr John Hawkins Knight," 1 December 1589, PRO SP 12/229/3, fol. 12-v. Four pinnaces are included in the list. "A note of such newe Sayles as are requisite to be made for furnishinge of her ma^ts shipps appoynted to the seas under the charge of Sr John Hawkyns knighte," 2 December 1589, PRO SP 12/229/2, fol. 11.

21. "A Memoriall for the Navy," 23 February 1589 (1590), PRO SP 12/230/80, fol. 119-v. The objections applied to other naval projects as well. Hawkins to Burghley, 1 March, 1589 (1590), PRO SP 12/231/2, fol. 4.

22. For details of these expenses see the estimates dated 4 October 1589, PRO SP 12/227/7, fol. 12; 10 October 1589, fols. 22-23; November 1589, HMC, *Twelfth Report, Coke,* appendix, part 1, 12-13; 1 December 1589, PRO SP 12/229/3, fol. 12-v; 2 December 1589, PRO SP 12/229/2, fol. 11; 9 February

1589 (1590), PRO SP 12/230/66, fols. 101–2; 14 March 1590, RPO SP 12/231/19, fol. 24.

23. Hawkins to Burghley, 16 April 1590, PRO SP 12/231/83, fol. 147–v.

24. Thomas Fleming to Privy Council, [19?] April 1590, PRO SP 12/231/93, fol. 166–v. 12/232/17. Council notes dated 24 April 1590, PRO SP 12/231/88, fols. 154–55. Council minutes of 23 April 1590, *Acts of the Privy Council,* 19:78–79. As it turned out, the new "war fleet" was really a convoy of hulks loaded with salt. See the minutes of April 24–30, ibid., 80–94.

25. The undated order to Hawkins is in the Longleat Devereux Papers, vol. 2, fol. 70, transcribed in Lloyd, "Hawkins's Instructions," 128. In his accounts for that year Hawkins gave 6 May 1590 as the beginning of his service at sea. PRO E 351/2227; notes kindly provided by Geoffrey Parker. Although the Frobisher order has not been found, Hawkins submitted new estimates for his own and Frobisher's ships. Hawkins, Palmer, Borough, and Gonson, "A note of the charge of her ma^{ts} shippes appointed to the seas under the charge of Sr J. Hawkins & Sr M. Fro: Knights," 7 May 1590, PRO SP 12/232/15, fol. 24–v; "The charge of wages for 12 of her ma^{ts} shippes and 27 C. M[ar]inars for 4 monethes," 17 May 1590, PRO SP 12/232/24, fols. 35–36v.

26. Lloyd, "Hawkins's Instructions," 128.

27. Hawkins, *Observations,* 2–3. McDermott, *Martin Frobisher,* 371–81. "The charge of wages for 12 of her ma^{ts} shippes and 27 C. M[ar]inars for 4 monethes," 17 May 1590, PRO SP 12/232/24, fols. 35–36v.

28. The date is from the accounts for provisions and wages submitted at the end of the voyage. "A note of the charge of vi of her highenes shippes bonnde to the southwardes under the conduction of Sr John Hawkins Knight," December 1590, PRO SP 122/234/74, fols. 144–45.

29. Privy Council to Hawkins and Frobisher, 11 June 1590, Acts of the Privy Council, 19:209–10.

30. John Hawkins, et al., "A [declaration] ordered by a conserte and meetinge of Sr John Hawkins Admyrall of her ma^{ts} shippes under his charge, the Mayor of Plymouth the Captaines and M^{rs} of the shippes, [the] Customer of Plymouth and Humfrey ffones being present," 3 and 4 July 1590, PRO SP 12/233/4, fols. 14–15. This is a very faint copy, apparently enclosed with the letter from Hawkins to Burghley, 31 October 1590, PRO SP 12/233/118, fols. 212–13.

31. Minutes, 20, 25, 26 July, 8, 16, 17, 22 August, 10, 29 September 1590, *Acts of the Privy Council,* 19:331–32, 334–35, 344, 346–47, 369, 383–84, 390–91, 398–99, 413, 429, 472.

32. Ricardo Burley to Alonso de Vaçan, 2 July 1590, AGS, Guerra y Marina 287, fol. 94. Richard Hawkins, *Observations,* 2–4.

33. Minutes, 25 October 1590, *Acts of the Privy Council*, 20:51–52. "An estimate of the charge for .ii. monthes Vituals for .1340. men Serving at the seas in .6. her m^ats ships specified in the margen Under the charge of Sir John Hawkyns Knight, Upon the coast and Islands of Spayne and Portingale," 7 November 1590, signed by Palmer, Borough, and Gonson, PRO SP 12/234/9, fol. 12.

34. Hawkins to Burghley, 31 October 1590, PRO SP 12/233/118, fols. 212–13. Minutes, 20 November 1590, *Acts of the Privy Council*, 20:81–83. Atkinson to Burghley (?), 2 November (?) 1590, PRO SP 12/234/2, fol. 4–v. Hawkins to Burghley, 8 December 1590, PRO SP 12/234/49, fol. 78.

35. "Sr John Hawkins and Sr Martyn Frobusher theire voyage undertaken this yeare 1590," BL Sloane 43, fols. 27v–29. Hawkins to Burghley, 31 October 1590, PRO SP 12/233/118, fol. 212.

36. Worth, "Sir John Hawkins," 272.

37. Hawkins to Burghley, 5 November 1590, BL Add. 9294, fol. 81. Hawkins to Howard, 5 November 1590, ibid., fol. 79.

38. Hawkins to Burghley, 10 November 1590, HMC, *Twelfth Report, Coke,* appendix, part 1, p. 14. Hawkins to Burghley, 8 December 1590, PRO SP 12/234/49, fol. 78. Henry Billingsley to Burghley, 7 January 1590 (1591), Hatfield ms., Cecil Papers, 18:88. Hawkins to Henry Maynard, 15 January 1590 (1591), HMC, *Twelfth Report, Coke,* appendix, part 1, p. 14. Hawkins to Burghley, 9 February 1590 (1591), ibid.

39. Hawkins to Burghley, 23 January 1590 (1591), HMC, *Twelfth Report, Coke,* appendix, part 1, p. 14. In his report on the voyage submitted at the end of December, Hawkins noted that receipts exceeded expenditures by £2,300. PRO SP 12/234/74, fols. 144–45.

40. Klarwill, *Fugger News-Letters, Second Series,* 212–13.

41. Hawkins to Burghley, 4 July 1591, HMC, *Twelfth Report, Coke,* appendix, part 1, p. 15. Richard Hawkins, *Observations,* 2. PRO AO 1, 1687/17. Notes kindly provided by Geoffrey Parker. Hawkins to Burghley, 8 July 1592, PRO SP 12/242/79, fols. 151–52.

42. Hasted, *County of Kent,* 218–19. Powell, "Chatham Chest," 174. Hawkins's exact role in founding the Chatham Chest is unclear, as is that of Drake and Howard. Laughton was skeptical. See his "John Hawkins," 218–19. In 1591 the queen provided a special allowance of six months' pay for widows whose husbands had been killed in the recent campaign. PRO E 351/2228; notes kindly provided by Geoffrey Parker.

43. Watkin, "Lady Hawkins," 118–20. Will of Margaret Hawkins, in Mary Hawkins, *Plymouth Armada Heroes,* 76–78. Her service to the queen is mentioned in the "fair table" she wrote to hang beside the Hawkins monument in the Church of St. Dunstan in the East. The original church no

longer exists, but the inscription was preserved by Stow in his *Survey of London*, 140–41.

44. Andrews, "Elizabethan Privateering," 13–16. Privy Council to Drake, 16 November 1590, in Dasent, *Acts of the Privy Council, 1590–91*, 20:79–80. Drake to Burghley, 8 October 1592, BL Lansdowne 70, no. 74, fol. 179.

45. Corbett, *Drake and the Tudor Navy*, 2:368. McDermott, *Martin Frobisher*, 391–93.

46. Sir John Burgh to Burghley, 17 August 1592, BL Lansdowne 70, no. 27, fol. 62. William Richard Drake, "The Great Carrack," 209–40. Oppenheim, *Monson's Naval Tracts*, 278–96. Kingsford, "Taking of the Madre de Dios," 85–121. Bovill, "The Madre de Dios," 129–51.

47. Burgh to Burghley, 17 August 1592, BL Lansdowne 70, no. 27, fol. 62. Royal warrant, (undated and unsigned), BL Lansdowne 70 no 26, fols. 60v–61. "Persons appointed at Plymouthe for to have care of the Prizes," 28 August 1592, BL Lansdowne 70, no. 28, fol. 64. Hawkins to Burghley, 11 September 1592, BL Lansdowne 70, no. 39, fol. 88. Dasent, *Acts of the Privy Council, 1592*, 23:181–82. Corbett, *Drake and the Tudor Navy*, 367–68. See also "An Estymate of the Carriques goodes, at Leaden Haulle," 15 December 1592, BL Lansdowne 70, fols. 208v–9, which shows the value as £141,000. In the Bath mss. the total is listed as £97,000. *Calendar of the Manuscripts of the Marquis of Bath*, 2:41.

48. Hawkins to Burghley 17 September 1592, BL Lansdowne 70, no. 43, fol. 96. Thompson to Hawkins, 27 August 1592, BL Lansdowne 70, no. 54, fol. 120.

49. Hawkins to Burghley, 25 September 1592, BL Lansdowne 70, no. 54, fol. 119. Testimony of surgeon John Pawson 7 October 1592, BL Lansdowne 70, no. 75, fol. 118; testimony of boatswain John Rogers, 13 October 1592, Lansdowne 70, no. 77, fol. 185. Richard Young to Sir Robert Cecil, 11 December 1592, Hatfield mss., Cecil Papers, 169:7; BL microfilm M.485/45.

50. Hawkins to Burghley, 17 September 1592, BL Lansdowne 70, no. 43, fols. 96–97. Richard Hawkins et al. to Burghley, 10 September 1592, BL Lansdowne 70, no. 34, fols. 78–79. Robert Cecil to Burghley, 19 September 1592, PRO SP 12/243/16, fol. 26.

51. Hawkins to Burghley, 25 September 1592, BL Lansdowne 70, no. 54, fol. 119.

52. Hawkins to Burghley, 30 September 1592, BL Lansdowne 70, no. 65, fol. 153.

53. Proclamation, 30 October 1592, Hatfield mss., Cecil Papers, 21:72, BL microfilm M.485/5. "An Estymate of the Carriques goodes," 15 December 1592, BL Lansdowne 70, no. 89, fol. 209. "The Names of the ships that weare at the taking of the Carrick with ther several tonnedge, and nombers

of men," 25 January 1592, BL Lansdowne 73, no. 10, fols. 38–39; "A Brief report of the grosse somes in severall accompts demaunded by suche as pretend interrest to the Carriques goods, as the same accompts were allowed," BL Lansdowne 73, no. 11, fols. 40–42. This may not have been the final total. A customs official gave other figures a few days later. See [Thomas Phelippes (?)] to Thomas Barnes, 3 February 1592 (1593), PRO SP 12/244/35, fol. 74.

54. Oppenheim explained the process in his *Administration of the Royal Navy,* 165–66, and others have done the same. The queen's share is usually given as £80,000. See, for example, Bovill, "Madre de Dios," 150.

55. Ralegh to Burghley, (late January 1592?), BL Lansdowne 70, no. 94, fol. 217. Indenture, 22 October 1592, Plymouth Record Office 277/10.

56. D'Ewes, *Journals,* 1:487, 519. BL Additional 41,140, fol. 193. Hampshire, "A Link with Hawkins," 323. Patent Roll, 36 Elizabeth, Part 17, cited in Williamson, *Hawkins,* 447. Ingpen, *Middle Temple Bench Book,* 115. Sturgess, *Register of Admissions,* 65.

57. Richard Hawkins, *Observations,* 2, 4

58. Ibid., 5–7, 11–13, 16–17. Without stating exactly how much he had invested, John Hawkins mentioned his investment in his will, dated 6 June 1595, PRO Prob 11/94, fols. 100–105.

59. Richard Hawkins, *Observations,* 18, 24–25, 27, 32–33.

60. Ibid., 37, 50–52, 54, 57–59, 70.

61. Ibid., 96, 100, 105, 117–20, 122–23, 125–26, 153–56.

62. "Mem^al traduzido de Françes en Español dado a la Reyna de Inglaterra de parte de Fran^co Draques y Juan Aquins pã hazer un viage para arruynar enteram^e los españoles," AGS Estado, K1566, B59, fol. 49. Burghley Diary, January 1592 (1593). Murdin, *Collection of State Papers,* 800.

63. Corbett, *Drake and the Tudor Navy,* 371–76.

64. Hawkins to Burghley, February 1593 (1594), PRO SP 12/247/27, fol. 45. Hawkins to Bughley, 23 August 1594, HMC, *Twelfth Report,* 1:15. Maynard, "Sir Francis Drake his Voyage 1595," BL Add. 5,209, fols. 2v–3.

65. Monson, *Naval Tracts,* 1:313. Andrews, *Drake's Voyages,* 159. The pertinent documents have been carefully transcribed and published, but without much of an introduction, in Andrews, *Last Voyage of Drake and Hawkins.*

66. Andrews, *Last Voyage of Drake and Hawkins,* 48–78. Queen to Drake and Hawkins, 29 January 1595, Inner Temple Library, ms. 538, 6:51, 97. The date is new style; a transcription from the patent rolls can be found in Marsden, *Documents Relating to Law and Custom of the Sea,* 1:284–87.

67. Queen to Drake and Hawkins, 29 January 1595, Inner Temple Library, ms. 538, 6:97. "Voyage truely discoursed, made by sir Francis Drake, and sir John Hawkins, chiefly pretended for some speciall service on the Islands

and maine of the West Indies," in Hakluyt, *Third and Last Volume of Voyages,* 583. Andrews, *Drake's Voyages,* 164.

68. Valdés to the king, 19 March 1593, BL Add. ms. 28,420, fol. 87–v. Andrews, *Drake's Voyages,* 163.

69. Medina-Sidonia to Antonio de Guevara, 7 June 1587, AGS Guerra Marina 198, fol. 92; 11 June 1587, fol. 93; and 3 June 1587, fol. 95. Clefford to Burghley, 26 July 1595, Hatfield ms., Cecil Papers, 172:35.

70. Howard to Cecil, 8 August 1595, Hatfield ms., Cecil Papers, 33:101. Queen to Drake, Hawkins, Thomas Gorges, and Thomas Baskerville, 11 August 1595, PRO SP Dom. Elizabeth, 12/253/76, fol. 110v.

71. Hawkins and Drake to Essex, 13 August 1595, Hatfield ms., Cecil Papers, 34:19. Hawkins, Drake, Gorges, and Baskerville to Robert Cecil, 13 August 1595, PRO SP 12/253/79, fol. 115. Hawkins and Drake to the queen, 13 August 1595, PRO SP 12/253/79.I, fol. 116–v. Burghley to Hawkins and Drake, 16 August 1595, PRO SP 12/253/87, fols. 127–28v, marked "directed to Sr Frā Drake and Sr Jhō Hawkȳs but not sent."

72. Drake and Hawkins to the queen, 16 August 1595, Hatfield ms., 35:30, transcribed in Andrews, *Last Voyage of Drake and Hawkins.* Burghley to Robert Cecil, 20 August 1595, PRO SP 12/253/88, fol. 129.

73. Thomas Maynarde, "Sir Francis Drake his Voyage, 1595," BL Add. ms. 5,209, fol. 2v–3.

74. Will of John Hawkins, 6 June 1595, and codicil, 16 June 1595, PRO Prob 11/94, fols. 100–105.

75. Ibid.

76. John Troughton, "Oͬ Juͬnall in año doñi 1595," PRO SP 12/257/48, fol. 77. In his will Hawkins called Troughton "my good friend." See also Thomas Maynarde, "Sir Francis Drake his Voyage, 1595," BL Add. ms. 5,209, fols. 3–5.

77. Untitled logbook, 1595–96, Bayerische Staatsbibliothek, Munich, codex angl. 2, fol. 8v. There is a transcription by Georg Martin Thomas (ed.), "Logbook eines Schiffes von der dritten Expedition Franz Drake's 28. August 1595–10. Mai 1596," in Friedrich Kunstmann, *Die Entdeckung Amerikas, nach den Ältesten Quellen Geschichtlich Dargestellt* (Munich: A. Asher, 1859), 101–22. See also "The voyage truely discoursed, made by sir Francis Drake, and sir John Hawkins, chiefly pretended for some speciall service on the Islands and maine of the West Indies," in Hakluyt, *Third and Last Volume of Voyages,* 583. Margaret Hawkins to Robert Cecil, Hatfield ms., Cecil Papers, 12 December 1595, 36:76, BL microfilm M.485/8.

78. Untitled logbook, 1595–1596, Bayerische Staatsbibliothek, Munich, codex angl. 2, fols. 8v–9. "The voyage truely discoursed, made by sir Francis Drake, and sir John Hawkins, chiefly pretended for some speciall service on

the Islands and maine of the West Indies," in Hakluyt, *Third and Last Volume of Voyages*, 584. Andrews, *Drake's Voyages*, 168.

79. John Troughton, "O^r Ju^{r}nall in año doñi 1595," PRO SP 12/257/48, fol. 77v. Untitled logbook, 1595–96, Bayerische Staatsbibliothek, Munich, codex angl. 2, fol. 10v. "The voyage truely discoursed, made by sir Francis Drake, and sir John Hawkins, chiefly pretended for some speciall service on the Islands and maine of the West Indies," in Hakluyt, *Third and Last Volume of Voyages*, 584. "Relación del Viage que hizieron las cinco Fragatas de Armada de su Magestad, yendo por Cabo dellas Don Pedro Tello de Guzmán, este presente Año de Noventa y cinco," facsimile in Kraus, *Sir Francis Drake*, 174.

80. Maynarde, "Sir Francis Drake his Voyage, 1595," BL Add. ms. 5,209. "De Juan Aquines que no quiso que vinieran tras las fragatas de la isla de guadalupe, luego que supo que le habian cojido el navio y venia a Puerto-Rico." See Alejandro Tapia y Rivera (ed.), "Relación de lo sucedido en S. Juan de Puerto-Rico de las Indias, con la armada inglesa, del cargo de Francisco Draque y Juan Aquines, a los 23 de Noviembre de 1595 años," in *Biblioteca Historica de Puerto-Rico* (Madrid: Imprenta Márquez, 1854), 411.

81. Untitled logbook, 1595–1596, Bayerische Staatsbibliothek, Munich, codex angl. 2, fol. 11. "The voyage truely discoursed, made by sir Francis Drake, and sir John Hawkins, chiefly pretended for some speciall service on the Islands and maine of the West Indies," in Hakluyt, *Third and Last Volume of Voyages*, 584. Andrews, *Drake's Voyages*, 169–70.

82. Will of John Hawkins, 6 June 1595, and codicil, 16 June 1595, PRO Prob 11/94, fols. 100–105; and codicil 8 November 1595, PRO Prob 11/87, fol. 384v.

83. Untitled logbook, 1595–1596, Bayerische Staatsbibliothek, Munich, codex angl. 2, fol. 11. "The voyage truely discoursed, made by sir Francis Drake, and sir John Hawkins, chiefly pretended for some speciall service on the Islands and maine of the West Indies," in Hakluyt, *Third and Last Volume of Voyages*, 584. In his brief account John Troughton seems to say that the death occurred on 7 November, but this is probably no more than an infelicitous sentence construction. See his account, "O^r Ju^{r}nall in año doñi 1595," PRO SP 12/257/48, fol. 77v.

84. Maynarde, "Sir Francis Drake his Voyage, 1595," BL Add. ms. 5,209. *Purchas his Pilgrimes*, 4:1185–86. In a brief but well-documented biography of Hawkins (DNB, 25:219), Laughton identified R.M. as Sir Robert Mansell. Later an admiral, Mansell would have been twenty-two years old at the time of the expedition.

85. Troughton to the queen, undated, Hatfield mss., Cecil Papers, 48:61, transcribed in Andrews, *Last Voyage*, 252.

10

Weighing Hawkins

1. Hawkins, *Troublesome Voyadge,* fols. A.iii, B.i, B.iii, and final page. Hakluyt, *Principall Navigations,* 521.
2. Flores, *Obra nuevamēte compuesta,* fol. 1v.
3. Davis, *Worldes Hydrographical Discription,* 12–13.
4. Roberts, *Trumpet of Fame,* 3.
5. Meteren, *Historia Belgica,* 423, 594. "Praeterea gens est natura sua audax inflata, animosa, impetuosa, in bello crudelis, primo congressu calida, mortis contemptrix, ad haec iactansior, dolosa, planeque dissimulationes aduiciae tum verbis tum moribus, quam illi pro summa habent prudentia, ut plurimum eloquens & hospitalis."
6. Howes, *Annales, or General Chronicles,* 806–7. Howes, *Annales* (1631), 1038. In this edition the following two statements appear on the same page: (1) "Sir Walter Raleigh was the first that brought tobacco to use." (2) Tobacco was first brought, & made known in England by Sir John Hawkins, about the yeere 1565, but not used by Englishmen in many yeeres after."
7. Holland, *Herωologia Anglica,* 101–5.
8. Richard Hawkins, *Observations,* 21–22. Purchas, *Purchas his Pilgrimes,* 4:1177–86, 1367–1417.
9. Camden, *Rerum Anglicarum Annales,* (1616), 134. "Ille [Hawkins] cum mercibus & Nigritis mancipiis Quorum frequens iam erat per Hispanos, & eorum exemplo, per Anglos in Africa venatio, & in America venditio (nescio quam honesta)." Camden, *Annales Rerum Anglicarum* (1625), 627–29, 646–47.
10. Stow, *Survey of London,* 139–41. "Johannes Hawkins; Eques auratus, clariss. Regiae Marinarum causarum Thesaurarius. Qui cum XLIIII annos muniis bellicis, & longis periculosisque navigationibus, detegendis novis regionibus, ad Patriae utilitatem, & suam ipsius gloriam, strenuam & egregiam operam navasset, in expeditione, cui Generalis praefuit ad Indiam occidentalem dum in Anchoris ad portum S. Joannis in insula Boriquena staret, placide in Domino ad coelestem patriam emigravit, 12 die Novembris anno salutis 1595. In cujus memoriam ob virtutem & res gestas, Domina Margareta Hawkins vxor mœstissima, hoc monumentum cum lachrymis posuit."
11. Prince, *Danmonii Orientals Illustres,* 472–76.
12. Campbell, *Lives of the Admirals,* 1:463–64.
13. González, *Apuntamientos,* 97–125.
14. Lingard, *History of England,* 6:235. Markham, *The Hawkins' Voyages,* viii–ix.
15. Froude, *History of England,* 9:508–21.

16. Smith, "Passages in the Life of Hawkins," 195–208. Smith was expanding upon a suggestion by Collier, "On the Charge of the ordinary," 191–94.

17. Worth, "Sir John Hawkins," 246, 256, 275. Markham, *The Hawkins' Voyages,* iii–xxi.

18. Mary Hawkins, *Plymouth Armada Heroes,* 76–77.

19. Laughton, "John Hawkins," 219.

20. Williamson, *Sir John Hawkins,* 490.

21. The first volume published by the Hakluyt Society was C. R. Drinkwater Bethune's book, *The Life of Sir Richard Hawkins, Knt., in His Voyage into the South Sea in the Year 1593* (London, 1847). Recognizing the limitations of the first effort, Sir Clements R. Markham included Richard's work in his book, *The Hawkins' Voyages,* vol. 57 of the Hakluyt Society *Works.*

22. Williamson, *Hawkins of Plymouth.*

23. G. R. G. Conway, *An Englishman and the Mexican Inquisition, 1556–1560* (Mexico, 1927). Unwin, *Defeat of John Hawkins,* 9.

24. C. Sanz Arizmendi, Cuatro Expediciones, 55–69. "Leal en sus tratos, magnánimo al devolver el tesoro de los españoles, generoso al indemnizar los daños por él ocasionados, respetando la propiedad agena, muy hábil marino y más que un corsario."

25. Rumeu de Armas, *Los Viajes de John Hawkins,* XVIII.

26. Lewis, *The Hawkins Dynasty.*

27. *Spanish Documents Concerning English Voyages to the Caribbean, 1527–1568,* second series, vol. 62. *Documents Concerning English Voyages to the Spanish Main, 1569–1580,* second series, vol. 71. *Sir Francis Drake's West Indian Voyage, 1585–86,* second series, vol. 148.

28. Laughton, *State Papers Relating to the Defeat of the Spanish Armada.* Corbett, *Papers Relating to the Navy During the Spanish War, 1585–1587.*

29. Gross, González-Aller Hierro, Dueñas Fontán, and Campo Mérida Valverde, *La Batalla del Mar Océano.*

30. Andrews, *Last Voyage,* 1–10.

Appendix 1
Latin Text of Hawkins's Damage Claim

1. PRO SP 12/53, fols. 6v–7v.

Appendix 2
Account of the Battle at San Juan de Ulúa

1. Flores, *Obra nueuamẽte compuesta sobre vna admirable victoria.*

Appendix 3
Inscription on the Memorial to Hawkins

1. Stow, *Survey of London*, 139–41.

Appendix 4
Portraits of Hawkins

1. Tenison, *Elizabethan England*, vol. 2, plate 14.
2. *Western Morning News* (Plymouth), 8 February 1933, p. 6.
3. The engraving does not appear in the Huntington Library or British Library copies, though it does appear on a separate sheet from the set in an extra-illustrated collection at the Huntington. See Granger, *Biographical History of England*, 3:111a.
4. Holland, 101-5.
5. Purchas, *Hakluytus Posthumus*. The Huntington Library copy of the 1625 edition (catalogue no. 3341) has the 1624 title page tipped in.

Bibliography

Manuscript Collections
Austria
Österreichische Nationalbibliothek, Vienna
Fugger News-Letters, Codex 8949.

England
British Library, London
Additional Manuscripts, 5209, 9294, 22047, 26056 (a, b, & c), 28336, 28340, 28341, 28346, 33740, 34729, 36316, 41140, 48023, 48126, 74210.
Cotton Manuscripts, Augustus I, Caligula C.III, Galba C.V, Galba D.VIII, Julius F.X, Vespasian C.XIII, Otho E.VIII, Otho E.IX.
Egerton Manuscript, 1512, 1525, 1694, 2047.
Harley Manuscripts, 6991, 7002.
Hatfield Manuscripts, Cecil Papers, microfilm, M.485.
Lansdowne Manuscripts, 21, 43, 52, 70, 113.
Nero Manuscript, 1.
Sloane Manuscripts, 43, 2177.

Cambridge University, Magdalene College, Pepys Library
Anthony Roll, MS 2991.
Volumes 2875, 2878.

Devon Record Office, Plymouth
Black Book.
Grant and Quitclaim, 710/674, 710/675, 710/676, 710/678.
St. Andrews Parish Register.

Inner Temple Library, London
MS 538.

LONDON GUILDHALL LIBRARY

Parish Register of St. Dunstan-in-the-East, MS7857.

PLYMOUTH PUBLIC LIBRARY

Clipping files.

PUBLIC RECORD OFFICE, LONDON

Calendar of Pardons, C82.
Calendar of Patent Rolls, C66/850, C66/1172.
High Court of Admiralty, 13/21, 15/22, 24/47, 25/1.
Plymouth Port Book, E 190/1010/18.
Probate 11/87, 11/94.
State Papers, Domestic, 12/37, 12/40, 12/43, 12/44, 12/48, 12/49, 12/53, 12/81,
    12/105, 12/111, 12/114, 12/127, 12/132, 12/133, 12/139, 12/142, 12/143, 12/144,
    12/148, 12/153, 12/156, 12/163, 12/170, 12/185, 12/186, 12/200, 12/201, 12/202,
    12/204, 12/206, 12/208, 12/209, 12/211, 12/212, 12/213, 12/214, 12/215, 12/216,
    12/217, 12/219, 12/223, 12/225, 12/227, 12/228, 12/229, 12/230, 12/231, 12/232,
    12/233, 12/234, 12/238, 12/242, 12/243, 12/244, 12/247, 12/253, 12/257.
State Papers, Foreign, 70/66, 70/73, 70/94, 70/99, 70/104A, 70/110, 70/111, 70/113,
    70/117, 70/119, 70/136, 70/288.
State Papers, Ireland, 63/27, 63/53.
State Papers, Spanish, 1/23, 94/9A.

WESTCOUNTRY STUDIES LIBRARY, EXETER

Clipping Files. Hawkins Collection.
Transcripts of Wills.

Germany

BAYERISCHE STAATSBIBLIOTHEK

Codex angl. 2.

Mexico

ARCHIVO GENERAL DE LA NACIÓN, MEXICO CITY

Ramo de Inquisición, tomos 1A, 26, 53, 55, 75, 121, 125, 149.

Spain

Archivo de Indias, Seville

Indiferente General 425, 433, 738, 858.
Justicia 93, 902, 908, 1000.
Mexico 168.
Patronato 265, 266, 267.
Santa Fe 72, 82, 89.
Santo Domingo 51, 71, 73, 78, 80, 89, 94, 118, 126, 169, 202, 206, 286.

Archivo General de Simancas

Estado 550, 594, 817, 818, 819, 820, 821, 822, 823, 824, 825, 827, 829, 830, 833, 835, 838, K.1564, K.1566, K.1567, K.1568, K.1569. K.1592.
Guerra Antigua 460, 520.
Guerra Marina 121, 122, 123, 198, 200, 208, 221, 245, 247, 287.

Archivo Historico Nacional, Madrid

Inquisición 762, 1048, 1824.
Ordenes Militares 3511/70.

Biblioteca de Francisco Zabálburu, Madrid

Colección Altamira, 153/153.

Biblioteca Nacional, Madrid

Juan Escalante de Mendoza, "*Itenerario de navegación de los mares y tierras occidentales.*"

Museo Canarias, Las Palmas, Canary Islands

Inquisición LIII-5, LXXX-12.

United States

Folger Shakespeare Library, Washington, D.C.

Mary Frear Keeler Collection.

Huntington Library, San Marino, Calif.

Ellesmere MS 1679.

LIBRARY OF CONGRESS, WASHINGTON, D.C.

Arthur Stanley Riggs Papers.
G. R. G. Conway Collection.
Hans P. Kraus Collection.

ST. LOUIS UNIVERSITY, VATICAN FILM LIBRARY

Urbinates Latini 1049, 1053, 1054, 1060, 1113, 1115, 2512.

Maps and Portraits

ARCHIVO GENERAL DE SIMANCAS

Map of Santo Domingo, GA 520219.
El castillo principal de la isla de Canaria, GA 460296.

BRITISH LIBRARY

Dockyard at Chatham (detail), Cotton Augustus I.152.

GUILDHALL LIBRARY

Ralph Agas, *Civitas Londinum.*

HUNTINGTON LIBRARY

Boazio Map of Cartagena (detail showing *Elizabeth Bonaventure*).

JOHN CARTER BROWN LIBRARY

Boazio Map of Cartagena (detail showing *Elizabeth Bonaventure*).

NATIONAL MARITIME MUSEUM

Portrait of Charles Lord Howard of Effingham, BHC 2786.
Portrait of Sir John Hawkins, BHC 2755 (Caird Collection).
Portrait of Sir Richard Hawkins, BHC 4186.
Portrait of Thomas Cavendish, Sir Francis Drake, and Sir John Hawkins, BHC
    2603 (Loan GH 94, Greenwich Hospital Collection).

PEPYS LIBRARY, MAGDALEN COLLEGE, CAMBRIDGE

Anthony Roll (views of *Jesus of Lubeck* and *Minion*), MS 32991.
Matthew Baker, "Fragments of Ancient English Shipwrightry" (view of Baker
    at drawing board; view of ship hull), MS 2820.

PLYMOUTH MUSEUM AND ART GALLERY

Portrait of John Hawkins by Federigo Zuccaro.

PUBLIC RECORD OFFICE

Smerwick Map (detail showing *Revenge, Swiftsure, Aid, Achates,* and *Merlin*),
    MPF 75.

Published Works

Adams, Simon. *The Armada Campaign of 1588.* London: Historical Associa-
    tion, 1988. Pamphlet.
———. "New Light on the 'Reformation' of John Hawkins: The Ellesmere
    Naval Survey of January 1584." *English Historical Review* 105 (1990):96–111.
Anderson, George W. *A New, Authentic, and Complete Collection of Voyages
    round the World.* London: For Alexander Hogg, 1781.
Andrews, Kenneth R. *Drake's Voyages: A Re-Assessment of Their Place in Eng-
    land's Maritime Expansion.* London: Weidenfeld and Nicolson, 1967.
———. *Trade, Plunder, and Settlement: Maritime Enterprise and the Genesis of
    the British Empire, 1480–1630.* New York: Cambridge University Press,
    1984.
———. "Elizabethan Privateering." *Raleigh in Exeter, 1985: Privateering and
    Colonisation in the Reign of Elizabeth I.* Ed. Joyce Youings. Exeter Studies in
    History, no. 10. Exeter: University of Exeter, 1985.
———. *Ships, Money, and Politics: Seafaring and Naval Enterprise in the Reign
    of Charles I.* New York: Cambridge University Press, 1991.
Arber, Edward (ed.). *The English Garner: Ingatherings from Our History and
    Literature.* Birmingham: E. Arber, 1882.
Arróniz, Othón. *La batalla naval de San Juan de Ulúa.* Xalapa, Mexico: Uni-
    versidad Veracruzana, 1982.
Bacon, Francis. "Considerations Touching a Warre with Spaine." *Certaine Mis-
    cellany Works of the Right Honourable Francis Lo[rd] Verulam, Viscount
    S[aint] Albans.* London: Printed by I. Haviland for Humphrey Robinson,
    1629.

Bagwell, Richard. *Ireland Under the Tudors: With a Succinct Account of the Earlier History*. London: Longmans, Green, 1885.

Barkham, Michael. "The Spanish Fleet, July 1588." In Rodríguez-Salgado, *Armada, 1588*, 154–63.

Barros Franco, José M. "La incursion de Richard Hawkins en Hispanomerica y su epílogo," *Revista de Historia Naval* 17 (1999):63–77.

Bigges, Walter. *A Summarie and True Discourse of Sir Francis Drakes West Indian Voyage*. London: Richard Field, 1589.

———. *A summarie and true discourse of Sir Francis Drake's West Indian voyage*. London: Nicholas Bourne, 1652.

Blatcher, Margaret. "Chatham Dockyard and a Little-known Shipwright, Matthew Baker, 1530–1613." *Archaeologia Cantiana* 107 (1990):155–72.

Bovill, E. W. "The Madre de Dios." *Mariner's Mirror* 54 (1968):129–52.

Boyd, William K. (ed.). *Calendar of State Papers Relating to Scotland and Mary, Queen of Scots, 1547–1603, Preserved in the Public Record Office, the British Museum, and Elsewhere in England*. Vol. 5, A.D. 1574–1581. Vol. 6, 1581–1583. Edinburgh: H. M. General Register House, 1907, 1910.

Bracken, C. W. *A History of Plymouth and Her Neighbors*. Plymouth: Underhill, 1931.

Brown, Horatio F. (ed.). *Calendar of State Papers and Manuscripts, Relating to English Affairs, Existing in the Archives and Collections of Venice, and in Other Libraries of Northern Italy*. Vol. 3. London: Her Majesty's Stationery Office, 1894.

Brown, Horatio F., and G. Cavendish Bentinck (eds.). *Calendar of the State Papers and Manuscripts Relating to English Affairs Existing in the Archives and Collections of Venice, and in Other Libraries of Northern Italy*. Vol. 7, 1558–1580. London: Her Majesty's Stationery Office, 1890.

Butler, Arthur J. (ed.). *Calendar of State Papers, Foreign Series, of the Reign of Elizabeth, January–June, 1583, and Addenda, Preserved in the Public Record Office*. London: Public Record Office, 1913.

Calderon Quijano, José Antonio. *Historia de las Fortificaciones en Nueva España*. Madrid: Gobierno del Estado de Veracruz, consejo Superior de Investigaciones Científicas, and Escuela de Estudios Hispanoamericanos, 1984.

Calvar Gross, Jorge, José Ignacio González-Aller Hierro, Marcelino de Dueñas Fontán, and Maria del Campo Mérida Valverde. *La Batalla del Mar Océano: Corpus Documental de las hostilidades entre España e Inglaterra, 1568–1604*. 5 vols. Madrid: Ministerio de Defensa, Armada Española, Instituto de Historia y Cultura Naval, Turner Libros, S.A., 1988–93.

Camden, William. *Britannia*. London: Ralph Newbery, 1586.

———. *Britannia sive florentissimorum regnorum Angliae, Scotiae, Hiberniae, et insularum adiacentum ex antiquitate chorographica descriptio.* London: George Bishop, 1594.

———. *Rerum Anglicarum Henrico VIII Edwardus VI et Maris regnantibus, Annales.* London: Officina Nortoniana, 1616.

———. *Annales Rerum Anglicarum, et Hibernicarum Regnante Elizabetha.* Lug. Batavorum, Officina Elzeviriana, 1625.

Campbell, John. *Lives of the Admirals and Other Eminent British Seamen.* 4 vols. London: John Applebee, 1742.

Clancy, Thomas H. *Papist Pamphleteers: The Allen-Parsons Party and the Political Thought of the Counter-Reformation in England, 1572–1615.* Chicago: Loyola University Press, 1964.

Clifford, Henry. *Life of Jane Dormer Duchess of Feria.* London: Burns and Oates, 1887.

Colección de documentos inéditos relatives al descubrimiento, conquista y organización de las antiguas posesiones de América y Oceania. Ser. 2, vols. 89–92. Madrid, 1866.

Collier, John P. "On the Charge of the ordinary and extraordinary Service of the English Navy in the middle of the reign of Queen Elizabeth; with a Letter and Report from Sir John Hawkins to Sir Walter Mildmay, on the subject of the needless expenditure of public money in 1583." *Archaeologia; or, Miscellaneous Tracts Relating to Antiquity Published by the Society of Antiquarians of London* 33 (1849):191–94.

Cooper, Charles P. *Correspondance Diplomatique de Bertrand de Salignac, de la Mothe Fénélon.* 7 vols. Paris: Imprimerie Panckoucke, 1838–40.

Corbett, Julian S. *Drake and the Tudor Navy: With a History of the Rise of England as a Maritime Power.* 2 vols. London: Longmans, Green, 1898.

——— (ed.). *Papers Relating to the Navy During the Spanish War, 1585–1587.* London: Navy Records Society, 1898; rpt. 1987.

Cox, Charles J. *Churchwardens' Accounts from the Fourteenth Century to the Close of the Seventeenth Century.* London: Methuen, 1913.

Crouch, Nathaniel. *The English Hero: or, Sir Francis Drake Reviv'd, Being a full Account of the dangerous Voyages, Admirable Adventures, Notable Discoveries, and Magnanimous Atchievements of that Valiant and Renowned Commander.* London: Printed for A. Bettsworth and C. Hitch[, 1681].

Darcie, Abraham. *Annales of the True and Royall History of the Famous Empress Elizabeth.* London: Benjamin Fisher, 1625.

Dasent, John R. (ed.). *Acts of the Privy Council of England.* New series, vols. 13–24. Norwich: Her Majesty's Stationery Office, 1899.

Davis, John. *The Worldes Hydrographical Discription.* London: Thomas Dawson, 1595.

A Declaration of the True Causes of the Great Troubles Presupposed to be Intended against the Realme of England. Cologne, 1592.

De rebus Gallicis, Belgicis, Italicis, Hispanicis, Constantinopolitanis &c. recens allata. Cologne, 1586.

Dietz, Brian. "The Royal Bounty and English Merchant Shipping in the Sixteenth and Seventeenth Centuries." *Mariner's Mirror* 77 (1991):7.

Drake, William Richard. "Notes upon the Capture of 'The Great Carrack,' in 1592." *Archaeologia; or Miscellaneous Tracts Relating to Antiquity Published by the Society of Antiquarians of London* 33 (1849):209–40.

Edwards, R. Dudley. *Ireland in the Age of the Tudors.* London: Croom Helm, 1977.

Eliott-Drake, Lady Elizabeth Fuller. *The Family and Heirs of Sir Francis Drake.* 2 vols. London: Smith, Elder, 1911.

Elizabethae, Angliae reginae haeresim calvinianam propugnantis, saevissimam in Catholicos sui regni edictum, quod in alios quoq; Reipub. Christianae Principe contumelias continet indignissimas: promulgatam Londini 29. Nouemb. 1591. Augsburg: Joannes Fabrus, 1592.

Ellis, Henry. "On certain Passages in the Life of Sir John Hawkins, temp. Elizabeth." *Archaeologia; or, Miscellaneous Tracts Relating to Antiquity Published by the Society of Antiquarians of London* 33 (1849):195–208.

Ellis, Steven G. *Tudor Ireland: Crown, Community, and the Conflict of Cultures, 1470–1603.* London: Longman, 1985.

Evans, John X. *The Works of Sir Roger Williams.* Oxford: Clarendon, 1972.

Expeditio Francisci Draki equitis Angli in Indias occidentales A.M.D. LXXXV. Leyden: Raphelengien, 1588.

Fernández-Armesto, Felipe. *The Spanish Armada: The Experience of War in 1588.* Oxford: Oxford University Press, 1989.

Fernández Duro, Cesáreo. *La Armada Invencible.* Madrid: Tipográfico de los sucessores de Rivadeneyra, 1884.

Finberg, H. P. R. *Tavistock Abbey: A Study in the Social and Economic History of Devon.* Cambridge: Cambridge University Press, 1951.

Flores, Alvaro. *Obra nueuamēte compuesta sobre vna admirable victoria que bono Don Francisco Lu xan contra don Juã d Acle lutherano capitán de la Reyna de Inglaterra. Compuesto por Aluaro de Flores natural de Malaga y vecino de Sebilla.* Burgos: Pedro de Sãtillana, 1570.

Froude, James. *English Seamen in the Sixteenth Century.* London: Longmans, Green, 1896.

Fuller, Thomas. *The Holy State.* Cambridge: Printed by Roger Daniel for John Williams, 1642.

Furnivall, Frederick J. *Early English Meals and Manners.* Early English Text Society, vol. 32. London: Edward Arnold, 1972.

Gairdner, James. *Letters and Papers, Foreign and Domestic, of the Reign of Henry VIII, Preserved in the Public Record Office, the British Museum, and Elsewhere in England.* Vol. 13, part 1, and vol. 17. London: Her Majesty's Stationery Office, 1892.

Glasgow, Tom, Jr. "The Shape of the Ships that Defeated the Spanish Armada." *Mariner's Mirror* 50 (1964):177–98.

———. "Elizabethan Ships Pictured on Smerwick Map, 1580: Background, Authentication, and Evaluation." *Mariner's Mirror* 52 (1966):157–65.

———. "The Origin of the First Royal Ship *Victory*, 1562." *Mariner's Mirror* 53 (1967):184–86.

———. "List of Ships in the Royal Navy from 1539 to 1588: The Navy from Its Infancy to the Defeat of the Spanish Armada." *Mariner's Mirror* 56 (1970):299–307.

———. "Comments on 'List of Ships in the Royal Navy from 1539 to 1588.'" *Mariner's Mirror* 61 (1975):351–53.

Granger, James A. *Biographical History of England.* 36 vols., extraillustrated. London: T. Davies, 1769. Huntington Library 283000.

Great Britain, Historical Manuscripts Commission. *Calendar of the Manuscripts of the Marquis of Bath Preserved at Longleat, Wiltshire.* Vol. 2. London: His Majesty's Stationery Office, 1907.

———. *Calendar of the Manuscripts of the Most Hon. the Marquis of Salisbury, &c., &c., &c., Preserved at Hatfield House, Hertfordshire.* Part 3, *Addenda.* London: His Majesty's Stationery Office, 1915.

———. *Manuscripts of the Right Honourable F. J. Savile Foljambe of Osberton.* 15th report, appendix, part 5. London: Her Majesty's Stationery Office, 1897.

———. *Report on the Manuscripts of His Grace the Duke of Portland, K.G., Preserved at Welbeck Abbey.* Vol. 9. London: His Majesty's Stationery Office, 1923.

———. *Report on the Manuscripts of Lord de L'Isle & Dudley, Preserved at Penhurst Place.* London: His Majesty's Stationery Office, 1925.

———. *Report on the Records of the City of Exeter.* London: His Majesty's Stationery Office, 1916.

Great Britain, House of Commons. *Journals of the House of Commons. From November the 8th, 1547, in the First Year of the Reign of King Edward the Sixth, to March 2d, 1628, in the Fourth Year of the Reign of King Charles the First.* Vol. 1. London: House of Commons, 1803.

Great Britain, Public Record Office. *Calendar of Patent Rolls Preserved in the Public Record Office. Edward VI.* Vol. 1, 1547–48; vol. 2, 1548–1549. London: His Majesty's Stationery Office, 1924.

———. *Calendar of Patent Rolls Preserved in the Public Record Office. Elizabeth.*

Vol. 2, *1560–1563*. London: His Majesty's Stationery Office, 1948.

———. *Eighth Report of the Deputy Keeper of the Public Records*. London: HMSO, 1847.

Greaves, Richard L. *Society and Religion in Elizabethan England*. Minneapolis: University of Minnesota Press, 1981.

Greepe, Thomas. *The True and Perfect Newes of that Valiant Knight Syr Fraun-cis Drake: Not Onely at Sancto Domingo, and Carthagena, but also Nowe at Cales, and uppon the Coast of Spayne*. London: I. Charlewood for Thomas Hackett, 1587.

Groetboecxken naden Nieuwen Stijl Waer in datmen tot allen Tijden Vinden mach de hooschde ende leechde der sonnen oft in wat graet de sonne alle dagen gaet: dit op de calculatie vanden nieuwen Almanach. Amsterdam: Cornelis Claesz, 1595(?).

Gunson, W. N. "Who Was Sir Richard Hawkins?" *Mariner's Mirror* 80 (1994):72–73.

Hakluyt, Richard. *Third and Last Volume of the Voyages, Navigations, Trafiques, and Discoveries of the English Nation*. London: George Bishop, Ralfe New-berie, and Robert Baker, 1600.

———. *Principall Navigations, Voiages and Discoveries of the English Nation*. London: George Bishop and Ralph Newberie, 1589.

Hampshire, A. Cecil. "A Link with Hawkins." Magazine article, clipping file, Plymouth Public Library.

Hasler, P. W. *History of Parliament: The House of Commons, 1558–1603*. Vol. 2, *Members D-L*. London: Her Majesty's Stationery Office, 1981.

Hasted, Edward. *The History and Topographical Survey of the County of Kent, Containing the Antient and Present State of It, Civil and Ecclesiastical; Col-lected from Public Records, and Other Authorities: Illustrated with Maps, Views, Antiquities, &c*. 2d ed. Canterbury: W. Bristow, 1798.

Hawkins, John. *A true declaration of the troublesome voyadge of M. John Haukins to the parties of Guynea and the west Indies, in the yeares of our Lord 1567. and 1568*. London: Thomas Purfoote for Lucas Harrison, 1569.

Hawkins, Mary. *Plymouth Armada Heroes: The Hawkins Family*. Plymouth: William Brendon and Son, 1888.

Hawkins, Richard. *The Observations of Sir Richard Hawkins, Knight, in His Voyage into the South Sea, Anno Domini, 1593*. London: I. D. for Iohn Iag-gard, 1622.

Herrera, Antonio de. *Descripción de las indias occidentales*. Madrid: Imprenta Real, 1601.

———. *Primera parte de la historia general del mundo, de XVII años del tiempo del rey don Felipe II el Prudente, desde el año de MDLIIII hasta el de MDLXX*. 2 vols. Valladolid: Juan Godínez de Millis, 1606.

———. *Segunda parte de la historia general del mundo, de XV años del tiempo del señor Rey don Felipe, el Prudente, desde el año de MDLXXI. hasta el de MDLXXXV*. Valladolid: Juan Godínez de Millis, 1606.

———. *Tercera parte de la historia general del mundo, de XIII años del tiempo del señor Rey don Felipe II el Prudente, desde el año de 1585 hasta el de 1598 que pasó a mejor vida*. Madrid: Alonso Martín de Balvoa, 1612.

Heyden, H. A. M. van der. "Emanuel van Meteren's History as Source for the Cartography of the Netherlands." *Querendo* 16 (1986):3–29.

Higham, Robert (ed.). *Security and Defence in South-West England Before 1800*. Exeter Studies in History, no. 19. Exeter: University of Exeter, 1987.

——— (ed.). *Landscape and Townscape in the South West*. Exeter Studies in History, no. 22. Exeter: University of Exeter, 1989.

Hoffman, Paul E. *The Spanish Crown and the Defense of the Caribbean, 1535–1585: Precedent, Patrimonialism, and Royal Parsimony*. Baton Rouge: Louisiana State University Press, 1980.

Holinshed, Raphaell. *The Third Volume of Chronicles*. London: John Harrison, George Bishop, Rafe Newberie, Henry Denham, and Thomas Woodcock, 1587.

Holinshed's Chronicles of England, Scotland, and Ireland. London: J. Johnson, 1807.

Holland, Henry. *Baziliⲱologia: A book of kings, being the true and liuely effigies of all our English kings from the Conquest vntill this present; with their seuerall coats of armes, impreses and devises; and a briefe chronologie of their liues and deaths*. London: Printed for H. Holland, 1618.

———. *Herⲱologia Anglica; hoc est clarissimorum et doctissimorum, aliquot anglorum, que florverunt ab anno Christi .M.D.C.XX*. Arnhem: Crispus Passeus, 1620.

Hortop, Job. *The Rare Travails of Job Hortop*. London: William Wright, 1591.

Hoskins, W. G. *A New Survey of England: Devon*. London: Collins, 1954.

Howes, Edmond. *The Annales or Generall Chronicle of England, Begun First by Maister John Stow, and after Him Continued and Augmented with Matters Forreyne, and Domestique, Ancient and Moderne, vnto the Ende of This Present Yeere 1614*. London: Thomas Adams, 1615.

———. *Annales, or Generall Chronicle of England, Begun by Iohn Stow: Continued and Augmented with Matters Forraigne and Domestique, Ancient and Moderne vnto the end of this Present Yeere 1631 by Edmund Howes*. London: Richard Meighen, 1631.

Hume, Martin A. S. (ed.). *Calendar of Letters and State Papers Relating to English Affairs Preserved Principally in the Archives of Simancas*. Vols. 2–4, *Elizabeth, 1580–1586*. London: Her Majesty's Stationery Office, 1896.

Hurstfield, Joel, and Alan G. R. Smith (eds.). *Elizabethan People, State, and Society*. London: Edward Arnold, 1972.

Ingpen, Arthur R. *The Middle Temple Bench Book, Being a Register of Benchers of the Middle Temple from the Earliest Records to the Present Time with Historical Introduction.* London: Chiswick, 1912.

Japikse, N. (ed.). *Resolution der Staten-General van 1576 tot 1609.* Vol. 41 of *Rijks Geschiedkundige Publicatiën.* The Hague: Martinus Nijhoff, 1918.

Kelsey, Harry. *Sir Francis Drake: The Queen's Pirate.* New Haven: Yale University Press, 1998.

Kingsford, Charles Lethbridge. "The Taking of the Madre de Dios, Anno 1592." *Naval Miscellany.* Ed. John K. Laughton. Naval Records Society Publications, vol. 40 (1912), 2:85–121.

——— (ed.). *A Survey of London by John Stow, Reprinted from the Text of 1603.* Oxford: Clarendon, 1908.

Klarwill, Victor. *Fugger-Zeitungen ungedruchte Briefe an dashaus Fuggeraus den jahren 1568–1605.* Vienna: Ritola Verlag, 1923.

Klarwill, Victor, and L. S. R. Byrne. *The Fugger News-Letters.* 2d series. London: John Lane, the Bodley Head, 1926.

Knighton, C. S., and David M. Loades (eds.). *The Anthony Roll of Henry VIII's Navy.* Pepys Library 2991 and British Library Additional MS 22047, with related documents. Aldershot: Ashgate for the Navy Records Society in association with the British Library and Magdalene College, Cambridge, 2000.

Latham, R. E. *Revised Medieval Latin Word-List from British and Irish Sources.* London: Oxford University Press, 1965.

Laudonnière, René. *L'Histoire notable de la Floride sitvee es Indes Occidentales.* Paris: Guillaume Auuray, 1586.

Laughton, John Knox. "John Hawkins." *Dictionary of National Biography,* ed. Leslie Stephen and Sidney Lee. London: Smith, Elder, 1891, 25:212–19.

———. *State Papers Relating to the Defeat of the Spanish Armada, Anno 1588.* Vols. 1 and 2 of Navy Records Society Publications. London: Navy Records Society, 1914.

Legg, John W. (ed.). *Missale ad usum ecclesie Westmonasteriensis.* 3 vols. London: Harrison and Sons, 1891–96.

Letters and Memorials of Father Robert Persons, S.J. London: Catholic Record Society, 1942.

Lewis, Frederic Christian. *The Scenery of the Rivers Tamar and Tavy, in Forty-Seven Subjects, Exhibiting the Most interesting Views on Their Banks from the Source to the Termination of Each; Including a View of the Breakwater at Plymouth.* London: John and Arthur Arch, 1823.

Lewis, Michael. "The Guns of the Jesus of Lubeck." *Mariner's Mirror* 22 (1936):324–45.

———. "Fresh Light on San Juan de Ulua." *Mariner's Mirror* 23 (1937):295–315.

———. *The Hawkins Dynasty: Three Generations of a Tudor Family*. London: Allen and Unwin, 1969.

Lingard, John. *The History of England from the First Invasion by the Romans to the Accession of William and Mary in 1688*. 10 vols. London: Charles Dolman, 1855.

Lloyd, Howell A. "Sir John Hawkins's Instructions, 1590." *Bulletin of the Institute of Historical Research* 44 (1971):125–28.

Loades, David. *The Tudor Navy: An Administrative, Political, and Military History*. Aldershot: Scolar, 1992.

Lomas, Sophie Crawford (ed.). *Calendar of State Papers, Foreign Series, in the Reign of Elizabeth Preserved in the Public Record Office*. London: His Majesty's Stationery Office, 1916.

López de Velasco, Juan. *Geografía y Descripción Universal de las Indias*. Ed. Marcos Jiménez de la Espada and María del Carmen González Muñoz. Madrid: Ediciones Atlas, 1971.

Maritiem Museum "Prins Hendrik." *Lof der Zeevaart: Collectie Dr. W. A. Engelbrecht*. Rotterdam: Maritiem Museum "Prins Hendrik," 1966.

Markham, Clements R. *The Hawkins' Voyages During the Reigns of Henry VIII, Queen Elizabeth, and James I*. London: Hakluyt Society, 1878.

Marsden, R. G. *Documents Relating to the Law and Customs of the Sea*. Vols. 49 and 50 of Navy Records Society Publications. London: Navy Records Society, 1915.

Martin, Colin, and Geoffrey Parker. *The Spanish Armada*. London: Penguin, 1988.

Martin, Paula. *Spanish Armada Prisoners*. Exeter Maritime Studies, no. 1. Exeter: University of Exeter Press, 1988.

Martínez del Río, Pablo. "La aventura Mexicana de Sir John Hawkins." *Memorias de la Academia Mexicana de la Historia* 2 (1943):241–95.

Mason, A. E. W. *The Life of Francis Drake*. London: Hodder and Stoughton, 1941.

Maura Gamazo, Gabriel. *El designio de Felipe II y el episodio de la armada invencible*. Madrid: Editorial Cultura Clásica y Moderna, 1957.

McGowan, A. P. *The Jacobean Commissions of Enquiry, 1608 and 1618*. Navy Records Society Publications, vol. 116. London: Navy Records Society, 1971.

Medina, J. T. (ed.). *Colección de documentos inéditos para la historia de Chile desde el viaje de Magallanes hasta la batalla de Maipo, 1518–1818*. Santiago de Chile: Imprenta Elzeviriana, 1901.

Merino, José P. "Graving Docks in France and Spain before 1800." *Mariner's Mirror* 71 (1985):35–58.

Meteren, Emanuel van. *Historia uund Abcontrafentung furnemlich der Nider-*

landischer geschichten und kriegshendelen mit hochsten fleisz beschrieben durch Merten von Manuel. Neurenberg: Hogenberg (?), 1593.

———. *Historiae unnd Abcontrafentung furnemblich der Niderlandischer geschichten unnd kriegshandelen, der anden theye mit hochsten fleiss beschrieben.* Neurenberg (?): Hogenberg (?), 1596.

———. *Beschryvinge vande overtresselijke ende wijdtvermaerde Zee-vaerdt vanden Edelen Heer ende Meester Thomas Candish, met drie schepen uytghevaren den 21. Julij 1586, ende met een schip wederom ghekeert in Pleymouth, den 9. September 1588.* Amsterdam: Cornelis Claesz, 1598.

———. *Historia Belgica nostri potissimum temporis, Belgii sub quatuor Burgundis & totidem Austriacis principibus coniunctionem & gubernationem breviter: turbas autem, bella et mutationes tempore Regis Philippi, Caroli V, Caesaris filii ad annum usque 1598, plenius complectens, conscripts: Senatui, populo Belgico, posterisq inscripta A. E. Meterano Belga.* Cologne (?), 1598 (?).

———. *Belgische ofte Nederlantsche historie van onsen tijden.* Delft: Jacob Cornelisz Vennencool, 1599.

Mexico, Archivo General de la Nación. *Corsarios Franceses e Ingleses en la inquisición de la Nueva España.* Mexico: Imprenta Universitaria, 1943.

Moes, E. W., and C. P. Burger, Jr. *De Amsterdamsche Boekdrukkers en Uitgevers in de Zestiende Eeuw.* Amsterdam: C. L. Van Langenhuysen, 1907.

Morton, Ann (ed.). *Calendar of the Patent Rolls Preserved in the Public Record Office: Elizabeth, 1580–1582.* Vol. 9. London: Her Majesty's Stationery Office, 1986.

Murdin, William A. (ed.). *A Collection of State Papers Relating to Affairs in the Reign of Queen Elizabeth for the Years 1571 to 1596 Transcribed from Original Paper and Other Authentic Manuscripts Never Before Published, Left by William Cecil, Lord Burghley and Deposited in the Library at Hatfield House.* London: William Bowyer, 1759.

Oppenheim, Michael. *A History of the Administration of the Royal Navy and of Merchant Shipping in Relation to the Navy.* Vol. 1, 1509–1660. London: John Lane, the Bodley Head. 1896.

———. *The Naval Tracts of Sir William Monson.* Navy Records Society, vol. 22. London: Navy Records Society, 1902–14.

———. *The Maritime History of Devon.* Exeter: University of Exeter, 1968.

Overall, William H. *Civitas Londinum. Ralph Agas. A Survey of the Cities of London and Westminster, the Borough of Southwark, and Parts Adjacent.* Published in Facsimile from the Original in the Guildhall Library. London: Adams and Francis, 1874.

Parker, Geoffrey. *The Grand Strategy of Philip II.* New Haven: Yale University Press, 1998.

———. "El Testamento Politico de Juan Martínez de Recalde." *Revista de Historia Naval*. Año 16, no. 60 (1998):7–44.

Peckham, George. *A True Reporte of the late discoveries and possession, taken in the right of the Crowne of Englande, of the New found Landes: By that valiaunt and worthye Gentleman Sir Humfrey Gilbert Knight*. London: Printed for I. C. by John Hinde, 1583.

Percyvall, Richard. *Bibliotheca Hispanica*. London: Richard Watkins, 1591.

Pérez, Antonio. *Relaciones de Antonio Pérez, Secretario de Estado, que fue, del Rey de España Don Phelippe II deste nombre*. Paris, 1598.

Perry, Ben E. *Aesopica: A Series of Texts Relating to Aesop or Ascribed to Him or Closely Connected with the Literary Tradition That Bears His Name*. Urbana: University of Illinois Press, 1952.

Phillips, Carla R. *Six Galleons for the King of Spain: Imperial Defense in the Early Seventeenth Century*. Baltimore: Johns Hopkins University Press, 1986.

Pierson, Peter. *Commander of the Armada, the Seventh Duke of Medina Sidonia*. New Haven: Yale University Press, 1989.

Portillo, Alvaro del. *Descubrimientos en las costas de California, 1532–1650*. Madrid: Ediciones Rialp, S.A., 1982.

Powell, Isobel G. "The Chatham Chest Under the Early Stuarts." *Mariner's Mirror* 8 (1922):174–82.

Prince, John. *Danmonii orientales Illustres, or, The Worthies of Devon*. 1701; rpt. London: Rees and Curtis, 1810.

Purchas, Samuel. *Hakluytus Posthumus, or Purchas His Pilgrimes*. London: William Stansby for Henrie Fetherstone, 1625.

Quinn, David B. *The Voyages and Colonising Enterprises of Sir Humfrey Gilbert*. Hakluyt Society *Works*, series 2, vols. 83–84. London: Hakluyt Society, 1940.

Quinn, David B., C. E. Armstrong, and R. A. Skelton. "The Primary Hakluyt Bibliography." *The Hakluyt Handbook*. Ed. David B. Quinn. Hakluyt Society *Works*, series 2, vol. 145. London: Hakluyt Society, 1974.

Quinn, David B., and A. N. Ryan. *England's Sea Empire, 1550–1642*. London: Allen and Unwin, 1983.

Ralegh, Walter. *The Works of Sir Walter Raleigh, Kt. Now First Collected: to Which are Prefixed the Lives of the Author by Oldys and Birch*. Vol. 8, *Miscellaneous Works*. Oxford: The University Press, 1829.

Read, Conyers. *Lord Burghley and Queen Elizabeth*. New York: Knopf, 1961.

Recopilacion de leyes de los reynos de las Indias. 2d ed. Madrid: Antonio Balbas, 1756.

Resolutien der Staten-General van 1576 tot 1609. Vol. 5 of *Rijks Geschiedkundige Publicatiën*, Grote Serie. The Hague: Martinus Nijhoff, 1921.

Rigg, J. M. (ed.). *Calendar of State Papers Relating to English Affairs, Preserved Principally at Rome in the Vatican Archives and Library*. Vol. 2, *Elizabeth, 1572–1578*. London: His Majesty's Stationery Office, 1926.

Risk, J. Erskine. "The Rise of Plymouth as a Naval Port." *Report and Transactions of the Devonshire Association for the Advancement of Science, Literature, and Art* (1898), 350–54.

Roberts, Henry. *The Trumpet of Fame: Or Sir Fraunces Drakes and Sir Iohn Hawkins Farewell: with an encouragement to all Sailers and Souldiers that are minded to go in this worthie enterprise. VVith the names of many Ships, and what they have done against our foes*. London: Thomas Creede, 1595.

Rodger, Nicholas A. M. *The Armada in the Public Records*. London: Her Majesty's Stationery Office, 1988.

———. *The Safeguard of the Sea: A Naval History of Britain*. New York: Norton, 1997.

Rodríguez-Salgado, María J. *Armada, 1588–1988: An International Exhibition to Commemorate the Spanish Armada*. London: Penguin, 1988.

———. Review of Petruccio Ubaldino's *La disfatta della flotta spagnola*. *English Historical Review* 105 (1990):404.

Rodríguez-Salgado, María J., and Ian Friel, "Battle at Sea." In Rodríguez-Salgado, *Armada*, 233–42.

Rose-Troupe, Frances. *The Western Rebellion of 1549: An Account of the Insurrection in Devonshire and Cornwall against Religious Insurrection in the Reign of Edward VI*. London: Smith, Elder, 1913.

Rumeu de Armas, Antonio. *Los viajes de John Hawkins a America, 1562–1595*. Seville: Escuela de Estudios Hispano-Americanos, 1947.

———. *Canarias y el Atlantico: Piraterias y Ataques Navales*. 5 vols. 1947–50; rpt. Las Palmas: Gobierno de Canarias, 1991.

Sanz Arizmendi, C. "Cuatro espediciones de Juan Haquines (John Hawkins)." *Boletín del Instituto de Estudios Americanistas* 1 (1918):55–69.

Scheurweghs, G. "On an Answer to the Articles of the Rebels of Cornwall and Devonshire (Royal MS. 18 B. XI)." *British Museum Quarterly* 8, no. 1 (1933–34):24–25.

Spain, Museo Naval. *Colección de documentos y manuscritos compilados por Fernández de Navarrete*. Vol. 15. Neudeln, Lichtenstein: Kraus-Thompson organization, 1971.

Spence, Richard T. *The Privateering Earl*. Stroud: Alan Sutton, 1955.

Stanislawski, Don. "Early Spanish Town Planning in the New World." *Geographical Review* 37 (1947):94–105.

Stoate, T. L. *Devon Lay Subsidy Rolls, 1524–27*. Bristol: T. L. Stoate, 1979.

Stow, John. *Annals of England, Faithfully Collected out of the Most Authenticall*

Authors, Records, and other Monuments of Antiquities, from the First Inhabitants untill the Present Yeere, 1592. London: Ralph Newbery, 1592.

———. *Annales or Generall Chronicle of England. Edited by Edmund Howes.* London: Thomas Adams, 1615.

———. *The Survey of London, edited by A.M. and H.D.* London: Elizabeth Purslow for Nicholas Browne, 1633.

Sturgess, H. A. C. *Register of Admissions to the Honourable Society of the Middle Temple from the Fifteenth Century to the Year 1944.* London: Butterworth, 1949.

Tenison, E. M. *Elizabethan England.* 13 vols. Royal Leamington Spa: Issued for the author, 1933–60.

Torres de Mendoza, Luís. *Colección de Documentos Inéditos relativos al descubrimiento, conquista y organización de las antiguas posesiones Españolas en América y Oceanía.* Vol. 5. Madrid: Frias, 1866.

Ubaldino, Petruccio. "Comentario della impresa fatta contra il regno d'Inghilterra del re catholica l'anno 1588." Trans. in Waters, *Elizabethan Navy,* 69–100.

Udall, Nicholas (?). *Troubles Connected with the Prayer Book of 1549.* Ed. Nicholas Pocock. New series, vol. 3. London: Camden Society, 1884.

Unwin, Rayner. *The Defeat of John Hawkins: A Biography of His Third Slaving Voyage.* London: Allen and Unwin, 1961.

Usherwood, Stephen. *The Great Enterprise: The History of the Spanish Armada as Revealed in Contemporary Documents.* London: Folio Society, 1978.

Valor Ecclesiasticus, Temp. Hen. VIII, Auctoritate Regia Institutus. London: Record Commission, 1831.

Vivian, J. L. *Visitations of the County of Devon, Comprising the Heralds, Visitations of 1531, 1564, and 1620.* Exeter: Henry S. Eland, 1895.

Voisin, Lancelot. *Les trois mondes.* Paris: Pierre L'Huillier, 1582.

Walling, R. A. J. "Sir John Hawkins." *Annual Report and Transactions of the Plymouth Institution* 14 (1904–5):143–63.

Waters, D. W. *The Elizabethan Navy and the Armada of Spain.* National Maritime Museum *Monographs and Reports,* no. 17 (1975).

Watkins, Hugh R. "Lady Hawkins." *Devon and Cornwall Notes and Queries* 14 (1926):118–20.

Wernham, R. B. *After the Armada: Elizabethan England and the Struggle for Western Europe, 1588–1595.* Oxford: Clarendon, 1984.

———. *The Expedition of Sir John Norris and Sir Francis Drake to Spain and Portugal, 1589.* Aldershot: Temple Smith for the Navy Records Society, 1988.

———. *The Return of the Armadas: The Last Years of the Elizabethan War*

Against Spain, 1595–1603. Oxford: Clarendon, 1994.

Whiting, Robert. *The Blind Devotion of the People: Popular Religion and the English Reformation*. Cambridge: Cambridge University Press, 1989.

Wieder, Frederick C. *De Reis van Mahu en de Cordes door de Straat van Magalhaes naar Zuid-Amerika en Japan, 1598–1600*. Vol. 22 of *Werken Uitgegeven door Linschoten Vereeniging*. The Hague: Martinus Nijhoff, 1924.

Williamson, James A. *Sir John Hawkins: The Time and the Man*. Oxford: Clarendon, 1927.

———. *The Age of Drake*. London: Adam and Charles Black, 1946.

———. *Hawkins of Plymouth: A New History of Sir John Hawkins and of the Other Members of His Family Prominent in Tudor England*. 2d ed. London: Adam and Charles Black, 1969.

Wingfield, Anthony. *A True Coppie of a Discourse written by a Gentleman employed in the late Voyage of Spaine and Portingale Sent to his particular friend, and by him published, for the better satisfaction of all such, as having been seduced by particular report, have entred into conceipts tending to the discredit of the enterprise and Actors of the same*. London: Thomas Woodcock, 1589.

Worth, R. N. "Sir John Hawkins: Sailor, Statesman, Hero." *Report and Transactions of the Devonshire Association* 15 (1883):246–85.

Wright, Irene A. *Spanish Documents Concerning English Voyages to the Caribbean, 1527–1568*. Hakluyt Society *Works*, series 2, vol. 62. London: Hakluyt Society, 1929.

———. *Further English Voyages to Spanish America*. Hakluyt Society *Works*, series 2, vol. 99. London: Hakluyt Society, 1951.

Wrightson, Keith. *English Society, 1580–1680*. London: Hutchinson, 1983.

Youings, Joyce A. *Tuckers Hall Exeter: The History of a Provincial City Company Through Five Centuries*. Exeter: University of Exeter, 1968.

———. "The South-Western Rebellion of 1549." *Southern History* 1 (1979):99–122.

———. *Sixteenth Century England*. London: Penguin, 1984.

———. "Bowmen, Billmen, and Hackbutters: The Elizabethan Militia in the South West." In Higham, *Security and Defence*, 51–68.

———. "Raleigh's Country and the Sea." *Proceedings of the British Academy* 70 (1989):27.

Zins, Henryk. *England and the Baltic in the Elizabethan Era*. Manchester: University of Manchester Press, 1972.

Index

Illustrations indicated by **boldface**.

Achates, 155, 159, 167

Adventure, 254

Africa: and William Hawkins, 4, 164; and slave trade, 13, 47; route to, **14;** and gold-mine story, 47, 50; and John Hawkins' third voyage to Indies, 60, 61, 71, 100

Aid, 155, 157, 202

Alas, Martín de, 327n29

Alba, Duke of, 100, 106, 108, 137, 143

Allen, Thomas, 195–200, 201, 354–55nn17, 18

Amydas, Joan, 4

Andalucía, 210

Andrews, Kenneth R., 280

Angel, 56, 57, 71, 77, 78, 102, 105

Antelope, 129, 155, 159, 161, 167, 202

Anthony, Thomas, 89

Antonio, Dom, **162,** 163–64, 174–75, 178, 231, 232

Arismendi, C. Sanz, 277

Ark Royal, 208, 214, 216, 217, 219, 235, 239

Armada: battles of, xiv, 160, 208, 211–14, **211,** 216–23, 225, 226, 228, 230, 272, 281; and Drake's war plan, 207–8; and duke of Medina-Sidonia, 208, 210; and Howard, 208–9, 210, 212, 213, 214, 216–22; strength of, 209–10, 223; and raiding of Spanish ports, 232

Atinas, Martin, 23, 30

Azores, 163, 181, 210, 231, 237, 244–45

Baeshe, Edward, 155, 190

Baker, Matthew: and John Hawkins, 151, 165, 173, 174; and navy contracts, 156, 165, 199; and ship design, 158, **158,** 159; and naval investigating commission, 166; and shipbuilding, 168, 178; and Burghley, 195; reports on condition of navy, 200–201, 202

Barrett, Robert: and John Hawkins' third voyage to Indies, 55, 64–65, 67, 68, 77; and San Juan de Ulúa, 88; and Inquisition, 133, **134**

Baskerville, Sir Thomas, 258, 259

Benit, William, 59

Benito, Tomás (Thomas Bennet), 54

Berin, Juan, 117

Berkeley, Edward, 179

Bernáldez, Alonzo, 26, 27

Bernáldez, Lorenzo, 15–16, 17

Bingham, Christopher, 54, 339n1

Birchet, Peter, 146–48

Blanco, Manuel, 179, 180–81

Bland, Captain (Paul Blondel), 62, 337n45

Boissard, Robert, 305, 306

Bolton, Robert, 41

Bolton, Thomas, 55, 111, 115

Bono, Juan, 132

Bontemps, Jean, 27, 43–45

Boone, John, 133

Borburata: and John Hawkins, 25–27, 30, 31, 33, 35–36, 74–81, 106; and Lovell, 42–44, 45

Boronel, Duarte, 97

Borough, William, 166, 173, 179, 181, 195, 205–6, 230, 232, 360n11

Bourgoigne, Adolf de, Baron DeWachen, 47, 48–50

Brazil, 4–5, 6, 164, 179, 181

Bristol, 38, 157

Brun, Juan (John Brown), 54

Buen Jesus, 179

Bull, 150, 155, 169

Burgh, Sir John, 245

Burghley, Lord (Sir W. Cecil): and Silva, 19, 38, 47; and DeWachen, 49, 50; and Fitzwilliams, 49, 126, 127, 138; and John Hawkins' third voyage to Indies, 98, 99; and John Hawkins' losses in battle of San Juan de Ulúa, 100, 107, 125–26, 274; and San Juan de Ulúa prisoners, 113, 136; and Ridolfi, 114, 124; and Spain, 119–20; and Stucley, 119, 120; portrait of, **121;** and John Hawkins' conversations with Spes, 137; and Hatton, 147; and John Hawkins' views on opening Spanish Indies to English ships, 150; and John Hawkins as treasurer of navy, 154, 155, 156, 160, 164–65, 168–69, 174, 206, 231, 232, 236–37, 253, 265; and John Hawkins' relationship with, 154, 203; and ordnance commission, 161; and Antonio, 163; and naval investigating commission, 166; and Winter, 173; and trust in John Hawkins, 177, 193, 194; and John Hawkins' illness, 184, 206; and Drake, 193; and Allen, 196; and Borough's report, 206; and Howard, 206, 209, 229; and John Hawkins' Armada accounts, 212; and John Hawkins' naval expenditures, 229, 234; and John Hawkins' reports and

plans, 230, 232–34, 236, 241; and John Hawkins' raiding of Spanish ships, 240; and John Hawkins' wife's death, 242; and privateers, 245, 248; and John Hawkins' last voyage, 259

Burrough, Sir John, 246

Bustamante, Francisco de, 84, 89

Camden, William, 271

Campbell, John, 267, 273

Canary Islands: and John Hawkins, 10–14, **11,** 18, 40–41, 57–59, 258–60; and Drake, 13, 176, 258–60; and Spanish officials, 18, 33, 57–58, 59; and Richard Hawkins, 251; castle of Gran Canaria, **259**

Cape Verde Islands, 23, 62, 67, 176, 251

Carleill, Christopher, 185

Cartagena, 82–83, 176, 255

Castellanos, Baltasar de, 44

Castellanos, Miguel de, 44, 45, 77–81, 139, 326n17

Castro, Beltrán de, 251

Cavendish, Thomas, 249, 270, 306

Cecil, Sir Robert, 247, 248, 249, 259, 260

Cecil, Sir William. *See* Burghley, Lord (Sir W. Cecil)

Challoner, Sir Thomas, 310n47, 311n48

Champernowne, Sir Arthur, 347n3

Chapman, Robert, 178, 195

Chatham: and ship repair, 160–61, 168, 170, 200, 202, 235; and John Hawkins' navy contract, 170, 172; and defenses, 184; and John Hawkins' reports, 187; Chatham Chest, 243, 363n42; Chatham Hospital, 249, 257, 304

Châtillon, Cardinal, 118, 150–51

Chichester, John, 38

Christóval, 129

Clara, 129

Clarke, William, 104

Clifford, Sir Nicholas, 258

Cola, 24

Conway, G. R. G., 277

Cook, William, 38

Cooke, Robert, 139

Corbett, Julian S., 279

Crane, 239

Cuba, 29, 95

Cumberland, Earl of, 234, 244, 245, 248

Cygnet, 186, 352n56

Dainty, 240, 241, 244–48, 250

Davis, John, 268–69

Defiance, 254

Delgadillo, Antonio, 86, 87, 89

Delight, 260, 261

Deptford, 154, 161, 168, 170, 172, 187, 235, 246

DeWachen, Baron, Adolfe de Bourgoigne, 47, 48–50

Dominica, 71

Don de Dieu, 62, 102, 105

Douglas, Margaret, 122

Dover, 47, 228, 229

Dragon, 245, 248

Drake, 186

Drake, Sir Francis: John Hawkins compared to, xiii, 256, 264, 269, 272; reputation of, xiii; and William Hawkins, 8, 164, 176; and Canary Islands, 13, 176, 258–60; and John Hawkins' first voyage to Indies, 15; and John Hawkins' second voyage to Indies, 19; and West Indies, 19, 41, 104, 149, 185, 252, 311n55; and religious beliefs, 42; and Río de la Hacha, 46, 77–78; and John Hawkins' third voyage to Indies, 56, 66, 77; and *Judith,* 56, 77, 90, 91,

104, 111, 115, 311n55; and Bland, 62; and San Juan de Ulúa, 90, 91, 93, 98, 105, 115, 281, 330n52; and Cuba, 95; and John Hawkins' losses at San Juan de Ulúa, 104, 141; and piracy, 149, 157, 230–31; John Hawkins's investment in Indies voyages of, 153; and Navy Board, 153, 190, 232; and Spanish ships, 157, 176, 191–92, 208, 230–31, 255–56, 261; and Antonio, 163, 232; and expeditions in Spanish waters, 175–77, 178, 185–86, 190–93, 194; and John Hawkins support of expeditions of, 175–76, 252; and Elizabeth, 176, 185, 186, 208, 232, 252, 253, 255; investigation of West Indies voyage, 185; warfare and profit motives, 204; and Armada, 207–8, 209, 212, 213–14, 217–18, 220, 222, 223; naval position of, 207, 208; and Plymouth, 207, 230; war plans of, 207, 208; and injured sailors, 243; as privateer, 244; and John Hawkins' purchase of rights to manor, 249; world-wide journeys of, 249; last voyage of, 252–64, 280; death of, 263; Peckham on, 268; Roberts on, 269; Holland on, 270; portraits of, 304, 306

Dreadnaught, 150, 156, 157, 159, 186, 239

Duck, 176

Ducket, Sir Lionel, 13

Dudley, Edward, 58–59, 60, 64–65, 67

Duquesa Santa Ana, 218

Echegoyan, 17

Edward (king of England), 145

Edward Bonaventure, 186

Elenor, 156

Elizabeth, 186

Elizabeth I (queen of England and Ire-
land): and slave trade, xiii, 18, 69;
and John Hawkins' second voyage to
Indies, 18, 26, 30, 35, 38, 311n48; and
Silva, 19, 37, 38, 47; John Hawkins'
commitment to, 33; and John
Hawkins as naval clerk of ships, 46;
and John Hawkins' third voyage to
Indies, 46, 48, 50, 53, 56, 58, 69; and
Bourgoigne, 47-48, 49; and John
Hawkins' piracy, 76, 149, 150; and
Philip II, 100, 118, 119, 149-50, 177;
and John Hawkins' negotiations for
prisoners, 113, 119, 139, 141; and
Ridolfi plot, 114-15, 119-29, 133,
137-38, 147, 177; and San Juan de
Ulúa prisoners, 119; and Stucley, 120;
and John Hawkins' religious beliefs,
122; and Mary, Queen of Scots,
125-26; excommunication of, 143;
and Ireland, 145-46; and Birchet,
147; and John Hawkins' stabbing,
147-48; approval of John Hawkins,
149; and John Hawkins' expenses
for, 150-51, **152**; and Navy Board,
153, 197; and Antonio, 163, 180; and
naval investigating commission,
165-68; and Drake, 176, 185, 186,
208, 232, 252, 253, 255; and Babington plot, 178, 185; and John Hawkins
as treasurer of navy, 193, 196,
236-37, 242, 265; and Howard, 228;
and naval expenditures, 230-31,
236-37; and privateers, 243-46, 248;
and John Hawkins' last voyage, 254,
255, 264
Elizabeth Bonaventure, 156, 186, 201,
203, **203**, 206, 239, 254
Elizabeth Jonas, 155, 159, 160, 161, 202,
209, 216
Ellines, Tomás, 132

Emery, John, 133
Enríquez, Martín, 86-88, 91, 106
Entens, Bartel, 144
Essex, Walter, Earl of, 145-46, 151, 254

Fancy, 250
Felipe, Diego, 84, 88
Fenner, George, 38
Fenner, Thomas, 179, 181, 208
Fenton, Edward, 164, 232
Feria, Duke and Duchess of: and San
Juan de Ulúa prisoners, 113, 122, 127,
128, 129-30, 132; and Fitzwilliams,
120-24, 126, 127, 128, 129, 131-32,
136, 137, 139, 149, 347n12; and Ridolfi
plot, 125, 130-31, 143
Fitzwilliams, George: and Burghley, 49,
126, 127, 138; and John Hawkins'
third voyage to Indies, 54; and Dudley, 58, 60, 67; and religious beliefs,
60, 117, 120, 122, 123; as San Juan de
Ulúa hostage, 113, 115, 117; and Spes,
117, 120, 128, 137; and San Juan de
Ulúa prisoners, 119, 122, 127, 129-30,
136; and duke and duchess of Feria,
120-24, 126, 127, 128, 129, 131-32,
136, 137, 139, 149, 347n12; and Mary,
Queen of Scots, 123, 124-26, 129,
131, 137; John Hawkins' betrayal of,
125, 126-27, 138, 139, 141; and Ridolfi,
133; and John Hawkins' expenses,
151
Flanders, 47-49, 123, 127, 131, 207
Flores, Alvaro, **85,** 268, 286-98,
329n47
Florida: and John Hawkins, 29; and
tobacco, 31; and France, 74; and John
Hawkins' third voyage to Indies, 83
Fones, Humphrey, 104
Foresight: and John Hawkins' plans for
attack on Spanish fleet, 150; and Ire-

land patrol, 157; and ship design, 159; and ship repair, 201, 235, 242; and John Hawkins' fleet command, 239; and Portuguese ships, 244, 245; and John Hawkins' last voyage, 254

Fortesque, Sir John, 248

Foxe, John, 108

France: and John Hawkins' piracy, 11, 148; French piracy, 27, 43–45, 60, 61, 74, 107, 110, 117, 118, 165; and trade, 61, 62, 144; and religious beliefs, 100; ending of civil war, 118; and San Juan de Ulúa prisoners, 132; and John Hawkins' trade with, 144; and Babington plot, 178; relations with England, 252, 253

Francis, 260, 261

French ships: John Hawkins' capture of, 11, 71, 83, 144, 148, 181, 239; and John Hawkins' second voyage to Indies, 27, 30; and Lovell's voyage, 43; and John Hawkins' third voyage to Indies, 61–62, 71, 83; and losses at San Juan de Ulúa, 112; and John Hawkins' fleet command, 178, 179

Frobisher, Martin: ships built for, 153; and Antonio, 163; and Drake, 185; and Allen, 195; and Armada battles, 208, 212, 214, 218, 219, 223, 230; and Spanish ships, 234, 237, 238–41; and Ralegh, 244; and Spanish siege of Brest, 252; Peckham on, 268; Holland on, 270

Froude, James Anthony, 274

Fuller, Thomas, 54, 81, 117, 122, 123, 339n1

Galleasses and galleons: and navy, 178, 179, 181, 217, 222; and Armada, 210, 217, 219, 221, 222

Garland, 244, 254

Garrard, Sir William, 53, 105

Garrett, John, 55

Garvey, William, 33

George Hoye, 156

Germany, 100

Gilbert, Sir Humphrey, 143, 144, 268, 347n3

Gillingham. *See* Chatham

Godard, Antonio (Anthony Godard), 53–54, 61, 72, 74, 82, 112

Golden Lion, 186, 238–39

Gonson, Benjamin, Senior, 13, 39, 150, 153

Gonson, Benjamin, Junior, 179, 232, 360n11

Gonson, Katherine, 12, 39

González, Bartolomé, 83–84

González, Tomás, 273

Goodwyn, Richard, 247

Gran Grifón, 217

Gravelines, 222, 223

Great Lighter, 156

Grimstone, Captain, 260

Grisling, Peter, 4

Gross, Jorge Calvar, 279

Guaras, Antonio, 148

Guinea: and William Hawkins, 4; and John Hawkins, 14, 26, 30–31, 39, 47, 50, 53, 62, **65**, 144; slave raids on Guinea Coast, **22, 65**; and Lovell, 42; and Richard Hawkins, 251

Guipúzcoa, 210, 212

Gundisalvo, Alvaro, 64

Gylbart, John, 133

Hakluyt, Richard, 2, 5, 14–15, 53, 108, 267–68, 271, 330n52

Hampton, James, 41

Hampton, John, 55

Hampton, Thomas, 13, 17, 41, 104

Handmaid, 156, 159

Hanseatic League, 239

Harte, John, 185

Hatton, Sir Christopher, 147, 161

Hawk, 250–51

Hawkins, 186

Hawkins, Catherine (Catalin Aquinza), 12

Hawkins, Henry, 4

Hawkins, Joan Trelawny, 7

Hawkins, Sir John: Drake compared to, xiii, 256, 264, 269, 272; and San Juan de Ulúa, xiii–xiv, 83–84, **85,** 86–93, 95, 100, 101, 233, 330n53, 331n60; accounts of/scholarship on, xiv, 267–81; and Armada battles, xiv, 208, 209, 212, 216, 218–19, 223, 226, 272; last voyage and death, xiv, 252–64, 271; and treason, xiv, 110, 114–15, 137, 139, 141, 147, 149, 177, 182, 195, 225–26, 242, 271, 272, 274, 281; birth and early life of, 4, 7, 10; inscription on memorial at St. Dunstan in the East, 7, 299–303; portraits of, 7, **192, 224,** 304, **305,** 306; voyages to Canaries, 10–14, **11,** 18, 40–41, 57–59, 258–60; marriage of, 12, 39–40, 51, 193, 199, 242; first voyage to Indies, 13, 15–18, 311n48; second voyage to Indies, 18–31, **25,** 33, 38, 43; accusations against, 23–24, 165, 193–202, 205–7; ties to Philip II, 27, 33, 35–38, 75–76, 242, 273; message to Elizabeth, 30; coat of arms, **32,** 33; and Silva, 35, 37–38, 41, 47, 49; home in London, 40, **40,** 51; Lovell's voyage, 40–45, 67, 69, 78, 317n27; third voyage to Indies, 46, 47, 48, 50, 53–69, 71–84, 86–87, 95–101, 321–22n22, 333n13; and DeWachen, 48–50; trial of Dudley, 58–59; voyage home from San Juan de Ulúa, 95–99, 115; *True*

Declaration, 107–8, **109,** 267; and Ridolfi Plot, 114–15, 119–29, 130, 131, 133, 137–38, **140,** 143, 147, 177; Philip II's pardon of, 131, 271; Philip II's assumptions about, 137, 138; as M.P. for Plymouth, 143–44; and Essex, 146, 151; stabbed by Birchet, 146–48; as treasurer of navy, 150, 153–61, 164, 168–73, 178, 184, 186–90, 193–96, 205–6, 225–26, 231, 232, 236–37, 243, 253, 264–65, 281; and naval contracts, 151, 153, 155–56, 161, 165, 168, 169–74, 178, 194, 195, 199–202, 206, 208; and Navy Board, 151, 153–54, 156, 158, 164, 165, 168, 174, 184, 195, 231, 234, 253; reports, ideas and plans, 151, 153–55, 157–60, 164, 174, 177, 186–90, 203–5, 230, 232–34, 236, 241; and naval expenditures, 154–55, 156, 228–29, 230, 232, 234, 236, 237; and Antonio, 163–64; and naval investigating commission, 166–68; naval fleet command of, 178–82, 237–41, 279; Plymouth fleet, 208, 209, 230, 239; Armada accounts, 212, 223; knighted, 219, 226; and the Dutch, 232, 239; Chatham Chest, 243, 363n42; second marriage, 243, 253, 256, 259–60, 262, 272; as privateer, 244, 245, 246, 247; Chatham Hospital, 249, 257, 304; will of, 256–57, **257,** 262–63. *See also* Piracy; Religious beliefs; Slave trade; Trade

Hawkins, Katherine, 35, 39, 315n9

Hawkins, Margaret, 35, 243, 256, 259–60, 262, 272, 363–64n43

Hawkins, Mary W. S., 275

Hawkins, Sir Richard: birth and early life, 12, 51; *Observations,* 50, 271, 276–77, 318n36; and ship design, 159, 160; and Brazil, 164; and Drake,

176–77, 191; portraits of, **192,** 306;
and *Revenge,* 238; relationship with
stepmother, 242; and *Madre de Dios,*
247; adventures at sea, 249–52, 257;
and rights to Drake's manor, 249;
and John Hawkins' will, 256–57;
Camden on, 271; Prince on, 272

Hawkins, William (first): early life, 4;
and national service, 4; and Plymouth affairs, 4; Brazil voyages, 5–6,
5; privateers, 6; and trade, 6–7, 8;
home of, 7–8; Mayor and M.P., 7;
and religious beliefs, 8–9; and
monastic property, 9; and piracy,
9–10; death, 10, 308n23; and Spanish
troops in Netherlands, 100; and Hakluyt, 268; letter to Cromwell, 307n2,
308n21

Hawkins, William (second): early life,
7, 10; Mayor of Plymouth, 7; and
Drake, 8, 164, 176; and Richard
Hawkins, 51; and John Hawkins'
third voyage to Indies, 53, 55, 98, 99;
and John Hawkins' losses at San
Juan de Ulúa, 98, 100, 104–5, 111; and
Châtillon, 118; and Ridolfi plot, 121;
and piracy, 144, 148, 149; and Brazil,
164; and ship repair, 202–3; and
naval expenditures, 230; death,
234–35

Henry VII (king of England), 145

Henry VIII (king of England), 9, 18,
40, 136, 145

Heyward, Rowland, 53

Holland, 3, 178

Holland, Henry, 270–71

Holstocke, William, 150, 166, 173, 174,
201–2, 230, 232

Hope: and John Hawkins as treasurer of
navy, 155; and ship design, 159; and
ship repair, 161, 202, 207, 229; and

John Hawkins' fleet command, 179,
239; and John Hawkins' last voyage,
254

Hortop, Job, 90, 133, **135,** 330n52

Howard, Lord Thomas, 216, 230

Howard of Effingham, Charles, Lord:
and naval investigating commission,
166; and Queenborough fleet, 203;
and John Hawkins as treasurer of
navy, 205–6, 207; and Burghley, 206,
209, 229; and Armada, 208–9, 210,
212, 213, 214, 216–22; and Plymouth
fleet, 208–9, 210; portrait of, **215;** and
sickness of men, 228; and fleet
demobilization, 229–30; and Drake,
231; and injured sailors, 243; and
John Hawkins' Panama expedition,
259

Howes, John, 270, 273

Huguenots, 30, 100, 118, 144, 148

Ingram, David, 112, 337n44

Inquisition, 133, **134,** 345n44

Ireland, 107, 110, 115, 119, 145, 151, 157,
255

Jesus of Lubeck: and John Hawkins'
second voyage to Indies, 18, 20, 21,
22, 39; and DeWachen, 48; sketch of,
48; and John Hawkins' third voyage
to Indies, 55, 57–58, 68, 71, 83, 110;
and San Juan de Ulúa, 84, 88, 89, 90;
and John Hawkins' claims for losses
at San Juan de Ulúa, 101, 102, 103,
104, 105; and ship design, 159, 160

John Baptist, 19

Jonas, 13

Judith: and John Hawkins' third voyage to Indies, 55–56, 57, 71, 77, 78;
and Drake, 56, 77, 90, 91, 104, 111,
115, 311n55; value of, 105

Keeler, Mary Frear, 279

La Rochelle, 100, 144, 145, 148, 151
Lader, Lewis, 149
Laudonnière, René de, 29, 30
Laughton, John K., 276, 279
Leicester, Earl of, 163, 176, 178
Levant, 210
Lewes, David, 38–39
Lewis, Michael, 278
Leyva, 218
Lincoln, Earl of, 153, 166
Lingard, John, 273–74
Lion, 156, 157, 179, 181, 201
Llerena, Christobal de, 29, 313n78
Lodge, Sir Thomas, 13
Lovell, John, 39, 40–46, 55, 56, 67, 69, 77, 78, 317n27
Low, William, 68
Luís, Anton, 318n33
Luxan, Francisco de, 86, 87, 88, 132, 329n47

Madeira, 20, 251, 258
Madre de Dios, 244, 245, 247
Magellan, Straits of, 251
Maldonado, Francisco, 83, 336n43
Marçana, Martín de, 84, 87
Marck, Count de la, 346n3
Margaret and John, 213–14
Margarita, 24, 42, 72–74, 164
María Juan, 223
Markham, Clements, 273–74, 275
Marks, Thomas, 133
Marlin, 239
Martin, Christopher, 181
Martínez, Juan, 14, 15
Martyn, Richard, 185
Mary, Queen of Scots: and Ridolfi plot, 114, 119, 120, 125, 131, 137; and Hawkins, 120, 122–23, 125, 128–29,

130, 137; and Fitzwilliams, 123, 124–26, 129, 131, 137; and San Juan de Ulúa prisoners, 129, 132; and Babington plot, 178
Mary Rose, 155, 214, 235, 239
Mary Tudor (queen of England and Ireland), 9, 27, 75, 145
Maynarde, Thomas, 256, 261, 264
Medina-Sidonia, Duke of, 208, 210, 211–13, 216–21, 223, 225
Mendoza, Juan de (Juan de Salvatierra): as captive, 107, 108, 110, 111, 115; and Spes, 111, 143; and San Juan de Ulúa prisoners, 114, 117; and Stucley, 120; identity of, 134, 136
Menéndez de Avilés, Pedro, 86
Merchant Royal, 186
Merlin, 20, 202
Meteren, Emanuel van, xiii, 269–70
Mexico. *See* New Spain
Mildmay, Sir Walter, 161, 166, 171, 195
Minion: and John Hawkins' second voyage to Indies, 19, 20; and John Hawkins' third voyage to Indies, 55, 56, 57, 60, 68, 69, 71, 96–99, 111; sketch of, **55;** and San Juan de Ulúa, 89, 90; and John Hawkins' claim for losses at San Juan de Ulúa, 101
Moon, 239
Morgan, Michael, 41–42

Navy: John Hawkins' reorganization of, xiv, 182, 225, 230, 274, 276; and Gonson, 13; John Hawkins as treasurer of, 150, 153–61, 164, 168–73, 178, 184, 186–90, 193–96, 205–6, 225–26, 231, 232, 236–37, 243, 253, 264–65, 281; Navy Board, 150, 151, 153–54, 156, 158, 165, 168, 179, 184, 195, 196–97, 231, 232, 234, 253, 360n11; and John Hawkins' naval contracts, 151, 153,

155–56, 161, 165, 168, 169–74, 178, 194, 195, 199–202, 206, 208; and expenditures, 154–55, 228–29; naval expenditures, 154–55, 156, 228–29, 230, 232, 234, 236, 237; and ship repair, 155, 156, 160, 168–71, 173, 188, 194, 195, 199–203, 206, 208, 209, 218, 229–30, 231, 242; and ship design, 158–60, 174, 178, 179; and investigating commission, 165–68, 169; defenses of, 174, **175,** 184–85, 203–5, 233; condition of, 177, 193, 195, 200–202, 206, 209; strength of, 209–10, 212; and Plymouth fleet, 210–11; and Armada, 211–14, **211,** 216–23, 225, 228; and capture of *Rosario,* 214; and sickness of men, 228–29, 249; and injured sailors, 243, 249; Spanish threat to, 252

Netherlands, 100, 113, 147, 149–50, 232, 239

New Bark, 151, 156

New Spain, 83, 133, 255

Nichols, Philip, 46

Nonpareil, 178, 179–80, 181, 201, 202, 216, 235, 239

Norris, Sir John, 231, 232, 252

Nuestra Señora del Rosario, 213, 214, 217

Olanda, Tomás, 97

Oliver, Isaac, 304

Oliver, Peter, 304, 306

O'Neill, Sir Brian MacPhelim, 146

Ottoman fleet, 36, 37, 149

Pallavicino, Horatio, 163

Palmer, Sir Henry, 232, 360n11

Panama, 251, 252–59

Parma, Duke of, 207, 208, 210, 216, 218, 219–20, 221, 223, 225

Pascoe, 41

Paul, 41

Pawson, John, 246

Peckham, George, 268

Perrott, Sir John, 156

Peter, 11

Pett, Peter: and John Hawkins, 151, 173, 194; and navy contracts, 156, 199; ship design, 158; and naval investigating commission, 166; and shipbuilding, 168, 178; and Burghley, 194, 195; reports on condition of navy, 200–201, 202

Philip and Mary, 155, 157, 159, 161, 167, 179

Philip II (king of Spain): and John Hawkins as pirate, 19, 27, 75–76, 106, 149; and John Hawkins' ties to, 27, 33, 35–38, 75–76, 242, 273; and Bourgoigne, 49, 50; and Spes, 76, 126–28, 137; and duke of Alba, 100, 106; and Elizabeth, 100, 118, 119, 149–50, 177; and John Hawkins' claim for losses at San Juan de Ulúa, 101, 106, 131, 151, 274; and John Hawkins' *True Declaration,* 108; and Stucley, 110, 114–15, 119, 137; and Spanish fleet in Netherlands, 113; and Ridolfi, 115, 119, 184; and Mary Queen of Scots, 122; and trust in John Hawkins, 126–27, 131–32; and Fitzwilliams/Feria agreement, 131–32, 149, 347n12; and John Hawkins' pardon, 131, 271; and John Hawkins' assumptions about, 137, 138; and Antonio, 163; and Drake, 176; invasion plans of, 185–86, 205; and Armada, 210; and Drake/Hawkins Panama expedition, 254

Phillips, Miles, 133

Pierson, Peter, 223

Piracy: and John Hawkins' third voyage to Indies, xiii, 62–64, 76, 78, 82, 95, 107; John Hawkins' involvement in, xiv, 178; and Plymouth, 3, 9, 100, 148; and William Hawkins (first), 9–10; and John Hawkins' capture of French ships, 11, 71, 83, 144, 148, 181, 239; and John Hawkins' first voyage to Indies, 14–15, 21; and John Hawkins' second voyage to Indies, 19, 21, 23–24, 27; French pirates, 27, 43–45, 60, 61, 74, 107, 110, 117, 118, 165; and Lovell, 42, 43; and Stucley, 114; and William Hawkins (second), 144, 148, 149; Drake's involvement in, 149, 157, 230–31; Richard Hawkins' involvement in, 191, 251; and privateers, 243–47; and John Hawkins as privateer, 244, 245, 246, 247–48; as revenue source, 244; and West Indies, 255

Pius V (pope), 143

Plymouth: description of, 2–4, 8; and piracy, 3, 9, 100, 148; view of, 3; William Hawkins as mayor of, 7; and Stucley, 119; John Hawkins as M.P. for, 143–44; and John Hawkins' control of mills, 148; and Drake's fleet, 207, 230; and Armada, 208, 209, 210–11; and Howard, 208–9, 210

Pole of Plymouth, 4, 6

Ponce de León, Pedro, 43

Ponce family, 10, 12–13

Ponte, Nicolaso, 21

Ponte, Pedro de, 14, 16, 18, 21, 57

Ponte family, 13–14, 18, 21

Portsmouth, 38, 168, 170, 172, 187, 200, 202

Portugal: and slave trade, 4, 23–24; and trade, 23–24, 30, 62, 64; and goldmine story, 47, 50; and Antonio, 163,

174–75, 178, 180; and English ships, 185; and Armada, 210; and Drake, 232; John Hawkins patrolling waters of, 239

Portuguese ships: and John Hawkins' first voyage to Indies, 14–15, 309–10n38; and John Hawkins' second voyage to Indies, 21, 23–24; and Lovell, 42; and John Hawkins' third voyage to Indies, 54, 60–64, 65, 69, 71, 83, 95; and privateers, 244–48

Potatoes, 31

Prayer Book Rebellion of *1549,* 9

Primrose, 164, 194

Prince, John, 272–73

Puerto Rico: and William Hawkins, 6, 164; and John Hawkins' last voyage, 254, 256, 260, 261–62, 263

Purchas, Samuel, 264, 271

Quince, Enrique, 54

Quittance, 239

Rainbow, 178, 186, 239, 242

Ralegh, Sir Walter, 160, 175, 176, 244, 245, 248–49, 368n6

Raunce, James, 41, 55, 97

Rayon, José Sancho, 279

Recalde, Juan Martínez de, 212, 218

Regazona, 216

Religious beliefs: and John Hawkins' religious indifference, xiv; and William Hawkins (first), 8–9; and John Hawkins' ties to Soler family, 12; and John Hawkins' second voyage to Indies, 21; and Lovell, 41–42; and John Hawkins' third voyage to Indies, 58–59, 60, 68, 80; and Fitzwilliams, 60, 117, 120, 122, 123; and Philip II, 100; and Ridolfi plot, 114, 117, 120, 122, 123; and William

Hawkins (second), 122, 235; and
duke of Feria, 123–24; and Hatton,
147; and Netherlands, 149; and John
Hawkins' plans for defense, 203–5;
and John Hawkins' attacks on Spanish ships, 241; and John Hawkins'
will, 257–58, 262

Repentance, 234, 242

Revenge: and John Hawkins as treasurer of navy, 156; and Ireland patrol,
157; and ship design, 159; and John
Hawkins' fleet command, 179, 239;
and ship repair, 202; and Armada
battles, 208, 214, 217–18, 222; and
Frobisher, 238

Ribault, Jean, 30

Ridolfi, Roberto: and Burghley, 114,
124; Ridolfi plot, 114–15, 117, 119–29,
130, 131, 133, 137–38, **140,** 143, 147,
177; and Philip II, 115, 119, 184; and
Stucley, 133–34

Río de la Hacha: and John Hawkins,
26, 27–28, 30, 31, 33, 77–81, 139; and
Lovell, 44–46, 77, 317n27; and Drake,
46, 77–78

Roberts, Henry, 269

Roberts, Humfrey, 133

Roebuck, 245

Rogers, John, 246

Rumeu de Armas, Antonio, 18, 277, 278

Sacharo, 42

Sale, 42

Salomon, 13, 18, 20, 23, 41, 260

Salvador, 129

Samson, 245

San Felipe, 222, 223

San Juan, 179, 181

San Juan de Portugal, 212

San Juan de Ulúa: and John Hawkins'
third voyage to Indies, xiii–xiv, 83–84,
85, 86–93, 95, 100, 101, 330n53,
331n60; and John Hawkins' claim for
losses, xiv, 100, 101–6, **105,** 108, 114,
131, 233, 283–85; hostages, 84, 87, 88,
90, 112–13, 117, 122, 329n42, 336n42;
and Spanish ships, 84, 86, 87–90, 118,
329n41; Flores' account of battle, **85,**
286–98; prisoners, 88, 91, **92,** 93,
100–101, 105, 107, 108, 110–15, 117,
118–19, 125, 127, 128, 131–33, 136, 139,
141, 274, 336n42; John Hawkins' voyage home from, 95–99, 115; and
William Hawkins, 98, 100, 104–5; and
John Hawkins' last voyage, 254

San Lorenzo, 221, 222

San Luís, 218–19

San Martín, 181, 217, 222

San Mateo, 222, 223

San Salvador, 212–13, 216

Santa Ana, 219

Santa Catalina, 213

Santa María (Rata Encoronada), 212

Santa Marta, 81–82, 327n27

Santiesteban, Cristóbal de, 16

Santo Domingo, 6, 15, 24, 37, 176, 181,
255

Sarmiento de Gamboa, Pedro, 179

Sarmiento de Valladares, Gregorio, 95,
332n10

Saunders, William, 54, 68

Savior, 129

Scout, 155, 159

Seymour, Lord Henry, 208, 210, 213,
220, 223, 230

Sheffield, Lord, 230

Shipbuilding, 153, 158–61, 173, 174, 178,
196–97, 200, 234

Ships. *See* Armada; French ships; Galleasses and galleons; Navy; Portuguese ships; Spanish ships; *and
specific ships*

Sias, Gregorio de, 96
Sierra Leone, 14, 15, 24, 31, 62, 66
Silva, Guzmán de, 19, 31, 33, 35-38, 41, 47, 49
Simon, Gregorio, 54
Slave trade: and John Hawkins' profits, xiii, 15, 16, 33, 47, 81; John Hawkins' involvement in, xiv, 271, 274-75, 276; and Brazil, 4; and John Hawkins in Canary Islands, 12-13; and Ponce family, 12-13; and John Hawkins' first voyage to Indies, 14-16, 268; and John Hawkins' second voyage to Indies, 18-20, 23, 25-28, 31, 33, 268; and slave raids on Guinea Goast, **22, 65**; and Lovell, 43-46, 56, 317n27; and John Hawkins' third voyage to Indies, 47, 55, 62, 64-69, **65,** 74, 78, 80-82, 86, 98, 267, 268, 324n42; and John Hawkins' losses at San Juan de Ulúa, 105, 111, 115, 336-37n43; and John Hawkins' injuries from, 148; and William Hawkins, 164. *See also* Trade
Smith, W. H., 274
Smythe, Thomas, 185
Soler, Pedro de, 12, 58, 59
Soler family, 10, 11, 12
Spain: and slave trade, 13; and trade, 30, 44, 100; Silva recruiting Hawkins for, 33, 36-37; and John Hawkins' third voyage to Indies, 95-96; and John Hawkins' claim for losses at San Juan de Ulúa, 100, 110, 113; and religious beliefs, 100; and John Hawkins as pirate, 149; and Babington plot, 178; and English ships, 185; and West Indies defense, 255. *See also* Armada; New Spain; Philip II (king of Spain)
Spanish/English relations: deterioration of, 17, 174-75; and trade, 26, 100, 106; changes in, 99-101; and Netherlands, 100, 113, 149-50, 239; and John Hawkins' claim for losses at San Juan de Ulúa, 108; and Ridolfi plot, 114-15, 119-20; and Huguenots, 118; and piracy, 157, 255; and England's defenses, 174-75, **175,** 184, 207; and Drake, 177, 207-8; and Spain's plans to invade England, 180, 185-86, 205, 207; and John Hawkins' plans for war, 233; and England's interdiction of naval stores, 239-40; and Spain's defense of Indies, 255; and John Hawkins' ties to Philip II, 273; and naval war, 279, 280. *See also* Armada
Spanish officials: and Santo Domingo, 15-16, 17, 24-25; and Canary Islands, 18, 33, 57-58, 59; and Borburata, 25-26, 30, 31, 33, 35-36, 75-81; and John Hawkins' second voyage to Indies, 25-31, 33, 312n68; and Río de la Hacha, 27-28, 30, 31, 33, 46, 77-81, 139; and John Hawkins' third voyage to Indies, 35, 37-38, 54, 57-58, 72, 96, 99; and Lovell, 43-46; and John Hawkins' slave trade, 47; and DeWachen, 49; and Margarita, 72-74; and Santa Marta, 81-82; and San Juan de Ulúa, 84, 86-89, 91, 93, 106-7; and San Juan de Ulúa prisoners, 112, 118-19; and John Hawkins' religious beliefs, 114; and Mendoza, 136
Spanish ships: and William Hawkins (first), 5; John Hawkins' capture of, 11, 83, 84, 179, 239; John Hawkins use of, 17, 18; John Hawkins' plans for attack of, 29, 113, 157, 174, 204, 235-36; and San Juan de Ulúa, 84, 86, 87-90, 118, 329n41; and French

pirates, 117; John Hawkins attack of, 149, 150, 179–80, **180**, 181, 237, **238, 239**–41, 362n25; and Drake, 157, 176, 191–92, 208, 230–31, 255–56, 261; and Antonio, 163; and William Hawkins (second), 164; and Cumberland, 234; and Richard Hawkins, 251; and John Hawkins' last voyage, 255–56, 261

Sparke, John, 28, 29, 31

Speake, George, 106

Spes, Guerau de: and John Hawkins as pirate, 76; and Philip II, 76, 126–28, 137; and San Juan de Ulúa, 106–7, 108; John Hawkins' negotiations with, 110, 113–14, 115, 117, 119, 128, 129, 137, 139, 143; and Mendoza, 111, 143; and Fitzwilliams, 117, 120, 128, 137; and Ridolfi plot, 125, 128, 138; John Hawkins' expenses caring for, 151

Spy, 186

Stevens, Gregory, 58, 60

Stow, John, 272

Stucley, Thomas: and Ireland, 110, 119, 145; and Philip II, 110, 114–15, 119, 137; and San Juan de Ulúa prisoners, 110, 111, 114–15; and John Hawkins, 120; Fitzwilliams' meetings with, 122, 127; and Fitzwilliams' meeting with Mary, Queen of Scots, 126; and Ridolfi, 133–34

Susan, 186

Swallow (30-ton ship), 13, 18, 19, 21, 309n34, 316n13

Swallow (80-ton ship): and Lovell's voyage, 39, 41; and John Hawkins' third voyage to Indies, 55, 56, 57, 71; and John Hawkins' claims for losses at San Juan de Ulúa, 101–2, 105; and John Hawkins as treasurer of navy, 155; and John Hawkins' plans for

attacks on Spanish ships, 157; and ship repair, 202; distinguished from 30-ton *Swallow,* 316n13

Swan, 251

Swiftsure, 156, 157, 159, 202, 235, 239, 242–43

Talbot, 194

Tello de Guzmán, Pedro, 260, 261

Tempul, Ricardo (Richard Temple), 54

Tenerife, 10, 13–14, 18, 20–21, 41, 56–58

Terceira, 163, 234

Thomas, 186, 220

Thompson, Captain, 246–47

Throckmorton, Elizabeth, 244

Tiger, 19, 155, 169, 245

Tipton, Hugh, 16, 112–13

Tobacco, 31, 270, 368n6

Tommes, John, 104

Torre, Juan de la, 96

Trade: and John Hawkins' profits, xiii, 16, 31, 33, 81; and Plymouth, 3; and William Hawkins (first), 4, 6–7, 8; and Canary Islands, 10–12; and John Hawkins' first voyage to Indies, 16–17; and Silva, 19, 310n44; and John Hawkins' second voyage to Indies, 24–29, 30, 33, 35, 38, 43; and Spanish/English relations, 26, 100, 106; and Lovell's voyage, 42–46; and John Hawkins' third voyage to Indies, 59–60, 72–83, **72,** 84, 98, 139; and France, 61, 62, 144; and *True Declarations,* 108; and John Hawkins' negotiations with Spes, 117; and John Hawkins as treasurer of navy, 161, 163; and William Hawkins (second), 161, 163; and John Hawkins' religious beliefs, 204. *See also* Slave trade

Tremontana, 178, 179

Triumphe, 155, 159, 160, 202, 209, 219
Troughton, John, 262, 264
Tureen, Jean, 104

Ubilla, Juan de, 88–89, 336–37n43
United Provinces of the Low Coun-
    tries, 231
Unwin, Rayner, 277
Upnor Castle, 170, 174, **175,** 184, 187
Urquiça, Juanes de, 27, 76

Valdés, Don Pedro de, 213, 214, 254,
    255
Vanguard, 178
Varenga, Francisco dal, 24
Vaughan, Margaret, 243
Verde, Valentín, 54
Victory, 155, 159, 178, 208, 209, 216, 234
Villanueva, Agustín de, 83, 88
Vizcaya, 208, 210

Walsingham, Sir Francis: and John
    Hawkins' work with, 161; and Anto-
    nio, 163; and Burghley, 165, 193, 194;
    and naval investigation commission,
    166; and investigation of Hawkins,
    195; and John Hawkins' plans for
    defense, 203–5, 233; and John
    Hawkins' report on Armada battles,
    223; and Drake, 231; and Ingram,
    337n44
Wendon, Raynold, 9
West Indies: John Hawkins' interest in,
    xiii–xiv; and William Hawkins, 6;
    John Hawkins' first voyage to, 13,
    15–18, 311n48; and slave trade, 13, 15;
    route to, **14;** John Hawkins' second
    voyage to, 18–31, **25,** 33, 38, 43; and
    Drake, 19, 41, 104, 149, 185, 252,
    311n55; and Lovell's voyage, 40–46,
    43; John Hawkins' third voyage to,
    46, 47, 48, 50, 53–69, 71–84, 86–87,

95–101, 321–22n22, 333n13; Spain's
    defense of, 255
White Bear, 155, 159, 160, 202, 209, 214,
    229
White Lion, 186
William and John, 55, 57, 71, 83, 104,
    105, 110, 111, 115
William of Orange, 100
Williams, Thomas, 68
Williamson, James A., 276–77, 278
Winter, George: and slave trade, 13;
    John Hawkins as successor of, 46;
    and John Hawkins' third voyage to
    Indies, 53; and John Hawkins' stab-
    bing, 146; and piracy, 149; and Navy
    Board, 150, 151, 188; and John
    Hawkins' charges against, 151, 154;
    and John Hawkins' help with dis-
    pute, 153; and Antonio, 163; John
    Hawkins as enemy of, 164, 165, 173,
    174, 194; and naval investigating com-
    mission, 166, 168; and ship repair,
    173, 230; and Drake, 185, 186; and
    Richard Hawkins, 191; John
    Hawkins as ally of, 195; and report
    on condition of navy, 201–2; and
    John Hawkins as treasurer of navy,
    205–6
Winter, Sir William: and Navy Board,
    150, 151, 153, 232, 360n11; and John
    Hawkins' help with dispute, 153; and
    Armada, 220; and naval expendi-
    tures, 230; death of, 232
Woolwich, 161, 168, 170, 172, 187
Worth, R. N., 275
Wright, Irene A., 277, 278, 279, 280

Yerba, Pedro de, 89

Zabálburu, Francisco de, 279
Zegri, Luís, 89
Zuccaro, Federigo, 304, 306